Cleaning Data for Ef[...] Data Science

Doing the other 80% of the work with Python, R, and command-line tools

David Mertz

BIRMINGHAM—MUMBAI

Cleaning Data for Effective Data Science

Producer: Shailesh Jain

Acquisition Editor – Peer Reviews: Saby D'silva

Project Editor: Rianna Rodrigues

Content Development Editor: Lucy Wan

Copy Editor: Safis Editing

Technical Editor: Aditya Sawant

Proofreader: Safis Editing

Indexer: Priyanka Dhadke

Presentation Designer: Pranit Padwal

First published: March 2021

Production reference: 1260321

Published by Packt Publishing Ltd.
Livery Place
35 Livery Street
Birmingham
B3 2PB, UK.

ISBN 978-1-80107-129-1

www.packt.com

Contributors

About the author

David Mertz, **Ph.D.** is the founder of KDM Training, a partnership dedicated to educating developers and data scientists in machine learning and scientific computing. He created a data science training program for Anaconda Inc. and was a senior trainer for them. With the advent of deep neural networks, he has turned to training our robot overlords as well.

He previously worked for 8 years with D. E. Shaw Research and was also a Director of the Python Software Foundation for 6 years. David remains co-chair of its Trademarks Committee and Scientific Python Working Group. His columns, *Charming Python* and *XML Matters*, were once the most widely read articles in the Python world.

I give great thanks to those people who have helped make this book better.

First and foremost, I am thankful for the careful attention and insightful suggestions of my development editor Lucy Wan, and technical reviewer Miki Tebeka. Other colleagues and friends who have read and provided helpful comments on parts of this book, while it was in progress, include Micah Dubinko, Vladimir Shulyak, Laura Richter, Alessandra Smith, Mary Ann Sushinsky, Tim Churches, and Paris Finley.

The text in front of you is better for their kindnesses and intelligence; all error and deficits remain mine entirely.

I also thank the thousands of contributors who have created the Free Software I used in the creation of this book, and in so much other work I do. No proprietary software was used by the author at any point in the production of this book. The operating system, text editors, plot creation tools, fonts, programming languages, shells, command-line tools, and all other software used belongs to our human community rather than to any exclusive private entity.

About the reviewer

Miki Tebeka is the CEO of 353solutions, and he has a passion for teaching and mentoring. He teaches many workshops on various technical subjects all over the world and also mentored many young developers on their way to success. Miki is involved in open source, has several projects of his own, and contributed to several more, including the Python project and the Go project. He has been writing software for 25 years.

Miki wrote *Forging Python, Python Brain Teasers, Go Brain Teasers, Pandas Brain Teasers* and is an author in LinkedIn Learning. He's an organizer of the Go Israel Meetup, GopherCon Israel, and PyData Israel Conference.

Table of Contents

Preface   vii

PART I - Data Ingestion   1

Chapter 1: Tabular Formats   3

Tidying Up   4
CSV   9
  Sanity Checks   10
  The Good, the Bad, and the Textual Data   13
    The Bad   13
    The Good   18
Spreadsheets Considered Harmful   21
SQL RDBMS   29
  Massaging Data Types   30
  Repeating in R   34
  Where SQL Goes Wrong (and How to Notice It)   36
Other Formats   42
  HDF5 and NetCDF-4   44
    Tools and Libraries   45
  SQLite   50
  Apache Parquet   52
Data Frames   54
  Spark/Scala   56
  Pandas and Derived Wrappers   58
  Vaex   59
  Data Frames in R (Tidyverse)   61
  Data Frames in R (data.table)   63
  Bash for Fun   64
Exercises   65
  Tidy Data from Excel   65
  Tidy Data from SQL   67
Denouement   68

Chapter 2: Hierarchical Formats — 71

JSON — **72**
What JSON Looks Like — 74
NaN Handling and Data Types — 78
JSON Lines — 82
GeoJSON — 85
Tidy Geography — 88
JSON Schema — 92
XML — **99**
User Records — 100
Keyhole Markup Language — 102
Configuration Files — **108**
INI and Flat Custom Formats — 109
TOML — 110
Yet Another Markup Language — 114
NoSQL Databases — **119**
Document-Oriented Databases — 121
Missing Fields — 123
Denormalization and Its Discontents — 125
Key/Value Stores — 127
Exercises — **130**
Exploring Filled Area — 130
Create a Relational Model — 131
Denouement — **133**

Chapter 3: Repurposing Data Sources — 135

Web Scraping — **136**
HTML Tables — 137
Non-Tabular Data — 140
Command-Line Scraping — 146
Portable Document Format — **148**
Image Formats — **153**
Pixel Statistics — 156
Channel Manipulation — 159
Metadata — 161
Binary Serialized Data Structures — **165**
Custom Text Formats — **170**
A Structured Log — 171
Character Encodings — 175
Exercises — **182**
Enhancing the NPY Parser — 182
Scraping Web Traffic — 183

Denouement   **185**

PART II - The Vicissitudes of Error   187

Chapter 4: Anomaly Detection   189

Missing Data   **191**
SQL   192
Hierarchical Formats   196
Sentinels   197
Miscoded Data   **201**
Fixed Bounds   **205**
Outliers   **210**
Z-Score   211
Interquartile Range   216
Multivariate Outliers   **219**
Exercises   **221**
A Famous Experiment   221
Misspelled Words   223
Denouement   **225**

Chapter 5: Data Quality   227

Missing Data   **228**
Biasing Trends   **232**
Understanding Bias   233
Detecting Bias   236
Comparison to Baselines   240
Benford's Law   244
Class Imbalance   **246**
Normalization and Scaling   **253**
Applying a Machine Learning Model   256
Scaling Techniques   257
Factor and Sample Weighting   262
Cyclicity and Autocorrelation   **267**
Domain Knowledge Trends   271
Discovered Cycles   278
Bespoke Validation   **282**
Collation Validation   283
Transcription Validation   287
Exercises   **291**
Data Characterization   291
Oversampled Polls   294
Denouement   **296**

PART III - Rectification and Creation — 297

Chapter 6: Value Imputation — 299

Typical-Value Imputation — **301**
Typical Tabular Data — 302
Locality Imputation — 309

Trend Imputation — **313**
Types of Trends — 314
A Larger Coarse Time Series — 317
  Understanding the Data — 318
  Removing Unusable Data — 321
  Imputing Consistency — 322
  Interpolation — 325
Non-Temporal Trends — 327

Sampling — **332**
Undersampling — 335
Oversampling — 339

Exercises — **345**
Alternate Trend Imputation — 345
Balancing Multiple Features — 346

Denouement — **348**

Chapter 7: Feature Engineering — 351

Date/Time Fields — **352**
Creating Datetimes — 354
Imposing Regularity — 355
Duplicated Timestamps — 358
Adding Timestamps — 359

String Fields — **364**
Fuzzy Matching — 367
Explicit Categories — 372

String Vectors — **379**
Decompositions — 388
Rotation and Whitening — 389
Dimensionality Reduction — 391
Visualization — 394

Quantization and Binarization — **398**

One-Hot Encoding — **406**

Polynomial Features — **409**
Generating Synthetic Features — 411
Feature Selection — 413

Exercises   **417**
  Intermittent Occurrences   417
  Characterizing Levels   418
Denouement   **419**

PART IV - Ancillary Matters   421

Closure   423
  What You Know   **423**
  What You Don't Know (Yet)   **424**
Glossary   427
Other Books You May Enjoy   463
Index   467

Preface

In order for something to become clean, something else must become dirty.

−*Imbesi's Law of the Conservation of Filth*

Doing the Other 80% of the Work

It is something of a truism in data science, data analysis, or machine learning that most of the effort needed to achieve your actual purpose lies in cleaning your data. The subtitle of this work alludes to a commonly assigned percentage. A keynote speaker I listened to at a data science conference a few years ago made a joke—perhaps one already widely repeated by the time he told it—about talking with a colleague of his. The colleague complained of data cleaning taking up half of her time, in response to which the speaker expressed astonishment that it could be so little as 50%.

Without worrying too much about assigning a precise percentage, in my experience working as a technologist and data scientist, I have found that the bulk of what I do is preparing my data for the statistical analyses, machine learning models, or nuanced visualizations that I would like to utilize it for. Although hopeful executives, or technical managers a bit removed from the daily work, tend to have an eternal optimism that the next set of data the organization acquires will be clean and easy to work with, I have yet to find that to be true in my concrete experience.

Certainly, some data is better and some is worse. But *all data is dirty*, at least within a very small margin of error in the tally. Even datasets that have been published, carefully studied, and that are widely distributed as canonical examples for statistics textbooks or software libraries, generally have a moderate number of data integrity problems. Even after our best pre-processing, a more attainable goal should be to make our data *less dirty*; making it *clean* remains unduly utopian in aspiration.

By all means we should distinguish *data quality* from *data utility*. These descriptions are roughly orthogonal to each other. Data can be dirty (up to a point) but still be enormously useful. Data can be (relatively) clean but have little purpose, or at least not be fit for purpose. Concerns about the choice of measurements to collect, or about possible selection bias, or other methodological or scientific questions are mostly outside the scope of this book. However, a fair number of techniques I present can *aid* in evaluating the utility of data, but there is often no mechanical method of remedying systemic issues. For example, statistics and other analyses may reveal—or at least strongly suggest—the unreliability of a certain data field. But the techniques in this book cannot generally automatically fix that unreliable data or collect better data.

The code shown throughout this book is freely available. However, the purpose of this book is not learning to use the particular tools used for illustration, but to understand the underlying purpose of data quality. The concepts presented should be applicable in any programming language used for data processing and machine learning. I hope it will be easy to adapt the techniques I show to your own favorite collection of tools and programming languages.

Types of Grime

There are roughly two families of problems we find in datasets. Not every problem neatly divides into these families, or at least it is not always evident which side something falls on without knowing the root cause. But in a general way, we can think of structural problems in the formatting of data versus content problems in the actual values recorded. On the structural branch a format used to encode a dataset might simply "put values in the wrong place" in one way or another. On the content side, the data format itself is correct, but implausible or wrong values have snuck in via flawed instruments, transcription errors, numeric overflows, or through other pitfalls of the recording process.

The several early chapters that discuss "data ingestion" are much more focused on structural problems in data sources, and less on numeric or content problems. It is not always cleanly possible to separate these issues, but as a question of emphasis it makes sense for the ingestion chapters to look at structural matters, and for later chapters on anomalies, data quality, feature engineering, value imputation, and model-based cleaning to direct attention to content issues.

In the case of structural problems, we almost always need manual remediation of the data. Exactly where the bytes that make up the data go wrong can vary enormously, and usually does not follow a pattern that lends itself to a single high-level description. Often we have a somewhat easier time with the content problems, but at the same time they are more likely to be irremediable even with manual work.

Consider this small comma-separated value (CSV) data source, describing a 6th grade class:

```
Student#,Last Name,First Name,Favorite Color,Age
1,Johnson,Mia,periwinkle,12
2,Lopez,Liam,blue,green,13
3,Lee,Isabella,,11
4,Fisher,Mason,gray,-1
5,Gupta,Olivia,9,102
6,,Robinson,,Sophia,,blue,,12
```

In a friendly way, we have a header line that indicates reasonable field names and provides a hint as to the meaning of each column. Programmatically, we may not wish to work with the punctuation marks and spaces inside some field names, but that is a matter of tool convenience that we can address with the APIs (application programming interfaces; the functions and methods of a library) that data processing tools give us (perhaps by renaming them).

Let us think about each record in turn. Mia Johnson, student 1, seems to have a problem-free record. Her row has five values separated by four commas, and each data value meets our intuitive expectations about the data type and value domain. The problems start hereafter.

Liam Lopez has too many fields in his row. However, both columns 4 and 5 seem clearly to be in the lexicon of color names. Perhaps a duplicate entry occurred or the compound color "blue-green" was intended. Structurally the row has issues, but several plausible remediations suggest themselves.

Isabella Lee is perhaps no problem at all. One of her fields is empty, meaning no favorite color is available. But structurally, this row is perfectly fine for CSV format. We will need to use some domain or problem knowledge to decide how to handle the missing value.

Mason Fisher is perhaps similar to Isabella. The recorded age of -1 makes no sense in the nature of "age" as a data field, at least as we usually understand it (but maybe the encoding intends something different). On the other hand, -1 is one of several placeholder values used very commonly to represent missing data. We need to know our specific problem to know whether we can process the data with a missing age, but many times we can handle that. However, we still need to be careful not to treat the -1 as a plain value; for example, the mean, minimum, or standard deviation of ages might be thrown off by that.

Olivia Gupta starts to present a trickier problem. Structurally her row looks perfect. But "9" is probably not a string in our lexicon of color names. And under our understanding of the data concerning a 6th grade class, we don't expect 102 year old students to be in it. To solve this row, we really need to know more about the collection procedure and the intention of the data. Perhaps a separate mapping of numbers to colors exists somewhere. Perhaps an age of 12 was mistranscribed as 102; but also perhaps a 102 year old serves as a teaching assistant in this class and not only students are recorded.

Sophia Robinson returns us to what looks like an obvious structural error. The row, upon visual inspection, contains perfectly good and plausible values, but they are separated by duplicate commas. Somehow, presumably, a mechanical error resulted in the line being formatted wrongly. However, most high-level tools are likely to choke on the row in an uninformative way, and we will probably need to remediate the issue more manually.

We have a pretty good idea what to do with these six rows of data, and even re-entering them from scratch would not be difficult. If we had a million rows instead, the difficulty would grow greatly, and would require considerable effort before we arrived at usable data.

Nomenclature

In this book I will use the terms feature, field, measurement, column, and occasionally variable more-or-less interchangeably. Likewise, the terms row, record, observation, and sample are also near synonyms. Tuple is used for the same concept when discussing databases (especially academically). In different academic or business fields, different ones of these terms are more prominent; and likewise different software tools choose among these.

Conceptually, most data can be thought of as a number of occasions on which we measure various attributes of a common underlying *thing*. In most tools, it is usually convenient to put these observations/samples each in a row; and correspondingly to store each of the measurements/features/fields pertaining to that thing in a column containing corresponding data for other comparable *things*.

Inasmuch as I vary the use of these roughly equivalent terms, it is simply better to fit with the domain under discussion and to make readers familiar with all the terms, which they are likely to encounter in various places for a similar intention. The choice among near synonyms is also guided by the predominant use within the particular tool, library, or programming community that is currently being discussed.

In many cases, a general concept has a strong overlap with the particular name a tool or library uses to implement or express that concept. Where relevant, I attempt to use the small typographic distinctions in the names to indicate focus. For example, I discuss *data frames* as a general paradigm for manipulating data, but refer to *DataFrame* when discussing Pandas or other libraries that use that spelling for the specific class used. Likewise, R's data.frame object is a specific implementation of the paradigm, and capitalization and punctuation will be adjusted for context.

Typography

As with most programming books, code literals will be set in a `fixed width` font, whether as excerpts inline or as blocks of code between paragraphs. For example, a code snippet, often a name, will appear as `sklearn.pipeline.Pipeline`. As a block, it would appear as:

```
scaler = sklearn.preprocessing.RobustScaler()
scaler.fit(X)
X_scaled = scaler.transform(X_train)
```

Input and output within a shell will be displayed like this:

```
sqlite> CREATE TABLE mytable(a SMALLINT, b VARCHAR(10), c REAL);
sqlite> INSERT INTO mytable(a, b, c) VALUES('123', 456, 789);
```

Names of software libraries, tools, and terms that are used in a special or distinctive sense within data science are shown with a dotted underline if they're defined in the *Glossary*. If not, these terms will be shown in **boldface** on first, or early, mention, but generally in the default typeface as common nouns elsewhere. *Italics* are used in places in the main text simply for emphasis of words or clauses in prose. In electronic versions of this book, underline will show that there is an embedded link to an external resource.

The names of software tools and libraries is a bit of a challenge to orthography (i.e. spelling). Capitalization, or lack thereof, is often used in a stylized way, and moreover sometimes these bits of software are rendered differently in different contexts. For example Python is a good proper name for a programming language, but the actual executable that launches a Python script is `python` in lower case. Tools or libraries that will usually be typed in literal form, at a command line or as a name in code, will be set in fixed width.

Still other tools have both an informal and a literal name. For example scikit-learn is stylized in lowercase, but is not the actual imported name of the library, which is `sklearn`. Moreover, the informal name would look out of place when referring to subpackages such as `sklearn.preprocessing`.

In general, the names of software libraries are actually pretty intuitive, but the *Glossary* lists the name variants used in slightly different contexts in this book.

aside

Sometimes, additional information or commentary is presented in asides that look like this, with superscripts in the text to mark their intended contexts.

Other times, tips, rules of thumb, and other things to remember look like this.

Taxonomy

Throughout this book, but especially in the first few chapters, I mention a large number of software tools and libraries that you might encounter in your work as a data scientist, developer, data analyst, or in another job title. The examples in the code of this book only use a relatively small fraction of those tools, mostly Python, and R, and a few libraries for those languages.

There are a much larger number of tools which you are fairly likely to encounter, and to need to use during your work. While this book does not specifically attempt to *document* the tools themselves, not even those tools that occur in many examples, I think it is valuable for readers to understand the general role of tools they may require in their specific tasks. When mentioning tools, I try to provide a general conceptual framework for what *kind* of thing that tool is, and point in the direction of the section or chapter that discusses purposes and tools most similar to it. You most certainly do not need to be familiar with any large number of the tools mentioned — potentially with none of them at all, not even the main programming languages used in examples.

The main lesson is "Don't Panic!", as Douglas Adams famously admonishes. You do not need to learn any specific tool discussed, but neither is any something you *cannot* learn when you need to or wish to. The *Glossary* of this book provides brief comments and definitions of terms and names used throughout this book, as well.

Included Code

In this book, I will primarily use Python and associated tools, such as Pandas, **sklearn.preprocessing**, and scipy.stats, to solve the data cleaning problems presented. R, and its Tidyverse tools, will often be shown as code alternatives. Some code samples will simply use **Bash** and the many text/data command-line processing tools available. Examples from other programming languages are occasionally mentioned, where relevant.

Quite a few additional libraries and tools are mentioned throughout this text, either only to introduce them briefly or even only to indicate they exist. Depending on your specific workplace, codebase, and colleagues, you may need to use some or all of these, even if they are not the main tools shown in this book. The *Glossary* describes (almost) all libraries mentioned, with brief descriptions of their purpose.

All of the code in this book is released to the Public Domain, or as Creative Commons CC0 (`https://creativecommons.org/share-your-work/public-domain/cc0/`) if your jurisdiction lacks a clear mechanism for placing content in the Public Domain. The URL `https://github.com/PacktPublishing/Cleaning-Data-for-Effective-Data-Science` contains the code directly printed in this book, and small modules or libraries supporting the techniques demonstrated, under the same terms. All of the datasets utilized are provided at the author's website at `https://www.gnosis.cx/cleaning/`. Some datasets may have different license terms, but only ones with reasonably open terms for use and modification are utilized. Because datasets are often large, this book will only reproduce directly very small datasets; I will often show a few representative sections of larger data in the text.

Running the Book

This book is itself written using Jupyter notebooks (`https://jupyter.org/`). This manner of creation allows for (almost) all the code within the book to be actively run before publication. The repository given above provides instructions and configuration files for creating a similar working environment. Code samples shown will usually be accompanied by the actual output of running them. For example, Python code:

```
from src.intro_students import data, cleaned
print(data)
```

```
Student#,Last Name,First Name,Favorite Color,Age
1,Johnson,Mia,periwinkle,12
2,Lopez,Liam,blue,green,13
3,Lee,Isabella,,11
```

```
4,Fisher,Mason,gray,-1
5,Gupta,Olivia,9,102
6,,Robinson,,Sophia,,blue,,12
```

```
cleaned
```

```
Student_No    Last_Name    First_Name    Favorite_Color    Age
         1      Johnson           Mia        periwinkle   12.0
         2        Lopez          Liam        blue-green   13.0
         3          Lee      Isabella         <missing>   11.0
         4       Fisher         Mason              gray    NaN
         5        Gupta        Olivia             sepia    NaN
         6     Robinson        Sophia              blue   12.0
```

Likewise in this configuration, I can run R code equally well. At times the code samples will show data being transferred between the R and Python kernels.

```
%load_ext rpy2.ipython
```

```
%%R -i cleaned
library('tibble')
# Select and rename columns
tibble(First=cleaned$First_Name,
       Last=cleaned$Last_Name,
       Age=cleaned$Age)
```

```
# A tibble: 6 x 3
  First     Last        Age
  <chr>     <chr>       <dbl>
1 Mia       Johnson       12
2 Liam      Lopez         13
3 Isabella  Lee           11
4 Mason     Fisher       NaN
5 Olivia    Gupta        NaN
6 Sophia    Robinson      12
```

Command-line tools will also be shown within code cells, for example:

```
%%bash
sed s/,,/,/g data/students.csv |
    cut -f2,3 -d, |
    tail -n +2 |
    tr , ' ' |
    sort
```

```
Fisher Mason
Gupta Olivia
Johnson Mia
Lee Isabella
Lopez Liam
Robinson Sophia
```

The code in this book was run using the following versions of the main programming languages used (Python and R). Other tools like Bash, shell utilities, or Scala in one section, are also used, but the first two are very stable across versions and should not vary in behavior. The large majority of the code shown will work at least a few versions back for the main languages; most likely the code will continue to work for several versions forward (but the future is unwritten). Specific libraries used, and the number touched on is numerous, may possibly change behaviors.

```
import sys
sys.version
```

```
'3.9.0 | packaged by conda-forge | (default, Oct 14 2020, 22:59:50)
\n[GCC 7.5.0]'
```

```
%%R
R.version.string
```

```
[1] "R version 4.0.3 (2020-10-10)"
```

Using this Book

Slovenliness is no part of data science...cleanliness is indeed next to godliness.

–cf. John Wesley

This book is intended to be suitable for use either by a self-directed reader or in more structured academic, training, or certification courses. Each chapter is accompanied by exercises at the bottom that ask readers or students to complete tasks related to what they just learned in the preceding material. The book repository contains additional discussion of some exercises, but will avoid presenting explicit solutions for mere copy-paste.

Instructors are encouraged to contact the author if they wish to plan course material around this book. Under a consulting arrangement, I am happy to provide solution code, suggestions on use of the exercises and other content, and so on.

The datasets and supporting materials for this book are available at the repository described above, and will be needed to engage fully with some of the more open ended problems presented. These extra materials will allow more interactive use of the book, and accompanying materials, than reading only would allow. However, sufficient explanation to understand the content based on the written material only will also be provided in the text.

Throughout this book I am *strongly opinionated* about a number of technical questions. I do not believe it will be difficult to distinguish my opinions from the *mere facts* I also present. I have worked in this area for a number of years, and I hope to share with readers the conclusions I have reached. Of course, even book authors are fallible beings, and if you decide to disagree with claims I make, I hope and wish that you will gain great benefit both from what you learn anew and what you are able to reformulate in strengthening your own opinions and conclusions.

This book does not use heavy mathematics or statistics, but there are references to concepts therein from time to time. Some concepts are described briefly in the *Glossary*. Readers who want to brush up on these concepts might consider these books:

- *Think Stats: Exploratory Data Analysis in Python* (`https://greenteapress.com/thinkstats2/thinkstats2.pdf`), Allen B. Downey, 2014 (O'Reilly Media; available both in free PDF and HTML versions, and as a printed book).

- *All of Statistics: A Concise Course in Statistical Inference*, Larry Wasserman, 2004 (Springer).

This book is also not focused on the *ethics of data visualization*, but I have tried to be conscientious in using plots, which I use throughout the text. Good texts that consider these issues include:

- *Data Visualization: A practical introduction* (`https://socviz.co/index.html`), Kieran Healy, 2018 (Princeton University Press; a non-final draft is available free online).

- *The Visual Display of Quantitative Information* (`https://www.edwardtufte.com/tufte/books_be`), Edward Tufte, 2001 (Graphics Press; all four of Tufte's visualization books are canonical in the field).

Data Hygiene

Throughout this book, I show you a variety of ways to modify datasets from the original versions you receive. Sometimes these transformations are between data formats or in-memory representations. At other times we impute, massage, sample, aggregate, or collate data.

Every time some transformation is made on data, we bring in certain assumptions or goals of our own; these may well be — and ideally should be — well motivated by task purpose or numeric and statistical analysis. However, they remain assumptions that could be wrong.

It is crucial to good practice of data science to version datasets as we work with them. When we draw some conclusion, or even simply when we prepare for the next transformation step, it is important to indicate which version of the data this action is based on. There are several different ways in which datasets may be versioned.

If a dataset is of moderate size, and if the transformations made are not themselves greatly time consuming, versioning within program flow is a good choice. For example, in Python-like pseudo-code:

```
data1 = read_format(raw_data)
data2 = transformation_1(data1)
data3 = transformation_2(data2)
# ... etc ...
```

When you use any version, anywhere else in a large program, it is clear from the variable name (or lookup key, etc.) which version is involved, and problems can be more easily diagnosed.

If a dataset is somewhat larger in size — to the point where keeping a number of near-copies in memory is a resource constraint — it is possible instead to track changes simply as metadata on the working dataset. This does not allow simultaneous access to multiple versions in code, but is still very useful for debugging and analysis. Again, in pseudo-code:

```
data = Annotated(read_format(raw_data))
inplace_transform_1(data)
data.version = "Transformed by step 1"
# ... actions on data ...
inplace_transform_2(data)
data.version = "Transformed by step 2"
# ... etc ...
```

At any part of an overall program, you can at least verify the version (or other metadata) associated with the dataset.

For transformations that you wish to persist longer than the run of a single program, use of **version control systems (VCSs)** is highly desirable. Most VCSs allow a concept of a *branch* where different versions of files can be maintained in parallel. If available, use of this capability is often desirable. Even if your dataset versions are strictly linear, it is possible to revert to a particular earlier version if necessary. Using accurate and descriptive commit messages is a great benefit to data versioning.

Most VCSs are intelligent about storing as few bytes as possible to describe changes. It is often possible for them to calculate a *"minimal change set"* to describe a transformation rather than simply storing an entirely new near-copy for each version. Whether or not your VCS does this with the formats you work with, data integrity and data provenance should be a more prominent concern than the potential need to allocate more disk space. Of late, Git is the most popular VCS; but the advice here can equally be followed using Apache Subversion, Mercurial, Perforce, Microsoft Visual SourceSafe, IBM Rational ClearCase, or any other modern VCS. Indeed, an older system like Concurrent Versions System (CVS) suffices for this purpose.

Exercises

None of the exercises throughout this book depend on using any specific programming language. In the discussion, Python is used most frequently, followed by R, with occasional use of other programming languages. But all exercises simply present one or more datasets and ask you to perform some task with that. Achieving those goals using the programming language of your choice is wonderful (subject to any constraints your instructor may provide if this book is used in formal pedagogy).

The toy tabular data on students given as an example is available at:

```
https://www.gnosis.cx/cleaning/students.csv
```

For this exercise, create a cleaned up version of the data following the assumptions illustrated in the code samples shown. Use your favorite programming language and tools, but the goal has these elements:

- Consistent doubled commas should be read as a single delimiter.
- Missing data in the *Favorite Color* field should be substituted with the string `<missing>`.
- Student ages should be between 9 and 14, and all other values are considered missing data.

- Some colors are numerically coded, but should be unaliased. The mapping is:

Number	Color	Number	Color
1	beige	6	alabaster
2	eggshell	7	sandcastle
3	seafoam	8	chartreuse
4	mint	9	sepia
5	cream	10	lemon

Using the small test dataset is a good way to test your code. But try also manually adding more rows with similar, or different, problems in them, and see how well your code produces a reasonable result. We have not discussed tools to accomplish this exercise yet, although you likely have used a programming language capable of solving it. Try to solve it now, but you can come back to this after later chapters if you prefer.

***

Download the example code files

The code bundle for the book is hosted on GitHub at `https://github.com/PacktPublishing/Cleaning-Data-for-Effective-Data-Science`. We also have other code bundles from our rich catalog of books and videos available at `https://github.com/PacktPublishing/`. Check them out!

Download the color images

We also provide a PDF file that has color images of the screenshots/diagrams used in this book. You can download it here: `https://static.packt-cdn.com/downloads/9781801071291_ColorImages.pdf`.

Get in touch

Feedback from our readers is always welcome.

General feedback: Email `feedback@packtpub.com`, and mention the book's title in the subject of your message. If you have questions about any aspect of this book, please email us at `questions@packtpub.com`.

Errata: Although we have taken every care to ensure the accuracy of our content, mistakes do happen. If you have found a mistake in this book we would be grateful if you would report this to us. Please visit http://www.packtpub.com/submit-errata, selecting your book, clicking on the Errata Submission Form link, and entering the details.

Piracy: If you come across any illegal copies of our works in any form on the Internet, we would be grateful if you would provide us with the location address or website name. Please contact us at copyright@packtpub.com with a link to the material.

If you are interested in becoming an author: If there is a topic that you have expertise in and you are interested in either writing or contributing to a book, please visit http://authors.packtpub.com.

Reviews

Please leave a review. Once you have read and used this book, why not leave a review on the site that you purchased it from? Potential readers can then see and use your unbiased opinion to make purchase decisions, we at Packt can understand what you think about our products, and our authors can see your feedback on their book. Thank you!

For more information about Packt, please visit packtpub.com.

PART I

Data Ingestion

1
Tabular Formats

Tidy datasets are all alike, but every messy dataset is messy in its own way.

–Hadley Wickham (cf. Leo Tolstoy)

A great deal of data both does and should live in tabular formats; to put it flatly, this means formats that have rows and columns. In a theoretical sense, it is possible to represent *every* collection of structured data in terms of multiple "flat" or "tabular" collections if we also have a concept of *relations*. Relational database management systems (RDBMSs) have had a great deal of success since 1970, and a very large part of all the world's data lives in RDBMSs. Another large share lives in formats that are not relational as such, but that are nonetheless tabular, wherein relationships may be imputed in an ad hoc, but uncumbersome, way.

As the Preface mentioned, the data ingestion chapters will concern themselves chiefly with structural or mechanical problems that make data dirty. Later in the book we will focus more on content or numerical issues in data.

This chapter discusses tabular formats including CSV, spreadsheets, SQL databases, and scientific array storage formats. The last sections look at some general concepts around data frames, which will typically be how data scientists manipulate tabular data. Much of this chapter is concerned with the actual mechanics of ingesting and working with a variety of data formats, using several different tools and programming languages. The Preface discusses why I wish to remain language-agnostic — or multilingual — in my choices. Where each format is prone to particular kinds of data integrity problems, special attention is drawn to that. Actually *remediating* those characteristic problems is largely left until later chapters; detecting them is the focus of our attention here.

As *The Hitchhiker's Guide to the Galaxy* is humorously inscribed: "Don't Panic!". We will explain in much more detail the concepts mentioned here.

***

We run the setup code that will be standard throughout this book. As the Preface mentions, each chapter can be run in full, assuming available configuration files have been utilized. Although it is not usually best practice in Python to use import *, we do so here to bring in many names without a long block of imports:

```
from src.setup import *
%load_ext rpy2.ipython

%%R
library(tidyverse)
```

With our various Python and R libraries now available, let us utilize them to start cleaning data.

Tidying Up

After every war someone has to tidy up.

–Maria Wisława Anna Szymborska

Concepts:

- Tidiness and database normalization
- Rows versus columns
- Labels versus values

Hadley Wickham and Garrett Grolemund, in their excellent and freely available book *R for Data Science* (`https://r4ds.had.co.nz/`), promote the concept of "tidy data." The Tidyverse collection of R packages attempt to realize this concept in concrete libraries. Wickham and Grolemund's idea of tidy data has a very close intellectual forebear in the concept of database normalization, which is a large topic addressed in depth neither by them nor in this current book. The canonical reference on database normalization is C. J. Date's *An Introduction to Database Systems* (Addison Wesley; 1975 and numerous subsequent editions).

In brief, tidy data carefully separates variables (the columns of a table, also called features or fields) from observations (the rows of a table, also called samples). At the intersection of these two, we find values, one data item (datum) in each cell. Unfortunately, the data we encounter is often not arranged in this useful way, and it requires *normalization*. In particular, what are really values are often represented either as columns or as rows instead. To demonstrate what this means, let us consider an example.

Returning to the small elementary school class we presented in the Preface, we might encounter data looking like this:

```
students = pd.read_csv('data/students-scores.csv')
students
```

	Last Name	First Name	4th Grade	5th Grade	6th Grade
0	Johnson	Mia	A	B+	A-
1	Lopez	Liam	B	B	A+
2	Lee	Isabella	C	C-	B-
3	Fisher	Mason	B	B-	C+
4	Gupta	Olivia	B	A+	A
5	Robinson	Sophia	A+	B-	A

This view of the data is easy for humans to read. We can see trends in the scores each student received over several years of education. Moreover, this format might lend itself to useful visualizations fairly easily:

```
# Generic conversion of letter grades to numbers
def num_score(x):
    to_num = {'A+': 4.3, 'A': 4, 'A-': 3.7,
              'B+': 3.3, 'B': 3, 'B-': 2.7,
              'C+': 2.3, 'C': 2, 'C-': 1.7}
    return x.map(lambda x: to_num.get(x, x))
```

This next cell uses a "fluent" programming style that may look unfamiliar to some Python programmers. I discuss this style in the section below on data frames. The fluent style is used in many data science tools and languages.

For example, this is typical Pandas code that plots the students' scores by year:

```
(students
     .set_index('Last Name')
     .drop('First Name', axis=1)
     .apply(num_score)
     .T
     .plot(title="Student score by year")
     .legend(bbox_to_anchor=(1, .75))
);
```

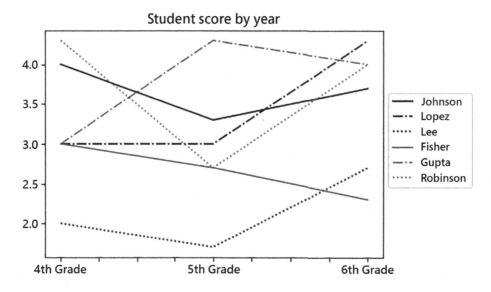

Figure 1.1: Student scores by year

This data layout exposes its limitations once the class advances to 7th grade, or if we were to obtain 3rd grade information. To accommodate such additional data, we would need to change the number and position of columns, not simply add additional rows. It is natural to make new observations or identify new samples (rows) but usually awkward to change the underlying variables (columns).

The particular class level (e.g. 4th grade) that a letter grade pertains to is, at heart, a value, not a variable. Another way to think of this is in terms of independent variables versus dependent variables, or in machine learning terms, features versus target. In some ways, the class level might correlate with or influence the resulting letter grade; perhaps the teachers at the different levels have different biases, or children of a certain age lose or gain interest in schoolwork, for example.

For most analytic purposes, this data would be more useful if we made it tidy (normalized) before further processing. In Pandas, the `DataFrame.melt()` method can perform this tidying. We pin some of the columns as `id_vars`, and we set a name for the combined columns as a variable and the letter grade as a single new column. This Pandas method is slightly magical and takes some practice to get used to. The key thing is that it preserves data, simply moving it between column labels and data values:

```
students.melt(
    id_vars=["Last Name", "First Name"],
    var_name="Level",
    value_name="Score"
).set_index(['First Name', 'Last Name', 'Level'])
```

```
First Name      Last Name       Level      Score
      Mia         Johnson    4th Grade        A
     Liam           Lopez    4th Grade        B
 Isabella             Lee    4th Grade        C
    Mason          Fisher    4th Grade        B
      ...             ...          ...      ...
 Isabella             Lee    6th Grade       B-
    Mason          Fisher    6th Grade       C+
   Olivia           Gupta    6th Grade        A
   Sophia        Robinson    6th Grade        A
18 rows × 1 columns
```

In the R Tidyverse, the procedure is similar. A tibble, which we see here, is simply a kind of data frame that is preferred in the Tidyverse:

```
%%R
library('tidyverse')

studentsR <- read_csv('data/students-scores.csv')
studentsR
```

```
── Column specification ──────────────────────────
cols(
  'Last Name' = col_character(),
  'First Name' = col_character(),
  '4th Grade' = col_character(),
  '5th Grade' = col_character(),
  '6th Grade' = col_character()
)
```

```
# A tibble: 6 x 5
  'Last Name' 'First Name' '4th Grade' '5th Grade' '6th Grade'
  <chr>       <chr>        <chr>       <chr>       <chr>
1 Johnson     Mia          A           B+          A-
2 Lopez       Liam         B           B           A+
3 Lee         Isabella     C           C-          B-
4 Fisher      Mason        B           B-          C+
5 Gupta       Olivia       B           A+          A
6 Robinson    Sophia       A+          B-          A
```

Within the Tidyverse, specifically within the **tidyr** package, there is a function pivot_longer() that is similar to Pandas' .melt(). The aggregation names and values have parameters spelled names_to and values_to, but the operation is the same:

```
%%R
studentsR <- read_csv('data/students-scores.csv')
studentsR %>%
  pivot_longer(c('4th Grade', '5th Grade', '6th Grade'),
               names_to = "Level",
               values_to = "Score")
```

```
── Column specification ─────────────────────────────────────
cols(
  'Last Name' = col_character(),
  'First Name' = col_character(),
  '4th Grade' = col_character(),
  '5th Grade' = col_character(),
  '6th Grade' = col_character()
)
```

```
# A tibble: 18 x 4
  'Last Name' 'First Name' Level     Score
  <chr>       <chr>        <chr>     <chr>
1 Johnson     Mia          4th Grade A
2 Johnson     Mia          5th Grade B+
3 Johnson     Mia          6th Grade A-
4 Lopez       Liam         4th Grade B
5 Lopez       Liam         5th Grade B
6 Lopez       Liam         6th Grade A+
7 Lee         Isabella     4th Grade C
8 Lee         Isabella     5th Grade C-
9 Lee         Isabella     6th Grade B-
```

```
10  Fisher     Mason     4th Grade  B
11  Fisher     Mason     5th Grade  B-
12  Fisher     Mason     6th Grade  C+
13  Gupta      Olivia    4th Grade  B
14  Gupta      Olivia    5th Grade  A+
15  Gupta      Olivia    6th Grade  A
16  Robinson   Sophia    4th Grade  A+
17  Robinson   Sophia    5th Grade  B-
18  Robinson   Sophia    6th Grade  A
```

The simple example above gives you a first feel for tidying tabular data. To reverse the tidying operation that moves variables (columns) to values (rows), the pivot_wider() function in tidyr can be used. In Pandas there are several related methods on DataFrames, including .pivot(), .pivot_table(), and .groupby() combined with .unstack(), which can create columns from rows (and do many other things too).

Having looked at the idea of tidiness as a general goal for tabular, let us begin looking at specific data formats, starting with comma-separated values and fixed-width files.

CSV

Speech sounds cannot be understood, delimited, classified and explained except in the light of the tasks which they perform in language.

–Roman Jakobson

Concepts:

- Delimited and fixed-width data
- Parsing problems
- Heuristics and "eyeballing"
- Inferring data types
- Escaping special characters
- Families of related CSV files

Delimited text files, especially comma-separated values (CSV) files, are ubiquitous. These are text files that put multiple values on each line and separate those values with some semi-reserved character, such as a comma. They are almost always the exchange format used to transport data between other tabular representations, but a great deal of data both starts and ends life as CSV, perhaps never passing through other formats.

Reading delimited files is not the fastest way of reading from disk into RAM memory, but it is also not the slowest. Of course, that concern only matters for large-ish datasets, not for the small datasets that make up most of our work as data scientists (small nowadays means roughly "fewer than 100k rows").

There are a great number of deficits in CSV files, but also some notable strengths. CSV files are the format second most susceptible to structural problems. All formats are generally equally prone to content problems, which are not tied to the format itself. Spreadsheets like Excel are, of course, *by a very large margin*, the worst format for every kind of data integrity concern.

At the same time, delimited formats — or fixed-width text formats — are also almost the only ones you can easily open and make sense of in a text editor or easily manipulate using command-line tools for text processing. Thereby delimited files are pretty much the only ones you can fix fully manually without specialized readers and libraries. Of course, formats that rigorously enforce structural constraints *do avoid some* of the need to do this. Later in this chapter, and in the next two chapters, a number of formats that enforce structure more are discussed.

One issue that you could encounter in reading CSV or other textual files is that the actual character set encoding may not be the one you expect, or the default on your current system. In this age of Unicode, this concern is diminishing, but only slowly, and archival files continue to exist. This topic is discussed in *Chapter 3*, *Repurposing Data Sources*, in the section *Custom Text Formats*.

Sanity Checks

As a quick example, suppose you have just received a medium-sized CSV file, and you want to perform a quick sanity check on it. At this stage, we are concerned about whether the file is formatted correctly at all. We can do this with command-line tools, even if most libraries are likely to choke on them (such as shown in the next code cell). Of course, we could also use Python, R, or another general-purpose language if we just consider the lines as text initially:

```
# Use try/except to avoid full traceback in example
try:
    pd.read_csv('data/big-random.csv')
except Exception as err:
    print_err(err)

ParserError
Error tokenizing data. C error: Expected 6 fields in line 75, saw 8
```

What went wrong there? Let us check.

```
%%bash
# What is the general size/shape of this file?
wc data/big-random.csv
```

```
 100000  100000 4335846 data/big-random.csv
```

Great! 100,000 rows; but there is some sort of problem on line 75 according to Pandas (and perhaps on other lines as well). Using a single piped Bash command that counts commas per line might provide insight. We could absolutely perform this same analysis in Python, R, or other languages; however, being familiar with command-line tools is a benefit to data scientists in performing one-off analyses like this:

```
%%bash
cat data/big-random.csv |
    tr -d -c ',\n' |
    awk '{ print length; }' |
    sort |
    uniq -c
```

```
   46 3
99909 5
   45 7
```

So we have figured out already that 99,909 of the lines have the expected 5 commas. But 46 have a deficit and 45 a surplus. Perhaps we will simply discard the bad lines, but that is not altogether too many to consider fixing by hand, even in a text editor. We need to make a judgement, on a per problem basis, about both the relative effort and reliability of automation of fixes versus manual approaches. Let us take a look at a few of the problem rows:

```
%%bash
grep -C1 -nP '^([^,]+,){7}' data/big-random.csv | head
```

```
74-squarcerai,45,quiescenze,12,scuoieremo,70
75:fantasmagorici,28,immischiavate,44,schiavizzammo,97,sfilzarono,49
76-interagiste,50,repentagli,72,attendato,95
--
712-resettando,58,strisciato,46,insaldai,62
713:aspirasse,15,imbozzimatrici,70,incanalante,93,succhieremo,41
714-saccarometriche,18,stremaste,12,hindi,19
--
8096-squincio,16,biascicona,93,solisti,70
8097:rinegoziante,50,circoncidiamo,83,stringavate,79,stipularono,34
```

Looking at these lists of Italian words and integers of slightly varying numbers of fields does not immediately illuminate the nature of the problem. We likely need more domain or problem knowledge. However, given that fewer than 1% of rows are a problem, perhaps we should simply discard them for now. If you do decide to make a modification such as removing rows, then versioning the data, with accompanying documentation of change history and reasons, becomes crucial to good data and process provenance.

The next cell uses a regular expression to filter the lines in the "almost CSV" file. The pattern may appear confusing, but regular expressions provide a compact way of describing patterns in text. The match in pat indicates that from the beginning of a line (^) until the end of that line ($) there are exactly five repetitions of character sequences that do not include commas, each followed by one comma ([^,]+,):

```
import re
pat = re.compile(r'^([^,]+,){5}[^,]*$')
with open('data/big-random.csv') as fh:
    lines = [l.strip().split(',')
             for l in fh if re.match(pat, l)]
pd.DataFrame(lines)
```

	0	1	2	3	4	5
0	infilaste	21	esemplava	15	stabaccavo	73
1	abbadaste	50	enartrosi	85	iella	54
2	frustulo	77	temporale	83	scoppianti	91
3	gavocciolo	84	postelegrafiche	93	inglesizzanti	63
...	...	...	...	...	...	...
99905	notareschi	60	paganico	64	esecutavamo	20
99906	rispranghiamo	11	schioccano	44	imbozzarono	80
99907	compone	85	disfronderebbe	19	vaporizzavo	54
99908	ritardata	29	scordare	43	appuntirebbe	24

99909 rows × 6 columns

In the code we managed, within Python, to read all rows without formatting problems. We could also have used the pd.read_csv() parameter error_bad_lines=False to achieve the same effect, but walking through it in plain Python and Bash gives you a better picture of why they are excluded.

The Good, the Bad, and the Textual Data

Let us return to some virtues and deficits of CSV files. Here when we mention CSV, we really mean any kind of delimited file. And specifically, text files that store tabular data nearly always use a single character for a delimiter, and end rows/records with a newline (or carriage return and newline in legacy formats). Other than commas, probably the most common delimiters you will encounter are tabs and the pipe character, |. However, nearly all tools are more than happy to use an arbitrary character.

Fixed-width files are similar to delimited ones. Technically they are different in that, although they are line-oriented, they put each field of data in specific character positions within each line. An example is used in the next code cell below. Decades ago, when Fortran and Cobol were more popular, fixed-width formats were more prevalent; my perception is that their use has diminished in favor of delimited files. In any case, fixed-width textual data files have most of the same pitfalls and strengths as do delimited ones.

The Bad

Columns in delimited or flat files do not carry a data type, being simply text values. Many tools will (optionally) make guesses about the data type, but these are subject to pitfalls. Moreover, even where the tools accurately guess the broad type category (i.e. string vs. integer vs. real number), they cannot guess the specific bit length desired, where that matters.

Likewise, the representation used for "real" numbers is not encoded—most systems deal with IEEE-754 floating-point numbers of some length, but occasionally decimals of some specific length are more appropriate for a purpose.

The most typical way that type inference goes wrong is where the initial records in some dataset have an apparent pattern, but later records deviate from this. The software library may infer one data type but later encounter strings that cannot be cast as such. "Earlier" and "later" here can have several different meanings.

For out-of-core data frame libraries like **Vaex** and **Dask** (Python libraries) that read lazily, type heuristics might be applied to a first few records (and perhaps some other sampling) but will not see those strings that do not follow the assumed pattern. However, later might also mean months later, when new data arrives.[partnum]

> *partnum*
>
> For example, in a former job of mine, we received client data about commercial products that had a "part number." That number was an actual integer, for many months, until it was not; it became a string that sometimes mixed letters with numerals. Unfortunately, other tooling had already made a wrong assumption about the undocumented data type (in this case an SQL schema, but it could be other code as well).

Most data frame libraries are greedy about inferring data types—although all will allow manual specification to shortcut inference.

For many layouts, data frame libraries can guess a fixed-width format and infer column positions and data types (where it cannot guess, we could manually specify). But the guesses about data types can go wrong. For example, viewing the raw text, we see a fixed-width layout in `parts.fwf`:

```
%%bash
cat data/parts.fwf
```

```
Part_No  Description          Maker              Price (USD)
12345    Wankle rotary engine  Acme Corporation   555.55
67890    Sousaphone           Marching Inc.      333.33
2468     Feather Duster       Sweeps Bros        22.22
A9922    Area 51 metal fragment  No Such Agency   9999.99
```

Reading this with Pandas correctly infers the intended column positions for the fields:

```
df = pd.read_fwf('data/parts.fwf', nrows=3)
df
```

```
   Part_No            Description              Maker  Price (USD)
0    12345  Wankle rotary engine   Acme Corporation       555.55
1    67890            Sousaphone      Marching Inc.       333.33
2     2468        Feather Duster        Sweeps Bros        22.22
```

```
df.dtypes
```

```
Part_No          int64
Description      object
Maker            object
Price (USD)      float64
dtype: object
```

We deliberately only read the start of the parts.fwf file. From those first few rows, Pandas made a type inference of int64 for the Part_No column.

Let us read the entire file. Pandas does the "right thing" here: Part_No becomes a generic object, i.e. string. However, if we had a million rows instead, and the heuristics Pandas uses, for speed and memory efficiency, happened to limit inference to the first 100,000 rows, we might not be so lucky:

```
df = pd.read_fwf('data/parts.fwf')
df
```

```
   Part_No              Description              Maker  Price (USD)
0    12345     Wankle rotary engine  Acme Corporation       555.55
1    67890               Sousaphone    Marching Inc.       333.33
2     2468            Feather Duster      Sweeps Bros        22.22
3    A9922  Area 51 metal fragment   No Such Agency      9999.99
```

```
df.dtypes   # type of 'Part_No' changed
```

```
Part_No          object
Description      object
Maker            object
Price (USD)      float64
dtype: object
```

R tibbles behave the same as Pandas, with the minor difference that data type imputation always uses 1,000 rows and will discard values if inconsistencies occur thereafter. Pandas can be configured to read all rows for inference, but by default reads a dynamically determined number. Pandas will sample more rows than R does, but still only approximately tens of thousands. The R collections data.frame and data.table are likewise similar. Let us read in the same file as above using R:

```
%%R
read_table('data/parts.fwf')
```

```
— Column specification ─────────────────────────────
cols(
  Part_No = col_character(),
  Description = col_character(),
```

```
    Maker = col_character(),
    'Price (USD)' = col_double()
)
# A tibble: 4 x 4
  Part_No Description          Maker               'Price (USD)'
  <chr>   <chr>                <chr>                       <dbl>
1 12345   Wankle rotary engine Acme Corporation             556.
2 67890   Sousaphone           Marching Inc.                333.
3 2468    Feather Duster       Sweeps Bros                   22.2
4 A9922   Area 51 metal fragment No Such Agency           10000.
```

Again, the first three rows are consistent with an integer data type, although this is inaccurate for later rows:

```
%%R
read_table('data/parts.fwf',
           n_max = 3,
           col_types = cols("i", "-", "f", "n"))

# A tibble: 3 x 3
  Part_No Maker            'Price (USD)'
    <int> <fct>                    <dbl>
1   12345 Acme Corporation          556.
2   67890 Marching Inc.             333.
3    2468 Sweeps Bros                22.2
```

***

Delimited files—but not so much fixed-width files—are prone to escaping issues. In particular, CSVs specifically often contain descriptive fields that sometimes contain commas within the value itself. When done right, this comma should be escaped. It is often not done right in practice.

CSV is actually a family of different dialects, mostly varying in their escaping conventions. Sometimes, spacing before or after commas is treated differently across dialects as well. One approach to escaping is to put quotes around either every string value, or every value of any kind, or perhaps only those values that contain the prohibited comma. This varies by tool and by the version of the tool. Of course, if you quote fields, there is potentially a need to escape those quotes; usually, this is done by placing a backslash before the quote character when it is part of the value.

An alternate approach is to place a backslash before those commas that are not intended as a delimiter but rather as part of a string value (or a numeric value that might be formatted, e.g. $1,234.56). Guessing the variant can be a mess, and even single files are not necessarily self-consistent between rows, in practice (often different tools or versions of tools have touched the data).

Tab-separated and pipe-separated formats are often chosen with the hope of avoiding escaping issues. This works to an extent. Both tabs and pipe symbols are far less common in ordinary prose. But both still wind up occurring in text occasionally, and all the escaping issues come back. Moreover, in the face of escaping, the simplest tools sometimes fail. For example, the Bash command `cut -d`, will not work in these cases, nor will Python's `str.split(',')`. A more custom parser becomes necessary, albeit a simple one compared to full-fledged grammars. Python's standard library `csv` module is one such custom parser.

The corresponding danger for fixed-width files, in contrast to delimited ones, is that values become too long. Within a certain line position range you can have any codepoints whatsoever (other than newlines). But once the description or name that someone thought would never be longer than, say, 20 characters becomes 21 characters, the format fails.

***

A special consideration arises around reading datetime formats. Data frame libraries that read datetime values typically have an optional switch to parse certain columns as datetime formats. Libraries such as Pandas support heuristic guessing of datetime formats; the problem here is that applying a heuristic to each of millions of rows can be *exceedingly slow*. Where a date format is uniform, using a manual format specifier can make it several orders of magnitude faster to read. Of course, where the format varies, heuristics are practically magic; and perhaps we should simply marvel that the dog can talk at all rather than criticize its grammar. Let us look at a Pandas attempt to guess datetimes for each row of a tab-separated file:

```
%%bash
# Notice many date formats
cat data/parts.tsv
```

Part_No	Description	Date	Price (USD)
12345	Wankle rotary	2020-04-12T15:53:21	555.55
67890	Sousaphone	April 12, 2020	333.33
2468	Feather Duster	4/12/2020	22.22
A9922	Area 51 metal	04/12/20	9999.99

```
# Let Pandas make guesses for each row
# VERY SLOW for large tables
```

```
parts = pd.read_csv('data/parts.tsv',
            sep='\t', parse_dates=['Date'])
parts
```

	Part_No	Description	Date	Price (USD)
0	12345	Wankle rotary	2020-04-12 15:53:21	555.55
1	67890	Sousaphone	2020-04-12 00:00:00	333.33
2	2468	Feather Duster	2020-04-12 00:00:00	22.22
3	A9922	Area 51 metal	2020-04-12 00:00:00	9999.99

We can verify that the dates are genuinely a datetime data type within the
DataFrame:

```
parts.dtypes
```

```
Part_No                 object
Description             object
Date            datetime64[ns]
Price (USD)            float64
dtype: object
```

We have looked at some challenges and limitations of delimited and fixed-width
formats; let us look at their considerable advantages as well.

The Good

The biggest strength of CSV files, and their delimited or fixed-width cousins, is the
ubiquity of tools to read and write them. Every library dealing with data frames or
arrays, across every programming language, knows how to handle them. Most of
the time the libraries parse the quirky cases pretty well. Every spreadsheet program
imports and exports as CSV. Every RDBMS—and most non-relational databases
as well—imports and exports as CSV. Most programmers' text editors even have
facilities to make editing CSV easier. Python has a standard library module called
csv that processes many dialects of CSV (or other delimited formats) as a line-by-line
record reader.

The fact that so very many structurally flawed CSV files live in the wild shows that
not *every* tool handles them entirely correctly. In part, that is probably because the
format is simple enough to *almost* work without custom tools at all. I have myself, in
a "throw-away script," written print(",".join([1,2,3,4]), file=csv) countless
times; that works well, until it doesn't. Of course, throw-away scripts become fixed
standard procedures for data flow far too often.

***

The lack of type specification is often a strength rather than a weakness. For example, the part numbers mentioned a few pages ago may have started out always being integers as an actual business intention, but later on a need arose to use non-integer "numbers." With formats that have a formal type specifier, we generally have to perform a migration and copy to move old data into a new format that follows the loosened or revised constraints.

One particular case where a data type change happens especially often, in my experience, is with finite-width character fields. Initially, some field is specified as needing 5, or 15, or 100 characters for its maximum length, but then a need for a longer string is encountered later, and a fixed table structure or SQL database needs to be modified to accommodate the longer length. Even more often — especially with databases — the requirement is under-documented, and we wind up with a dataset filled with truncated strings that are of little utility (and perhaps permanently lost data).

Text formats in general are usually flexible in this regard. Delimited files — but not fixed-width files — will happily contain fields of arbitrary length. This is similarly true of JSON data, YAML data,*config* XML data, log files, and some other formats that simply utilize text, often with line-oriented records. In all of this, data typing is very loose and only genuinely exists in the data processing steps. That is often a great virtue.

config

YAML usually contains relatively short configuration information rather than *data* in the prototypic sense. TOML is a similar format in this regard, as is the older INI format. All of these are really intended for hand editing, and hence are usually of small size, even though good APIs for reading and writing their data are common. While you could put a million records into any of these formats, you will rarely or never encounter that in practice.

***

A related "looseness" of CSV and similar formats is that we often indefinitely aggregate multiple CSV files that follow the same informal schema. Writing a different CSV file for each day, or each hour, or each month, of some ongoing data collection is very commonplace. Many tools, such as Dask and **Spark**, will seamlessly treat collections of CSV files (matching a glob pattern on the file system) as a single dataset. Of course, in tools that do not directly support this, manual concatenation is still not difficult. But under the model of having a directory that contains an indefinite number of related CSV snapshots, presenting it as a single common object is helpful.

The libraries that handle families of CSV files seamlessly are generally lazy and distributed. That is, with these tools, you do not typically read in all the CSV files at once, or at least not into the main memory of a single machine. Rather, various cores or various nodes in a cluster will each obtain file handles to individual files, and the schema information will be inferred from only one or a few of the files, with actual processing deferred until a specific (parallel) computation is launched. Splitting processing of an individual CSV file across cores is not easily tractable, since a reader can only determine where a new record begins by scanning until it finds a newline.

While details of the specific APIs of libraries for distributed data frames is outside the scope of this book, the fact that parallelism is easily possible given an initial division of data into many files is a significant strength for CSV as a format. Dask in particular works by creating many Pandas DataFrames and coordinating computation upon all of them (or those needed for a given result) with an API that exactly copies the same methods of individual Pandas objects:

```
# Generated data files with random values
from glob import glob
# Use glob() function to identify files matching pattern
glob('data/multicsv/2000-*.csv')[:8] # ... and more
```

```
['data/multicsv/2000-01-27.csv',
 'data/multicsv/2000-01-26.csv',
 'data/multicsv/2000-01-06.csv',
 'data/multicsv/2000-01-20.csv',
 'data/multicsv/2000-01-13.csv',
 'data/multicsv/2000-01-22.csv',
 'data/multicsv/2000-01-21.csv',
 'data/multicsv/2000-01-24.csv']
```

We read this family of CSV files into one virtualized DataFrame that acts like a Pandas DataFrame, even if loading it with Pandas would require more memory than our local system allows. In this specific example, the collection of CSV files is not genuinely too large for a modern workstation to read into memory; but when it becomes so, using some distributed or out-of-core system like Dask is necessary to proceed at all:

```
import dask.dataframe as dd
df = dd.read_csv('data/multicsv/2000-*-*.csv',
                 parse_dates=['timestamp'])
print("Total rows:", len(df))
df.head()
Total rows: 2592000
```

	Timestamp	id	name	x	y
0	2000-01-01 00:00:00	979	Zelda	0.802163	0.166619

```
1  2000-01-01 00:00:01  1019  Ingrid  -0.349999   0.704687
2  2000-01-01 00:00:02  1007  Hannah  -0.169853  -0.050842
3  2000-01-01 00:00:03  1034  Ursula   0.868090  -0.190783
4  2000-01-01 00:00:04  1024  Ingrid   0.083798   0.109101
```

When we require some summary to be computed, Dask will coordinate workers to aggregate on each individual DataFrame, then aggregate those aggregations. There are more nuanced issues of which operations can be reframed in this "map-reduce" style and which cannot, but that is the general idea (and the Dask or Spark developers have thought about this for you so you do not have to):

```
df.mean().compute()
```

```
id    999.965606
x       0.000096
y       0.000081
dtype: float64
```

Having looked at some pros and cons of working with CSV data, let us turn to another format where a great deal of data is stored. Unfortunately, for spreadsheets, there are almost exclusively cons.

Spreadsheets Considered Harmful

Drugs are bad, m'kay. You shouldn't do drugs, m'kay. If you do them you're bad, because drugs are bad, m'kay. It's a bad thing to do drugs, so don't be bad by doing drugs, m'kay.

–Mr. Mackay (South Park)

Concepts:

- Non-enforced field/column identity
- Computational opacity
- Semi-tabular data
- Non-contiguous data
- Invisible data and data type discrepancies
- User interface as attractive nuisance

Edward Tufte, that brilliant doyen of information visualization, wrote an essay called *The Cognitive Style of PowerPoint: Pitching Out Corrupts Within* (`https://www.edwardtufte.com/tufte/powerpoint`). Among his observations is that the manner in which slide presentations, and PowerPoint specifically, hides important information more than it reveals it was a major or even main cause of the 2003 Columbia space shuttle disaster. PowerPoint is anathema to clear presentation of information.

To no less of a degree, spreadsheets in general, and Excel in particular, are anathema to effective data science. While perhaps not as much as in CSV files, a great share of the world's data lives in Excel spreadsheets. There are numerous kinds of data corruption that are the special realm of spreadsheets. As a bonus, data science tools read spreadsheets much more slowly than they do every other format, while spreadsheets also have hard limits on the amount of data they can contain that other formats do not impose.

Most of what spreadsheets do to make themselves convenient for their users makes them bad for scientific reproducibility, data science, statistics, data analysis, and related areas.*computation* Spreadsheets have apparent rows and columns in them, but nothing enforces consistent use of them, even within a single sheet. Some particular feature often lives in column F for some rows, but the equivalent thing is in column H for other rows, for example. Contrast this with a CSV file or an SQL table; for these latter formats, while all the data in a column is not necessarily *good* data, it generally must pertain to the same feature.

computation

Another danger of spreadsheets is not around data ingestion, per se, at all. Computation within spreadsheets is spread among many cells in no obvious or easily inspectable order, leading to numerous large-scale disastrous consequences (loss of billions in financial transactions (`https://www.businessinsider.com/excel-partly-to-blame-for-trading-loss-2013-2`); a worldwide economic planning debacle (`https://theconversation.com/the-reinhart-rogoff-error-or-how-not-to-excel-at-economics-13646`); a massive failure of Covid-19 contact tracing (`https://www.bbc.com/news/technology-54423988`) in the UK). The European Spreadsheet Risks Interest Group (`http://www.eusprig.org/`) is an entire organization devoted to chronicling such errors. They present a number of lovely quotes, including this one:

> There is a literature on denial, which focuses on illness and the fact that many people with terminal illnesses deny the seriousness of their condition or the need to take action. Apparently, what is very difficult and unpleasant to do is difficult to contemplate. Although denial has only been studied extensively in the medical literature, it is likely to appear whenever required actions are difficult or onerous. Given the effortful nature of spreadsheet testing, developers may be victims of denial, which may manifest itself in the form of overconfidence in accuracy so that extensive testing will not be needed.

–Ray Panko, 2003 (`https://arxiv.org/abs/0804.0941`)

In procedural programming (including object-oriented programming), actions flow sequentially through code, with clear locations for branches or function calls; even in functional paradigms, compositions are explicitly stated. In spreadsheets it is anyone's guess what computation depends on what else, and what data ranges are actually included. Errors can occasionally be found accidentally, but program analysis and debugging are *nearly* impossible. Users who know only, or mostly, spreadsheets will likely object that *some* tools exist to identify dependencies within a spreadsheet; this is technically true in the same sense as that many goods transported by freight train could also be carried on a wheelbarrow.

Moreover, every cell in a spreadsheet can have a different data type. Usually, the type is assigned by heuristic guesses within the spreadsheet interface. These are highly sensitive to the exact keystrokes used, the order cells are entered, whether data is copy/pasted between blocks, and numerous other things that are both hard to predict and that change between every version of every spreadsheet software program. Infamously, for example, Excel interprets the gene name SEPT2 (Septin 2) as a date (at least in a wide range of versions). Compounding the problem, the interfaces of spreadsheets make determining the data type for a given cell uncomfortably difficult.

Let us start with an example. The screenshot below is of a commonplace and ordinary-looking spreadsheet. Yes, some values are not aligned in their cells exactly consistently, but that is purely an aesthetic issue. The first problem that jumps out at us is the fact that one sheet is being used to represent two different (in this case related) tables of data. Already this is going to be difficult to make tidy:

	A	B	C	D
1	timestamp	id	name	x
2	2000-01-01 0:00:00	979	Zelda	0.802163
3	2000-01-01 0:00:01	1020	Ingrid	-0.349999
4	2000-01-01 0:00:02	1007	Hannah	-0.169853
5	2000-01-01 0:00:03	1034	Ursula	0.86809
6				
7				
8	timestamp	id	name	y
9	2000-01-01 0:00:02	1007	Hannah	-0.050842
10	2000-01-01 0:00:03	1034	Ursula	-0.190783
11	2000-01-01 0:00:04	1024	Ingrid	0.109101

Figure 1.2: Excel pitfalls

If we simply tell Pandas (or specifically the supporting **openpyxl** library) to try to make sense of this file, it makes a sincere effort and applies fairly intelligent heuristics. It does not crash, to its credit. Other DataFrame libraries will be similar, with different quirks you will need to learn. But what went wrong that we can see initially?

```
# Default engine 'xlrd' might have bug in Python 3.9
pd.read_excel('data/Excel-Pitfalls.xlsx',
              sheet_name="Dask Sample", engine="openpyxl")
```

```
            Timestamp      id      name        x
0   2000-01-01 00:00:00    979     Zelda    0.802163
1   2000-01-01 0:00:01    1019.5   Ingrid   -0.349999
2   2000-01-01 00:00:02   1007     Hannah   -0.169853
3   2000-01-01 00:00:03   1034     Ursula   0.86809
4            timestamp      id      name        y
5   2000-01-01 00:00:02   1007     Hannah   -0.050842
6   2000-01-01 00:00:03   1034     Ursula   -0.190783
7   2000-01-01 00:00:04   1024     Ingrid   0.109101
```

Right away we can notice that the id column contains a value 1019.5 that was invisible in the spreadsheet display. Whether that column is intended as a floating-point or an integer is not obvious at this point. Moreover, notice that visually the date on that same row looks slightly wrong. We will come back to this.

As a first step, we can, with laborious manual intervention, pull out the two separate tables we actually care about. Pandas is actually a little bit *too smart* here—it will, by default, ignore the data typing actually in the spreadsheet and do inference similar to what it does with a CSV file. For this purpose, we tell it to use the data type actually stored by Excel. Pandas' inference is not a panacea, but it *is* a useful option at times (it can fix *some*, but not *all*, of the issues we note below; however, other things are made worse). For the next few paragraphs, we wish to see the raw data types stored in the spreadsheet itself:

```
df1 = pd.read_excel('data/Excel-Pitfalls.xlsx',
                    nrows=5, dtype=object, engine="openpyxl")
df1.loc[:2] # Just look at first few rows
```

```
            Timestamp      id      name        x
0   2000-01-01 00:00:00    979     Zelda    0.802163
1   2000-01-01 00:00:01   1019.5   Ingrid   -0.349999
2   2000-01-01 00:00:02   1007     Hannah   -0.169853
```

We can read the second implicit table as well by using the `pd.read_excel()` parameter `skiprows`:

```
pd.read_excel('data/Excel-Pitfalls.xlsx', skiprows=7,
engine="openpyxl")
```

```
            Timestamp    id    name          y
0    2000-01-01 00:00:02  1007  Hannah  -0.050842
1    2000-01-01 00:00:03  1034  Ursula  -0.190783
2    2000-01-01 00:00:04  1024  Ingrid   0.109101
```

If we look at the data types read in, we will see they are all Python objects to preserve the various cell types. But let us look more closely at what we actually have:

```
df1.dtypes
```

```
timestamp     datetime64[ns]
id                    object
name                  object
x                     object
dtype: object
```

The timestamps in this particular small example are all reasonable to parse with Pandas. But real-life spreadsheets often provide something much more ambiguous, often impossible to parse as dates. Look above at *Figure 1.2* to notice that the data type is invisible in the spreadsheet itself. We can find the Python data type of the generic object stored in each cell:

```
# Look at the stored data type of each cell
tss = df1.loc[:2, 'timestamp']
for i, ts in enumerate(tss):
    print(f"TS {i}: {ts}\t{ts.__class__.__name__}")
```

```
TS 0: 2000-01-01 00:00:00        Timestamp
TS 1: 2000-01-01 00:00:01        Timestamp
TS 2: 2000-01-01 00:00:02        Timestamp
```

The Pandas `to_datetime()` function is idempotent[idempotent] and would have run if we had not specifically disabled it by using `dtype=object` in the `pd.read_excel()` call. However, many spreadsheets are far messier, and the conversion will simply not succeed, producing an `object` column in any case. Particular cells in a column might contain numbers, formulae, or strings looking nothing like dates (or sometimes strings looking just enough like date string that a human, but not a machine, might guess the intent; say "Decc 23,, 201.9").

idempotent

The word and concept *idempotent* is a useful one in mathematics, computer science, and programming in general. It means that calling the same function again on its own output will continue to produce the same answer. This is related to the even fancier concept in mathematics of an *attractor*. In ordinary programming terms, this means that you do not have to worry as much about potentially modifying a value repeatedly in an idempotent way, which may emerge from the vicissitudes of program flow. In other words, whatever the initial x is, you know that: python pd.to_datetime(x) == pd.to_datetime(pd.to_datetime(x))

Let's look at using `pd.to_datetime()`:

```
pd.to_datetime(tss)
```

```
0    2000-01-01 00:00:00
1    2000-01-01 00:00:01
2    2000-01-01 00:00:02
Name: timestamp, dtype: datetime64[ns]
```

Other columns pose a similar difficulty. The values that look identical in the spreadsheet view of the `id` column are actually a mixture of integers, floating-point numbers, and strings. It is *conceivable* that such was the intention, but in practice it is almost always an accidental result of the ways that spreadsheets hide information from their users. By the time these datasets arrive on your data science desk, they are merely messy, and the causes are lost in the sands of time. Let us look at the data types in the `id` column:

```
# Look at the stored data type of each cell
ids = df1.loc[:3, 'id']
for i, id_ in enumerate(ids):
    print(f"id {i}: {id_}\t{id_.__class__.__name__}")
```

```
id 0: 979          int
id 1: 1019.5    float
id 2: 1007         int
id 3: 1034         str
```

Of course, tools like Pandas can type cast values after reading them, but we require domain-specific knowledge of the dataset to know what cast is appropriate. Let us cast data using the .astype() method:

```
ids.astype(int)
```

```
0      979
1      1019
2      1007
3      1034
Name: id, dtype: int64
```

Putting together the cleanup we mention, we might carefully type our data in a manner similar to the following:

```
# Only rows through index '3' are useful
# We are casting to more specific data types
#    based on domain and problem knowledge
df1 = df1.loc[0:3].astype(
    {'id': np.uint16,
     'name': pd.StringDtype(),
     'x': float})
# datetimes require conversion function, not just type
df1['timestamp'] = pd.to_datetime(df1.timestamp)
print(df1.dtypes)
```

```
timestamp      datetime64[ns]
id                     uint16
name                   string
x                     float64
dtype: object
```

```
df1.set_index('timestamp')
```

```
              timestamp      id      name         x
2000-01-01 00:00:00         979     Zelda     0.802163
2000-01-01 00:00:01        1019    Ingrid    -0.349999
2000-01-01 00:00:02        1007    Hannah    -0.169853
2000-01-01 00:00:03        1034    Ursula     0.868090
```

What makes spreadsheets harmful is not principally their underlying data formats. Non-ancient versions of Excel (`.xlsx`), LibreOffice (OpenDocument, `.ods`), and Gnumeric (`.gnm`) have all adopted a similar format at the byte level. That is, they all store their data in XML formats, then compress those to save space. As I mentioned, this is slower than other approaches, but that concern is secondary.

If one of these spreadsheet formats were used purely as an exchange format among structured tools, they would be perfectly suitable to preserve and represent data. It is instead the social and user interface (UI) elements of spreadsheets that make them dangerous. The "tabular" format of Excel combines the worst elements of untyped CSV and strongly typed SQL databases. Rather than assigning a data type by column/feature, it allows type assignments per cell.

Per-cell typing is almost always the wrong thing to do for any data science purpose. It neither allows flexible decisions by programming tools (either using inference or type declaration APIs) nor does it enforce consistency of different values that should belong to the same feature at the time data is stored. Moreover, the relatively free-form style of entry in the UIs of spreadsheets does nothing to guide users away from numerous kinds of entry errors (not only data typing, but also various misalignments within the grid, accidental deletions or insertions, and so on). Metaphorically, the danger posed by spreadsheet UIs resembles the concept in tort law of an "attractive nuisance" — they do not directly create the harm, but they make harm exceedingly likely with minor inattention.

Unfortunately, there do not currently exist any general-purpose data entry tools in widespread use. Database entry forms could serve the purpose of enforcing structure on data entry, but they are limited for non-programmatic data exploration. Moreover, the use of structured forms, whatever the format where the data might be subsequently stored, currently requires at least a modicum of software development effort, and many general users of spreadsheets lack this ability. Something similar to a spreadsheet, but that allowed locking data type constraints on columns, would be a welcome addition to the world. Perhaps one or several of my readers will create and popularize such tools.

For now, the reality is that many users will create spreadsheets that you will need to extract data from as a data scientist. This will inevitably be more work for you than if you were provided a different format. But think carefully about the block regions and tabs/sheets that are of actual relevance, about the problem-required data types for casts, and about how to clean unprocessable values. With effort the data will enter your data pipelines.

We can turn now to well structured and carefully date typed formats; those stored in relational databases.

SQL RDBMS

At the time, Nixon was normalizing relations with China. I figured that if he could normalize relations, then so could I.

–E. F. Codd (inventor of relational database theory)

Concepts:

- Python DB-API and SQL drivers
- Data type impedance mismatches
- Manually casting to exact data types
- Truncation and overflow
- Wrapping versus clipping

Relational database management systems (RDBMSs) are enormously powerful and versatile. For the most part, their requirement of strict column typing and frequent use of formal foreign keys and constraints is a great boon for data science. While specific RDBMSs vary greatly in how well normalized, indexed, and designed they are—not every organization has or utilizes a database engineer specifically—even somewhat informally assembled databases have many desirable properties for data science. Not all relational databases are *tidy*, but they all take you several large steps in that direction.

Working with relational databases requires some knowledge of **Structured Query Language** (**SQL**). For small data, and perhaps for medium-sized data, you can get by with reading entire tables into memory as data frames. Operations like filtering, sorting, grouping, and even joins can be performed with data frame libraries. However, it is much more efficient if you are able to do these kinds of operations directly at the database level; it is an absolute necessity when working with big data. A database that has millions or billions of records, distributed across tens or hundreds of related tables, can itself quickly produce the hundreds of thousands of rows (tuples) that you need for the task at hand. But loading all of these rows into memory is either unnecessary or simply impossible.

There are many excellent books and tutorials on SQL. I do not have a specific one to recommend over others, but finding a suitable text to get up to speed—if you are not already—is not difficult. The general concepts of GROUP BY, JOIN, and WHERE clauses are the main things you should know as a data scientist.

If you have a bit more control over the database you pull data from, knowing something about how to intelligently index tables, and optimize slow queries by reformulation and looking at EXPLAIN output, is helpful. However, it is quite likely that you, as a data scientist, will not have full access to database administration. If you do have such access: be careful!

For this book, I use a local PostgreSQL server to illustrate APIs. I find that PostgreSQL is vastly better at query optimization than is its main open source competitor, MySQL. Both behave equally well with careful index tuning, but generally PostgreSQL is much faster for queries that must be optimized on an ad hoc basis by the query planner. In general, almost all of the APIs I show will be nearly identical across drivers in Python or in R (and in most other languages) whether you use PostgreSQL, MySQL, Oracle DB, DB2, SQL Server, or any other RDBMS. The Python DB-API, in particular, is well standardized across drivers. Even the single-file RDBMS SQLite3, which is included in the Python standard library, is almost DB-API compliant (and .sqlite is a very good storage format).

Within the setup.py module that is loaded by each chapter and is available within the source code repository, some database setup is performed. If you run some of the functions contained therein, you will be able to create generally the same configuration on your system as I have on the one where I am writing this. Actual installation of an RDBMS is not addressed in this book; see the instructions accompanying your database software. But a key and simple step is creating a *connection* to the database:

```
# Similar with adapter other than psycopg2
con = psycopg2.connect(database=db, host=host,
            user=user, password=pwd)
```

This connection object will be used in subsequent code in this book. We also create an engine object that is an SQLAlchemy wrapper around a connection that adds some enhancements. Some libraries like Pandas require using an engine rather than only a connection. We can create that as follows:

```
engine = create_engine(
    f'postgresql://{user}:{pwd}@{host}:{port}/{db}')
```

Massaging Data Types

I used the Dask data created earlier in this chapter to populate a table with the following schema. These metadata values are defined in the RDBMS itself. Within this section, we will work with the elaborate and precise data types that relational databases provide:

Column	Data Type	Data Width
index	integer	32
timestamp	timestamp without time zone	None
id	smallint	16
name	character	10
x	numeric	6
y	real	24

This is the same data structure created in the previous Dask discussion, but I have somewhat arbitrarily imposed more specific data types on the fields. The PostgreSQL "data width" shown is a bit odd; it mixes bit length with byte length depending on the type. Moreover, for the floating-point y, it shows the bit length of the mantissa, not of the entire 32-bit memory word. But in general we can see that different columns have different specific types.

When designing tables, database engineers generally try to choose data widths that are sufficient for the purpose, but also as small as the requirement allows. If you need to store billions of person ages, for example, a 256-bit integer could certainly hold those numbers, but an 8-bit integer can also hold all the values that can occur, using 1/32 as much storage space.

Using the Python DB-API loses some data type information. It does *pretty well*, but Python does not have a full range of native types. The fractional numbers are accurately stored as either `Decimal` or native floating-point, but the specific bit lengths are lost. Likewise, the integer is a Python integer of unbounded size. The `name` strings are always 10 characters long, but for most purposes we probably want to apply `str.rstrip()` (strip whitespace at right end) to take off the surrounding whitespace:

```
# Function connect_local() spelled out in Chapter 4 (Anomaly Detection)
con, engine = connect_local()
cur = con.cursor()
cur.execute("SELECT * FROM dask_sample")
pprint(cur.fetchmany(2))
```

```
[(3456,
  datetime.datetime(2000, 1, 2, 0, 57, 36),
  941,
  'Alice     ',
  Decimal('-0.612'),
  -0.636485),
 (3457,
```

```
datetime.datetime(2000, 1, 2, 0, 57, 37),
1004,
'Victor    ',
Decimal('0.450'),
-0.687718)]
```

Unfortunately, we lose even more data type information using Pandas (at least as of Pandas 1.0.1 and SQLAlchemy 1.3.13, current as of this writing). Pandas is able to use the full type system of NumPy, and even adds a few more custom types of its own. This richness is comparable to—but not necessarily identical to—the type systems provided by RDBMSs (which, in fact, vary from each other as well, especially in extension types). However, the translation layer only casts to basic string, float, int, and date types.

Let us read a PostgreSQL table into Pandas, and then examine what native data types were utilized to approximate that SQL data:

```
df = pd.read_sql('dask_sample', engine, index_col='index')
df.tail(3)
```

index	timestamp	id	name	x	y
5676	2000-01-02 01:34:36	1041	Charlie	-0.587	0.206869
5677	2000-01-02 01:34:37	1017	Ray	0.311	0.256218
5678	2000-01-02 01:34:38	1036	Yvonne	0.409	0.535841

The specific dtypes within the DataFrame are:

```
df.dtypes
```

```
timestamp     datetime64[ns]
id                     int64
name                  object
x                    float64
y                    float64
dtype: object
```

Although it is a bit more laborious, we can combine these techniques and still work with our data within a friendly data frame, but using more closely matched types (albeit not perfectly matched to the database). The two drawbacks here are:

- We need to make manual decisions about the best type for each column
- Operations in Pandas will be much slower with object columns

Let us endeavor to choose better data types for our data frame. We probably need to determine the precise types from the documentation of our RDBMS, since few people have the PostgreSQL type codes memorized. The DB-API cursor object has a `.description` attribute that contains column type codes:

```
cur.execute("SELECT * FROM dask_sample")
cur.description
```

```
(Column(name='index', type_code=23),
 Column(name='timestamp', type_code=1114),
 Column(name='id', type_code=21),
 Column(name='name', type_code=1042),
 Column(name='x', type_code=1700),
 Column(name='y', type_code=700))
```

We can introspect to see the Python types used in the results. Of course, these do not carry the bit lengths of the database with them, so we will need to manually choose them. Datetime is straightforward enough to put into Pandas' `datetime64[ns]` type:

```
rows = cur.fetchall()
[type(v) for v in rows[0]]
```

```
[int, datetime.datetime, int, str, decimal.Decimal, float]
```

Working with `Decimal` numbers is tricker than other types. Python's standard library `decimal` module complies with IBM's General Decimal Arithmetic Specification (http://speleotrove.com/decimal/); unfortunately, databases do not. In particular, the IBM 1981 spec (with numerous updates) allows each *operation* to be performed within some chosen "decimal context" that gives precision, rounding rules, and other things. This is simply *different* from having a decimal precision *per column*, with no specific control of rounding rules. We can usually ignore these nuances; but when they bite us, they can bite hard. The issues arise more in civil engineering and banking/finance than they do with data science as such, but these are concerns to be aware of.

In the next cell, we cast several columns to specific numeric data types with specific bit widths:

```
# Read the data with no imposed data types
df = pd.DataFrame(rows,
                  columns=[col.name for col in cur.description],
                  dtype=object)

# Assign specific int or float lengths to some fields
types = {'index': np.int32, 'id': np.int16, 'y': np.float32}
```

```
df = df.astype(types)

# Cast the Python datetime to a Pandas datetime
df['timestamp'] = pd.to_datetime(df.timestamp)
df.set_index('index').head(3)
```

```
index            timestamp   id    name      x         y
 3456  2000-01-02 00:57:36  941   Alice  -0.612  -0.636485
 3457  2000-01-02 00:57:37 1004  Victor   0.450  -0.687718
 3458  2000-01-02 00:57:38  980   Quinn   0.552   0.454158
```

We can verify those data types are used.

```
df.dtypes
```

```
index                int32
timestamp    datetime64[ns]
id                   int16
name                object
x                   object
y                  float32
dtype: object
```

The Pandas "object" type hides the differences of the underlying classes of the Python objects stored. We can look at those more specifically:

```
pprint({repr(x): x.__class__.__name__
        for x in df.reset_index().iloc[0]})
```

```
{"'Alice      '": 'str',
 '-0.636485': 'float32',
 '0': 'int64',
 '3456': 'int32',
 '941': 'int16',
 "Decimal('-0.612')": 'Decimal',
 "Timestamp('2000-01-02 00:57:36')": 'Timestamp'}
```

Repeating in R

For the most part, the steps for reading in SQL data in R are similar to those in Python. And so are the pitfalls around getting data types just right. We can see that the data types are the same rough approximations of the actual database types as Pandas produced. Obviously, in real code you should not specify passwords as literal values in the source code but use some tool for secrets management:

```R
%%R
require("RPostgreSQL")
drv <- dbDriver("PostgreSQL")
con <- dbConnect(drv, dbname = "dirty",
                 host = "localhost", port = 5432,
                 user = "cleaning", password = "data")
sql <- "SELECT id, name, x, y FROM dask_sample LIMIT 3"
data <- tibble(dbGetQuery(con, sql))
data
```

```
# A tibble: 3 x 4
      id name              x      y
   <int> <chr>         <dbl>  <dbl>
1    941 "Alice      " -0.612 -0.636
2   1004 "Victor     "  0.45  -0.688
3    980 "Quinn      "  0.552  0.454
```

What is interesting to look at is that we might produce data frames that are not directly database tables (nor simply the first few rows, as in examples here), but rather some more complex manipulation or combination of that data. Joins are probably the most interesting case here since they take data from multiple tables. But grouping and aggregation is also frequently useful, and might reduce a million rows to a thousand summary descriptions, for example, which might be our goal:

```R
%%R
sql <- "SELECT max(x) AS max_x, max(y) AS max_y,
               name, count(name)
        FROM dask_sample
        WHERE id > 1050
        GROUP BY name
        ORDER BY count(name) DESC
        LIMIT 12;"
# Here we simply retrieve a data.frame
# rather than convert to tibble
dbGetQuery(con, sql)
```

```
    max_x    max_y      name   count
1   0.733  0.768558    Hannah     10
2   0.469  0.849384   Norbert     10
3   0.961  0.735508     Wendy      9
4   0.950  0.673037     Quinn      8
5   0.892  0.853494   Michael      7
6   0.772  0.989233    Yvonne      7
```

```
 7  0.958  0.859792    Patricia      6
 8  0.953  0.865918     Ingrid       6
 9  0.998  0.980781     Oliver       6
10  0.050  0.501860      Laura       6
11  0.399  0.808572      Alice       5
12  0.604  0.826401      Kevin       5
```

Where SQL Goes Wrong (and How to Notice It)

For the following example, I started with a dataset that described Amtrak train stations in 2012. Many of the fields initially present were discarded, but some others were manipulated to illustrate some points. Think of this as "fake data" even though it is derived from a genuine dataset. In particular, the column Visitors is invented whole cloth; I have never seen visitor count data, nor do I know if it is collected anywhere. It is just numbers that will have a pattern:

```
amtrak = pd.read_sql('bad_amtrak', engine)
amtrak.head()
```

	Code	StationName	City	State	Visitors
0	ABB	Abbotsford-Colby	Colby	WI	18631
1	ABE	Aberdeen	Aberdeen	MD	12286
2	ABN	Absecon	Absecon	NJ	5031
3	ABQ	Albuquerque	Albuquerque	NM	14285
4	ACA	Antioch-Pittsburg	Antioch	CA	16282

On the face of it—other than the telling name of the table we read in—nothing looks out of place. Let us look for problems. Notice that the tests below will, in a way, be anomaly detection, which is discussed in a later chapter. However, the anomalies we find are specific to SQL data typing.

String fields in RDBMSs are prone to truncation if specific character lengths are given. Modern database systems also have a VARCHAR or TEXT type for unlimited length strings, but often specific lengths are used in practice. To a certain degree, database operations can be more efficient with known text lengths, so the choice is not simple foolishness. But whatever the reason, you will find such fixed lengths frequently in practice. In particular, the StationName column is defined as CHAR(20). The question is: is that a problem?

Knowing the character length will not automatically answer the question we care about. Perhaps Amtrak regulation requires a certain length of all station names. This is domain-specific knowledge that you may not have as a data scientist. In fact, the domain experts may not have it either, because it has not been analyzed or because rules have changed over time. Let us analyze the data itself.

Moreover, even if a database field is currently variable length or very long, it is quite possible that a column was altered over the life of a database, or that a migration occurred. Unfortunately, multiple generations of old data that may each have been corrupted in their own ways can obscure detection.

One place you may encounter this problem data history is with dates in older datasets where two-digit years were used. The "Y2K" issue had to be addressed two decades ago for active database systems—for example, I spent the calendar year of 1998 predominantly concerned with this issue—but there remain some infrequently accessed legacy data stores that will fail on this ambiguity. If the character string '34' is stored in a column named YEAR, does it refer to something that happened in the 20th century or an anticipated future event a decade after this book is being written? Some domain knowledge is needed to answer this.

Some rather concise Pandas code can tell us something useful. A first step is cleaning the padding in the fixed-length character field. The whitespace padding is not generally useful in our code. After that we can look at the length of each value, count the number of records per length, and sort by those lengths, to produce a histogram:

```
amtrak['StationName'] = amtrak.StationName.str.strip()
hist = amtrak.StationName.str.len().value_counts().sort_index()
hist
```

```
4        15
5        46
6       100
7       114

    ...

17       15
18       17
19       27
20      116
Name: StationName, Length: 17, dtype: int64
```

The pattern is even more striking if we visualize it. Clearly station names bump up against that 20 character width. This is not quite yet a smoking gun, but it is very suggestive:

```
hist.plot(kind='bar',
          title="Lengths of Station Names");
```

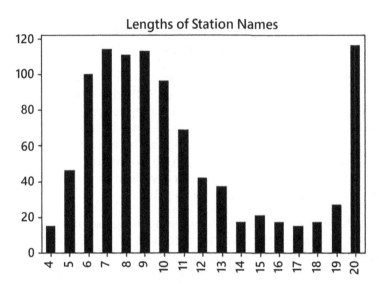

Figure 1.3: Histogram showing lengths of station names

We want to be careful not to attribute an underlying phenomenon as a data artifact. For example, in preparing this section, I started analyzing a collection of Twitter 2015 tweets. Those naturally form a similar pattern of "bumping up" against 140 characters—but I realized that they do this because of a limit in the accurate underlying data, not as a data artifact. However, the Twitter histogram curve looks similar to that for station names. I am aware that Twitter doubled its limit in 2018; I would expect an aggregated collection over time to show asymptotes at both 140 and 280, but as a "natural" phenomenon.

If the character width limit changed over the history of our data, we might see a pattern of multiple soft limits. These are likely to be harder to discern, especially if those limits are significantly larger than 20 characters to start with. Before we absolutely conclude that we have a *data artifact* rather than, for example, an Amtrak naming rule, let us look at the concrete data.

This is not impractical when we start with a thousand rows, but it becomes more difficult with a million rows. Using Pandas' `.sample()` method is often a good way to view a random subset of rows matching some filter, but here we just display the first and last few:

```
amtrak[amtrak.StationName.str.len() == 20]
```

	Code	StationName	City	State	Visitors
28	ARI	Astoria (Shell Stati	Astoria	OR	27872
31	ART	Astoria (Transit Cen	Astoria	OR	22116
42	BAL	Baltimore (Penn Stat	Baltimore	MD	19953
50	BCA	Baltimore (Camden St	Baltimore	MD	32767
...	...	...	...	...	...
965	YOC	Yosemite - Curry Vil	Yosemite National Park	CA	28352
966	YOF	Yosemite - Crane Fla	Yosemite National Park	CA	32767
969	YOV	Yosemite - Visitor C	Yosemite National Park	CA	29119
970	YOW	Yosemite - White Wol	Yosemite National Park	CA	16718

116 rows × 5 columns

It is reasonable to conclude from our examined data that truncation is an authentic problem here. Many of the samples have words terminated in their middle at character length. Remediating it is another decision and more effort. Perhaps we can obtain the full texts as a followup; if we are lucky the prefixes will uniquely match full strings. Of course, quite likely, the real data is just lost. If we only care about uniqueness, this is likely not to be a big problem (the three-letter codes are already unique). However, if our analysis concerns the missing data itself we may not be able to proceed at all. Perhaps we can decide in a problem-specific way that prefixes nonetheless are a representative sample of what we are analyzing.

***

A similar issue arises with numbers of fixed lengths. Floating-point numbers might lose desired precision, but integers might wrap and/or clip. We can examine the Visitors column and determine that it stores a 16-bit SMALLINT. Which is to say, it cannot represent values greater than 32,767. Perhaps that is more visitors than any single station will plausibly have.

Or perhaps we will see data corruption:

```
max_ = amtrak.Visitors.max()
amtrak.Visitors.plot(
        kind='hist', bins=20,
        title=f"Visitors per station (max {max_})");
```

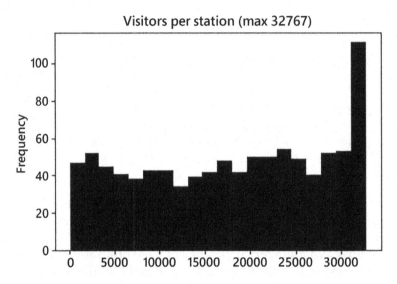

Figure 1.4: Histogram showing visitors per station

In this case, the bumping against the limit is a strong signal. An extra hint here is the specific limit reached. It is one of those special numbers you should learn to recognize. Signed integers of bit-length N range from -2^{N-1} up to $2^{N-1}-1$. Unsigned integers range from 0 to 2^N. 32,767 is $2^{16}-1$. However, for various programming reasons, numbers one (or a few) shy of a data type bound also frequently occur. In general, if you ever see a measurement that is exactly one of these bounds, you should take a second look and think about whether it might be an artifactual number rather than a genuine value. This is a good rule even outside the context of databases.

A possibly more difficult issue to address is when values wrap instead. Depending on the tools you use, large positive integers might wrap around to negative integers. Many RDBMSs—including PostgreSQL—will simply refuse transactions with unacceptable values rather than allowing them to occur. But different systems vary. Wrapping on sign is obvious in the case of counts that are non-zero by their nature, but for values where both positive and negative numbers make sense, detection is harder.

For example, in this Pandas Series example, which is cast to a short integer type, we see values around positive and negative 15 thousand, both as genuine elements and as artifacts of a type cast:

```
ints = pd.Series(
    [100, 200, 15_000, 50_000, -15_000, -50_000])
ints.astype(np.int16)
```

```
0      100
1      200
2     15000
3    -15536
4    -15000
5     15536
dtype: int16
```

In a case like this, we simply need to acquire enough domain expertise to know whether the out-of-bounds values that might wrap can ever be sensible measurements. I.e. is 50,000 reasonable for this hypothetical measure? If all reasonable observations are of numbers in the hundreds, wrapping at 32,000 is not a large concern. It is *conceivable* that some reasonable value got there as a wrap from an unreasonable one; but wrong values can occur for a vast array of reasons, and this would not be an unduly large concern.

Note that integers and floating-point numbers only come, on widespread computer architectures, in sizes of 8, 16, 32, 64, and 128 bits. For integers those might be signed or unsigned, which would halve or double the maximum number representable. These maximum values representable within these different bit widths are starkly different from each other. A rule of thumb, if you can choose the integer representation, is to leave an order-of-magnitude padding from the largest magnitude you *expect* to occur. However, sometimes even an order of magnitude does not set a good bound on unexpected (but accurate) values.

For example, in our hypothetical visitor count, perhaps a maximum of around 20,000 was reasonably anticipated, but over the years, that got as high as 35,000, leading to the effect we see in the *Figure 1.4* plot (of hypothetical data). Allowing for 9,223,372,036,854,775,807 (2^{63}-1) visitors to a station might have seemed like unnecessary overhead to the initial database engineers. However, a 32-bit integer, with a maximum of 2,147,483,647 (2^{31}-1), would have been a better choice, even though the actual maximum remains far larger than will ever be observed.

Let us turn now to some other data formats you are likely to work with, generally binary data formats, often used for scientific requirements.

Other Formats

Let a hundred flowers bloom; let a hundred schools of thought contend.

–Confucian saying

Concepts:

- Binary columnar data files
- Hierarchical array data
- Single-file RDBMS

A variety of data formats that you may encounter can be used for holding tabular data. For the most part these do not introduce any special new cleanliness concerns that we have not addressed in earlier sections. Properties of the data themselves are discussed in later chapters. The data type options vary between storage formats, but the same kinds of general concerns that we discussed with RDBMSs apply to all of them. In the main, from the perspective of this book, these formats simply require somewhat different APIs to get at their underlying data, but all provide data types per column. The formats addressed herein are not an exhaustive list, and clearly new ones may arise or increase in significance after the time of this writing. But the principles of access should be similar for formats not discussed.

The closely related formats HDF5 and NetCDF (discussed below) are largely interoperable, and both provide ways of storing multiple arrays, each with metadata associated and also allowing highly dimensional data, not simply tabular 2-D arrays. Unlike with the data frame model, arrays within these scientific formats are of homogeneous type throughout. That is, there is no mechanism (by design) to store a text column and a numeric column within the same object, nor even numeric columns of different bit-widths. However, since they allow multiple arrays in the same file, full generality is available, just in a different way than within the SQL or data frame model.

SQLite (discussed below) is a file format that provides a relational database, consisting potentially of multiple tables, within a single file. It is extremely widely used, being present and used everywhere from every iOS and Android device up to the largest supercomputer clusters. An interface for SQLite is part of the Python standard library and is available for nearly all other programming languages.

Apache Parquet (discussed below) is a column-oriented data store. What this amounts to is simply a way to store data frames or tables to disk, but in a manner that optimizes common operations that typically vectorize along columns rather than along rows.

A similar philosophy motivates columnar RDBMSs like Apache Cassandra and MonetDB, both of which are SQL databases, simply with different query optimization possibilities. kdb+ is an older, and non-SQL, approach to a similar problem. PostgreSQL and MariaDB*MariaDB* also both have optional storage formats that use column organization. Generally, these internal optimizations are not direct concerns for data science, but Parquet requires its own non-SQL APIs.

MariaDB

MariaDB is a fork of MySQL, created by MySQL creator Monty Widenius. It was motivated by intellectual property freedom concerns after Oracle acquired MySQL in 2009. For the most part, the design and features are similar to those of MySQL, although some advanced features have diverged since that split. You may be using MariaDB, in fact, even if you are unaware of doing so, since the shell tool and drivers still generally retain the name `mysql` for compatibility.

***

There are a number of binary data formats that are reasonably widely used, but I do not specifically discuss them in this book. Many other formats have their own virtues, but I have attempted to limit the discussion to the handful that I feel you are *most likely* to encounter in regular work as a data scientist. Some additional formats are listed below, with characterization mostly adapted from their respective home pages. You can see in the descriptions which discussed formats they most resemble, and generally the identical data integrity and quality concerns apply as in the formats I discuss. Differences are primarily in performance characteristics: how big the files are on disk, how fast can they be read and written under different scenarios, and so on:

- **Feather** (and **Arrow**): Feather is basically a direct serialization of the Arrow in-memory format for storage on disk with a very thin adaptor layer. Apache Arrow is a development platform for in-memory analytics. It specifies a standardized language-independent columnar memory format for flat and hierarchical data, organized for efficient analytic operations on modern hardware, as described by the Arrow documentation (`https://arrow.apache.org/docs/`).

- **Apache Avro**: Avro is a data serialization system that provides rich data structures, a compact, fast, binary data format, and a container file, to store persistent data. It integrates with dynamic languages without code generation being needed (unlike in similar systems such as **Thrift** and **Protocol Buffers**). (Paraphrased from the Apache Avro documentation. `https://avro.apache.org/docs/1.3.3/`)

- **bcolz**: bcolz provides columnar, chunked data containers that can be compressed either in-memory and on-disk. Column storage allows for efficiently querying tables, as well as for cheap column addition and removal. It is based on NumPy, and uses it as the standard data container to communicate with bcolz objects, but it also comes with support for import/export facilities to/from HDF5/PyTables tables and Pandas dataframes, as described by the bcolz documentation (`https://github.com/Blosc/bcolz`).

- **Zarr**: Zarr provides classes and functions for working with N-dimensional arrays that behave like NumPy arrays but whose data is divided into chunks and each chunk is compressed. If you are already familiar with HDF5 then Zarr arrays provide similar functionality, but with some additional flexibility, as described by the Zarr documentation (`https://zarr.readthedocs.io/en/stable/tutorial.html`).

HDF5 and NetCDF-4

There is a slightly convoluted history of the Hierarchical Data Format (HDF), which was begun by the National Center for Supercomputing Applications (NCSA) in 1987. HDF4 was significantly over-engineered and is far less widely used now. HDF5 simplified the file structure of HDF4. It consists of *datasets*, which are multidimensional arrays of a single data type, and *groups*, which are container structures holding datasets and other groups. Both groups and datasets may have attributes attached to them, which are any pieces of named metadata. What this does, in effect, is emulate a file system within a single file. The nodes or "files" within this virtual file system are array objects. Generally, a single HDF5 file will contain a variety of related data for working with the same underlying problem.

The Network Common Data Form (NetCDF) is a library of functions for storing and retrieving array data. The project itself is nearly as old as HDF and is an open standard that was developed and supported by a variety of scientific agencies. As of version 4, it supports using HDF5 as a storage back-end; earlier versions used some other file formats, and current NetCDF software requires continued support for those older formats. Occasionally NetCDF-4 files do enough special things with their contents that reading them with generic HDF5 libraries is awkward.

Generic HDF5 files typically have an extension of `.h5`, `.hdf5`, `.hdf`, or `.he5`. These should all represent the same binary format, and other extensions occur sometimes too. Some corresponding extensions for HDF4 also exist. Oddly, even though NetCDF can consist of numerous underlying file formats, they all seem standardized on the `.nc` extension.

Tools and Libraries

Although I generally do not rely on GUI tools, in the case of viewing the fairly complex structure of HDF5, they can help. For example, a file from NASA's Earth Science Data collection is included in this book's sample data repository. Users can freely register to obtain datasets from NASA, which in aggregate is petabytes of information. This particular HDF5/NetCDF file contains datasets for surface pressure, vertical temperature profiles, surface and vertical wind profiles, tropopause pressure, boundary layer top pressure, and surface geopotential for a 98-minute period. In particular, some of the data is spatially 3-dimensional.

A view of a small portion of the data using the open source viewer HDF Compass (`https://hdf-compass.readthedocs.io/en/latest/index.html`) illustrates some of the structure. The particular dataset viewed is 1 of 16 in the file. This DELP dataset is about *pressure thickness*, and contains both an array of 32-bit values and 8 attributes describing the dataset. You can see in the screenshot below that this particular GUI tool presents the 3rd dimension as a selection widget, and the first two dimensions in a tabular view.

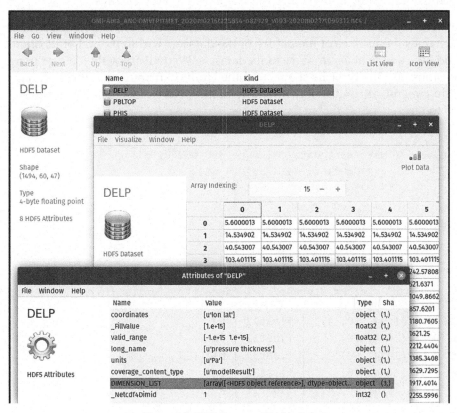

Figure 1.5: HDF Compass NASA data

Within Python, there are two popular open source libraries for working with HDF5, PyTables and h5py. For working with NetCDF specifically, there is a netcdf4-python library as well. If you wish to read data from HDF5 files, and not to add NetCDF specific metadata, one of the general HDF5 tools is fine (h5py handles special metadata better than PyTables).

PyTables and h5py have moderately different attitudes. H5py stays close to the HDF5 spec itself while PyTables attempts to provide a higher-level "Pythonic" interface. PyTables has the advantage that its data model borrows from, and acknowledges, a library for XML access that this author wrote way back in 2000; however, that advantage may be less relevant for general readers than for me personally. In the R world, the library rhdf5 is available.

In libraries for working with HDF5 data, a degree of laziness is allowed when dealing with large datasets. In the Python interfaces, datasets are virtualized NumPy arrays; importantly you can perform slice operations into these arrays, and only actually read into memory the indicated data. You may be dealing with terabytes of underlying information but process or modify only megabytes at a time (or at all), with efficient reading and writing from regions of on disk arrays.

The names for data files used by NASA are verbose but contain detailed indication in the names themselves of the nature of the datasets within them. Let us open one file and take a look at a summary of its datasets. We will show the dataset name, its dimensions, its data type, its shape, and the "units" attribute that these all happen to have. In general, attributes may have any names, but NASA has conventions about which to use:

```python
import h5py
h5fname = ('data/earthdata/OMI-Aura_ANC-OMVFPITMET'
           '_2020m0216t225854-o82929_v003'
           '-2020m0217t090311.nc4')


data = h5py.File(h5fname, mode='r')

for name, arr in data.items():
    print(f"{name:6s} | {str(arr.shape):14s} | "
          f"{str(arr.dtype):7s} | {arr.attrs['units'][0]}")
```

```
DELP   | (1494, 60, 47) | float32 | Pa
PBLTOP | (1494, 60)     | float32 | Pa
PHIS   | (1494, 60)     | float32 | m+2 s-2
PS     | (1494, 60)     | float32 | Pa
T      | (1494, 60, 47) | float32 | K
TROPPB | (1494, 60)     | float32 | Pa
```

U	(1494, 60, 47)	float32	m s-1
U10M	(1494, 60)	float32	m s-1
V	(1494, 60, 47)	float32	m s-1
V10M	(1494, 60)	float32	m s-1
lat	(1494, 60)	float32	degrees_north
lev	(47,)	int16	1
line	(1494,)	int16	1
lon	(1494, 60)	float32	degrees_east
sample	(60,)	int16	1
time	(1494,)	float64	seconds since 1993-01-01 00:00:00

We can lazily create a memory view into only part of one of the dataset arrays. In the example, we have opened in read-only mode, but if we had opened using the `'r+'` or `'a'` modes we could change the file. Use the `'w'` mode with extreme caution since it will overwrite an existing file. If the mode allows modification on disk, calling `data.flush()` or `data.close()` will write any changes back to the HDF5 source.

Let us create a view of only a small section of the 3-dimensional V dataset. We are not particularly concerned here with understanding the domain of the data, but just demonstrating the APIs. In particular, notice that we have used a stride in one dimension to show that the general NumPy style of complex memory views is available. Only the data referenced is actually put into main memory while the rest stays on disk:

```
# A 3-D block from middle of DELP array
middle = data['V'][::500, 10:12, :3]
middle
```

```
array([[[17.032158  , 12.763597  ,  3.7710803 ],
        [16.53227   , 12.759642  ,  4.1722884 ]],

       [[ 4.003829  , -1.0843939 , -6.7918572 ],
        [ 3.818467  , -1.0030019 , -6.6708655 ]],

       [[-2.7798688 ,  0.24923703, 20.513933  ],
        [-2.690715  ,  0.2226392 , 20.473366  ]]], dtype=float32)
```

If we modify the data in the view `middle`, it will be written back when we flush or close the handle (if not in read-only mode). We might also use our data slice for other computations or data science purposes. For example, perhaps such a selection acts as tensors that are input into a neural network.

In a simpler case, perhaps we simply want to find some statistics or reduction/ abstraction on the data:

```
middle.mean(axis=1)

  array([[16.782215  , 12.76162   ,  3.9716845 ],
         [ 3.911148  , -1.0436978 , -6.7313614 ],
         [-2.735292  ,  0.23593812, 20.493649  ]], dtype=float32)
```

***

Working with HDF5 files in R—or most any other language—is generally similar to doing so from Python. Let us take a look with the R library `rhdf5`:

```
%%R -i h5fname
library(rhdf5)
h5ls(h5fname)
```

	group	name	otype	dclass	dim
0	/	DELP	H5I_DATASET	FLOAT	47 x 60 x 1494
1	/	PBLTOP	H5I_DATASET	FLOAT	60 x 1494
2	/	PHIS	H5I_DATASET	FLOAT	60 x 1494
3	/	PS	H5I_DATASET	FLOAT	60 x 1494
4	/	T	H5I_DATASET	FLOAT	47 x 60 x 1494
5	/	TROPPB	H5I_DATASET	FLOAT	60 x 1494
6	/	U	H5I_DATASET	FLOAT	47 x 60 x 1494
7	/	U10M	H5I_DATASET	FLOAT	60 x 1494
8	/	V	H5I_DATASET	FLOAT	47 x 60 x 1494
9	/	V10M	H5I_DATASET	FLOAT	60 x 1494
10	/	lat	H5I_DATASET	FLOAT	60 x 1494
11	/	lev	H5I_DATASET	INTEGER	47
12	/	line	H5I_DATASET	INTEGER	1494
13	/	lon	H5I_DATASET	FLOAT	60 x 1494
14	/	sample	H5I_DATASET	INTEGER	60
15	/	time	H5I_DATASET	FLOAT	1494

You may notice that the order of dimensions is transposed in R versus Python, so we have to account for that in our selection of a region of interest. However, generally the operation of slicing in R is very similar to that in NumPy. The function `h5save()` is used to write data that was modified back to disk.

```
%%R -i h5fname
V = h5read(h5fname, 'V')
V[1:2, 10:12, 10:11]
```

```
, , 1

        [,1]     [,2]     [,3]
[1,]  17.69524 17.23481 16.57238
[2,]  12.46370 12.44905 12.47155


, , 2

        [,1]     [,2]     [,3]
[1,]  17.71876 17.25898 16.56942
[2,]  12.42049 12.40599 12.43139
```

***

The NASA data shown does not use group hierarchies, only top-level datasets. Let us look at a toy data collection that nests groups and datasets.

```
make_h5_hierarchy()  # initialize the HDF5 file
f = h5py.File('data/hierarchy.h5', 'r+')
dset = f['/deeply/nested/group/my_data']
print(dset.shape, dset.dtype)
```

```
(10, 10, 10, 10) int32
```

We see that we have a 4-dimensional array of integer data. Perhaps some metadata description was attached to it as well. Let us also view — and then modify — some section of the data since we have opened in 'r+' mode. After we change the data, we can write it back to disk. We could similarly change or add attributes in a regular dictionary style, for instance:

```
dset.attrs[mykey] = myvalue
```

Let us show a slice from the dataset.

```
for key, val in dset.attrs.items():
    print(key, "→", val)
print()
print("Data block:\n", dset[5, 3, 2:4, 8:])
```

```
author      David Mertz
citation    Cleaning Data Book
shape_type  4-D integer array

Data block:
 [[-93 -53]
 [ 18 -37]]
```

Now we modify the same slice of data we displayed, then close the file handle to write it back to disk:

```
dset[5, 3, 2:4, 8:] = np.random.randint(-99, 99, (2, 2))
print(dset[5, 3, 2:4, 8:])
f.close()                    # write change to disk

[[-45 -76]
 [-96 -21]]
```

We can walk the hierarchy in Python's h5py package, but it is somewhat manual to loop through paths. R's rhdf5 provides a nice utility function, h5ls(), that lets us see more of the structure of this test file:

```
%%R
library(rhdf5)
h5ls('data/hierarchy.h5')
```

	group	name	otype	dclass	dim
0	/	deeply	H5I_GROUP		
1	/deeply	nested	H5I_GROUP		
2	/deeply/nested	group	H5I_GROUP		
3	/deeply/nested/group	my_data	H5I_DATASET	INTEGER	10 x 10 x 10 x 10
4	/deeply	path	H5I_GROUP		
5	/deeply/path	elsewhere	H5I_GROUP		
6	/deeply/path/elsewhere	other	H5I_DATASET	INTEGER	20
7	/deeply/path	that_data	H5I_DATASET	FLOAT	5 x 5

SQLite

In essence, SQLite is simply another RDBMS from the point of view of a data scientist. For a developer or systems engineer, it has some special properties, but for readers of this book, you will get data from an SQLite file via SQL queries. Somewhat similarly to HDF5, an SQLite file—often given extensions .sqlite, .db, or .db3 (but not as standardized as with some file types)—can contain many tables. In SQL, we automatically get joins and subqueries to combine data from multiple tables, whereas there is no similar standard for combining data from multiple HDF5 datasets.

The SQLite3 data format and server is extremely efficient, and queries are usually fast. As with other SQL databases, it operates with *atomic transactions* that succeed or fail in their entirety. This prevents a database from reaching a logically inconsistent state. However, it does not have a concurrent access model.

Or rather, it does not allow multiple simultaneous writers to a common database in the way that server-based RDBMSs do. Many reader clients may open the same file simultaneously without difficulty; it only bogs down when many clients wish to perform write transactions. There are ways to address this situation, but they are outside the scope of this particular book.

An important advantage of SQLite over other RDBMSs is that distributing the single file that makes up the database is dead simple. With other systems, you need to add credentials, and firewall rules, and the like, to give new users access; or alternately you need to export the needed data to another format, typically CSV, that is both slow and somewhat lossy (i.e. data types).

Data typing in SQLite is something of a chimera. There are few basic data types, which we will discuss. However, unlike nearly every other SQL database, SQLite carries data types per value, not per column. This would seem to run into the same fragility that was discussed around spreadsheets, but in practice it is far less of a problem than with those. One reason the types-per-value is not as much of a concern is because of the interface used to populate them; it is highly unusual to edit individual values in SQLite interactively, and far more common to issue programmatic SQL commands to INSERT or UPDATE many rows with data from a common source.

However, apart from the data types, SQLite has a concept called *type affinity*. Each column is given a preferred type that does not *prevent* other data types from occurring, but does nudge the preference toward the affinity of the column. We can run the tool `sqlite` from the command line to get to the interactive SQLite prompt. For example (adapted from SQLite documentation):

```
sqlite> CREATE TABLE mytable(a SMALLINT, b VARCHAR(10), c REAL);
sqlite> INSERT INTO mytable(a, b, c) VALUES('123', 456, 789);
```

Here a row will be inserted with an integer in the a column, TEXT in the b column, and a floating-point in the c column. SQL syntax itself is loosely typed, but the underlying database makes type/casting decisions. This is true of other RDBMSs too, but those are stricter about column data types. So we can also run this in SQLite, which will fail with other databases:

```
sqlite> INSERT INTO mytable(a, b, c) VALUES('xyz', 3.14, '2.71');
```

Let us see what results:

```
sqlite> SELECT * FROM mytable;
123|456|789.0
xyz|3.14|2.71
```

The SQLite interactive shell does not make data types entirely obvious, but running a query in Python will do so.

```
import sqlite3
db = sqlite3.connect('data/affinity.sqlite')
cur = db.cursor()
cur.execute("SELECT a, b, c FROM t1")
for row in cur:
    print([f"{x.__class__.__name__} {x}" for x in row])

['int 123', 'str 456', 'float 789.0']
['str xyz', 'str 3.14', 'float 2.71']
```

Column a prefers to hold an integer if it is set with something it can interpret as an integer, but will fall back to a more general data type if required. Likewise, column c prefers a float, and it can interpret either an unquoted integer or a float-like string as such.

The actual data types in SQLite are *exclusively* NULL, INTEGER, REAL, TEXT, and BLOB. However, most of the type names in other SQL databases are aliases for these simple types. We see that in the example, where VARCHAR(10) is an alias for TEXT and SMALLINT is an alias for INTEGER. REAL values are always represented as 64-bit floating-point numbers. Within INTEGER values, bit lengths of 1, 2, 3, 4, 6, or 8 are chosen for storage efficiency. There is no datetime type in SQLite storage, but time-oriented SQL functions are happy to accept any of TEXT (ISO-8601 strings), REAL (days since November 24, 4714 B.C), or INTEGER (seconds since 1970-01-01T00:00:00).

The overall takeaway for working with SQLite databases is that possibly a little extra care is needed in double-checking your data types when reading data, but for the most part you can pretend it is strongly typed per column. Truncation, clipping, and wrap-around issues will not occur. There is no actual decimal data type, but only aliases; for data science — versus accounting or finance — this is rarely a concern. But usual caveats about floating-point rounding issues will apply.

Apache Parquet

The Parquet format grew out of the **Hadoop** ecosystem, but at heart is simply an optimized, column-oriented file format for storing table-like data. Parquet has a type system that focuses on numeric types. It is not quite as simplified as SQLite but also eschews providing every possible bit length, as NumPy or C/C++ do, for example. All integer types are signed. Everything that is not numeric is a byte-array that is cast for the needed purpose at the application level (i.e. not the storage format level).

Having grown out of Hadoop tools, Parquet is especially well optimized for parallel computation. A Parquet "file" is actually a directory containing a number of data files, with a _metadata file in that directory describing the layout and other details.

```bash
%%bash
ls -x data/multicsv.parq
```

```
_common_metadata  _metadata         part.0.parquet    part.10.parquet
part.11.parquet   part.12.parquet   part.13.parquet   part.14.parquet
part.15.parquet   part.16.parquet   part.17.parquet   part.18.parquet
part.19.parquet   part.1.parquet    part.20.parquet   part.21.parquet
part.22.parquet   part.23.parquet   part.24.parquet   part.25.parquet
part.26.parquet   part.27.parquet   part.28.parquet   part.29.parquet
part.2.parquet    part.3.parquet    part.4.parquet    part.5.parquet
part.6.parquet    part.7.parquet    part.8.parquet    part.9.parquet
```

Sometimes the file system is a parallel and distributed system such as **Hadoop File System** (HDFS) that further supports computational efficiency on large datasets. In such case, Parquet does various clever sharding of data, efficient compression (using varying strategies), optimization of contiguous reads, and has been analyzed and revised to improve its typical use cases, for both speed and storage size.

Some of the tools or libraries supporting Parquet are **Apache Hive**, **Cloudera Impala**, **Apache Pig**, and **Apache Spark**, all of which live in the parallel computation space. However, there are available interfaces for Python and R as well (and other languages). Many of the higher-level tools address Parquet data with an SQL layer.

For Python, the libraries pyarrow and **fastparquet** provide a direct interface to the file format. While these libraries are general, they are designed primarily to translate Parquet data into data frames (usually Pandas, sometimes Dask, Vaex, or others). Within the R world, **sparklyr** is an interface into Spark but requires a running Spark instance (a local installation is fine). The **arrow** package is a direct reader, similar to the Python libraries.

In general, if you are working with genuinely big data, the Hadoop or Spark tools — accompanied by appropriate computing clusters — are a good choice. Dask is an approach to parallelism on Python, which is very good; other approaches like MPI are available for R, Python, and many other languages. However, Hadoop and Spark are the tools to which the most attention has been paid in regard to efficient and large scale parallel computation.

Even if you only need to worry about medium-sized data (hundred of thousands to millions of rows) rather than big data (hundreds of millions to billions of rows), Parquet is still a fast format to work with. Moreover, it has the generally desirable property of typing data by column that makes data at least one small step closer to being clean and tidy.

As an example, let us read the medium-sized dataset we generated earlier with Dask. Both Pandas and Dask will use either `pyarrow` or `fastparquet`, depending on what is installed.

```
pd.read_parquet('data/multicsv.parq/')
```

index	timestamp	id	name	x	y
0	2000-01-01 00:00:00	979	Zelda	0.802163	0.166619
1	2000-01-01 00:00:01	1019	Ingrid	-0.349999	0.704687
2	2000-01-01 00:00:02	1007	Hannah	-0.169853	-0.050842
3	2000-01-01 00:00:03	1034	Ursula	0.868090	-0.190783
...	...	...	...	...	...
86396	2000-01-10 23:59:56	998	Jerry	0.589575	0.412477
86397	2000-01-10 23:59:57	1011	Yvonne	0.047785	-0.202337
86398	2000-01-10 23:59:58	1053	Oliver	0.690303	-0.639954
86399	2000-01-10 23:59:59	1009	Ursula	0.228775	0.750066

2592000 rows × 5 columns

We could distribute the above read using `dask.dataframe` and just the same syntax, i.e. `dd.read_parquet(...)`. For large datasets this could keep the inactive segments out of core and distribute work over all the cores on the local machine. However, for medium to small data like this, Pandas is faster in avoiding the coordination overhead.

Although we have utilized the concept of data frames already, using both Python with Pandas and R with tibbles, it is worth looking at just what the underlying abstraction consists of. We will briefly look at a number of different data frame implementations in varying programming languages to understand what they have in common (which is a lot).

Data Frames

Whenever you set out to do something, something else must be done first.

— *Murphy's (First) Corollary*

Concepts:

- Filter/transform/group/aggregate
- Spark data frames
- Pandas and derivatives
- Other Python data frames
- R Tidyverse
- R data.tables
- The Unix philosophy

A large number of libraries across almost as many programming languages support the data frame abstraction. Most data scientists find this abstraction to be powerful and even their preferred way of processing data. Data frames allow an easy expression of many of the same fundamental concepts or operations as does SQL, but within the particular programming language and memory space of the rest of their program. SQL—even when it actually addresses a purely local database such as SQLite—is always more of a "remote fetch" than interactive exploration that data frames allow.

These operations consist, in the main, of filtering, grouping, aggregation, sorting, and vectorized function application. Generally, all data frame libraries allow for a "fluent" programming style that chains together these operations in some order to produce a final result; that final (or at least working) result is usually itself either a data frame or a scalar value. Sometimes a visualization is relevant for such a processed result, and most data frame tools integrate seamlessly with visualization libraries.

The goal, of course, of these fluent chained operations is to describe a reproducible workflow. Exploration of various data modifications can be built up step by step, with intermediate results often providing hints that you might have gone wrong or a degree of reassurance that your path is correct. At the end of that exploration, you will have an expression of a composite transformation of data that can be reused with new data from the domain and problem you are addressing. Comments in code and accompanying these chains, or pipelines, always make life easier for both you and other readers of code.

Those libraries that are distributed and/or out-of-core allow working with large datasets rather seamlessly, which is to say that the data frame abstraction scales almost unboundedly, even if particular libraries have some rough limits. In this section, I will present similar code using a number of data frame libraries, commenting briefly on the strengths, weaknesses, and differences among them.

This book generally utilizes Python with Pandas, and to a somewhat lesser extent R with tibbles. We will see the conceptual and usage similarity of those libraries with other libraries in Python/R (Vaex, `data.table`), and even with other programming languages such as Scala/Spark or Bash with coreutils. Many data scientists use Spark in particular; whatever specific tools you use, the concepts throughout should translate easily, especially where data frame approaches are available.

Most of the code in this book will use Pandas. Python is, as of this writing, the most widely used language for data science, and Pandas is, by a large margin, its most widely used data frame library. In fact, several of the "competing" libraries themselves utilize Pandas as an internal component. However, in this section, I would like to illustrate and emphasize how similar all of these libraries are. For that purpose, I am going to perform the same task using a number of these libraries.

There are a great many operations and pipelines, many quite complex, that can be accomplished with data frames. This brief section is not a tutorial on any of the specific libraries, but only a glimpse into the shared style of expressing data manipulation and the smaller differences among the different tools.

With each data frame library, we will do the following:

1. Filter based on a comparison of two columns, x and y
2. Vectorize derived value from one column of the comparison, y
3. Group data having common value in another column, name
4. Aggregate data in a grouped column, x
5. Sort data based on a computed column, Mean_x
6. For illustration, display the first 5 rows of result

Spark/Scala

As a starting point, I would like to illustrate a pipeline of steps using the distributed computing framework, Spark, and its native programming language, Scala. Bindings into Spark from Python, R, and other languages also exist, but incur a certain degree of translation overhead that slows operations. This pipeline takes the sample Dask dataset shown in other examples in this chapter and performs all of the basic operations mentioned on the dataset.[setup]

setup

Configuring and replicating the environment used by this book for the Python and R code is described in the accompanying repository. However, configuring Hadoop and Spark are separate steps that are not quite so easy to encapsulate in a few configuration files. The steps are not *difficult*, but you will need to follow the official documentation accompanying these tools, or other tutorials available online.

The next few lines were run inside the Spark shell. For the composition of this book, a local instance of Hadoop and Spark were running, but this could as easily be a connection to a remote cluster. Upon launch you will see something similar to this:

```
Spark context Web UI available at http://popkdm:4040
Spark context available as 'sc' (master = local[*], app id =
local-1582775303458).
Spark session available as 'spark'.
Welcome to
      ____              __
     / __/__  ___ _____/ /__
    _\ \/ _ \/ _ `/ __/  '_/
   /___/ .__/\_,_/_/ /_/\_\   version 2.4.5
      /_/

Using Scala version 2.11.12 (OpenJDK 64-Bit Server VM, Java 11.0.6)
Type in expressions to have them evaluated.
Type :help for more information.
```

In the shell, we can read in the collection of CSV files in a common directory. Many other data sources are likewise available under a similar interface. We allow inference of data types and use of the column headers to name fields. The pipe symbols (|) are simply part of the Spark shell interface to indicate a continuation line; they are not themselves the Scala code:

```scala
scala> val df = spark.read.        // Local file or Hadoop resource
     |     options(Map("inferSchema"->"true","header"->"true")).
     |     csv("data/multicsv/")  // Directory of multiple CSVs
df: org.apache.spark.sql.DataFrame = [
    timestamp: timestamp, id: int ... 3 more fields]
```

The fluent code below simply performs the intended steps in order:

```scala
scala> df.  // Working with loaded DataFrame
     | filter($"x" > ($"y" + 1)).  // x more than y+1 (per row)
     | groupBy($"name").            // group together same name
     | agg(avg($"x") as "Mean_x").  // mean within each group
     | sort($"Mean_x").             // order data by new column
     | show(5)


+------+------------------+
|  name|            Mean_x|
+------+------------------+
|   Ray|0.6625697073245446|
|Ursula|0.6628107271270461|
|Xavier|0.6641165295855926|
| Wendy|0.6642381725604264|
| Kevin| 0.664836301676443|
+------+------------------+
only showing top 5 rows
```

Pandas and Derived Wrappers

A number of libraries either emulate the Pandas API or directly utilize it as a dependency. Dask and **Modin** both directly wrap Pandas, and partition one native DataFrame into many separate Pandas DataFrames. A method on the native DataFrame is usually dispatched to the underlying corresponding Pandas method per DataFrame. Although Modin can use either Dask or **Ray** as its parallel/cluster execution back-end, Modin differs from Dask in being eager in its execution model.

Dask is a general-purpose execution back-end, with its `dask.dataframe` subpackage being only one component. Much of what Dask does is similar to the library Ray, which Modin may also use if desired (benchmarks as of this writing mildly favor Ray, depending on the use case). Most Pandas API method calls in Dask initially only build a **directed acyclic graph** (**DAG**) of the required operations. Computation is only performed when the `.compute()` method of a built DAG is called. The example below uses Dask, but it would look exactly the same with Modin except for the final `.compute()` and an initial `import modin.pandas as pd`.

cuDF is another library that follows Pandas' API very closely, but it executes methods on CUDA GPUs. Since the underlying execution is on an entirely different kind of chip architecture, cuDF does not share code with Pandas nor wrap Pandas. But almost all API calls will be identical, but often vastly faster if you have a recent CUDA GPU on your system.

Like Pandas and Modin, cuDF is eager in its execution model:

```
import dask.dataframe as dd
dfd = dd.read_csv('data/multicsv/*.csv', parse_dates=['timestamp'])
```

The operations in the Pandas style below look very similar to those in Spark. The accessor .loc overloads several selection styles, but a predicate filter is such a permitted one. Another is used on the same line to select columns, i.e. a sequence of names. Grouping is nearly identical, other than the capitalization of the method name. Pandas even has an .agg() method to which we could pass a mean function or the string 'mean'; we just chose the shortcut. Columns are not automatically renamed in aggregation, so we do that to match more precisely. Instead of sorting and showing, we take the 5 smallest in a single method. In effect, the conceptual elements are identical, and spelling varies only mildly:

```
(dfd
    .loc[dfd.x > dfd.y+1,           # Row predicate
        ['name', 'x']]             # Column list
    .groupby("name")               # Grouping column(s)
    .mean()                        # Aggregation
    .rename(columns={'x': 'Mean_x'}) # Naming
    .nsmallest(5, 'Mean_x')        # Selection by order
).compute()                        # Concretize
```

```
Name        Mean_x
Ray         0.662570
Ursula      0.662811
Xavier      0.664117
Wendy       0.664238
Kevin       0.664836
```

Vaex

Vaex is a Python library completely independent of Pandas, but that uses a largely similar API. A fair amount of code will just work identically with either style of data frame, but not so much that you can simply drop in one for the other. The philosophy of Vaex is somewhat different from Pandas. On the one hand, Vaex emphasizes lazy computation and implicit parallelism; expressions are eagerly evaluated, but with attention to not touching those portions of data that are not needed for a given operation. This goes hand in hand with the mostly out-of-core operation. Rather than reading data into memory, Vaex memory maps the data on disk, only loading those parts required for an operation.

Vaex consistently avoids making data copies, in effect expressing selections as views. It has a concept of *expressions* and of *virtual columns*. For example, a computation on several columns, even if assigned to a new column, does not use any significant new memory since only the functional form is stored rather than the data. Only when that data is needed is the computation performed, and only for those rows affected. The overall result is that Vaex can be very fast on large datasets; however, Vaex parallelizes only over multiple cores on one machine, not over clusters of machines.

Because of its memory-mapped approach, Vaex does not really want to deal directly with CSV files internally. Unlike serialized Feather or HDF5, which put each datum at a predictable location on disk, CSV is inherently ragged in layout on disk. While a .read_csv() method will read a single file into memory, for working with a family of CSVs in a directory, you will want to convert them to a corresponding family of HDF5 files. Fortunately, the method .read_csv_and_convert() does this automatically for you. The result is that the first time you read such a collection, the conversion takes a while, but subsequent opens utilize the existing HDF5 files and open instantly (no actual read into memory, just memory maps):

```
import vaex
dfv = vaex.read_csv_and_convert('data/multicsv/*.csv', copy_
index=False)
```

Another difference from Pandas is that Vaex data frames are *tidy* (as described at the start of this chapter). Many operations on Pandas rely on their row index, which might even be a hierarchical index comprising multiple nested columns. The "index," such as it is, in Vaex is simply the row number. You can do filtering, and grouping, and sorting, and so on, but always based on regular columns. This philosophy is shared with tibble and data.table in R, both of which reject that aspect of the older data.frame:

```
print(
dfv
    [dfv.x > dfv.y + 1]    # Predicate selection of rows
    [['name', 'x']]        # List selection of columns
    .groupby('name')       # Grouping
    .agg({'x': 'mean'})    # Aggregation
    .sort('x')             # Sort (Vaex does not have .nsmallest() method)
    .head(5)               # First 5
)

#   name              x
0   Ray         0.66257
1   Ursula     0.662811
2   Xavier     0.664117
```

```
3    Wendy     0.664238
4    Kevin     0.664836
```

Let us remove those temporary HDF5 files for discussion of libraries other than Vaex:

```
%%bash
rm -f data/multicsv/*.hdf5
```

Let us now turn to analogous data frame options within R.

Data Frames in R (Tidyverse)

In the Tidyverse, tibbles are the preferred data frame objects, and **dplyr** is an associated library for—often chained—pipelined data manipulations. The way that dplyr achieves a fluent style is not based on chained method calls. Indeed, object-oriented programming is rarely used in R in general. Instead, dplyr relies on the "pipe" operator (%>%), which treats the result of the prior expression as the first argument to the next function called. This allows for rewriting compact but deeply nested expressions, such as the following:

```
round(exp(diff(log(x))), 1)
```

In fluent style this becomes:

```
x %>%
  log() %>%
  diff() %>%
  exp() %>%
  round(1)
```

First we can read in the collection of CSV files that was generated earlier. The 2.5 million total rows in this data are still medium-sized data, but the patterns in the below code could be applied to big data:

```
%%R
files <- dir(path = "data/multicsv/", pattern = "*.csv", full.names =
TRUE)
read_csv_quiet <- function(file) {
    read_csv(file, col_types = cols("T", "n", "f", "n", "n"), progress
= FALSE) }

data <- files    %>%
  # read_csv() on each file, reduce to one DF with rbind
  map(read_csv_quiet) %>%
```

```
  # If this were genuinely large data, we would process each file
individually
  reduce(rbind)

data
```

```
# A tibble: 2,592,000 x 5
   timestamp                id name        x        y
   <dttm>                <dbl> <fct>    <dbl>    <dbl>
 1 2000-01-01 00:00:00     979 Zelda    0.802    0.167
 2 2000-01-01 00:00:01    1019 Ingrid  -0.350    0.705
 3 2000-01-01 00:00:02    1007 Hannah  -0.170   -0.0508
 4 2000-01-01 00:00:03    1034 Ursula   0.868   -0.191
 5 2000-01-01 00:00:04    1024 Ingrid   0.0838   0.109
 6 2000-01-01 00:00:05     955 Ingrid  -0.757    0.308
 7 2000-01-01 00:00:06     968 Laura    0.230   -0.913
 8 2000-01-01 00:00:07     945 Ursula   0.265   -0.271
 9 2000-01-01 00:00:08    1020 Victor   0.512   -0.481
10 2000-01-01 00:00:09     992 Wendy    0.862   -0.599
# ... with 2,591,990 more rows
```

The dplyr pipes into functions that filter, modify, group, and aggregate data look nearly identical to the chained methods used in other data frame libraries. A few function names are slightly different than in other libraries, but the steps performed are identical:

```
%%R
summary <- data    %>%
  filter(x > y+1) %>%    # Predicate selection of rows
  select(name, x) %>%    # Selection of columns
  group_by(name)  %>%    # Grouping
                         # Aggregation and naming
  summarize(Mean_x = mean(x)) %>%
  arrange(Mean_x) %>%    # Sort data
  head(5)                # First 5

summary
```

```
'summarise()' ungrouping output (override with '.groups' argument)
# A tibble: 5 x 2
  name    Mean_x
  <fct>    <dbl>
1 Ray      0.663
```

```
2 Ursula   0.663
3 Xavier   0.664
4 Wendy    0.664
5 Kevin    0.665
```

Data Frames in R (data.table)

Outside the Tidyverse, the main approach to working with tabular data in modern R is data.table. This is a replacement for the older, but standard, R data.frame. I do not separately discuss data.frame in this book since new code should always prefer either tibbles or data.tables.

Unlike most other approaches to data frames, data.table does not use a fluent or chained style. Instead, it uses an extremely compact *general form* of DT[i, j, by] that captures a great many of the manipulations possible. Not every collection of operations can be expressed in a single general form, but a great many of them can. Moreover, because data.table is able to optimize over the entire general form, it can often be significantly faster on large datasets than those libraries performing operations in a sequenced manner.

Each element of the general form may be omitted to mean "everything." If used, the i is an expression describing the rows of interest; often this i will consist of several clauses joined by logic connectors & (and), | (or), and ! (not). Row ordering may also be imposed within this expression (but not on derived columns). For example:

```
dt[(id > 999 | date > '2020-03-01') & !(name == "Lee")]
```

The column selector j can refer to columns, including derived columns:

```
dt[ , .(id, pay_level = round(log(salary), 1)]
```

Finally, the by form is a grouping description that allows for calculations per row subset. Groups can follow either categorical values or computed cuts:

```
dt[, mean(salary), cut(age, quantile(age, seq(0,100,10)))]
```

Putting those forms together, we can produce the same summary as with other data frame libraries. However, the final ordering has to be performed as a second step:

```
%%R
library(data.table)

dt <- data.table(data)
summary <- dt[
```

```
    i = x > y + 1,         # Predicate selection of rows
                           # Aggregation and naming
    j = .(Mean_x = mean(x)),
    by = .(name)]          # Grouping

# Sort data and first 5
summary[order(Mean_x), .SD[1:5]]
```

```
      name    Mean_x
1:     Ray 0.6625697
2: Ursula 0.6628107
3: Xavier 0.6641165
4:  Wendy 0.6642382
5:  Kevin 0.6648363
```

Bash for Fun

For readers who are accustomed to performing pipelined filtering and aggregation at the command line, the piped or fluent style used by data frames will seem very familiar. In fact, it is not difficult to replicate our example using command-line tools. The heavy lifter here is **awk**, but the code it uses is very simple. Conceptually, these steps exactly match those we used in data frame libraries. The small tools that combine, using pipes, under the Unix philosophy, can naturally replicate the same basic operations used in data frames:

```
%%bash
COND='{if ($4 > $5+1) print}'
SHOW='{for(j in count) print j,sum[j]/count[j]}'
AGG='{ count[$1]++; sum[$1]+=$2 }'" END $SHOW"

cat data/multicsv/*.csv |    # Create the "data frame"
  grep -v ^timestamp    |    # Remove the headers
  awk -F, "$COND"        |    # Predicate selection
  cut -d, -f3,4          |    # Select columns
  awk -F, "$AGG"         |    # Aggregate by group
  sort -k2               |    # Sort data
  head -5                     # First 5
```

```
Ray 0.66257
Ursula 0.662811
Xavier 0.664117
Wendy 0.664238
Kevin 0.664836
```

Jeroen Janssens wrote a delightful book entitled *Data Science at the Command Line* (`https://www.datascienceatthecommandline.com/`) that is both wonderfully written and freely available online. You should also buy the printed or ebook edition to support his work. In this subsection, and at various places in this book, I make only small gestures in the direction of the types of techniques that that book talks about in detail.

The data frame and fluent programming style is a powerful idiom, and is especially widely used in data science. Every one of the specific libraries I discuss are excellent choices with equivalent power. Which fits you best is largely a matter of taste, and perhaps of what your colleagues use.

Exercises

Putting together much of what we have learned in this chapter, the below exercises should allow you to utilize the techniques and idioms you have read about.

Tidy Data from Excel

An Excel spreadsheet with some brief information on awards given to movies is available at:

```
https://www.gnosis.cx/cleaning/Film_Awards.xlsx
```

In a more fleshed-out case, we might have data for many more years, more types of awards, more associations that grant awards, and so on. While the organization of this spreadsheet is much like a great many you will encounter "in the wild," it is very little like the tidy data we would rather work with. In the simple example, only 63 data values occur, and you could probably enter them into the desired structure by hand as quickly as coding the transformations. However, the point of this exercise is to write programming code that could generalize to larger datasets of similar structure:

	A	B	C	D	E	F	G
1	Best Picture						
2	Year	Academy Award	Director	Golden Globe - Drama	Director	Golden Globe - Musical or Comedy	Director
3	2019	Parasite	Bong Joon-ho	1917	Sam Mendes	Once Upon a Time in Hollywood	Quentin Tarantino
4	2018	Green Book	Peter Farrelly	Bohemian Rhapsody	Bryan Singer	Green Book	Peter Farelly
5	2017	The Shape of Water	Guillermo del Toro	Three Billboards Outside Ebbing, Missouri	Martin McDonagh	Lady Bird	Greta Gerwig
6							
7							
8	Best Actor						
9	Year	Academy Award	Film	Golden Globe - Drama	Film	Golden Globe - Musical or Comedy	Film
10	2019	Joaquin Phoenix	Joker	Joaquin Phoenix	Joker	Taron Egerton	Rocketman
11	2018	Rami Malek	Bohemian Rhapsody	Rami Malek	Bohemian Rhapsody	Christian Bale	Vice
12	2017	Gary Oldman	Darkest Hour	Gary Oldman	Darkest Hour	James Franco	The Disaster Artist
13							
14							
15	Best Actress						
16	Year	Academy Award	Film	Golden Globe - Drama	Film	Golden Globe - Musical or Comedy	Film
17	2019	Renée Zellweger	Judy	Renée Zellweger	Judy	Awkwafina	The Farewell
18	2018	Olivia Colman	The Favourite	Glenn Close	The Wife	Olivia Coleman	The Favourite
19	2017	Frances McDormand	Three Billboards Outsi	Frances McDormand	Three Billboards Outside E	Saoirse Ronan	Lady Bird

Figure 1.6: Film awards spreadsheet

Your task in this exercise is to read this data into a single well-normalized data frame, using whichever language and library you are most comfortable with. Along the way, you will need to remediate whatever data integrity problems you detect. As examples of issues to look out for:

- The film *1917* was stored as a number, not a string, when naïvely entered into a cell.

- The spelling of some values is inconsistent. Olivia Colman's name is incorrectly transcribed as "Coleman" in one occurrence. There is a spacing issue in one value you will need to identify.

- Structurally, an apparent parallel is not really so. Person names are sometimes listed under the name of the association, but other times under another column. Film names are sometimes listed under association, other times elsewhere.

- Some column names occur multiple times in the same tabular area.

When thinking about good data frame organization, think of what the independent and dependent variables are. In each year, each association awards for each category. These are independent dimensions. A person name and a film name are slightly tricky since they are not exactly independent, but at the same time some awards are to a film and others to a person. Moreover, one actor might appear in multiple films in a year (not in this sample data, but do not rule it out). Likewise, at times multiple films have used the same name at times in film history. Some persons are both director and actor (in either the same or different films).

Once you have a useful data frame, use it to answer these questions in summary reports:

- For each film involved in multiple awards, list the award and year it is associated with.

- For each actor/actress winning multiple awards, list the film and award they are associated with.

- While not occurring in this small dataset, sometimes actors/actresses win awards for multiple films (usually in different years). Make sure your code will handle that situation.

- It is manual work, but you may want to research and add awards given in other years; in particular, adding some data will show actors with awards for multiple films. Do your other reports correctly summarize the larger dataset?

Tidy Data from SQL

An SQLite database with roughly the same brief information as in the prior spreadsheet is available at:

```
https://www.gnosis.cx/cleaning/Film_Awards.sqlite
```

However, the information in the database version is relatively well normalized and typed. Also, additional information has been included on a variety of entities included in the spreadsheet. Only slightly more information is included in this schema than in the spreadsheet, but it should be able to accommodate a large amount of data on films, actors, directors, and awards, and the relationships among those data:

```
sqlite> .tables
actor      award      director   org_name
```

As was mentioned in the prior exercise, the same name for a film can be used more than once, even by the same director. For example, Abel Gance used the title *J'accuse!* for both his 1919 and 1938 films with connected subject matter:

```
sqlite> SELECT * FROM director WHERE year < 1950;
Abel Gance|J'accuse!|1919
Abel Gance|J'accuse!|1938
```

Let us look at a selection from the actor table, for example. In this table we have a column gender to differentiate beyond name. As of this writing, no transgender actor has been nominated for a major award both before and after a change in gender identity, but this schema allows for that possibility. In any case, we can use this field to differentiate the "actor" versus "actress" awards that many organizations grant:

```
sqlite> .schema actor
CREATE TABLE actor (name TEXT, film TEXT, year INTEGER, gender
CHAR(1));

sqlite> SELECT * FROM actor WHERE name="Joaquin Phoenix";
Joaquin Phoenix|Joker|2019|M
Joaquin Phoenix|Walk the Line|2006|M
Joaquin Phoenix|Hotel Rwanda|2004|M
Joaquin Phoenix|Her|2013|M
Joaquin Phoenix|The Master|2013|M
```

The goal in this exercise is to create the same tidy data frame that you created in the prior exercise and answer the same questions that were asked there. If some questions can be answered directly with SQL, feel free to take that approach instead. For this exercise, only consider awards for the years 2017, 2018, and 2019. Some others are included in an incomplete way, but your reports are for those years:

```
sqlite> SELECT * FROM award WHERE winner="Frances McDormand";
Oscar|Best Actress|2017|Frances McDormand
GG|Actress/Drama|2017|Frances McDormand
Oscar|Best Actress|1997|Frances McDormand
```

Denouement

All models are wrong, but some models are useful.

–George Box

Topics covered in this chapter: Delimited Files; Spreadsheet Dangers; RDBMS; HDF5; Data Frames.

This chapter introduced the data formats that make up the large majority of all the structured data in the world. While I do not have hard data, exactly, on this breakdown of data volume—nor can anyone, apart perhaps from some three-letter agencies specializing in bulk data acquisition—I still feel like it is a safe assertion. Between all the scientific data stored in HDF5 and related formats, all the business data stored in spreadsheets, all the transactional data stored in SQL databases, and everything exported from almost everywhere to CSV, this makes up almost everything a working data scientist encounters on a regular basis.

In presenting formats, we addressed the currently leading tools for ingestion of those data sources in several languages. The focus throughout this book will remain on Python and R, which are the main programming languages for data science. Perhaps that will change in the future, and almost certainly some new libraries will arise for addressing this huge bulk of data in faster and more convenient ways. Even so, most of the conceptual issues about the strengths and limits of formats—concerns largely about data types and storage artifacts—will remain for those new languages and libraries. Only spelling will change mildly.

An extended, but nonetheless dramatically incomplete, discussion looked at the data frame abstraction used in a great many tools. Here again, new variations may arise, but I am confident that the general abstraction will be the primary one used in data science for several decades after this writing. In presenting a number of slightly different libraries, I have only scratched the surface of any one of them.

In fact, even if this entire chapter was about just one of the mentioned libraries, it would be incomplete compared with those excellent books that spend their whole length discussing one particular data frame library. Nonetheless, I hope that this introduction to thinking about data processing problems in terms of the steps of filtering, grouping, aggregation, naming, and ordering will serve readers well in their articulation of many ingestion tasks.

One limit of the data frame abstraction that we used in reading all the formats discussed in this chapter is that none look at data streaming in any meaningful way. For the most part, data science needs are not streaming needs, but occasionally they overlap. If your needs lie at that particular edge, check the documentation for streaming protocols like ActiveMQ, RabbitMQ, and Kafka (among others); but your concern will not chiefly be in the data formats themselves, but rather in event processing, and in evolving detection of anomalies and bad data, such as is discussed in *Chapters 4* and *5*, and perhaps value imputation, discussed in *Chapter 6*.

In the next chapter, we turn to data formats that are hierarchically organized rather than tabular.

2
Hierarchical Formats

No gods, no masters.

–Louis Auguste Blanqui

When we utilize machine learning models, and indeed when we perform general statistical analyses, we almost always assume our data is tabular. Observations and features; rows and columns. And yet, there are a number of very popular ways of storing data that resemble trees rather than plowed fields. Data objects belong to other data objects which belong to yet other data objects, with no specific limit on the depth or names of branches. Both for economy of understanding and, in the case of database systems, for efficiency of access, hierarchical data formats very often make more sense for a broad class of data.

There are many domains that simply map more naturally to hierarchies than to tables. Yes, the relational algebra—the conceptual structure that underpins SQL and relational databases—is in some way able to represent every possible structure. But it feels awkward for naturally hierarchical data. For example, file systems have nested paths that eventually lead to actual files at their leaves. Directories along the way might have indefinitely many subdirectories, with names at every level expressing something meaningful, until we get to the files, which may themselves have hierarchical, tabular, or other arrangements of data.

Likewise, if we make a graph of connected web pages—or indeed of *any* kind of network, whether social, electronic communications, ecological interactions, or another—it is closer to a hierarchy than to a table. Yes, not all, or most, graphs are directed acyclic graphs (DAGs), but still less are they rows and columns.

Or imagine you had a "book of life" that described many biological organisms, organized by Linnaean taxonomy—domain, kingdom, phylum, class, order, family, genus, species (and perhaps sometimes subspecies, superfamily, subfamily, or tribe, for example). Not only is this hierarchical structure important data, but the leaf attributes are largely different for varying species. Information on the dentation of prokaryotes is not going to be relevant. Teeth are only attributes of organisms within the Chordata phylum, and mostly only within the subphylum Vertebrata. Correspondingly, attributes about hyphae are only relevant within the Fungi, Oomycota, or Actinobacteria (crossing domains, kingdoms, and phyla, but still only within a small fragment of the hierarchy).

For better or worse, when we do data science with hierarchical data sources, that generally means that we construct a tabular abstraction of the underlying data. Depending on our purpose, either or both of the leaf attributes and branching structure might be relevant. In either case, we want to encode these as columns of variables and rows of records. This contrasts somewhat with many purposes outside of data science; for other purposes, it is often simply a matter of "drilling down" into the relevant leaf or distant branch and presenting or modifying the small amount of information at that level. Data science is much more often about generalizing over many different data points, concerning many different objects.

***

Before we get to the sections of this chapter, let us run our standard setup code:

```
from src.setup import *
%load_ext rpy2.ipython
```

```
%%R
library(tidyverse)
```

Now let us dive into JavaScript Object Notation as the first hierarchical format of this chapter.

JSON

She's a germ free adolescent
Cleanliness is her obsession
Cleans her teeth ten times a day
Scrub away scrub away scrub away
The S.R. way...

–Poly Styrene

Concepts:

- JSON is a syntax not a semantics
- REST queries and responses
- The command-line tool jq
- Safe JSON readers
- NaNs, Infinities, and overflows
- Aggregating JSON records
- Working with large, deeply nested JSON
- Extracting a tabular summary of JSON data
- Validating structure with JSON Schema

JavaScript Object Notation (JSON) is a widely used data exchange format. As the name suggests, it is a format derived from JavaScript, but it is strictly language-neutral. JSON is currently specified by Internet Engineering Task Force (IETF) RFC 8259. While it can be and is used for many purposes, it is especially prevalent as a way for computer services to communicate with each other. Hence, a large share of JSON data consists of transient messages that do not necessarily ever live on permanent storage such as files on disk or values in a database. Of course, sometimes those messages are logged or somehow stored, and become fruitful for data science purposes.

JSON is supported by a great many programming languages, in their standard library, as built-ins, or with widely available libraries for those languages. In syntax, JSON is very similar to, but neither exactly a superset nor subset of, native data structures in JavaScript, and to a large extent to those in Python. An important thing to understand about JSON is that it specifies a syntax, but not a semantics. Each language has to make decisions about how to process text conforming with JSON grammar.

There are exactly four value types defined in JSON, and three literal values. Whitespace is ignored throughout JSON.

- `false`, `true`, and `null` are literal values.
- An *object* is a grammatical structure that is enclosed in curly braces, { and }, with strings for keys, separated by a colon from values of any syntactic type. Multiple key/value pairs are separated by commas.
- An *array* is a grammatical structure that is enclosed in square brackets, [and], with any syntactic values separated by commas.

- A *number* optionally starts with a minus sign, followed by a sequence of digits, optionally followed by a fractional part after a decimal portion, optionally followed by an exponent. This is mostly the same as the spelling of numbers in languages like Python, R, JavaScript, Julia, C, etc., but slightly more restrictive.

- A *string* is a grammatical structure enclosed by double quotes (the code point U+0022) that may contain almost any characters. Unicode code points may be indicated as, for example, \u0022, and a few special characters must be escaped with a backslash.

For example, the following fragment utilizes all four value types. The example contains an object with a string key, whose value is an array containing one each of the literal values, and two numbers:

```
{"key": [true, false, null, 15, 55.66]}
```

What JSON Looks Like

JSON is frequently used to interactively communicate messages among computer systems. On my local machine, I have a small demonstration web service running. In the book repository, the directory `node-server/` contains all the code to launch it. It happens to be written in JavaScript/Node, but it could be written in any programming language. The key thing about it is that it provides a Representational State Transfer (RESTful) interface in which clients may send JSON messages and will receive other JSON messages back. The short document shown in the output below is fairly typical of such uses:

```
# A response to an HTTP request
response = requests.get('http://localhost:3001/users')

# Show status code, content-type, and JSON body
print(response.status_code, response.headers['Content-Type'])
response.text
200 application/json; charset=utf-8
```

```
'{"1":{"name":"Guido van Rossum","password":"unladenswallow","details":{"profession":"ex-BDFL"}},"2":{"name":"Brendan Eich","password":"nontransitiveequality","details":{"profession":"Mozillan"}},"3":{"name":"Ken Thompson","password":"p/q2-q4!","details":{"profession":"Unix Creator"}}}'
```

Whitespace is not significant in JSON, but it can definitely make it more readable for human examination. For example, a small function in the setup module for this book can do that:

```
pprint_json(response.text)
```

```
{
  "1": {
    "name": "Guido van Rossum",
    "password": "unladenswallow",
    "details": {
      "profession": "ex-BDFL"
    }
  },
  "2": {
    "name": "Brendan Eich",
    "password": "nontransitiveequality",
    "details": {
      "profession": "Mozillan"
    }
  },
  "3": {
    "name": "Ken Thompson",
    "password": "p/q2-q4!",
    "details": {
      "profession": "Unix Creator"
    }
  }
}
```

A command-line tool called jq is very useful for working with JSON data, either streamed or on disk. A data scientist or developer who frequently works with JSON should consider learning the slightly arcane, but compact, query language jq provides; that is outside the scope of this book, however. The home page (https://stedolan.github.io/jq/) for the tool, as of the time of writing, contains a very nice blurb for it:

> jq is like sed for JSON data - you can use it to slice and filter and map and transform structured data with the same ease that sed, awk, grep and friends let you play with text.

One very simple task jq can accomplish is pretty-printing (indentation, line breaks, colorization, and so on):

```
with open('data/3001.json', 'w') as fh:
    fh.write(response.text)

!jq . data/3001.json
```

```
{
  "1": {
    "name": "Guido van Rossum",
    "password": "unladenswallow",
    "details": {
      "profession": "ex-BDFL"
    }
  },
  "2": {
    "name": "Brendan Eich",
    "password": "nontransitiveequality",
    "details": {
      "profession": "Mozillan"
    }
  },
  "3": {
    "name": "Ken Thompson",
    "password": "p/q2-q4!",
    "details": {
      "profession": "Unix Creator"
    }
  }
}
```

Despite its close similarity to native spelling of data structures in Python and JavaScript (and other languages), you must use a read/parse function to convert JSON to native data. At times, a function like eval() in JavaScript, Python, or some other languages will successfully convert a string to native data. However, this is a *very bad idea*; on the one hand, it sometimes fails (even within JavaScript). The other hand is more crucial: trying this can potentially execute malicious code contained within JSON (or pseudo-JSON). Almost all programming languages have JSON readers/parsers as part of their standard library or widely available.

For example, in JavaScript, using the Node.js runtime we could write:

```
%%bash
js="
const fs = require('fs');
let raw = fs.readFileSync('data/3001.json');
let users = JSON.parse(raw);
console.log(users);
"
echo $js | node
```

```
{ '1':
   { name: 'Guido van Rossum',
     password: 'unladenswallow',
     details: { profession: 'ex-BDFL' } },
  '2':
   { name: 'Brendan Eich',
     password: 'nontransitiveequality',
     details: { profession: 'Mozillan' } },
  '3':
   { name: 'Ken Thompson',
     password: 'p/q2-q4!',
     details: { profession: 'Unix Creator' } } }
```

In Python, the equivalent is:

```
with open('data/3001.json') as fh:
    # Could also call 'json.load(fh)' to read file
    raw = fh.read()
    users = json.loads(raw)
users
```

```
{'1': {'name': 'Guido van Rossum',
  'password': 'unladenswallow',
  'details': {'profession': 'ex-BDFL'}},
 '2': {'name': 'Brendan Eich',
  'password': 'nontransitiveequality',
  'details': {'profession': 'Mozillan'}},
 '3': {'name': 'Ken Thompson',
  'password': 'p/q2-q4!',
  'details': {'profession': 'Unix Creator'}}}
```

In R, we do not have a direct equivalent for the dictionary or hashmap structure as a standard data structure. Hence the representation is as a *named list* (generally a nested one). Here we only display the third element of that list for illustration:

```
%%R
library(rjson)
result <- fromJSON(file = "data/3001.json")
result[3]
```

```
$'3'
$'3'$name
[1] "Ken Thompson"

$'3'$password
[1] "p/q2-q4!"

$'3'$details
$'3'$details$profession
[1] "Unix Creator"
```

Other programming languages will have different spellings, but libraries or standard functions can convert between native data and JSON.

NaN Handling and Data Types

The semi-formal description of the grammar of JSON had a covert purpose underlying its direct information. Readers might notice things that are *missing* from it. In particular, there is a single syntactic type named "number," but there are no distinctions among integers, floating-points, decimals, complex numbers, fractions/rationals, or the bit length of represented numbers. The decision of how to interpret numeric values is strictly left to libraries, or to individual users.

It may not be as obvious, but there are also some important floating-point "numbers" missing altogether. IEEE-754 floating-point numbers include the special values **Not-a-Number** (**NaN**) and Infinity/-Infinity. To be pedantic, the binary standard represents a great many distinct bit patterns as meaning "NaN," although just one each for +Infinity and -Infinity (negative zero is another oddball number, but is less important). JSON cannot represent those values, even though many or most programming languages have a way of spelling those values; in programming languages, typically NaN has a single spelling, such as NaN, rather than millions of them for all the bit patterns.

In Python, the standard library and other common JSON parsers make a heuristic assumption that numbers that contain either a decimal point or an exponent are intended to represent floating-points, and numbers without them are meant to represent integers. There are edge cases where these assumptions can fail. Numbers like 1e309 that would fit perfectly well and exactly into Python's unlimited-size integers are treated as floats, and fail as such (they *could*, however, be spelled with hundreds of trailing zeros and no decimal point to be interpreted as integers). Probably more often relevant is that by treating JSON numbers as floats, their precision is limited to the native floating-point type. In 64-bits, this works out to 17 decimal digits; in 32-bits it is only 9 digits. Readers normally simply lose this potential precision.

A simple example shows some of these overflow or truncation issues. Here, Python and R are identical; other languages may behave differently (but most are similar):

```
# An interpreted float, an overflow, and a truncation
json_str = "[1e308, 1e309, 1.2345678901234567890]"
json.loads(json_str)
```

```
[1e+308, inf, 1.2345678901234567]
```

```
%%R -i json_str
options(digits = 22)
fromJSON(json_str)
```

```
[1] 1.000000000000000010979e+308                    Inf
[3]   1.234567890123456690432e+00
```

An inclination you could easily be forgiven is to think that this issue is no more than inherent in the nature of floating-point rounding. After all, the value that is 10^{308} is also only approximate, as we see in the long representation in the R output. However, Python at least provides a natural alternative that more closely matches the JSON number syntax in the decimal module. Unfortunately, producing values of the type Decimal in the standard library is cumbersome (but possible). Fortunately, the third-party module simplejson makes this easy, as we see below:

```
simplejson.loads(json_str, use_decimal=True)
```

```
[Decimal('1E+308'), Decimal('1E+309'), Decimal('1.2345678901234567890')]
```

Other languages, such as JavaScript and R, lack a standard decimal or unlimited precision data type, and will simply lose precision in representing some syntactically valid JSON numbers.

A wrinkle in this story is that the default "JSON" libraries in languages like Python do not *actually* read and write JSON by default. They read a superset of JSON, but that might include the additional literals NaN, Infinity, and -Infinity. The *JSON5* proposal includes these extensions and a few others, but is not an official standard currently. The Python standard library, for example, does not support literals of nan, Nan inf, +Infinity, or other spellings that might seem reasonable; at least not as of this writing. Exactly what literals other languages and libraries support is up to them, and may change. Let us try some special values:

```
specials = "[NaN, Infinity, -Infinity]"
vals = json.loads(specials)
vals
```

```
[nan, inf, -inf]
```

Several libraries in R represent these special IEEE-754 values in a manner different from what Python libraries do. I use rjson in these examples, but RJSONIO and jsonlite use similar conventions. The R solution to the underspecification is to spell its special values as strings with special suggestive values, as in the third line of output below:

```
%%R -i vals
vals = c(NaN, Inf, -Inf)
print(vals)
print("R version of 'enhanced JSON':")
rjson_str = toJSON(vals)  # function from rjson library
print(rjson_str)
```

```
[1]  NaN  Inf -Inf
[1] "R version of 'enhanced JSON':"
[1] "[\"NaN\",\"Inf\",\"-Inf\"]"
```

This technique fails on round-tripping, even within rjson itself, unless you write custom code to interpret strings. We read back the content simply as strings rather than as special numeric values:

```
%%R
print("Read back in 'enhanced JSON':")
fromJSON(rjson_str)
```

```
[1] "Read back in 'enhanced JSON':"
[1] "NaN"   "Inf"   "-Inf"
```

***

We can see strict JSON-compliant behavior using the JavaScript reader:

```
%%bash
js="JSON.parse('[NaN, Infinity, -Infinity]');"
echo $js | node | cat

undefined:1
[NaN, Infinity, -Infinity]
 ^

SyntaxError: Unexpected token N in JSON at position 1
    at JSON.parse (<anonymous>)
    at [stdin]:1:6
    at Script.runInThisContext (vm.js:122:20)
    at Object.runInThisContext (vm.js:329:38)
    at Object.<anonymous> ([stdin]-wrapper:6:22)
    at Module._compile (internal/modules/cjs/loader.js:778:30)
    at evalScript (internal/bootstrap/node.js:590:27)
    at Socket.<anonymous> (internal/bootstrap/node.js:323:15)
    at Socket.emit (events.js:203:15)
    at endReadableNT (_stream_readable.js:1145:12)
```

We can also use a slightly misnamed, and cumbersome, parameter (parse_constant) to enforce strict mode in the Python standard library. This catches only those specific values of special floating-point numbers spelled in the manner shown below:

```
json.loads("[NaN, Infinity, -Infinity]", parse_constant=lambda _:
"INVALID")

['INVALID', 'INVALID', 'INVALID']
```

In other words, not just any hypothetical literal outside these particular spellings will be handed to the parse_constant function:

```
try:
    json.loads("[nan, +Inf, Foobar]", parse_constant=lambda _:
"INVALID")
except Exception as err:
    print_err(err)

JSONDecodeError
Expecting value: line 1 column 2 (char 1)
```

The tool jq has an odd "semi-strict" behavior. Infinity is recognized, under several spellings, but is not treated as the actual IEEE-754 value "infinity." None of these choices are right or wrong per se, but incompatibilities are dangers to stay alert for:

```
%%bash
echo "[NaN, inf, -Infinity]" | jq .

[
  null,
  1.7976931348623157e+308,
  -1.7976931348623157e+308
]
```

JSON Lines

In the next subsection, we look at JSON documents of substantial size and structure. However, as we saw in the slightly fanciful example in the previous subsection, JSON is often used to encode small bundles of data. One area where we very often encounter "small bundles of data" is in log files, such as are discussed in *Chapter 7, Feature Engineering, Chapter 3, Repurposing Data Sources,* and other places in this book. The entries in log files are generally similar, and are usually arranged one per line; however, frequently, different entries are required to hold different fields. This tends to require a lot of conditional logic when parsing a log file.

JSON streaming is a very useful and widely used approach to reducing this burden. Since whitespace is ignored in JSON, every document can be contained in a single line (newlines encoded as \n), and any structures and field names can be expressed with JSON syntactic structures. This does not remove all conditional logic since the disposition of a particular entry will still often depend on the data inside it, but at least it removes the concern from the parsing step itself.

To be precise, the syntax called **Newline Delimited JSON (ndjson)** or **JSON Lines** is one of several approaches to aggregating (small) JSON documents. Newline delimitation is the most widely used style, and is easiest to work with using command-line text processing tools which are usually line-oriented. However, you may encounter several other styles occasionally:

- **Record separator-delimited**: The Unicode character INFORMATION SEPARATOR TWO (U+001E) used as a delimiter (RFC 7464), that is, newlines may occur inside JSON document entries.

- **Concatenated JSON**: No delimiters used, and each JSON entry is an object or array. This allows a streaming parser to recognize the matching } or] that will terminate the top-level structure. Every JSON Lines stream is automatically also a concatenated JSON stream.

- **Length-prefixed JSON**: Each entry consists of an integer indicating the number of bytes in the remainder of the entry, followed by a JSON object or array (in principle, a string would work too). This has an advantage over plain concatenation in that the reader does not need to test on each character read whether a structure is completed.

Let us consider a JSON Lines example based on one in the current version of the Wikipedia article on JSON streaming (`https://en.wikipedia.org/wiki/JSON_streaming`). The lines are somewhat larger than the width of these margins, so a small Bash pipeline will format for a presentation length. As shown, each line is displayed with a leading integer (which is not part of the line) and subsequent displayed lines without a leading number are part of the same line on disk (many text editors use a similar approach):

```
%%bash
cat -n data/jsonlines.log | fmt -w55 | tr -d " "

1       {"ts":"2020-06-18T10:44:13",
"logged_in":{"username":"foo"},
"connection":{"addr":"1.2.3.4","port":5678}}
2       {"ts":"2020-06-18T10:44:15",
"registered":{"username":"bar","email":"bar@example.com"},
"connection":{"addr":"2.3.4.5","port":6789}}
3       {"ts":"2020-06-18T10:44:16",
"logged_out":{"username":"foo"},
"connection":{"addr":"1.2.3.4","port":5678}}
4       {"ts":"2020-06-18T10:47:22",
"registered":{"username":"baz","email":"baz@example.net"},
"connection":{"addr":"3.4.5.6","port":7890}}
```

The three JSON documents, one per line, contain somewhat different fields. All share the fields `"ts"` and `"connection"` to mark when they occurred, and from what client address. Different kinds of events, however, require different additional fields. This can allow command-line processing.

For example, using generic text processing tools, we might list (as a JSON document) the username and email of all newly registered users:

```
%%bash
# Extract registrations
grep "registered" data/jsonlines.log |
    sed 's/^.*registered"://' |
    sed 's/}.*/}/'
```

```
{"username":"bar","email":"bar@example.com"}
{"username":"baz","email":"baz@example.net"}
```

You've probably noticed already that the above command line could have gone wrong (because we did not choose the best tool). If a registration object contained nested objects (that is, more closing braces, }) we would not match the "registered" event that we actually wanted. For that matter, if some "username" field were the string "registered", we would go awry as well. To do this correctly, we need to actually parse the JSON. Here again, from the command line, jq is a useful tool:

```
%%bash
jq '.registered | select(.username != null)' data/jsonlines.log
```

```
{
  "username": "bar",
  "email": "bar@example.com"
}
{
  "username": "baz",
  "email": "baz@example.net"
}
```

Most likely, following initial exploration of a dataset, for which these command-line tools are useful, we would like to perform these kinds of tasks in a general-purpose programming language. A third-party Python module called jsonlines exists, but simply using the standard library is more than sufficient, as we see below:

```
with open('data/jsonlines.log') as log:
    for line in log:
        record = json.loads(line)
        if 'registered' in record:
            user = record['registered']
            if 'username' in user:
                print(user)
```

```
{'username': 'bar', 'email': 'bar@example.com'}
{'username': 'baz', 'email': 'baz@example.net'}
```

In a more fleshed-out version, of course, we would do something beyond just printing out the registrant information. If one of the other variants for JSON streaming were used rather than JSON Lines, the code would be somewhat more difficult, but still reasonable to program manually.

GeoJSON

GeoJSON is a format for encoding a variety of geographic data structures that is described in IETF RFC 7946. This book is not able to address the numerous programming and data issues that are specific to Geographic Information Systems (GISes). A variety of specialized programming tools, books, and other learning material is available to explore this field. For our purposes, we merely need to understand that a GeoJSON file is a JSON file that often contains a large amount of data, and is moderately nested. In contrast to some other formats JSON is used for, the hierarchies available in GeoJSON are not of unlimited depth, but simply consist of a variety of optional keys at several levels of nesting.

The particular data we will utilize in this subsection was generated by Eric Celeste from data published by the United States Census Bureau, describing the counties in the United States. The public domain data was originally provided by the Census Bureau as shapefiles (.shp). The GeoJSON discussed here, and the **Keyhole Markup Language** (**KML**) discussed in the next section, are mechanical transformations of the original data (the data should be equivalent). For the example here, I've used the lowest resolution shape definitions, which nonetheless amounts to fairly substantial data.

Notice that the JSON file we read, from the 2010 census, was encoded as ISO-8859-1. In those days of yore, we were young and naïve, and the then-current JSON standard had not yet mandated encoding as UTF-8. See *Chapter 3, Repurposing Data Sources*, for a discussion on determining and working with different character encodings; I, myself, in fact, had to utilize those techniques to determine how to read this data without raising exceptions. Let us explore the concepts slightly:

```
with open('data/gz_2010_us_050_00_20m.json', encoding='ISO-8859-1') as
fh:
    counties = json.load(fh)

counties.keys()

dict_keys(['type', 'features'])
```

At the top level, the JSON object has a key called "type" and another called "features". The former is simply a descriptive string, the latter where the bulk of the data on the 3221 counties in the United States in 2010 lives, as we deduce from the output below:

```
counties['type'], type(counties['features']), len(counties['features'])

('FeatureCollection', list, 3221)
```

Let us look at one of those features. We can see that it has some metadata under the key "properties". The main data is the geographic position of the boundaries of the particular county, under the key "geometry". The higher-resolution data files contain the same metadata and structure of their data; the difference is that the shapes are defined by polygons with more sides, which hence more accurately describe the shape of the county in question. What we use is more than large enough to support the examples. The actual shape, in Python terms, is a list-of-lists-of-lists:

```
counties['features'][999]

{'type': 'Feature',
 'properties': {'GEO_ID': '0500000US19153',
  'STATE': '19',
  'COUNTY': '153',
  'NAME': 'Polk',
  'LSAD': 'County',
  'CENSUSAREA': 573.795},
 'geometry': {'type': 'Polygon',
  'coordinates': [[[-93.328614, 41.507824],
    [-93.328486, 41.49134],
    [-93.328407, 41.490921],
    [-93.41226, 41.505549],
    [-93.790612, 41.511916],
    [-93.814282, 41.600448],
    [-93.815527, 41.863419],
    [-93.698032, 41.86337],
    [-93.347933, 41.863104],
    [-93.348681, 41.600999],
    [-93.328614, 41.507824]]]}}
```

Each leaf list is simply a longitude/latitude position, a list of those is a polygon, but a county potentially has discontiguous regions that need multiple polygons to define.

As I have mentioned, there are a plethora of tools for GIS and geospatial data processing. These include a more specialized Python module called geojson; within the broader Python GIS space, **Cartopy** is a well-maintained package with many capabilities, and is built on top of **PROJ**, NumPy, and **Shapely**. Among other capabilities, these types of GIS tools allow visualization of longitude/latitude coordinates onto many map projections, with optional rendering of geographic and political features, and calculations based on Haversine distances rather than inaccurate Cartesian distances. To focus just on the JSON data though, with apologies to the cartographers among my readers, let us make a flat-footed rendering to visualize USA counties.

The code below simply creates a Matplotlib figure and axis, loops through each of the features in the GeoJSON data, drills down to the coordinates, and maps the counties as patches. Visualization helps us understand the "shape" of the data we are working with. The details of the Matplotlib API are not important here. The relevant aspect is the way that we *descend* into the nested data that was read from JSON. For example:

```
polk = counties['features'][999]['geometry']['coordinates'][0]
```

This would load the list-of-lists describing the boundaries of Polk County, Iowa:

```
fig, ax = plt.subplots(figsize=(8, 5))
patches, colors, ncolor = [], [], 8

for n, county in enumerate(counties['features']):
    # Only use first polygon if multiple discontiguous regions
    poly = np.array(county['geometry']['coordinates'][0])
    poly = poly.reshape(-1, 2)
    polygon = Polygon(poly)
    patches.append(polygon)
    colors.append(n % ncolor)

p = PatchCollection(patches, cmap=cm.get_cmap('Greys', ncolor))
p.set_array(np.array(colors))
ax.add_collection(p)

ax.set_ylim(24, 50)
ax.set_ylabel("Latitude")
ax.set_xlim(-126, -67)
ax.set_xlabel("Longitude")
ax.set_title("Counties of the United States");
```

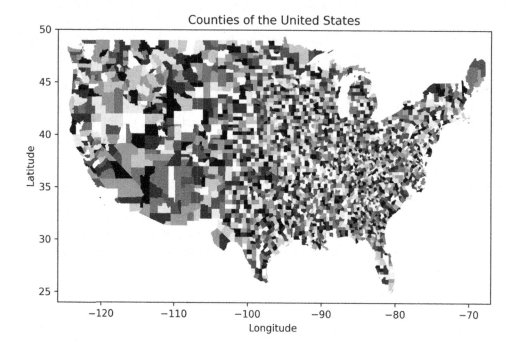

Figure 2.1: Plot of counties of the United States

This is certainly not the best map of the United States, but the contours as a plot help us understand the dataset.

Tidy Geography

As an example of utilizing this data, apart from the visualization, we would like to create a tabular data frame that has the following columns:

- State name
- County name
- Area (square kilometers of land)
- Northernmost latitude
- Southernmost latitude
- Westernmost longitude
- Easternmost longitude

This subsection will demonstrate a bit more *code* than most do. When dealing with hierarchical data, it is difficult to avoid some messiness. Testing various data attributes at various levels almost always requires loops or recursion, temporary containers, lookups and memorization of data, and a number of steps that can often be handled at a much higher level with methods of a tidy data frame.

For a starting point, we can notice that the USA census provides (land) area measurements in square miles; we can use the conversion constant 2.59 for mi^2/km^2. A less direct conversion is determining the state name from the Federal Information Processing Standards (FIPS) code given for the state. Looking online at government data sources, we can locate a tab-separated description of this correspondence that we can use:

```
fips = pd.read_csv('data/FIPS.tsv', sep='\t')
fips
```

	Name	Postal Code	FIPS
0	Alabama	AL	1
1	Alaska	AK	2
2	Arizona	AZ	4
3	Arkansas	AR	5
...	...	...	...
51	Guam	GU	66
52	Northern Mariana Islands	MP	69
53	Puerto Rico	PR	72
54	Virgin Islands	VI	78

55 rows × 3 columns

We would like to transform this DataFrame into a Series that takes a key of FIPS and maps to the state name. Once we have crawled the data and levels of the JSON hierarchy, we can make that mechanical transformation:

```
fips_map = fips.set_index('FIPS').Name
fips_map
```

```
FIPS
1          Alabama
2           Alaska
4          Arizona
5         Arkansas
           ...
66            Guam
```

```
69      Northern Mariana Islands
72                   Puerto Rico
78                 Virgin Islands
Name: Name, Length: 55, dtype: object
```

Luckily for the task at hand, we know we need to descend at fixed depths to find the data items of interest. In other situations, we may wish to use a recursive approach instead, with nested function calls corresponding to nested keys at indeterminate depth. We can simply loop through counties, much as we did to create the visualization, and gather data into plain lists as a first step.

In order to factor out the processing a bit, let us first define a function called `extremes()` that will take the collection of polygons and return the extremes for the cardinal directions:

```python
def extremes(coords):
    lat, lon = [], []
    # Expect a list of lists of lists
    for region in coords:
        for point in region:
            lat.append(point[1])
            lon.append(point[0])
    # We are assuming western hemisphere here
    north = max(lat)
    south = min(lat)
    east = max(lon)
    west = min(lon)
    return north, south, east, west
```

Next we would like a function to produce a DataFrame from the GeoJSON dictionary.

```python
def county_summary(features):
    geo_id = []
    state, county_name, area = [], [], []
    north, south, east, west = [], [], [], []

    for county in features:
        props = county['properties']
        polys = county['geometry']['coordinates']
        geo_id.append(props['GEO_ID'])
        # District of Columbia not US state (default to None)
```

```
            state_name = fips_map.get(int(props['STATE']), None)
            state.append(state_name)
            county_name.append(props['NAME'])
            area.append(props['CENSUSAREA'] * 2.59)
            n, s, e, w = extremes(polys)
            north.append(n)
            south.append(s)
            east.append(e)
            west.append(w)

    df = pd.DataFrame({
            'geo_id': geo_id,
            'state': state,
            'county': county_name,
            'area': area,
            'northmost': north,
            'southmost': south,
            'eastmost': east,
            'westmost': west
        })
    return df.set_index('geo_id')
```

Although the code is fairly straightforward, it has enough in it that we would like to provide a sanity check in a unit test:

```
def test_counties(df):
    assert (df.northmost > df.southmost).all()
    assert (df.westmost < df.eastmost).all()
    assert (df.area > 0).all()
```

We can convert the JSON hierarchy into a tidy data frame using the county_summary() function we've just written, and check our boundary assumptions:

```
census_counties = county_summary(counties['features'])

# Sanity checks (if no assertion violated, we are happy)
test_counties(census_counties)
census_counties
```

geo_id	state	county	area	northmost
0500000US01001	Alabama	Autauga	1539.58924	32.7074
0500000US01009	Alabama	Blount	1669.96984	34.2593
0500000US01017	Alabama	Chambers	1545.01529	33.1081
0500000US01021	Alabama	Chilton	1794.49186	33.0719
...	...	...	...	...
0500000US51021	Virginia	Bland	926.50775	37.2935
0500000US51027	Virginia	Buchanan	1302.15617	37.5378
0500000US51037	Virginia	Charlotte	1230.95189	37.2488
0500000US51041	Virginia	Chesterfield	1096.33923	37.5626

geo_id	southmost	eastmost	westmost
0500000US01001	32.3408	-86.4112	-86.9176
0500000US01009	33.7653	-86.3035	-86.9634
0500000US01017	32.7285	-85.1234	-85.5932
0500000US01021	32.6617	-86.375	-87.0192
...	...	...	...
0500000US51021	36.9524	-80.8546	-81.4622
0500000US51027	37.0417	-81.7384	-82.3059
0500000US51037	36.6979	-78.4433	-78.9046
0500000US51041	37.2227	-77.2442	-77.8551

3221 rows × 7 columns

Exactly what analysis or modeling is relevant at this point is driven by your task. But in general, obtaining tidy data will be a similar matter of crawling through the hierarchical structure and pulling out relevant information from varying levels.

JSON Schema

When we tidied some GeoJSON data in the previous subsection, we made a number of assumptions about exactly which keys we would encounter at which levels, nested within objects. If these assumptions had been violated, various exceptions would be raised, or other errors would occur, in the processing functions. It is, of course, possible to check for these situations with conditional branches, exception handling, use of methods like Python's dict.get(), and other similar techniques. However, code that is cluttered with a great many such error handling constructs can have its underlying processing logic obscured.

One approach to enforcing assumptions about JSON documents is to use a JSON Schema to validate documents prior to passing them to data extraction functions. Configure Unify Execute (CUE) (`https://cuelang.org/`) is a promising newer approach to validation, but I do not address it in this book. A JSON Schema is itself a JSON document following certain specifications. At its simplest, it needs to specify a type for the JSON being validated. Within that, it can indicate what keys might occur inside objects, which are required, the cardinality of arrays, and a number of other elements, including recursive structures. An approach of "validate, then process" is often useful; here validation merely describes the *structure* of a JSON document. It is not intended to make any claims about it containing *good data*, such as is discussed in *Chapter 4*, *Anomaly Detection*, and *Chapter 5*, *Data Quality*.

The examples below use the Python third-party module **jsonschema**, but wrap its API in a slightly different function, `not_valid()`, imported from this book's `setup.py` module. This function will return `False` if everything is fine, but returns a descriptive error message if a problem was encountered. For example, we might validate the USA county data using the official GeoJSON schema:

```
response = requests.get('https://geojson.org/schema/GeoJSON.json')
geojson_schema = json.loads(response.text)

if msg := not_valid(counties, geojson_schema):
    print(msg)
else:
    print("Everything is Happy!")
```

```
Everything is Happy!
```

As hoped, the United States Census department data is valid. The GeoJSON schema is quite large, so I present as an example below a smaller one I developed myself. The small "user database" web server that was queried above sends user records that are expected to follow a certain format, but the format, as development usually occurs, might only be informally specified in email threads and telephone conversations between developers. Before running scripts to process these user records, it is useful to identify users or potential user documents that will violate the assumptions embedded in our code logic.

Let us see what information we can obtain from our example schema:

```python
user_schema = json.loads("""
{
    "$schema": "http://json-schema.org/draft-07/schema#",
    "$id": "http://kdm.training/user-schema.json",
    "title": "User",
    "description": "A User of Our Computer System",
    "type" : "object",
    "required": ["name", "password"],
    "properties" : {
        "name" : {"type" : "string"},
        "password": {
            "description": "Use special characters and mixed case",
            "type": "string"},
        "lucky_numbers": {
            "description": "Up to 6 favorite numbers 1-100",
            "type": "array",
            "items": {
                "type": "number",
                "minimum": 1,
                "maximum": 100
            },
            "uniqueItems": true,
            "minItems": 0,
            "maxItems": 6
        }
    }
}
""")
```

This simple "User" schema does not exercise *all* the capabilities in JSON Schema, but it is a good representation. Some metadata is contained in the keys "$schema", "$id", "title", and "description". All of these are optional in the JSON Schema specification, but their names are standard, if used. The only key that is strictly required is "type", which must be one of the four JSON data types. Within an object, keys may be required or optional; however, JSON Schema has no mechanism to *exclude* other keys that are not described. The schema merely states that *if* a key is present, it must have values of a certain sort.

The keys "name" and "password" are required, and are both strings. The optional description of "password" indicates a desire for passwords to be "good" in the sense that many computer systems enforce, but JSON Schema does not itself have a mechanism to check programmatic rules of that sort. The key "lucky_numbers" describes quite a bit; not only must it have an array as a value, but that array must consist of numbers between 1 and 100, and have no more than 6 of them. Let us look at a document that passes validation:

```
david = json.loads("""
{
  "name": "David Mertz",
  "password": "badpassword",
  "details": {
    "profession": "Data Scientist",
    "employer": "KDM"
  },
  "lucky_numbers": [12, 42, 55, 87]
}
""")

if msg := not_valid(david, user_schema):
    print(msg)
```

The top-level key "details" is not mentioned in the schema, and hence may contain anything whatsoever (anything which is valid JSON, of course). This document validates successfully, so perhaps we would want to process it downstream. Let us consider a few documents that fail as users:

```
barbara_feldon = json.loads("""
{
  "name": 99,
  "password": "1ibydieZ!S@8"
}
""")

if msg := not_valid(barbara_feldon, user_schema):
    print(msg)
```

```
99 is not of type 'string'

Failed validating 'type' in schema['properties']['name']:
    {'type': 'string'}

On instance['name']:
    99
```

The diagnosis of the failure will hopefully provide information relevant to remediation. The JSON below fails in a somewhat different manner, and with a more verbose description of the problem:

```python
intruder = json.loads("""
{
  "password": "P4cC!^*8chWz8",
  "profession": "Hacker"
}
""")

if msg := not_valid(intruder, user_schema):
    print(msg)
```

```
'name' is a required property

Failed validating 'required' in schema:
    {'$id': 'http://kdm.training/user-schema.json',
     '$schema': 'http://json-schema.org/draft-07/schema#',
     'description': 'A User of Our Computer System',
     'properties': {'lucky_numbers': {'description': 'Up to 6 favorite '
                                                     'numbers 1-100',
                                      'items': {'maximum': 100,
                                                'minimum': 1,
                                                'type': 'number'},
                                      'maxItems': 6,
                                      'minItems': 0,
                                      'type': 'array',
                                      'uniqueItems': True},
                    'name': {'type': 'string'},
                    'password': {'description': 'Use special characters '
                                                'and mixed case',
                                 'type': 'string'}},
     'required': ['name', 'password'],
     'title': 'User',
     'type': 'object'}

On instance:
    {'password': 'P4cC!^*8chWz8', 'profession': 'Hacker'}
```

Let us look through a few more failure messages:

```python
the_count = json.loads("""
{
  "name": "Count von Count",
  "password": "fourbananas",
  "lucky_numbers": ["one", "two", "three"]
}
""")

if msg := not_valid(the_count, user_schema):
    print(msg, "\n--------------------")
```

```
'one' is not of type 'number'

Failed validating 'type' in schema['properties']['lucky_numbers']
['items']:
    {'maximum': 100, 'minimum': 1, 'type': 'number'}

On instance['lucky_numbers'][0]:
    'one'
--------------------
```

We failed on the data type of the nested array. Its cardinality is checked as well:

```python
george = json.loads("""
{
  "name": "Georg Cantor",
  "password": "omega_aleph",
  "lucky_numbers": [1, 2, 3, 4, 5, 6, 7, 8]
}
""")

if msg := not_valid(george, user_schema):
    print(msg)
```

```
[1, 2, 3, 4, 5, 6, 7, 8] is too long

Failed validating 'maxItems' in schema['properties']['lucky_numbers']:
    {'description': 'Up to 6 favorite numbers 1-100',
     'items': {'maximum': 100, 'minimum': 1, 'type': 'number'},
     'maxItems': 6,
```

```
            'minItems': 0,
            'type': 'array',
            'uniqueItems': True}

    On instance['lucky_numbers']:
        [1, 2, 3, 4, 5, 6, 7, 8]
```

In one final example, we see that uniqueness can be validated in an array. This provides a way of distinguishing a set from a sequence, even though JSON itself does not distinguish those data types:

```
revolution_9 = json.loads("""
{
    "name": "Yoko Ono",
    "password": "grapefruit",
    "lucky_numbers": [9, 9, 9]
}
""")

if msg := not_valid(revolution_9, user_schema):
    print(msg)

[9, 9, 9] has non-unique elements

Failed validating 'uniqueItems' in schema['properties']['lucky_
numbers']:
    {'description': 'Up to 6 favorite numbers 1-100',
     'items': {'maximum': 100, 'minimum': 1, 'type': 'number'},
     'maxItems': 6,
     'minItems': 0,
     'type': 'array',
     'uniqueItems': True}

On instance['lucky_numbers']:
    [9, 9, 9]
```

It is time to move on to another, much scarier hierarchical topic.

XML

XML is like violence – if it doesn't solve your problems, you are not using enough of it.

–Anonymous

Concepts:

- Defining eXtensible Markup Language
- Dialects and schemata
- Attributes and elements
- Dealing with deep and ragged nesting

The almost mandatory epigraph accompanying this section, and extending Ludwig von Rochau's notion of *Realpolitik*, is, of course, underlyingly deplorable, albeit presumably meant ironically. I take violence to always be unacceptable, and XML only mostly so. Both remain far too common in our world. This corrective paraphrase only partially fixes the concern: "XML is like violence: useful only in specific situations, and totally unacceptable everywhere else."

eXtensible Markup Language (XML) is a complex format that might appear simple on its surface. A large number of books longer than this one have been written to discuss just one or two tools or technologies associated with XML. In particular, XML is not really one format so much as it is a meta-format with many dialects. Syntactically, XML is a relatively simple format that defines elements with angle bracketed tags (less-than and greater-than signs), allows attributes within tags, and has a few other syntactic forms for special entities and directives. The user records that appear shortly below provide a minimal example. As a rough approximation, XML is a generalization of HTML; or more accurately, HTML is a dialect of XML (to be pedantic, however, recent versions of HTML are not precisely XML dialects in some technical details).

An XML dialect is usually defined by a schema that specifies exactly which tags and attributes are permitted, and the manners in which they may nest inside one another. A schema may also define the data type interpretation of particular fields. Hundreds of such dialects are widely used; for example, all modern word processors and publication systems use an XML dialect to define their documents (with a compression layer wrapped around the underlying XML). Many other non-document formats use XML as well, including, for example, scientific data formats.

Several different schema languages can be used to define particular XML dialects. All of them are outside the scope of this book. However, as a general procedure, validating an XML document prior to further processing it is almost always a good idea, if a schema is available. This is closely analogous to the discussion in the previous section about using JSON Schema, but different tools and libraries will be used. Probably the most commonly used means of defining an XML schema is a **Document Type Definition** (DTD). More modern alternatives are XML Schema and RELAX NG. Notice that while XML Schema and RELAX NG allow the declaration and validation of data types, I am not aware of any widely used tool or library that uses those type declarations when converting XML into native data structures. Validation may assure you that a given data value, for example, "looks like an integer," but you will still need to cast it as such within your code when you want to use it that way.

User Records

As a small example, I will formulate one of the user records discussed in the JSON section as an XML document. I do not here create or specify a schema, but in principle it would be possible to have one that defined all the constraints of a valid document. As in JSON, whitespace is not (usually) significant, but can aid readability:

```xml
<?xml version="1.0" encoding="utf-8" ?>
<users>
  <user>
    <name>David Mertz</name>
    <password>badpassword</password>
    <details>
      <profession employer="KDM" duration="26" units="months">
      Data Scientist</profession>
      <telephone>+1 323 863 5571</telephone>
    </details>
    <lucky-numbers>
      <item>12</item>
      <item>42</item>
      <item>55</item>
      <item>87</item>
    </lucky-numbers>
  </user>
  <user> ... </user>
</users>
```

In XML, we have a somewhat underdetermined decision about whether to put a given datum within an element body or within an attribute. The example shows both.

For this section, I will use the Python standard XML library ElementTree. Other APIs exist, even within the Python standard library, and various other programming languages have a variety of libraries and APIs available for working with XML. ElementTree makes a reasonable compromise between feeling like Python and feeling like XML. However, if you want to work in a *more Pythonic* style with XML trees, the **lxml** library comes with an API called lxml.objectify.

The lxml.objectify API is, in turn, based on much earlier work by my colleague Uche Ogbuji on Amara Bindery, and by me even earlier on gnosis.xml.objectify. Neither of those old projects are currently maintained, but xml.objectify is very similar and intuitive to work with. In general, lxml is a fast and well-tested XML library, built on **libxml2** and **libxslt**, that provides both the objectify interface and an enhanced and faster version of ElementTree.

The two styles of data representation within an XML document is something you need to keep in mind. There is no fundamental difference to us, as data scientists, whether data lives in an XML attribute or is the body of an element (tag). To clarify, a *tag* is the actual word inside angle brackets (e.g. <item>), while an *element* is everything occurring between an opening tag and the corresponding closing tag (e.g. <item>55</item>). Both elements and attributes can equally be useful for us. However, in most APIs, they are accessed differently. Let us show both in a code example:

```python
import xml.etree.ElementTree as ET
tree = ET.parse('data/users.xml')

# Let us first find the attributes and text of a profession
prof = tree.find('user').find('details').find('profession')
print("Body (title):", prof.text.strip())
print("Attributes:  ", prof.attrib)
```

```
Body (title): Data Scientist
Attributes:   {'employer': 'KDM', 'duration': '26', 'units': 'months'}
```

Within attributes, we have a perfectly regular native Python dictionary that we can extract field values from. Notice that all keys and values are simply strings. If we wished, for example, to treat 'duration' as an integer, we could cast it within our code. Additionally, we often wish to loop through elements at the same level of the document hierarchy to treat them similarly.

As we saw with JSON, elements might be ragged and contain different children, even if they share the same parent tag:

```
items = tree.find('user').find('lucky-numbers').findall('item')
lucky_numbers = [int(item.text) for item in items]
lucky_numbers
```

```
[12, 42, 55, 87]
```

Nested or recursive traversal, for example by calling `.findall()` at various levels of the hierarchy, is a common approach to walking an XML document. XML documents can be very large, and for those, an incremental approach is available in `ElementTree` and other libraries. In the next section, as a slightly more fleshed out example, we will process the same geographic data as we did in the JSON section.

Keyhole Markup Language

KML is an XML format that is generally functionally equivalent to shapefiles or GeoJSON. As with those other formats, more specialized GIS tools will do more than we show in this subsection. We will need to do a little bit of magic to look for tags within the KML namespace that defines the tags within this document. We can see that some schema and namespace information is defined at the top of the file before we get the real "data" of the file (the `"Placemark"` elements):

```
<?xml version="1.0" encoding="utf-8" ?>
<kml xmlns="http://www.opengis.net/kml/2.2">
<Document>
  <Folder>
    <name>gz_2010_us_050_00_20m</name>
    <Schema name="gz_2010_us_050_00_20m" id="gz_2010_us_050_00_20m">
      <SimpleField name="Name" type="string"></SimpleField>
      <SimpleField name="Description" type="string"></SimpleField>
      <SimpleField name="GEO_ID" type="string"></SimpleField>
      <SimpleField name="STATE" type="string"></SimpleField>
      <SimpleField name="COUNTY" type="string"></SimpleField>
      <SimpleField name="NAME" type="string"></SimpleField>
      <SimpleField name="LSAD" type="string"></SimpleField>
      <SimpleField name="CENSUSAREA" type="float"></SimpleField>
    </Schema>
    <Placemark>
      <name>Autauga</name>
      <Style>
        <LineStyle><color>ff0000ff</color></LineStyle>
```

```
    <PolyStyle><fill>0</fill></PolyStyle>
  </Style>
  <ExtendedData>
    <SchemaData schemaUrl="#gz_2010_us_050_00_20m">
      <SimpleData name="Name">Autauga</SimpleData>
      <SimpleData name="GEO_ID">0500000US01001</SimpleData>
      <SimpleData name="STATE">01</SimpleData>

... more content, eventual closing tags ...
```

An XML file can contain many namespaces that different tags live within. So `ElementTree` allows us to define a dictionary mapping short names to namespace URLs to allow more convenient access. We drill down a few levels, where just one parent node occurs, to find the "`Folder`" that contains the "`Placemark`" elements that we really care about. These were called "`features`" in GeoJSON:

```
ns = {'kml': "http://www.opengis.net/kml/2.2"}
document = ET.parse('data/gz_2010_us_050_00_20m.kml')

root = document.getroot()
kml_doc = root.find('kml:Document', ns)
folder = kml_doc.find('kml:Folder', ns)

# Make sure we have the same number of counties as with GeoJSON
placemarks = folder.findall('kml:Placemark', ns)
print("Count of placemarks:", len(placemarks))
# Show one Placemark element object
placemarks[0]
```

```
Count of placemarks: 3221
<Element '{http://www.opengis.net/kml/2.2}Placemark' at 0x7fe220289680>
```

Pulling out the somewhat obscurely nested data is a bit more work than is ideal. Let us look at what we want from the first county child node:

```
# The name of the county is comparatively straightforward
print("County name:", placemarks[0].find('kml:name', ns).text)

# Other county info is only distinguished by attribute
sdata = (placemarks[0].find('kml:ExtendedData', ns)
                      .find('kml:SchemaData', ns)
                      .findall('kml:SimpleData', ns))
```

```
# We are going to want GEO_ID, STATE and CENSUSAREA
for record in sdata:
    print(record.attrib, record.text)

County name: Autauga
{'name': 'Name'} Autauga
{'name': 'GEO_ID'} 0500000US01001
{'name': 'STATE'} 01
{'name': 'COUNTY'} 001
{'name': 'LSAD'} County
{'name': 'CENSUSAREA'} 594.436000000000035
```

The actual name of the county is redundantly encoded in two places. Our below function, kml_county_summary(), should check for data integrity (that is, consistent values). Now we need to drill into a slightly different part of the hierarchy to locate the polygon:

```
coords = (placemarks[0].find('kml:Polygon', ns)
                       .find('kml:outerBoundaryIs', ns)
                       .find('kml:LinearRing', ns)
                       .find('kml:coordinates', ns))
pprint(coords.text)

('-86.497916734108713,32.346347937379285,123.940341341309249 '
 '-86.719045580223096,32.404719907202413,124.507383406162262 '
 '-86.816062031841554,32.342711234558017,124.433184524998069 '
 '-86.891734835750142,32.50487314981855,125.151479452848434 '
 '-86.918751525796665,32.666059588245083,125.785741473548114 '
 '-86.714541775531544,32.66362459160964,125.451970156282187 '
 '-86.715371359148733,32.707584324141543,125.614226697944105 '
 '-86.414261392701192,32.709278995622782,125.144079957157373 '
 '-86.41231357529395,32.411845326016262,124.046804890967906 '
 '-86.497916734108713,32.346347937379285,123.940341341309249')
```

If we consult the KML documentation, we can determine that within KML, within a "LinearRing" element, the coordinates (polygon) take the form of lon,lat[,alt] structures separated by spaces. For our task of finding the northernmost, southernmost, easternmost, and westernmost points—as we did in the GeoJSON case—the altitude will not interest us. However, we *do* need to parse the structured raw text to get the actual boundary. We will do that with the function kml_extremes(). Since most of the actual logic is the same as in the GeoJSON version in the previous section, kml_extremes() can merely massage the data format slightly before calling the earlier extremes() function:

```
def kml_extremes(coordinates):
    "Pass in a KML coordinates ElementTree object"
    text_points = coordinates.text.split()
    points = [p.split(',') for p in text_points]
    points = [[float(p[0]), float(p[1])] for p in points]
    # We pass a list-of-list-of-lists here
    return extremes([points])


kml_extremes(coords)
```

```
(32.70927899562278, 32.34271123455802, -86.41231357529395,
-86.91875152579667)
```

Next, we would like a function to produce a DataFrame from the KML data. It will be similar to that for the GeoJSON, but digging out the data is moderately different (and generally more cumbersome):

```
def kml_county_summary(placemarks, ns=ns):
    geo_id = []
    state, county_name, area = [], [], []
    north, south, east, west = [], [], [], []

    for placemark in placemarks:
        # Get county name here and below to assure consistency
        name = placemark.find('kml:name', ns).text

        # Other county info is distinguished by XML attribute
        sdata = (placemark.find('kml:ExtendedData', ns)
                          .find('kml:SchemaData', ns)
                          .findall('kml:SimpleData', ns))
        # We want Name, GEO_ID, STATE and CENSUSAREA
        for record in sdata:
            rectype = record.attrib['name']  # XML attrib
            if rectype == 'Name':  # String 'Name' (county)
                # If name is recorded differently, problem!
                assert record.text == name
                county_name.append(name)
            elif rectype == 'GEO_ID':
                geo_id.append(record.text)
            elif rectype == 'CENSUSAREA':
                # Convert to km^2 from mi^2
                area.append(float(record.text) * 2.59)
            elif rectype == 'STATE':
```

```
                # District of Columbia is not a US state
                state_name = fips_map.get(int(record.text), None)
                state.append(state_name)

        # We are going to "cheat" here a little bit.
        # Sometimes a placemark has a top level <MultiGeometry>
        # with several Polygons; we will skip that calculation
        try:
            coordinates = (placemark
                    .find('kml:Polygon', ns)
                    .find('kml:outerBoundaryIs', ns)
                    .find('kml:LinearRing', ns)
                    .find('kml:coordinates', ns))
            n, s, e, w = kml_extremes(coordinates)
        except AttributeError:
            n, s, e, w = None, None, None, None

        north.append(n); south.append(s);
        east.append(e); west.append(w)

    df = pd.DataFrame({
            'geo_id': geo_id, 'state': state,
            'county': county_name, 'area': area,
            'northmost': north, 'southmost': south,
            'eastmost': east, 'westmost': west
        })
    return df.set_index('geo_id')
```

We can convert the KML hierarchy into a tidy data frame. Working with XML is often persnickety; often the main cause of this is not the physical format per se, but a tendency among creators of XML dialects to nest elements especially deeply and utilize very complex schemata. That is somewhat the case with this KML example.

```
kml_counties = kml_county_summary(placemarks)
kml_counties
```

geo_id	state	county	area	northmost
0500000US01001	Alabama	Autauga	1539.58924	32.709279
0500000US01009	Alabama	Blount	1669.96984	34.261131
0500000US01017	Alabama	Chambers	1545.01529	33.109960
0500000US01021	Alabama	Chilton	1794.49186	33.073731
...	...	...	...	...
0500000US51021	Virginia	Bland	926.50775	37.295189
0500000US51027	Virginia	Buchanan	1302.15617	37.539502
0500000US51037	Virginia	Charlotte	1230.95189	37.250505
0500000US51041	Virginia	Chesterfield	1096.33923	37.564372

geo_id	southmost	eastmost	westmost
0500000US01001	32.342711	-86.412314	-86.918752
0500000US01009	33.767154	-86.304677	-86.964531
0500000US01017	32.730429	-85.124537	-85.594308
0500000US01021	32.663625	-86.376119	-87.020318
...	...	...	...
0500000US51021	36.954152	-80.855694	-81.463294
0500000US51027	37.043415	-81.739470	-82.306981
0500000US51037	36.699679	-78.444320	-78.905600
0500000US51041	37.224467	-77.245139	-77.856138

```
3221 rows × 7 columns
```

Let us now make a great leap forward to the hundred flowers that make up configuration formats.

Configuration Files

The wonderful thing about standards is that there are so many of them to choose from.

–Grace Murray Hopper[attrib]

> *attrib*
>
> The provenance of this quote is uncertain, though widely attributed to Admiral Hopper. It is sometimes also credited to Andrew Tanenbaum, Patricia Seybold, or Ken Olsen. The first of these did, indeed, use it in his *Computer Networks* (1981), but perhaps not as an original comment.

Concepts:

- A surfeit of slightly different formats
- Namespaces may simulate hierarchy
- INI and TOML
- YAML

Small data often lives in configuration files. Probably the most popular of these, at least for programming projects, is now YAML Ain't Markup Language; formerly Yet Another Markup Language (YAML). The informal INI format is also common, especially in the Windows world (but mostly in older software). **Tom's Obvious, Minimal Language (TOML)** is very similar to INI, but contains a few enhancements and a stricter definition. Sometimes JSON or XML are also used for the same purpose, although both are distinctly less human-editable. The greatest difficulty comes with numerous software projects that have, for various reasons (few of them good), adopted their own custom configuration format.

These configuration formats typically have a certain degree of hierarchy. Depending on the format, this hierarchy might be of fixed or unlimited depth. However, most formats allow unlimited nesting, and hence crawling them is similar to techniques we saw with JSON and XML.

INI and Flat Custom Formats

The exceptions to unlimited depth seem to be either env (.env) files—which are also an informal convention rather than a standard—and INI files. Env files are (usually) not actually hierarchical at all, but are simply assignments of values to names in a flat fashion. Sometimes this can be identical to defining environment variables in a shell configuration, but often the need for quoting a value containing whitespace is omitted and character escaping rules can vary. An INI file is often taken to allow a single level of hierarchy between the sections marked with square brackets ([and]) and assignments marked with a name and equals sign on a single line. Let us look at a simple INI example given in the Wikipedia article on INI files (https://en.wikipedia.org/wiki/INI_file):

```
; last modified 1 April 2001 by John Doe
[owner]
name=John Doe
organization=Acme Widgets Inc.

[database]
; use IP address in case network name resolution is not working
server=192.0.2.62
port=143
file="payroll.dat"
```

At times, INI files simulate deeper hierarchies by, in concept, namespacing their section names. So such a file might contain the sections [owner.database.systems] and [owner.vcs.developers], which could be manually decoded into a hierarchy of "owners." The Python standard library comes with a parser for this format called configparser. This is one of the older modules in the standard library, and its API is a bit creaky:

```
import configparser
cfg = configparser.ConfigParser()
cfg.read('data/example.ini')

print("Sections:    ", cfg.sections())
print("Owner keys: ", [k for k in cfg['owner']])
print("Owner/name: ", cfg['owner']['name'])
print("Port #:     ", cfg['database'].getint('port'))

Sections:    ['owner', 'database']
Owner keys:  ['name', 'organization']
Owner/name:  John Doe
Port #:      143
```

Data typing is limited as well. The special methods `.getboolean()`, `.getint()`, and `.getfloat()` simply do the equivalent of the obvious type constructors. However, Booleans, as cast with the methods, are case-insensitive and recognize `yes`/`no`, `on`/`off`, `true`/`false`, and `1`/`0`.

While this API is not the most natural, at least the module exists. When tools define their own formats, you may need to drop to the level of manual text processing, such as is discussed in *Chapter 3, Repurposing Data Sources*, in the section *Custom Text Formats*. For example, on my system, the archaic text-based web browser **w3m** has a custom configuration format in `$HOME/.w3m/config` that contains lines such as these (and about 150 others):

```
tabstop 8
display_charset UTF-8
cookie_avoid_wrong_number_of_dots
accept_encoding gzip, compress, bzip, bzip2, deflate
extbrowser7 wget -c
extbrowser8 url=%s && printf %s "$url" | xsel && printf %s "$url" |
xsel -b & ssl_ca_path /etc/ssl/certs
```

In general, it *appears* that the key is some alphanumeric characters followed by a space. But what comes next might be nothing at all; it might be a string or a number, it might be a comma-separated list with more spaces, or it might even be a shell command that involves pipes, processes, and so on. If we wanted to analyze a million users' config files, we would need to use a number of manual heuristics, or find explicit documentation of what values each key can take (if such documentation exists).

TOML

TOML formalizes a number of conventions that have been used by various tools utilizing their own INI format. Sections are marked in the same fashion, but may be nested for indefinite hierarchy. A reasonable range of data types are formally specified by the parser. Not every data structure can be represented straightforwardly in TOML, but most of the most common ones can be. A great many programming languages have libraries supporting TOML, albeit as of this writing, some are only at the v0.5.0 level of support rather than v1.0.0-rc.1 (but the differences are very small).

The following is an example given in the TOML documentation:

```toml
# This is a TOML document.

title = "TOML Example"

[owner]
name = "Tom Preston-Werner"
dob = 1979-05-27T07:32:00-08:00 # First class dates

[database]
server = "192.168.1.1"
ports = [ 8001, 8001, 8002 ]
connection_max = 5000
enabled = true

[servers]

  # Indentation (tabs and/or spaces) is allowed but not required
  [servers.alpha]
  ip = "10.0.0.1"
  dc = "eqdc10"

  [servers.beta]
  ip = "10.0.0.2"
  dc = "eqdc10"

[clients]
data = [ ["gamma", "delta"], [1, 2] ]

# Line breaks are OK when inside arrays
hosts = [
  "alpha",
  "omega"
]
```

Having a formal parser available avoids a great deal of the manual logic of custom formats. Moreover, the API here is quite modern in that it simply converts a configuration file to a native data structure, with no need for unusual special methods to get at the underlying data. Having native support for a datetime data type is a handy convenience (which JSON lacks); strings, numbers (float/int), lists, and dictionaries are supported. The top level of every TOML document is always a mapping; however, that might be represented in a particular programming language. Let us take a look at an example:

```
import toml
toml.load(open('data/example.toml'))

{'title': 'TOML Example',
 'owner': {'name': 'Tom Preston-Werner',
  'dob': datetime.datetime(1979, 5, 27, 7, 32, tzinfo=<toml.tz.TomlTz
object at 0x7fe20bc4e490>)},
 'database': {'server': '192.168.1.1',
  'ports': [8001, 8001, 8002],
  'connection_max': 5000,
  'enabled': True},
 'servers': {'alpha': {'ip': '10.0.0.1', 'dc': 'eqdc10'},
  'beta': {'ip': '10.0.0.2', 'dc': 'eqdc10'}},
 'clients': {'data': [['gamma', 'delta'], [1, 2]],
  'hosts': ['alpha', 'omega']}}}
```

One big advantage of having a parser available is that typically it will report (relatively) helpfully on what went wrong. I created a slightly wrong version of the same TOML file, intended to resemble errors human typists might often make. The error message itself does not, perhaps, provide complete clarity about what went wrong; at least it tells us where to look for it though:

```
with open('data/example-bad.toml') as fh:
    try:
        cfg = toml.load(fh)
    except Exception as err:
        print_err(err)

TomlDecodeError
invalid literal for int() with base 0: '2] []
hosts = [    "alpha"' (line 27 column 1 char 433)
```

Let us print part of the TOML file:

```
!cat -n data/example-bad.toml | tail -8
```

```
    26  [clients]
    27  data = [ ["gamma", "delta"], [1, 2] []
    28
    29  # Line breaks are OK when inside arrays
    30  hosts = [
    31    "alpha",
    32    "omega"
    33  ]
```

With human eyes, we can detect the problem easily enough. Line 27 has some formatting problems, although exactly what was intended is not entirely obvious. Generally, manual remediation is required to reconstruct the original intention.

Just to demonstrate another programming language, reading TOML into R is very similar. Specifically, this also gives us a (nested) native data structure with a single call:

```
%%R
library(RcppTOML)
parseTOML("data/example.toml")
```

```
List of 5
 $ clients :List of 2
  ..$ data :List of 2
  .. ..$ : chr [1:2] "gamma" "delta"
  .. ..$ : int [1:2] 1 2
  ..$ hosts: chr [1:2] "alpha" "omega"
 $ database:List of 4
  ..$ connection_max: int 5000
  ..$ enabled       : logi TRUE
  ..$ ports         : int [1:3] 8001 8001 8002
  ..$ server        : chr "192.168.1.1"
 $ owner   :List of 2
  ..$ dob : POSIXct[1:1], format: "1979-05-27 15:32:00"
  ..$ name: chr "Tom Preston-Werner"
 $ servers :List of 2
  ..$ alpha:List of 2
  .. ..$ dc: chr "eqdc10"
  .. ..$ ip: chr "10.0.0.1"
  ..$ beta :List of 2
```

```
.. ..$ dc: chr "eqdc10"
.. ..$ ip: chr "10.0.0.2"
$ title  : chr "TOML Example"
```

Yet Another Markup Language

YAML occupies a similar space as JSON and XML, but with a heavy emphasis on human readability and editability. Both of the latter had an initial impetus, in part, to be human-readable and editable formats, but neither succeeds well in such a goal; yes they are textual, but for both it is easy to make subtle syntax or grammatical mistakes. YAML comes much closer.

In their basic form, YAML documents are quite readable and present an intuitive view of their structure. Things can get more complicated with tags and directives, and by the time you get to language-specific schemata, much of the generic readability is diminished. However, 99% of YAML documents utilize only the very accessible subset that remains simple, yet powerful. Let us look at an example adapted from the YAML tutorial:

```
invoice: 34843
date   : 2001-01-23
bill-to: &id001
    given  : Chris
    family : Dumars
    address:
        lines: |
            458 Walkman Dr.
            Suite #292
        city   : Royal Oak
        state  : MI
        postal : 48046
ship-to: *id001
product:
    - sku         : BL394D
      quantity    : 4
      description : Basketball
      price       : 450.00
    - sku         : BL4438H
      quantity    : 1
      description : Super Hoop
      price       : 2392.00
tax  : 251.42
total: 4443.52
```

```
comments:
    Late afternoon is best.
    Backup contact is Nancy
    Billsmer @ 338-4338.
```

There are a few subtleties in this simple document. A very large variety of data types are recognized based on syntactic patterns, much as we can spell constants of many types in programming languages, which a parser distinguishes. Quoting is rarely needed, but is permitted (for example, if a string happens to contain numeric digits only, and you do not wish it to be treated as a number).

The overall structure of this document is a mapping from several names to their values. In some cases, those values are themselves sequences or mappings, in other cases they are scalars. Strings may be multiline, with a pleasant subtlety that beginning with a pipe (|) indicates that newlines should be preserved (but other indentation is ignored). The address lines in the above example show this. In the case of the key comments, the string occupies multiple lines, but newlines are not preserved.

A powerful feature is the availability of anchors and references. These are vaguely inspired by C-family languages that have references and pointers. The idea is that a fragment of a document may be named (an anchor) and referenced elsewhere. This avoids repetition but also, more importantly, assures consistency in the contents. We see this where a person with an address is defined in relation to bill-to but referenced under the key ship-to.

Let us see what the data looks like when read into native Python data structures:

```
import yaml
order = yaml.load(open('data/example.yaml'))
order
```

```
{'invoice': 34843,
 'date': datetime.date(2001, 1, 23),
 'bill-to': {'given': 'Chris',
  'family': 'Dumars',
  'address': {'lines': '458 Walkman Dr.\nSuite #292\n',
   'city': 'Royal Oak',
   'state': 'MI',
   'postal': 48046}},
 'ship-to': {'given': 'Chris',
  'family': 'Dumars',
  'address': {'lines': '458 Walkman Dr.\nSuite #292\n',
   'city': 'Royal Oak',
```

```
    'state': 'MI',
    'postal': 48046}},
  'product': [{'sku': 'BL394D',
    'quantity': 4,
    'description': 'Basketball',
    'price': 450.0},
   {'sku': 'BL4438H',
    'quantity': 1,
    'description': 'Super Hoop',
    'price': 2392.0}],
  'tax': 251.42,
  'total': 4443.52,
  'comments': 'Late afternoon is best. Backup contact is Nancy Billsmer
@ 338-4338.'}
```

As with TOML, dates are handled natively. The anchor and reference are expanded into references to the same nested dictionary. Some numbers are parsed as floats, others as ints, using the same spelling rules as most programming languages. Notice that an initial dash introduces an item of a sequence/list as opposed to a key in a mapping/dictionary. Look back at the YAML version of the invoice to see this.

We can verify that referenced objects are simply references, not full copies:

```
# Is nested dict same object under different keys?
order['ship-to'] is order['bill-to']
```

```
True
```

Remember that several different enhancements are used to enable JSON streaming, the most common being JSON Lines. YAML thought of this in its initial design, and inherently builds in specific elements for multiple documents in the same stream, while still allowing each component document to use whatever whitespace makes it the most readable (obviously, subject to the grammar of YAML, but it is flexible). For example, here is a single file that contains multiple documents; it could equally be any other Python file-like object with a .read() method though (i.e. including an infinite stream):

```
%YAML 1.1
---
# YAML can contain comments like this
name: David
```

```
age: 55
---
name: Mei
age: 50        # Including end-of-line
---
name: Juana
age: 47
...
---
name: Adebayo
age: 58
...
```

The version directive at the start is optional, but is good practice. Three dashes alone on a line indicate the start of a document. Starting a new document suffices to indicate the last one has ended. However, three dots are also available to explicitly mark the end of a document. We might loop through these multiple documents, and process each one in some manner, as in the code below. In a data science context, we generally expect each document to contain similar structure and "fields," but that is not a constraint of the YAML format itself:

```
with open('data/multidoc.yaml') as stream:
    docs = yaml.load_all(stream)
    print(docs, '\n')
    for doc in docs:
        print(doc)
```

```
<generator object load_all at 0x7fe20bc2edd0>

{'name': 'David', 'age': 55}
{'name': 'Mei', 'age': 50}
{'name': 'Juana', 'age': 47}
{'name': 'Adebayo', 'age': 58}
```

As we discussed with TOML, one of the biggest advantages to working with a formally specified format with developed tools—even, or especially, if it is a format often manually edited by humans—is that parsers will hopefully produce meaningful messages about formatting problems without us needing to catch them manually:

```
try:
    yaml.load(open('data/example-bad.yaml'))
except Exception as err:
    print_err(err)
```

```
ScannerError
mapping values are not allowed here    in "data/example-bad.yaml", line
17, column 31
```

With the error message in hand, we might look at the portion of the document that indicates a problem. It is not too difficult to identify the problem on line 17. In this case, the error is intentionally obvious:

```
%%bash
cat -n data/example-bad.yaml | sed '15,19p;d'
```

```
    15        - sku         : BL394D
    16          quantity    : 4
    17          description : Basketball: ERROR
    18          price       : 450.00
    19        - sku         : BL4438H
```

Similarly, if we try to parse a YAML stream, it will succeed up until the point that it encounters the bad document. This has to be true, since the grammatically incorrect document in the stream is not even *read* until the iterator gets to it. We can confirm this by trying to print out each document as it is read:

```
try:
    for doc in yaml.load_all(open('data/multidoc-bad.yaml')):
        print(doc)
except Exception as err:
    print_err(err)
```

```
{'name': 'David', 'age': 55}
{'name': 'Mei', 'age': 50}
ScannerError
mapping values are not allowed here    in "data/multidoc-bad.yaml",
line 10, column 12
```

We have looked at the most important configuration file formats; let us return to big data.

NoSQL Databases

Das ist nicht nur nicht richtig; es ist nicht einmal falsch!

–Wolfgang Pauli[not wrong]

> **not wrong**
>
> In English: "That is not only not right; it is not even wrong." Pauli's colorful phrase is usually circulated simply as the description "not even wrong." In general understanding, his intent is taken as meaning "unfalsifiable."

Concepts:

- Graph databases
- Document-oriented databases
- Missing fields in ragged documents
- Denormalization and data integrity
- Key/value stores
- Informal hierarchies

A number of database systems avoid the relational model, usually with the goal of better performance within a particular domain. As well, many RBDMSs now include JSON and XML data types. In overview, these systems break down into document-oriented databases, graph databases, and key/value stores. Specific server software may combine elements of these—or indeed elements of relational databases—and the specific performance characteristics, design philosophy, and general limitations vary among each project.

Most "NoSQL" database systems have a prominent attribute suggested by the moniker; namely, using query languages other than SQL. However, even there, some of them nonetheless implement at least a subset of SQL as a method of accessing data. These other query languages are sometimes unique to a particular database system, but in some cases are somewhat standardized. For example, the graph query languages Gremlin, SPARQL (SPARQL Protocol and RDF Query Language), and GQL (Graph Query Language; formerly *Cypher*) are each supported by several different database systems. Among open source graph databases, the most well known are perhaps Neo4j and OrientDB, but numerous others exist, including many proprietary ones.

Beyond mentioning here that they exist, I will not discuss in this book anything specific about data cleanliness issues that are characteristic of graph databases. The types of data analyses performed on graphs are typically somewhat specialized and outside the scope of what I can discuss here. But you may encounter data in these formats. I will discuss in somewhat more detail document-oriented databases and key/value stores, both of which you are more likely to find yourself working with (for most readers; individual needs and jobs vary, of course).

In broad concept, graph databases consist of nodes, and edges that connect nodes; both nodes and edges can usually hold attributes or properties, either freeform per object or defined by a schema. For example, the node representing me might contain my name ("David"), my occupation ("Data Scientist"), and my current home state ("Maine"). In turn, I have a "social graph" that includes my connection/edge labeled "Friend" (that perhaps contains other properties) to the node "Brad." I also have a connection labeled "Publisher" to the node "Packt." A complete social graph may consist of millions of nodes and edges, with various attributes attached to each.

A small illustration in the public domain was created by user Ahzf for the Wikimedia Commons:

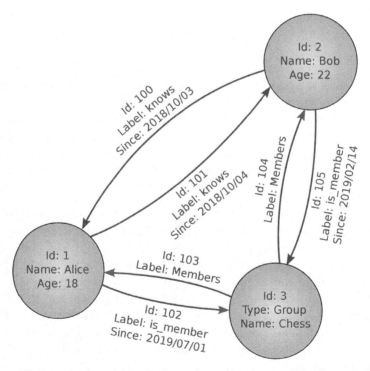

Figure 2.2: Example of a social graph. Source: https://commons.wikimedia.org/wiki/File:GraphDatabase_PropertyGraph.png

Document-Oriented Databases

Document-oriented databases typically store and communicate their data using XML, JSON, or Binary JSON (BSON). In a sense, you can think of these databases simply as single giant files in one of these formats, which just happen to have mechanisms to index and optimize queries into them. In actual implementation, this will not be true, but as a conceptual model it does not go far astray. The key thing to understand in document-oriented databases is that their data is hierarchically organized. This can make some access patterns very efficient, but it comes with all the same pitfalls as other hierarchical formats.

Popular open source document-oriented databases include MongoDB, CouchDB, CrateDB, Elasticsearch, and Solr. This software space is well occupied, and a large number of other tools, both open source and proprietary, are not included in my list. In broad concept, especially in terms of data cleanliness concerns, these different projects are similar.

The main pitfall in hierarchical data is simply that it is ragged. Particular fields at particular levels of nesting might be missing. Let us illustrate with an example inspired by a MongoDB blog post about restaurants with reviews. For these illustrations we use MongoDB, which is based around JSON. The same concepts would apply to any document-oriented database. As with other examples in this book, security configuration and login credentials will be part of normal usage, but are not addressed here:

```
# Assume that MongoDB is running on local system
from pymongo import MongoClient
client = MongoClient('mongodb://localhost:27017')
```

We can check what databases exist on this server. Other than "business", the others are administrative in nature, and simply exist by default on every MongoDB installation.

```
# What databases exist on the local server?
client.database_names()
```

```
['admin', 'business', 'config', 'local']
```

The "business" database has two branches at its top level: one for reviews, another for info.

> A document-oriented database is typically organized in a hierarchy of server → database → collection → document. For comparison, a relational database is organized as server → database → table → row.

Let us look at a few documents from each. General "info" on the first few restaurants:

```
db_biz = client.business
print("Restaurants:", db_biz.info.count())
for biz in db_biz.info.find(limit=3):
    pprint(biz)
```

```
Restaurants: 50
{'_id': ObjectId('5f30928db504836031a2c2a1'),
 'cuisine': 'Mexican',
 'name': 'Kitchen Tasty Inc.',
 'phone': '+1 524 555 9265'}
{'_id': ObjectId('5f30928db504836031a2c2a2'),
 'cuisine': 'Sandwich',
 'name': 'Sweet Salty Take-Out',
 'phone': '+1 408 555 6924'}
{'_id': ObjectId('5f30928db504836031a2c2a3'),
 'cuisine': 'Vegetarian',
 'name': 'City Kitchen Inc.',
 'phone': '+1 528 555 8923'}
```

Similarly, here are the first few reviews. Each review pertains to one of the listed restaurants in the "info" branch:

```
print("Reviews:", db_biz.reviews.count())
for review in db_biz.reviews.find(limit=3):
    pprint(review)
```

```
Reviews: 5000
{'_id': ObjectId('5f30928db504836031a2c2d3'),
 'name': 'Tasty Sweet Inc.',
 'price': 'cheap',
 'rating': 1}
{'_id': ObjectId('5f30928db504836031a2c2d4'),
 'name': 'Big Big Restaurant',
 'price': 'cheap',
 'rating': 6}
{'_id': ObjectId('5f30928db504836031a2c2d5'),
 'name': 'Goat Big Take-Out',
 'price': 'reasonable',
 'rating': 8}
```

We might make a more specific inquiry. For example, perhaps we are interested in those reviews of "City Kitchen Inc." that consider the price "cheap". We can see that different diners who evaluated the price the same rated the restaurant differently. In principle, other data might be attached to each of these documents, of course. MongoDB's query language is itself expressed as JSON (or as Python dictionaries from the Python interface):

```
query = {'price': 'cheap', 'name': 'City Kitchen Inc.'}
for review in db_biz.reviews.find(query, limit=4):
    pprint(review)
```

```
{'_id': ObjectId('5f30928db504836031a2c2ea'),
 'name': 'City Kitchen Inc.',
 'price': 'cheap',
 'rating': 3}
{'_id': ObjectId('5f30928db504836031a2c435'),
 'name': 'City Kitchen Inc.',
 'price': 'cheap',
 'rating': 7}
{'_id': ObjectId('5f30928db504836031a2c553'),
 'name': 'City Kitchen Inc.',
 'price': 'cheap',
 'rating': 3}
{'_id': ObjectId('5f30928db504836031a2c5d6'),
 'name': 'City Kitchen Inc.',
 'price': 'cheap',
 'rating': 1}
```

Missing Fields

In our general preview of the "business" database, everything was completely regular. We might jump into writing some code that crawls through records of a certain sort, perhaps matching a certain filter, with the intention of performing aggregation or modeling on corresponding data fields. For example, perhaps we would like to generate a histogram of the ratings given to "City Kitchen Inc.". The danger here is that some reviews might not *have* ratings, which we handle below using a try/except block:

```
ratings = []
query = {'name': 'City Kitchen Inc.'}
for review in db_biz.reviews.find(query):
    try:
```

```
            ratings.append(review['rating'])
        except KeyError:
            pass

n = len(ratings)
pd.Series(ratings).plot(kind="hist", title=f"{n} ratings");
```

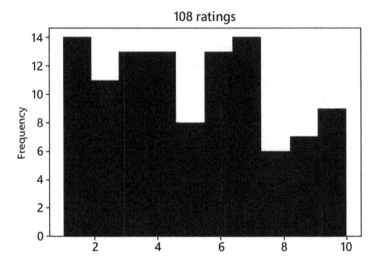

Figure 2.3: Histogram of ratings and their frequencies

We can see what is missing if we ask MongoDB for the actual number of rows. Our loop indeed skipped some data:

```
db_biz.reviews.find({'name': 'City Kitchen Inc.'}).count()
```

```
110
```

MongoDB—or any other hierarchical database (with perhaps some variation in API)—will let you match documents based on missing fields. In this small example, there is not that much other data in each document to consider, but in real-world cases, there might be many, and diverse, fields in similar documents. Let us list the reviews that do not have an associated rating:

```
list(db_biz.reviews.find({'name': 'City Kitchen Inc.', 'rating':
None}))
```

```
[{'_id': ObjectId('5f30928db504836031a2c3fa'),
  'name': 'City Kitchen Inc.',
  'price': 'expensive'},
```

```
{'_id': ObjectId('5f30928db504836031a2c6b6'),
 'name': 'City Kitchen Inc.',
 'price': 'reasonable'}]
```

Whether or not you need to worry about these two reviews with missing ratings is problem- and domain-driven. You might want to ignore them. You might want to perform techniques such as those discussed in *Chapter 5, Data Quality*, and *Chapter 6, Value Imputation*. In any event, you should be conscious of the fact that your data is incomplete.

Denormalization and Its Discontents

For performance reasons that are analogous to those in relational databases, sometimes data is denormalized in document-oriented databases. Querying within one branch will be faster, and querying just one document will be much faster again. Hence, administrators of document-oriented databases will commonly duplicate information into a location "closer" to where it is typically accessed.

In querying a document-oriented database, we might use code similar to this:

```
def has_best_review(name, db=db_biz):
    "Return phone if restaurant has at least one 10 rating"
    query = {'name': name, 'rating': 10}
    review = None

    # Fast path has phone in local results
    for review in db.reviews.find(query):
        phone = review.get('phone')
        if phone:
            return f"Call {name} at {phone}! (FAST query)"

    # If there were no ratings of 10, we don't like it!
    if not review:
        return f"Do not bother with {name}!"

    # MUCH SLOWER path is second query
    info = db.info.find_one({'name': name})
    return f"Call {name} at {info['phone']}! (SLOW query)"
```

Perhaps when a review is consulted numerous times (for example, if it had an actual description field), the database administrator may cache the phone number that is usually wanted within the actual review document.

Let us see how several inquiries behave:

```
has_best_review('Salty Big Take-Out')

'Call Salty Big Take-Out at +1 354 555 8317! (FAST query)'

has_best_review('City Kitchen Inc.')

'Call City Kitchen Inc. at +1 528 555 8923! (SLOW query)'

has_best_review('Out of Business')

'Do not bother with Out of Business!'
```

On its face, this all seems like reasonable performance optimization. The problem is that *duplicated* information is information that *might be* inconsistent. Here we will use the database itself to look for non-absent fields (the example function could be improved using this query element also):

```
query = {'name': 'Salty Big Take-Out',
         'rating': 10, 'phone':{"$ne":None}}

db_biz.reviews.find_one(query)

{'_id': ObjectId('5f30928db504836031a2c7c9'),
 'name': 'Salty Big Take-Out',
 'price': 'reasonable',
 'rating': 10,
 'phone': '+1 354 555 8317'}
```

However, let us take a look at the "info" branch for this restaurant rather than the "reviews" branch we have focused on so far:

```
db_biz.info.find_one({'name': 'Salty Big Take-Out'})

{'_id': ObjectId('5f30928db504836031a2c2aa'),
 'name': 'Salty Big Take-Out',
 'cuisine': 'Mexican',
 'phone': '+1 967 555 5487'}
```

At this point, we are faced with a data integrity problem. Presumably, at *some point* the telephone number was copied into the review document. It is *plausible* that the phone number was copied from the "info" branch to the "reviews" branch at the time the review was created (or maybe on the thousandth access to it?); that would suggest that the "info" branch is more current. However, it is also *possible* that the phone number was entered with the review itself as an option.

Determining the cause of the data integrity problem, unfortunately, depends on understanding not only the code that might have run in the past, but also even the human or automated entry processes that might have occurred.

Key/Value Stores

The simplest possible database system is a key/value store. These systems do nothing more than map some key (usually a string) to a value (sometimes a string, sometimes compound types). Often these systems are used as in-memory data stores to allow the fastest possible access, often as a form of caching. However, most of the systems that usually operate in-memory — including among distributed servers — also have some persistence mechanism such as virtual memory or snapshotting. Other variations of key/value stores are primarily on-disk formats, but they might in turn reside primarily in cache memory, hence achieving similar speed.

Redis (Remote Dictionary Server) and Memcached are popular in-memory systems (with persistence mechanisms on the side). Memcached, as its name suggests, is most commonly used as a cache, and is hence much less commonly a "source of knowledge." That is, a cache frequently sits between a client and a server and simply records the previous result from a client. If an identical request occurs again (possibly limited to some "staleness" period) then the complex database query, difficult computation, or access to additional resources external to the server can be skipped and the cached result is returned instead. Redis is sometimes used this way, but is also often used as a definitive or sole source of knowledge for some element of the data needed by a server.

To illustrate this caching in pseudo-code, a server proxy might contain code similar to this:

```
request = get_client_request()
key = hash(request)    # Collision resistant hash

# See if FAST PATH is available
if result := check_for_cache(key):
    send_to_client(result)

# SLOW PATH as fallback
else:
    result = expensive_operation(request)
    send_to_client(result)
    store_to_cache(key, result, expiration=duration)
```

Other key/value stores are derived from the early Unix **Database Manager** (DBM) system. These include Lightning Memory-Mapped Database (LMDB), GNU dbm (GDBM), and Berkeley DB. All of these simply map byte strings to other byte strings, without addressing more complex data structures. In contrast, for example, Redis allows for values to have a rich collection of data types, including collections allowing nesting. In practice, however, bytes are sufficient to hold any kind of data; it is just a matter of those bytes representing some serialization format, such as JSON text or Python pickles (the Python shelve module, for example, is basically just DBM coupled with pickles).

Being primarily single files on disk that store key/value pairs, DBM-family libraries occupy a similar application space with SQLite single-file databases. Both are a way to encapsulate related data into a format that can be read universally and depends only on a single file to be shared. Obviously, the manner of use is different between relational and key/value stores, but the same information can easily be represented in either, and both provide their own kind of querying and updating interfaces.

In a sense, key/value stores are simple enough that they do not lend themselves to data integrity problems. Obviously, it is always possible to store values that are simply *wrong* no matter what format is used. But there is nothing in the structure of a mapping itself that adds special concerns. Or so it would seem.

Problems arise in practice because users actually *want* hierarchy in their data. Most keys are not useful as completely flat names. Developers commonly invent ad hoc hierarchies in the keys used within key/value stores; this is not necessarily or usually a bad habit by developers, it usually reflects a genuine requirement of the problem space. However, these hierarchies can be especially fragile.

For example, I have created a DBM file that contains similar information to the restaurant database discussed above in its MongoDB format. The hierarchy of branches is represented here using namespacing of the keys with delimiters. This approach is quite commonplace among creators of key/value store systems. Let us look at a few of the keys in this key/value store. I have used a random seed that happens to sample some keys of interest:

```
biz = dbm.open('data/keyval.db')
seed(6)
# Keys are bytes; could convert to strings if desired
sample(list(biz.keys()), 10)

[b'Big Sweet Take-Out::info::phone',
 b'Big Sweet Inc.::ratings',
 b'Goat Sweet Inc.::info::phone',
 b'Fish City Restaurant//ratings',
 b'Delight Goat Inc.::ratings',
```

```
b'DESCRIPTION',
b'Salty Delight Take-Out::ratings',
b'Sweet Tasty Restaurant::info::phone',
b'Delight Salty Restaurant::info::phone',
b'Tasty Fish Inc.::info::cuisine']
```

We can query on various informally hierarchical keys.

```
name = b"Tasty Fish Inc."
print("Overview:", biz[b"DESCRIPTION"])
print("Cuisine: ", biz[name + b"::info::cuisine"] )
print("Ratings: ", biz[name + b"::ratings"][:30], "...")

Overview: b'Restaurant information'
Cuisine:  b'Mexican'
Ratings:  b'2;1;1;10;5;7;1;4;8;10;7;7;6;8;' ...
```

As is common, I have created an informal sequence in the "ratings" value by using delimiters. Consumers of the data will simply have to be aware that a particular value is formatted that way. We might even use a small amount of code to pull related keys out from the ad hoc hierarchy:

```
for key, val in biz.items():
    if key.startswith(b'Tasty Fish Inc.::'):
        print(key.decode(), '\t', val[:30].decode())

Tasty Fish Inc.::ratings        2;1;1;10;5;7;1;4;8;10;7;7;6;8;
Tasty Fish Inc.::info::phone    +1 935 555 8029
Tasty Fish Inc.::info::cuisine  Mexican
```

The main problem that arises here is that over the course of using the database, an inconsistent convention for hierarchical keys was used. This is a general concern, and occurs frequently in real data; it is probably especially prominent in multi-user, multi-consumer systems like Redis that are likely to communicate with tools written by many people, in many languages, over time. Data integrity failures just tend to seep in. For example:

```
for key, val in biz.items():
    if key.startswith(b'Fish City Restaurant'):
        print(key, val[:30])

b'Fish City Restaurant::ratings' b'6;10;4;3;10;5;1;4;7;8;5;2;1;5;'
b'Fish City Restaurant//ratings' b'9'
b'Fish City Restaurant::info::phone' b'+1 851 555 1082'
b'Fish City Restaurant::info::cuisine' b'American'
```

Although the intent of the differently delimited hierarchical keys is easy to discern as human readers, detecting such inconsistencies can be laborious, and you risk missing information with inadequate remediation. For these types of key/value stores, if you need to utilize their data source, a good first examination is to analyze the structure of keys themselves. They will not always utilize an ad hoc hierarchy, but doing so is frequent. Even if there are millions of keys rather than the hundreds in my example, that initial approach can at least assure that consistent path components exist using consistent delimiters (or other formatting of keys).

We have covered a large number of different hierarchical formats, and even so left out much possible discussion of others. An in-depth look at graph databases will need to live in a different book. Also, many volumes have been written on the myriad APIs and dialects of XML that this chapter only gestures at. However, I hope this has given you a feel for the kinds of concerns that arise with this family of data sources.

Exercises

The first exercise here deals with refining the processing of the geographic data that is available in several formats. The second exercise addresses moving between a key/value and a relational model for data representation.

Exploring Filled Area

Using the United States county data, we created tidy data frames that contained the extents of counties as simple cardinal direction limits; we also were provided with the "census area" of each county. Unfortunately, the data available here does not specifically address water bodies and their sizes, which might be relevant to some counties.

The census data can be found at:

```
https://www.gnosis.cx/cleaning/gz_2010_us_050_00_20m.json

https://www.gnosis.cx/cleaning/gz_2010_us_050_00_20m.kml

https://www.gnosis.cx/cleaning/gz_2010_us_050_00_20m.zip
```

In this exercise, you will create an additional column in the data frame illustrated in the text to hold the percentage of the "bounding box" of a county that is occupied by the census area. The trick, of course, is that the surface area enclosed by latitude/longitude corners is not a simple rectangle, nor even a trapezoid, but rather a portion of a spherical surface. County shapes themselves are typically not rectangular, and may include discontiguous regions.

To complete this exercise, you may either reason mathematically about this area (the simplifying assumption that the Earth is a sphere is acceptable) or identify appropriate GIS software to do this calculation for you. The result of your work will be a data frame like that presented in the chapter, but with a column called "occupied" that contains 3221 floating-point values between 0 and 1.

For extra credit, you can investigate or improve a few additional data integrity issues. The shapefile in the ZIP archive is the canonical data provided by the US Census Bureau. The code we saw in this chapter to process GeoJSON and KML actually produces slightly different results for latitude/longitude locations, at the third decimal place. Presumably, the independent developer whom I downloaded these conversions from allowed some data error to creep in somehow. Diagnose which version, if either, matches the original .shp file, and try to characterize the reason for and degree of the discrepancy.

For additional extra credit, fix the kml_county_summary() function presented in this chapter so that it correctly handles <MultiGeometry> county shapes rather than skipping over them. How often did this problem occur among the 3221 United States counties?

Create a Relational Model

The key/value data in the DBM restaurant data is organized in a manner that might provide very fast access in Redis or similar systems. But there is certainly a mismatch with the implicit data model. Keys have structure in their hierarchy, but it is a finite and shallow hierarchy. Values may be of several different implicit data types; in particular, ratings are stored as strings, but they really represent sequences of small integer values. Other fields are simple strings (albeit stored as bytes in the DBM).

The dbm module in the shown example uses Python's fallback "dumb DBM" format, which does not depend on external drivers like GDBM or LDBM. For the example with hundreds of records, this is quite fast; if you wished to use millions of records, other systems would scale well and are preferred. This "dumb" format actually consists of three separate files, but sharing the keyval.db prefix; the three are provided as a ZIP archive:

```
dbm.whichdb('data/keyval.db')
```

```
'dbm.dumb'
```

The `dbm.dumb` format is not necessarily portable to other programming languages. It is, however, simple enough that you could write an adapter rather easily. To provide the identical data in a more universal format, a CSV of the identical content is also available:

https://www.gnosis.cx/cleaning/keyval.zip

https://www.gnosis.cx/cleaning/keyval.csv

For this assignment, you should transform the key/value data in this example into relational tables, using foreign keys where appropriate and making good decisions about data types. SQLite is an excellent choice for a database system to target; it is discussed in *Chapter 1, Tabular Formats*. Any other RDBMS is also a good choice if you have administrative access (i.e. table creation rights). Before transforming the data model, you will need to clean up the inconsistencies in the hierarchical keys that were discussed in this chapter.

The names of restaurants are promised to be distinct; however, for foreign key relationships, you may wish to normalize using a short index number standing for the restaurants uniformly. The separate ratings should definitely be stored as distinct data items in a relevant table. To get a feel for more fleshed-out data, invent timestamps for the reviews, such that each is mostly distinct. A real-world dataset will generally contain review dates; for the example, no specific dates are required, just the form of them.

Although this data is small enough that performance will not be a concern, think about what indices are likely to be useful in a hypothetical version of this data that is thousands or millions of times larger. Imagine you are running a popular restaurant review service and you want your users to have fast access to their common queries.

Using the relational version of your data model, answer some simple queries, most likely using SQL:

- What restaurant received the most reviews?
- What restaurants received reviews of 10 during a given time period (the relevant range will depend on which dates you chose to populate)?
- What style of cuisine received the highest mean review?

For extra credit, you may go back and write code to answer the same questions using only the key/value data model.

Denouement

Simple is better than complex.
Complex is better than complicated.
Flat is better than nested.
Sparse is better than dense.
Readability counts.

–Tim Peters (The Zen of Python)

Topics covered in this chapter: JSON; JSON Lines; JSON Schema; XML; YAML and Configuration Files; Document-Oriented Databases; Key/Value Stores.

Hierarchical data often provides a much better representation of *entities* that have attributes and relationships to each other than does flat data. In object-oriented programming, but also simply in ordinary taxonomies and ontologies, the relationships *is-a* and *has-a* are frequently fundamental, and neither of those is whatsoever tabular. Or at best, even the attributes captured by *has-a* relationships are ragged and sparse, and definitely not tidy. Moreover, *is-a* relationships are hierarchical at their core.

There is often—even usually—an impedance mismatch between hierarchical data and data science. Much of these issues comes down to *access patterns*. For many software applications, what interests us are particular entities that carry with them heterogeneous bundles of data, each bundle pertaining to the kind of thing the entity is an instance of. In utilizing such applications, we only care about one *thing* (or a handful of things) at a given time. When that is the case, hierarchical data structures can often be both more efficient and conceptually closer to the underlying ideas the data represents.

When we do data science, whether it is general statistics, data visualization, or machine learning models, we are concerned with collections of records or samples that are homogeneous in regard to our purpose or goal. Yes, there may be missing data concerns such as those that will be addressed in *Chapter 4, Anomaly Detection*, and *Chapter 5, Data Quality*, but those do not dominate our analysis. Data science is about summarization and aggregation. It is almost never about individual entities in themselves.

Therefore, when provided with hierarchical data, as data scientists we need to articulate what a tree represents that can be expressed in terms of homogeneous samples. What fields or features abstract from the hierarchical structure and express something in common among numerous entities? Those entities need not be leaves of the trees (although that is common); they might also be properties that can be extracted or extrapolated from different branches, which are useful and meaningful to summarize, model, and aggregate.

In the next chapter, we look at a number of additional data formats, including web data, PDFs, images, and custom text and binary formats.

3
Repurposing Data Sources

All language is but a poor translation.

–Franz Kafka

Sometimes, data lives in formats that take extra work to ingest. For common and explicitly data-oriented formats, common libraries already have readers built into them. Data frame libraries, for example, read a huge number of different file types. At worst, slightly less common formats have their own more specialized libraries that provide a relatively straightforward path between the original format and the general purpose data processing library you wish to use.

A greater difficulty often arises because a given format is not *per se* a data format, but exists for a different purpose. Nonetheless, often there is data somehow embedded or encoded in the format that we would like to utilize. For example, web pages are generally designed for human readers and rendered by web browsers with "quirks modes" that deal with not-quite-HTML, as is often needed. Portable Document Format (PDF) documents are similar in having human readers in mind, and yet also often containing tabular or other data that we would like to process as data scientists. Of course, in both cases, we would rather have the data itself in some separate, easily ingestible, format; but reality does not always live up to our hopes. Image formats likewise are intended for the presentation of pictures to humans, but we sometimes wish to characterize or analyze collections of images in some data science or machine learning manner. There *is* a bit of a difference between **Hypertext Markup Language** (HTML) and PDF, on one hand, and images on the other hand. With the former, we hope to find tables or numeric lists that are incidentally embedded inside a textual document.

With the images, we are interested in the format itself as data: what is the pattern of pixel values and what does that tell us about characteristics of the image as such?

Still other formats are indeed intended as data formats, but they are unusual enough that common readers for the formats will not be available. Generally, custom text formats are manageable, especially if you have some documentation of what the rules of the format are. Custom binary formats are usually more work, but possible to decode if the need is sufficiently pressing and other encodings do not exist. Mostly, such custom formats are legacy in some way, and a one-time conversion to more widely used formats is the best process.

***

Before we get to the sections of this chapter, let us run our standard setup code:

```
from src.setup import *
%load_ext rpy2.ipython
```

```
%%R
library(imager)
library(tidyverse)
library(rvest)
```

Web Scraping

Important letters which contain no errors will develop errors in the mail.

–Anonymous

Concepts:

- HTML tables
- Non-tabular data
- Command-line scraping

A great deal of interesting data lives on web pages, and often, unfortunately, we do not have access to the same data in more structured data formats. In the best cases, the data we are interested in at least lives within HTML tables inside a web page; however, even where tables are defined, often the content of the cells has more than just the numeric or categorical values of interest to us. For example, a given cell might contain commentary on the data point or a footnote providing a source for the information. At other times, of course, the data we are interested in is not in HTML tables at all, but structured in some other manner across a web page.

In this section, we will first use the R library rvest to extract some tabular data, and then use BeautifulSoup in Python to work with some non-tabular data. This shifting tool choice is not because one tool or the other is uniquely capable of doing the task we use it for, nor even is one necessarily better than the other at it. I simply want to provide a glimpse into a couple of different tools for performing a similar task.

In the Python world, the framework Scrapy is also widely used—it does both more and less than BeautifulSoup. Scrapy can actually pull down web pages and navigate dynamically among them, while BeautifulSoup is only interested in the parsing aspect, and it assumes you have used some other tool or library (such as Requests) to actually obtain the HTML resource to be parsed. For what it does, BeautifulSoup is somewhat friendlier and is remarkably well able to handle malformed HTML. In the real world, what gets called "HTML" is often only loosely conformant to any actual format standards, and hence web browsers, for example, are quite sophisticated (and complicated) in providing reasonable rendering of only vaguely structured tag soups.

At the time of writing, in 2020, the Covid-19 pandemic is ongoing, and the exact contours of the disease worldwide are changing on a daily basis. Given this active change, the current situation is too much of a moving target to make a good example (and too politically and ethically laden). Let us look at some data from a past disease though to illustrate web scraping. While there are surely other sources for similar data we could locate, and some are most likely in immediately readable formats, we will collect our data from the Wikipedia article on the 2009 flu pandemic.

A crucial fact about web pages is that they can be and often are modified by their maintainers. There are times when the Wayback Machine (`https://archive.org/web/`) can be used to find specific historical versions. Data that is available at a given point in time may not continue to be in the future at a given URL. Or even where a web page maintains the same underlying information, it may change details of its format that would change the functionality of our scripts for processing the page. On the other hand, many changes represent exactly the updates in data values that are of interest to us, and the dynamic nature of a web page is exactly its greatest value. These are trade-offs to keep in mind when scraping data from the web.

HTML Tables

Wikipedia has a great many virtues, and one of them is its versioning of its pages. While a default URL for a given topic has a friendly and straightforward spelling that can often even be guessed from the name of a topic, Wikipedia also provides a URL parameter in its query strings that identifies an exact version of the web page that should remain bitwise identical for all time.

There are a few exceptions to this permanence; for example, if an article is deleted altogether, it may become inaccessible. Likewise, if a template is part of a renaming, as unfortunately occurred during the writing of this book, a "permanent" link can break. Let us examine the Wikipedia page we will attempt to scrape in this section:

```
# Same string composed over two lines for layout
# XXXX substituted for actual ID because of discussed breakage
url2009 = ("https://en.wikipedia.org/w/index.php?"
          "title=2009_flu_pandemic&oldid=XXXX")
```

The particular part of this page that we are interested in is an info box about halfway down the article. It looks like this in my browser:

2009 flu pandemic data	
Area	Confirmed deaths
Worldwide (total)	**14,286**
European Union and EFTA	2,290
Other European countries and Central Asia	457
Mediterranean and Middle East	1,450
Africa	116
North America	3,642
Central America and Caribbean	237
South America	3,190
Northeast Asia and South Asia	2,294
Southeast Asia	393
Australia and Pacific	217
Source: ECDC – January 18, 2010	
Further information: Cases and deaths by country	
Note: The ratio of confirmed deaths to total deaths due to the pandemic is unknown. For more information, see "Data reporting and accuracy".	
V • T • E	

Figure 3.1: Wikipedia info box in the article entitled "2009 Flu Pandemic"

Constructing a script for web scraping inevitably involves a large amount of trial and error. In concept, it might be possible to manually read the underlying HTML before processing it, and correctly identify the positions and types of the element of interest. In practice, it is always quicker to eyeball the partially filtered or indexed elements and refine the selection through repetition.

For example, in this first pass below, I determined by trial and error that the "cases by region" table was number 4 on the web page by enumerating through earlier numbers and visually ruling them out. As rendered by a web browser, it is not always apparent what element is a table; it is also not necessarily the case that an element being rendered visually above another actually occurs earlier in the underlying HTML.

This first pass also already performs a little bit of cleanup in value names. Through experimentation, I determined that some region names contain an HTML <br/>, which is stripped in the following code, leaving no space between words. In order to address that, I replace the HTML break with a space, and then need to reconstruct an HTML object from the string and select the table again:

```
%%R
page <- read_html(url2009)
table <- page %>%
    html_nodes("table") %>%
    .[[4]] %>%
    str_replace_all("<br>", " ") %>%
    minimal_html() %>%
    html_node("table") %>%
    html_table(fill = TRUE)
head(table, 3)
```

This code produced the following (before the template change issue):

	2009 flu pandemic data	2009 flu pandemic data	2009 flu pandemic data
1	Area	Confirmed deaths	<NA>
2	Worldwide (total)	14,286	<NA>
3	European Union and EFTA	2,290	<NA>

Although the first pass still has problems, all the data is basically present, and we can clean it up without needing to query the source further. Because of the nested tables, the same header is incorrectly deduced for each column. The more accurate headers are relegated to the first row.

Moreover, an extraneous column that contains footnotes was created (it has content in some rows below those shown by head()). Because of the commas in numbers over a thousand, integers were not inferred. Let us convert the data.frame to a tibble:

```
data <- as_tibble(table,
        .name_repair = ~ c("Region", "Deaths", "drop")) %>%
    select(-drop) %>%
    slice(2:12) %>%
    mutate(Deaths = as.integer(gsub(",", "", Deaths)),
           Region = as.factor(Region))
data
```

And this might give us a helpful table like:

```
# A tibble: 11 x 2
   Region                                   Deaths
   <fct>                                     <int>
 1 Worldwide (total)                         14286
 2 European Union and EFTA                    2290
 3 Other European countries and Central Asia   457
 4 Mediterranean and Middle East             1450
 5 Africa                                      116
 6 North America                             3642
 7 Central America and Caribbean              237
 8 South America                             3190
 9 Northeast Asia and South Asia             2294
10 Southeast Asia                             393
11 Australia and Pacific                      217
```

Obviously this is a very small example that could easily be typed in manually. The general techniques shown might be applied to a much larger table. More significantly, they might also be used to scrape a table on a web page that is updated frequently. 2009 is strictly historical, but other data is updated every day, or even every minute, and a few lines like the ones shown could pull down current data each time it needs to be processed.

Non-Tabular Data

For our processing of a non-tabular source, we will use Wikipedia as well. Again, a topic that is of wide interest and not prone to deletion is chosen. Likewise, a specific historical version is indicated in the URL, just in case the page changes its structure by the time you read this. In a slightly self-referential way, we will look at the article that lists HTTP status codes in a term/definition layout.

A portion of that page renders in my browser like this:

415 Unsupported Media Type (RFC 7231⊘)

The request entity has a media type which the server or resource does not support. For example, the client uploads an image as image/svg+xml, but the server requires that images use a different format.[49]

416 Range Not Satisfiable (RFC 7233⊘)

The client has asked for a portion of the file (byte serving), but the server cannot supply that portion. For example, if the client asked for a part of the file that lies beyond the end of the file.[50] Called "Requested Range Not Satisfiable" previously.[51]

417 Expectation Failed

The server cannot meet the requirements of the Expect request-header field.[52]

418 I'm a teapot (RFC 2324⊘, RFC 7168⊘)

This code was defined in 1998 as one of the traditional IETF April Fools' jokes, in RFC 2324⊘, *Hyper Text Coffee Pot Control Protocol*, and is not expected to be implemented by actual HTTP servers. The RFC specifies this code should be returned by teapots requested to brew coffee.[53] This HTTP status is used as an Easter egg in some websites, including Google.com.[54][55]

421 Misdirected Request (RFC 7540⊘)

The request was directed at a server that is not able to produce a response[56] (for example because of connection reuse).[57]

Figure 3.2: HTTP status codes, Wikipedia definition list

Numerous other codes are listed in the articles that are not in the screenshot. Moreover, there are section divisions and other descriptive elements or images throughout the page. Fortunately, Wikipedia tends to be very regular and predictable in its use of markup. The URL we will examine is:

```
url_http = ("https://en.wikipedia.org/w/index.php?"
            "title=List_of_HTTP_status_codes&oldid=947767948")
```

The first thing we need to do is actually retrieve the HTML content. The Python standard library module `urllib` is perfectly able to do this task. However, even its official documentation (`https://docs.python.org/3/library/urllib.request.html#module-urllib.request`) recommends using the third-party package Requests for most purposes. There is nothing you *cannot* do with `urllib`, but often the API is more difficult to use, and is unnecessarily complicated for historical/legacy reasons. For simple things, like what is shown in this book, it makes little difference; for more complicated tasks, getting in the habit of using Requests is a good idea.

Let us open a page and check the status code returned:

```
import requests
resp = requests.get(url_http)
resp.status_code
```

```
200
```

The raw HTML we retrieved is not especially easy to work with. Even apart from the fact it is compacted to remove extra whitespace, the general structure is a "tag soup" with various things nested in various places, and in which basic string methods or regular expressions do not help us very much in identifying the parts we are interested in. For example, here is a short segment from somewhere in the middle:

```
pprint(resp.content[43400:44000], width=55)
```

```
(b'ailed</dt>\n<dd>The server cannot meet the requir'
 b'ements of the Expect request-header field.<sup i'
 b'd="cite_ref-53" class="reference"><a href="#cite'
 b'_note-53">&#91;52&#93;</a></sup></dd>\n<dt><span '
 b'class="anchor" id="418"></span><a href="/wiki/HT'
 b'TP_418" class="mw-redirect" title="HTTP 418">418'
 b' I\'m a teapot</a> (<a class="external mw-magicli'
 b'nk-rfc" rel="nofollow" href="https://tools.ietf.'
 b'org/html/rfc2324">RFC 2324</a>, <a class="extern'
 b'al mw-magiclink-rfc" rel="nofollow" href="https:'
 b'//tools.ietf.org/html/rfc7168">RFC 7168</a>)</dt'
 b'>\n<dd>This code was defined in 1998 as one of th'
 b'e traditional <a href="/')
```

What we would like is to make the tag soup beautiful instead. The steps in doing so are first creating a "soup" object from the raw HTML, then using methods of that soup to pick out the elements we care about for our dataset. As with the R and rvest version—as indeed, with any library you decide to use—finding the right data in the web page will involve trial and error:

```
from bs4 import BeautifulSoup
soup = BeautifulSoup(resp.content)
```

As a start, upon our examination, we notice that the status codes themselves are each contained within an HTML <dt> element. Below we display the first and last few of the elements identified by this tag. Everything so identified is, in fact, a status code, but I only know that from manual inspection of all of them (fortunately, eyeballing fewer than 100 items is not difficult; doing so with a million would be infeasible).

However, if we look back at the original web page itself, we will notice that two AWS custom codes at the end are not captured because the page formatting is inconsistent for those. In this section, we will ignore those, having determined they are not general-purpose anyway:

```
codes = soup.find_all('dt')
for code in codes[:5] + codes[-5:]:
    print(code.text)
```

```
100 Continue
101 Switching Protocols
102 Processing (WebDAV; RFC 2518)
103 Early Hints (RFC 8297)
200 OK
524 A Timeout Occurred
525 SSL Handshake Failed
526 Invalid SSL Certificate
527 Railgun Error
530
```

It would be nice if each <dt> were matched with a corresponding <dd>. If it were, we could just read all the <dd> definitions and zip them together with the terms. Real-world HTML is messy. It turns out—and I discovered this while writing, not by planning the example—that there are sometimes more than one (and potentially sometimes zero) <dd> elements following each <dt>. Our goal then will be to collect all of the <dd> elements that follow a <dt> until other tags occur.

In the BeautifulSoup API, the empty space between elements is a node of plain text that contains exactly the characters (including whitespace) inside that span. It is tempting to use the API node.find_next_siblings() in this task. We *could* succeed doing this, but this method will fetch too much, including all subsequent <dt> elements after the current one. Instead, we can use the .next_sibling property to get each one, and stop when needed:

```
def find_dds_after(node):
    dds = []
    sib = node.next_sibling
    while True:        # Loop until a break
        # Last sibling within page section
        if sib is None:
            break
        # Text nodes have no element name
        elif not sib.name:
            sib = sib.next_sibling
```

```
                continue
            # A definition node
            if sib.name == 'dd':
                dds.append(sib)
                sib = sib.next_sibling
            # Finished <dd> the definition nodes
            else:
                break
    return dds
```

The custom function I wrote above is straightforward, but special to this purpose. Perhaps it is extensible to similar definition lists one finds in other HTML documents. BeautifulSoup provides numerous useful APIs, but they are building blocks for constructing custom extractors rather than foreseeing every possible structure in an HTML document. To understand it, let us look at a couple of the status codes:

```
for code in codes[23:26]:
    print(code.text)
    for dd in find_dds_after(code):
        print("   ", dd.text[:40], "...")
```

```
400 Bad Request
    The server cannot or will not process th ...
401 Unauthorized (RFC 7235)
    Similar to 403 Forbidden, but specifical ...
    Note: Some sites incorrectly issue HTTP   ...
402 Payment Required
    Reserved for future use. The original in ...
```

The HTTP 401 response contains two separate definition blocks. Let us apply the function across all the HTTP code numbers. What is returned is a list of definition blocks; for our purpose, we will join the text of each of these with a newline. In fact, we construct a data frame with all the information of interest to us in the next cells:

```
data = []
for code in codes:
    # All codes are 3 character numbers
    number = code.text[:3]
    # Parenthetical is not part of status
    text, note = code.text[4:], ""
    if " (" in text:
        text, note = text.split(" (")
```

```
    note = note.rstrip(")")
    # Compose description from list of strings
    description = "\n".join(t.text for t in find_dds_after(code))
    data.append([int(number), text, note, description])
```

From the Python list of lists, we can create a Pandas DataFrame for further work on the dataset:

```
(pd.DataFrame(data,
            columns=["Code", "Text", "Note", "Description"])
    .set_index('Code')
    .sort_index()
    .head(8))
```

Code	Text	Note	Description
100	Continue		The server has received the request headers an...
101	Switching Protocols		The requester has asked the server to switch p...
102	Processing	WebDAV; RFC 2518	A WebDAV request may contain many sub-requests
103	Checkpoint		Used in the resumable request proposal to res...
103	Early Hints	RFC 8297	Used to return some response headers before fi...
200	OK		Standard response for successful HTTP requests...
201	Created		The request has been fulfilled, resulting in t...
202	Accepted		The request has been accepted for processing, ...

Clearly, the two examples this book walked through in some detail are not general to all the web pages you may wish to scrape data from. Organization into tables and into definition lists are certainly two common uses of HTML to represent data, but many other conventions might be used. Particular domain-specific — or likely page-specific — class and id attributes on elements is also a common way to mark the structural role of different data elements.

Libraries such as rvest, BeautifulSoup, and scrapy all make identification and extraction of HTML by element attributes straightforward as well. Simply be prepared to try many variations on your web scraping code before you get it right. Generally, your iteration will be a narrowing process; each stage *needs to* include the information desired, and it becomes a process of removing the parts you do not want through refinement.

Command-Line Scraping

Another approach that I have often used for web scraping is to use the command-line web browsers lynx and links. Install either or both with your system package manager. These tools can dump HTML contents as text that is, in turn, relatively easy to parse if the format is simple. There are many times when just looking for patterns of indentation, vertical space, searching for particular keywords, or similar text processing will get the data you need more quickly than the trial and error of parsing libraries like rvest or BeautifulSoup. Of course, there is always a certain amount of eyeballing and retrying commands. For people who are well versed in text processing tools, this approach is worth considering.

The two similar text-mode web browsers both share a -dump switch that outputs non-interactive text to STDOUT. Both of them have a variety of other switches that can tweak the rendering of the text in a variety of ways. The output from these two tools is similar, but the rest of your scripting will need to pay attention to the minor differences. Each of these browsers will do a very good job of dumping 90% of web pages as text that is easy to process. Of the problem 10% (a hand waving percentage, not a real measure), often one or the other tool will produce something reasonable to parse. In certain cases, one of these browsers may produce useful results and the other will not. Fortunately, it is easy simply to try both for a given task or site.

Let us look at the output from each tool against a portion of the HTTP response code page. Obviously, I experimented to find the exact line ranges of output that would correspond. You can see that only incidental formatting differences exist in this friendly HTML page. First, with lynx:

```bash
%%bash
base='https://en.wikipedia.org/w/index.php?title='
url="$base"'List_of_HTTP_status_codes&oldid=947767948'
lynx -dump $url | sed -n '397,406p'
```

```
      requester put on the request header fields.^[170][44]^[171][45]
```

```
  413 Payload Too Large ([172]RFC 7231)
          The request is larger than the server is willing or able to
          process. Previously called "Request Entity Too Large".^[173][46]
```

```
  414 URI Too Long ([174]RFC 7231)
          The [175]URI provided was too long for the server to process.
          Often the result of too much data being encoded as a
          query-string of a GET request, in which case it should be
```

And the same part of the page again, but this time with `links`:

```bash
%%bash
base='https://en.wikipedia.org/w/index.php?title='
url="$base"'List_of_HTTP_status_codes&oldid=947767948'
links -dump $url | sed -n '377,385p'
```

```
      requester put on the request header fields.^[44]^[45]
```

```
  413 Payload Too Large (RFC 7231)
          The request is larger than the server is willing or able to
          process. Previously called "Request Entity Too Large".^[46]
```

```
  414 URI Too Long (RFC 7231)
          The URI provided was too long for the server to process. Often the
          result of too much data being encoded as a query-string of a GET
```

The only differences here are one space difference in indentation of the definition element and some difference in the formatting of footnote links in the text. In either case, it would be easy enough to define some rules for the patterns of terms and their definitions. Something like this:

- Look for a line that starts with 3 spaces followed by a 3-digit number
- Accumulate all non-blank lines following that; stop at the blank line
- Strip the footnote/link markers from the texts
- Split the code number and text in the same manner as in the previous example

Let us wave goodbye to the Scylla of HTML, as we pass by, and fall into the Charybdis of PDF.

Portable Document Format

This functionary grasped it in a perfect agony of joy, opened it with a trembling hand, cast a rapid glance at its contents, and then, scrambling and struggling to the door, rushed at length unceremoniously from the room and from the house.

–Edgar Allan Poe

Concepts:

- Identifying tabular regions
- Extracting plain text

There are a great many commercial tools for extracting data that has become hidden away in PDF files. Unfortunately, many organizations—government, corporate, and others—issue reports in PDF format but do not provide data formats more easily accessible to computer analysis and abstraction. This is common enough to have provided impetus for a cottage industry of tools for semi-automatically extracting data back out of these reports. This book does not recommend the use of proprietary tools, about which there is no guarantee of maintenance and improvement over time; as well, of course, those tools cost money and are an impediment to cooperation among data scientists who work together on projects without necessarily residing in the same "licensing zone."

There are two main elements that are likely to interest us in a PDF file. An obvious one is tables of data, and those are often embedded in PDFs. Otherwise, a PDF can often simply be treated as a custom text format, as we discuss in a section below. Various kinds of lists, bullets, captions, or simply paragraph text might have data of interest to us.

There are two open source tools I recommend for extraction of data from PDFs. One of these is the command-line tool pdftotext, which is part of the Xpdf and derived Poppler software suites. The second is a Java tool called **tabula-java**. tabula-java is, in turn, the underlying engine for the GUI tool Tabula, and also has language bindings for Ruby (**tabula-extractor**), Python (**tabula-py**), R (**tabulizer**), and Node.js (**tabula-js**). Tabula creates a small web server that allows interaction within a browser to do operations like creating lists of PDFs and selecting regions where tables are located. The Python and R bindings also allow the direct creation of data frames or arrays, with the R binding incorporating an optional graphical widget for region selection.

For this discussion, we do not use any of the language bindings, nor the GUI tools. For one-off selection of single-page datasets, the selection tools could be useful, but for automation of recurring document updates or families of similar documents, scripting is needed.

Moreover, while the various language bindings are perfectly suitable for scripting, we can be somewhat more language agnostic in this section by limiting ourselves to the command-line tool of the base library.

As an example for this section, let us use a PDF that was output from the preface of this book itself. There may have been small wording changes by the time you read this, and the exact formatting of the printed book or ebook will surely be somewhat different from this draft version. However, this nicely illustrates tables rendered in several different styles that we can try to extract as data. There are three tables, in particular, that we would like to capture:

```
[1]:          Last_Name First_Name Favorite_Color    Age
    Student_No
    1            Johnson        Mia      periwinkle   12.0
    2             Lopez        Liam      blue-green   13.0
    3              Lee     Isabella       <missing>   11.0
    4            Fisher       Mason            gray    NaN
    5             Gupta      Olivia           sepia    NaN
    6          Robinson      Sophia            blue   12.0
```

Likewise in this configuration, I can run R code equally well. At times the code samples will show data being transferred between the R and Python kernels.

```
[2]: %load_ext rpy2.ipython
```

```
[3]: %%R -i cleaned
     library('tibble')
     tibble(First=cleaned$First_Name,
            Last=cleaned$Last_Name,
            Age=cleaned$Age)
```

```
# A tibble: 6 x 3
  First     Last         Age
  <chr>     <chr>
<dbl>
1 Mia       Johnson       12
2 Liam      Lopez         13
3 Isabella  Lee           11
4 Mason     Fisher       NaN
5 Olivia    Gupta        NaN
6 Sophia    Robinson      12
```

Figure 3.3: Page 5 of the book's preface

On page 5 of the draft preface, a table is rendered by both Pandas and tibble, with corresponding minor presentation differences. On page 7, another table is included that looks somewhat different again:

- Missing data in the *Favorite Color* field should be substituted with the string `<missing>`.
- Student ages should be between 9 and 14, and all other values are considered missing data.
- Some colors are numerically coded, but should be dealiased. The mapping is:

Number	Color	Number	Color
1	beige	6	alabaster
2	eggshell	7	sandcastle
3	seafoam	8	chartreuse
4	mint	9	sepia
5	cream	10	lemon

Using the small test data set is a good way to test your code. But try also manually adding more rows with similar, or different, problems in them, and see how well your code produces a reasonable result.

Figure 3.4: Page 7 of the book's preface

Running tabula-java requires a rather long command line, so I have created a small Bash script to wrap it on my personal system:

```bash
#!/bin/bash
# script: tabula
# Adjust for your personal system path
TPATH='/home/dmertz/git/tabula-java/target'
JAR='tabula-1.0.4-SNAPSHOT-jar-with-dependencies.jar'
java -jar "$TPATH/$JAR" $@
```

Extraction will sometimes automatically recognize tables per page with the `--guess` option, but you can get better control by specifying a portion of a page where tabula-java should look for a table. We simply output to STDOUT in the following code cells, but outputting to a file is just another option switch:

```
%%bash
tabula -g -t -p5 data/Preface-snapshot.pdf
```

```
[1]:,,Last_Name,First_Name,Favorite_Color,Age
"",Student_No,,,,
"",1,Johnson,Mia,periwinkle,12.0
"",2,Lopez,Liam,blue-green,13.0
"",3,Lee,Isabella,<missing>,11.0
```

```
"",4,Fisher,Mason,gray,NaN
"",5,Gupta,Olivia,sepia,NaN
"",6,Robinson,Sophia,blue,12.0
```

Tabula does a good, but not perfect, job. The Pandas style of setting the name of the index column below the other headers threw it off slightly. There is also a spurious first column that is usually empty strings, but has a header as the output cell number. However, these small defects are very easy to clean up, and we have a very nice CSV of the actual data in the table.

Remember from just above, however, that page 5 actually had *two tables* on it. Tabula-java only captured the first one, which is not unreasonable, but is not all the data we might want. Slightly more custom instructions (determined by moderate trial and error to determine the region of interest) can capture the second one:

```
%%bash
tabula -a'%72,13,90,100' -fTSV -p5 data/Preface-snapshot.pdf
```

```
First     Last      Age
<chr>     <chr>
bl>
Mia       Johnson   12
Liam      Lopez     13
Isabella  Lee       11
Mason     Fisher    NaN
Olivia    Gupta     NaN
Sophia    Robinson  12
```

To illustrate the output options, we chose tab-delimited rather than comma-separated for the output. A JSON output is also available. Moreover, by adjusting the left margin (as percent, but as typographic points is also an option), we can eliminate the unnecessary row numbers. As before, the ingestion is good but not perfect. The tibble formatting of data type markers is superfluous for us. Discarding the two rows with unnecessary data is straightforward.

Finally, for this example, let us capture the table on page 7 that does not have any of those data frame library extra markers. This one is probably more typical of the tables you will encounter in real work. For the example, we use points rather than page percentage to indicate the position of the table:

```
%%bash
tabula -p7 -a'120,0,220,500' data/Preface-snapshot.pdf
```

```
Number,Color,Number,Color
1,beige,6,alabaster
```

```
2,eggshell,7,sandcastle
3,seafoam,8,chartreuse
4,mint,9,sepia
5,cream,10,lemon
```

The extraction here is perfect, although the table itself is less than ideal in that it repeats the number/color pairs twice. However, that is likewise easy enough to modify using data frame libraries.

The tabula-java tool, as the name suggests, is only really useful for identifying tables. In contrast, pdftotext creates a *best-effort* purely text version of a PDF. Most of the time this is quite good. From that, standard text processing and extraction techniques usually work well, including those that parse tables. However, since an entire document (or a part of it selected by pages) is output, this lets us work with other elements such as bullet lists, raw prose, or other identifiable data elements of a document:

```
%%bash
# Start with page 7, tool writes to .txt file
# Use layout mode to preserve horizontal position
pdftotext -f 7 -layout data/Preface-snapshot.pdf
# Remove 25 spaces from start of lines
# Wrap other lines that are too wide
sed -E 's/^ {,25}//' data/Preface-snapshot.txt |
    fmt -s |
    head -20
```

```
• Missing data in the Favorite Color field should be substituted with
the string <missing>.
• Student ages should be between 9 and 14, and all other values are
considered missing data.
• Some colors are numerically coded, but should be dealiased. The
mapping is:
```

Number	Color	Number	Color
1	beige	6	alabaster
2	eggshell	7	sandcastle
3	seafoam	8	chartreuse
4	mint	9	sepia
5	cream	10	lemon

```
Using the small test data set is a good way to test your code. But try
also manually adding more rows with similar, or different, problems in
them, and see how well your code produces a reasonable result.
```

The tabular part in the middle would be simple to read as a fixed width format. The bullets at the top or the paragraph at the bottom might be useful for other data extraction purposes. In any case, it is plain text at this point, which is easy to work with.

Let us turn now to analyzing images, mostly for their metadata and overall statistical characteristics.

Image Formats

As the Chinese say, 1001 words is worth more than a picture.

–John McCarthy picture

picture

The quote McCarthy plays off of is not, of course, of ancient Chinese origin. Like much early 20th century American sinophilia—inevitably tinged with sinophobia—it originated with an advertising agency. Henrik Ibsen had said "A thousand words leave not the same deep impression as does a single deed" prior to his 1906 death. This was adapted in March 1911 by Arthur Brisbane speaking to the Syracuse Advertising Men's Club, as "Use a picture. It's worth a thousand words." Later repetitions added the alleged source as a "Chinese proverb" or even a false attribution to Confucius specifically, presumably to lend credence to the slogan.

Concepts:

- OCR and image recognition (outside scope)
- Color models
- Pixel statistics
- Channel preprocessing
- Image metadata

For certain purposes, raster images are themselves the datasets of interest to us. "Raster" just means rectangular collections of pixel values. The field of machine learning around image recognition and image processing is far outside the scope of this book. The few techniques in this section might be useful to get your data ready to the point of developing input to those tools, but no further than that.

Also not considered in this book are other kinds of recognition of the *content* of images at a high-level. For example, optical character recognition (OCR) tools might recognize an image as containing various strings and numbers as rendered fonts, and those values might be the data we care about.

If you have the misfortune of having data that is only available in printed and scanned form, you most certainly have my deep sympathy. Scanning the images using OCR is likely to produce noisy results with many misrecognitions. Detecting those is addressed in *Chapter 4, Anomaly Detection*; essentially, you will get either wrong strings or wrong numbers when these errors happen, and ideally the errors will be identifiable. However, the specifics of those technologies are not within the current scope.

For this section, we merely want to present tools to read in images as numeric arrays, and perform a few basic processing steps that might be used in your downstream data analysis or modeling. Within Python, the library Pillow is the go-to tool (backward-compatible successor to **PIL**, which is deprecated). Within R, the imager library seems to be most widely used for the general-purpose tasks of this section. As a first task, let us examine and describe the raster images used in the creation of this book:

```
from PIL import Image, ImageOps

for fname in glob('img/*'):
    try:
        with Image.open(fname) as im:
            print(fname, im.format, "%dx%d" % im.size, im.mode)
    except IOError:
        pass
```

```
img/Flu2009-infobox.png PNG 607x702 RGBA
img/Konfuzius-1770.jpg JPEG 566x800 RGB
img/UMAP.png PNG 2400x2400 RGBA
img/DQM-with-Lenin-Minsk.jpg MPO 3240x4320 RGB
img/HDFCompass.png PNG 958x845 RGBA
img/t-SNE.png PNG 2400x2400 RGBA
img/preface-2.png PNG 945x427 RGBA
img/DQM-with-Lenin-Minsk.jpg_original MPO 3240x4320 RGB
img/PCA.png PNG 2400x2400 RGBA
img/Excel-Pitfalls.png PNG 551x357 RGBA
img/gnosis-traffic.png PNG 1064x1033 RGBA
img/Film_Awards.png PNG 1587x575 RGBA
img/HTTP-status-codes.png PNG 934x686 RGBA
img/preface-1.png PNG 988x798 RGBA
```

We see that mostly PNG images were used, with a smaller number of JPEGs. Each has certain spatial dimensions, by width then height, and each is either RGB, or RGBA if it includes an alpha channel. Other images might be HSV format. Converting between color spaces is easy enough using tools like Pillow and imager, but it is important to be aware of which model a given image uses. Let us read one in, this time using R:

```
%%R
library(imager)
confucius <- load.image("img/Konfuzius-1770.jpg")
print(confucius)
plot(confucius)
```

Image. Width: 566 pix Height: 800 pix Depth: 1 Colour channels: 3

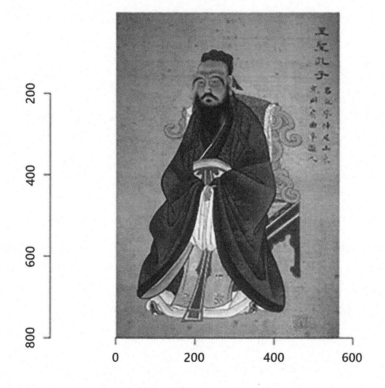

Figure 3.5: Confucius

Let us analyze the contours of the pixels.

Pixel Statistics

We can work on getting a feel for the data, which at heart is simply an array of values, with some tools the library provides. In the case of imager, which is built on **CImg**, the internal representation is 4-dimensional. Each plane is an X by Y grid of pixels (left-to-right, top-to-bottom). However, the format can represent a stack of images—for example, an animation—in the depth dimension. The several color channels (if the image is not grayscale) are the final dimension of the array. The Confucius example is a single image, so the third dimension is of length one. Let us look at some summary data about the image:

```
%%R
grayscale(confucius) %>%
    hist(main="Luminance values in Confucius drawing")
```

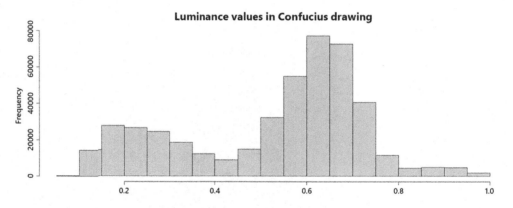

Figure 3.6: Histogram of luminance values in the Confucius drawing

Perhaps we would like to look at the distribution only of one color channel instead:

```
%%R
B(confucius) %>%
    hist(main="Blue values in Confucius drawing")
```

Blue values in Confucius drawing

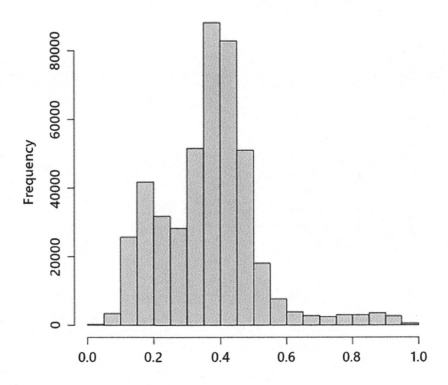

Figure 3.7: Histogram of blue values in the Confucius drawing

The preceding histograms simply utilize the standard R histogram function. There is nothing special about the fact that the data represents an image. We could perform whatever statistical tests or summarizations we wanted on the data to make sure it *makes sense* for our purpose; a histogram is only a simple example to show the concept. We can also easily transform the data into a tidy data frame. As of this writing, there is an "impedance error" in converting directly to a tibble, so the cell below uses an intermediate `data.frame` format.

Tibbles are *often* but not *always* drop-in replacements when functions were written to work with data.frame objects:

```
%%R
data <- as.data.frame(confucius) %>%
    as_tibble %>%
    # channels 1, 2, 3 (RGB) as factor
    mutate(cc = as.factor(cc))
data
```

```
# A tibble: 1,358,400 x 4
          x     y cc    value
      <int> <int> <fct> <dbl>
   1      1     1 1     0.518
   2      2     1 1     0.529
   3      3     1 1     0.518
   4      4     1 1     0.510
   5      5     1 1     0.533
   6      6     1 1     0.541
   7      7     1 1     0.533
   8      8     1 1     0.533
   9      9     1 1     0.510
  10     10     1 1     0.471
# ... with 1,358,390 more rows
```

With Python and PIL/Pillow, working with image data is very similar. As in R, the image is an array of pixel values with some metadata attached to it. Just for fun, we use a variable name with Chinese characters to illustrate that such is supported in Python:

```
# Courtesy name: Zhòngní (仲尼)
# "Kǒng Fūzǐ" (孔夫子) was coined by 16th century Jesuits
仲尼 = Image.open('img/Konfuzius-1770.jpg')
data = np.array(仲尼)
print("Image shape:", data.shape)
print("Some values\n", data[:2, :, :])
```

```
Image shape: (800, 566, 3)
Some values
 [[[132  91  69]
  [135  94  74]
  [132  91  71]

  ...
```

```
       [148    98    73]
       [142    95    69]
       [135    89    63]]

      [[131    90    68]
       [138    97    75]
       [139    98    78]
       ...
       [147   100    74]
       [144    97    71]
       [138    92    66]]]
```

In the Pillow format, images are stored as 8-bit unsigned integers rather than as floating-point numbers in the [0.0, 1.0] range. Converting between these is easy enough, of course, as is other normalization. For example, for many neural network tasks, the preferred representation is values centered at zero with a standard deviation of one. The array used to hold Pillow images is 3-dimensional since it does not have provision for stacking multiple images in the same object.

Channel Manipulation

It might be useful to perform manipulation of image data before processing. The following example is contrived, and similar to one used in the library tutorial. The idea in the next few code lines is that we will mask the image based on the values in the blue channel, but then use that to selectively zero-out red values. The result is not visually attractive for a painting, but one can imagine it might be useful for medical imaging or false-color radio astronomy images, for example (I am also working around making a transformation that is easily visible in a monochrome book as well as in full color).

The convention used in the .paste() method below is a bit odd. The rule is: where the mask is 255, copied as is; where mask is 0, preserve current value (blend if intermediate). The effect overall in the color version is that in the mostly red-tinged image, the greens dominate at the edges where the image had been most red. In grayscale, it mostly just darkens the edges:

```
# split the Confucius image into individual bands
source = 仲尼.split()
R, G, B = 0, 1, 2

# select regions where blue is less than 100
mask = source[B].point(lambda i: 255 if i < 100 else 0)
source[R].paste(0, None, mask)
```

```
im = Image.merge(仲尼.mode, source)
ImageOps.scale(im, 0.5)
```

Figure 3.8: Processed Confucius image (left), original image (right)

Another example we mentioned is that transformation of the color space might be useful. For example, rather than look at the colors red, green, and blue, it might be that hue, saturation, and lightness are better features for your modeling needs. This is a deterministic transformation of the data, but emphasizing different aspects. It is something analogous to decompositions such as principal component analysis, which is discussed in *Chapter 7, Feature Engineering*. Here we convert from an RGB to HSL representation of the image:

```
%%R
confucius.hsv <- RGBtoHSL(confucius)
data <- as.data.frame(confucius.hsv) %>%
    as_tibble %>%
    # channels 1, 2, 3 (HSV) as factor
    mutate(cc = as.factor(cc))
data
```

```
# A tibble: 1,358,400 x 4
        x     y cc    value
    <int> <int> <fct> <dbl>
  1     1     1 1      21.0
  2     2     1 1      19.7
```

```
 3      3     1 1      19.7
 4      4     1 1      19.7
 5      5     1 1      19.7
 6      6     1 1      19.7
 7      7     1 1      19.7
 8      8     1 1      19.7
 9      9     1 1      19.7
10     10     1 1      20
# ... with 1,358,390 more rows
```

Both the individual values and the shape of the space have changed in this transformation. The transformation is lossless, beyond minor rounding issues. A summary by channel will illustrate this:

```
%%R
data %>%
    mutate(cc = recode(
        cc, '1'="Hue", '2'="Saturation", '3'="Value")) %>%
    group_by(cc) %>%
    summarize(Mean = mean(value), SD = sd(value))
```

```
'summarise()' ungrouping output (override with '.groups' argument)
# A tibble: 3 x 3
  cc             Mean      SD
  <fct>         <dbl>   <dbl>
1 Hue            34.5    59.1
2 Saturation    0.448   0.219
3 Value         0.521   0.192
```

Let us now look at perhaps the most important aspect of images to data scientists.

Metadata

Photographic images may contain metadata embedded inside them. Specifically, the **Exchangeable Image File Format (Exif)** specifies how such metadata can be embedded in JPEG, TIFF, and WAV formats (the last is an audio format). Digital cameras typically add this information to the images they create, often including details such as timestamp and latitude/longitude location.

Some of the data fields within an Exif mapping are textual, numeric, or tuples; others are binary data. Moreover, the *keys* in the mapping are from ID numbers that are not meaningful to humans directly; this mapping is a published standard, but some equipment makers may introduce their own IDs as well.

The binary fields contain a variety of types of data, encoded in various ways. For example, some cameras may attach small preview images as Exif metadata, but simpler fields are also encoded.

The function below will utilize Pillow to return two dictionaries, one for the textual data, the other for the binary data. Tag IDs are expanded to human-readable names, where available. Pillow uses "camel case" for these names, but other tools have different variations on capitalization and punctuation within the tag names. The casing by Pillow is what I like to call Bactrian case—as opposed to Dromedary case— both of which differ from Python's usual "snake case" (e.g. BactrianCase versus dromedaryCase versus snake_case):

```python
from PIL.ExifTags import TAGS

def get_exif(img):
    txtdata, bindata = dict(), dict()
    for tag_id in (exifdata := img.getexif()):
        # Lookup tag name from tag_id if available
        tag = TAGS.get(tag_id, tag_id)
        data = exifdata.get(tag_id)
        if isinstance(data, bytes):
            bindata[tag] = data
        else:
            txtdata[tag] = data
    return txtdata, bindata
```

Let us check whether the Confucius image has any metadata attached:

```python
get_exif(仲尼)  # Zhòngní, i.e. Confucius
```

```
({}, {})
```

We see that this image does not have any such metadata. Let us look instead at a photograph taken of the author next to a Lenin statue in Minsk:

```python
# Could continue using multi-lingual variable names by
# choosing 'Ленин', 'Ульянов' or 'Мінск'
dqm = Image.open('img/DQM-with-Lenin-Minsk.jpg')
ImageOps.scale(dqm, 0.1)
```

Figure 3.9: The Author after keynote at PyCon Belarus

This image, taken with a digital camera, indeed has Exif metadata. These generally concern photographic settings, which are perhaps valuable to analyze in comparing images. This example also has a timestamp, although not in this case a latitude/longitude position (the camera used did not have a GPS sensor). Location data, where available, can obviously be valuable for many purposes:

```
txtdata, bindata = get_exif(dqm)
txtdata
```

```
{'CompressedBitsPerPixel': 4.0,
 'DateTimeOriginal': '2015:02:01 13:01:53',
 'DateTimeDigitized': '2015:02:01 13:01:53',
 'ExposureBiasValue': 0.0,
 'MaxApertureValue': 4.2734375,
 'MeteringMode': 5,
 'LightSource': 0,
 'Flash': 16,
 'FocalLength': 10.0,
 'ColorSpace': 1,
 'ExifImageWidth': 3240,
 'ExifInteroperabilityOffset': 10564,
 'FocalLengthIn35mmFilm': 56,
 'SceneCaptureType': 0,
 'ExifImageHeight': 4320,
```

```
    'Contrast': 0,
    'Saturation': 0,
    'Sharpness': 0,
    'Make': 'Panasonic',
    'Model': 'DMC-FH4',
    'Orientation': 1,
    'SensingMethod': 2,
    'YCbCrPositioning': 2,
    'ExposureTime': 0.00625,
    'XResolution': 180.0,
    'YResolution': 180.0,
    'FNumber': 4.4,
    'ExposureProgram': 2,
    'CustomRendered': 0,
    'ISOSpeedRatings': 500,
    'ResolutionUnit': 2,
    'ExposureMode': 0,
    34864: 1,
    'WhiteBalance': 0,
    'Software': 'Ver.1.0  ',
    'DateTime': '2015:02:01 13:01:53',
    'DigitalZoomRatio': 0.0,
    'GainControl': 2,
    'ExifOffset': 634}
```

One detail we notice in the textual data is that the tag ID 34864 was not unaliased by Pillow. I can locate external documentation indicating that the ID should indicate "Exif.Photo.SensitivityType", but Pillow is apparently unaware of that ID. The bytes strings may contain data you wish to utilize, but the meaning given to each field is different and must be compared to reference definitions. For example, the field ExifVersion is defined as ASCII bytes, but *not* as UTF-8 encoded bytes like regular text field values. We can view that using:

```
bindata['ExifVersion'].decode('ascii')
```

```
'0230'
```

In contrast, the tag named ComponentsConfiguration consists of four bytes, with each byte representing a color code. The get_exif() function produces separate text and binary dictionaries (txtdata and bindata). Let us decode bindata with a new special function:

```
def components(cc):
    colors = {0: None,
```

```
                1: 'Y', 2: 'Cb', 3: 'Cr',
                4: 'R', 5: 'G', 6: 'B'}
    return [colors.get(c, 'reserved') for c in cc]
components(bindata['ComponentsConfiguration'])
```

```
['Y', 'Cb', 'Cr', None]
```

Other binary fields are encoded in other ways. The specifications are maintained by the Japan Electronic Industries Development Association (JEIDA). This section intends only to give you a feel for working with this kind of metadata, and is by no means a complete reference.

Let us turn our attention now to the specialized binary data formats we sometimes need to work with.

Binary Serialized Data Structures

I usually solve problems by letting them devour me.

–Franz Kafka

Concepts:

- Prefer existing libraries
- Bytes and struct data types
- Offset layout of data

There are a great many binary formats that data might live in. Everything very popular has grown good open source libraries, but you may encounter some legacy or in-house format for which this is not true. Good general advice is that unless there is an ongoing and/or performance sensitive need for processing an unusual format, try to leverage existing parsers. Custom formats can be tricky, and if one is uncommon, it is as likely as not also to be underdocumented.

If an existing tool is only available in a language you do not wish to use for your main data science work, nonetheless see if that can be easily leveraged to act only as a means to export to a more easily accessed format. A fire-and-forget tool might be all you need, even if it is one that runs recurringly, but asynchronously with the actual data processing you need to perform.

For this section, let as assume that the optimistic situation is not realized, and we have nothing beyond some bytes on disk, and some possibly flawed documentation to work with. Writing the custom code is much more the job of a systems engineer than a data scientist; but we data scientists need to be polymaths, and we should not be daunted by writing a little bit of systems code.

For this relatively short section, we look at a simple and straightforward binary format. Moreover, this is a real-world data format for which we do not actually need a custom parser. Having an actual well-tested, performant, and bullet-proof parser to compare our toy code with is a good way to make sure we do the right thing. Specifically, we will read data stored in the NumPy NPY format (`https://docs.scipy.org/doc/numpy/reference/generated/numpy.lib.format.html#module-numpy.lib.format`), which is documented as follows (abridged):

- The first 6 bytes are a magic string: exactly \x93NUMPY

- The next 1 byte is an unsigned byte: the major version number of the file format, e.g. \x01

- The next 1 byte is an unsigned byte: the minor version number of the file format, e.g. \x00.

- The next 2 bytes form a little-endian unsigned short int: the length of the header data HEADER_LEN

- The next HEADER_LEN bytes are an ASCII string that contains a Python literal expression of a dictionary

- Following the header comes the array data

First, we read in some binary data using the standard reader, using Python and NumPy, to understand what type of object we are trying to reconstruct. It turns out that the serialization was of a 3-dimensional array of 64-bit floating-point values. A small size was chosen for this section, but of course, real-world data will generally be much larger:

```
arr = np.load(open('data/binary-3d.npy', 'rb'))
print(arr, '\n', arr.shape, arr.dtype)

[[[ 0.  1.  2.]
  [ 3.  4.  5.]]

 [[ 6.  7.  8.]
  [ 9. 10. 11.]]]
(2, 2, 3) float64
```

Visually examining the bytes is a good way to have a better feel for what is going on with the data. NumPy is, of course, a clearly and correctly documented project, but for some hypothetical format, this is an opportunity to potentially identify problems with the documentation not matching the actual bytes. More subtle issues may arise in the more detailed parsing; for example, the meaning of bytes in a particular location can be contingent on flags occurring elsewhere. Data science is, in surprisingly large part, a matter of eyeballing data:

```
%%bash
hexdump -Cv data/binary-3d.npy
```

```
00000000  93 4e 55 4d 50 59 01 00  76 00 7b 27 64 65 73 63  |.NUMPY..v.{'desc|
00000010  72 27 3a 20 27 3c 66 38  27 2c 20 27 66 6f 72 74  |r': '<f8', 'fort|
00000020  72 61 6e 5f 6f 72 64 65  72 27 3a 20 46 61 6c 73  |ran_order': Fals|
00000030  65 2c 20 27 73 68 61 70  65 27 3a 20 28 32 2c 20  |e, 'shape': (2, |
00000040  32 2c 20 33 29 2c 20 7d  20 20 20 20 20 20 20 20  |2, 3), }        |
00000050  20 20 20 20 20 20 20 20  20 20 20 20 20 20 20 20  |                |
00000060  20 20 20 20 20 20 20 20  20 20 20 20 20 20 20 20  |                |
00000070  20 20 20 20 20 20 20 20  20 20 20 20 20 20 20 0a  |               .|
00000080  00 00 00 00 00 00 00 00  00 00 00 00 00 00 f0 3f  |...............?|
00000090  00 00 00 00 00 00 00 40  00 00 00 00 00 00 08 40  |.......@.......@|
000000a0  00 00 00 00 00 00 10 40  00 00 00 00 00 00 14 40  |.......@.......@|
000000b0  00 00 00 00 00 00 18 40  00 00 00 00 00 00 1c 40  |.......@.......@|
000000c0  00 00 00 00 00 00 20 40  00 00 00 00 00 00 22 40  |...... @......"@|
000000d0  00 00 00 00 00 00 24 40  00 00 00 00 00 00 26 40  |......$@......&@|
000000e0
```

As a first step, let us make sure the file really does match the type we expect in having the correct "magic string." Many kinds of files are identified by a characteristic and distinctive first few bytes. In fact, the common utility on Unix-like systems, `file`, uses exactly this knowledge via a database describing many file types. For a hypothetical rare file type (i.e. not NumPy), this utility may not know about the format; nonetheless, the file might still have such a header:

```
%%bash
file data/binary-3d.npy
```

```
data/binary-3d.npy: NumPy array, version 1.0, header length 118
```

With that, let us open a file handle for the file and proceed with trying to parse it according to its specification. For this, in Python, we will simply open the file in bytes mode, so as not to convert to text, and read various segments of the file to verify or process portions.

For this format, we will be able to process it strictly sequentially, but in other cases it might be necessary to seek to particular byte positions within the file. The Python struct module will allow us to parse basic numeric types from bytestrings. The ast module will let us create Python data structures from raw strings without a security risk that eval() can encounter:

```python
import struct, ast
binfile = open('data/binary-3d.npy', 'rb')

# Check that the magic header is correct
if binfile.read(6) == b'\x93NUMPY':
    vermajor = ord(binfile.read(1))
    verminor = ord(binfile.read(1))
    print(f"Data appears to be NPY format, "
          f"version {vermajor}.{verminor}")
else:
    print("Data in unsupported file format")
    print("*** ABORT PROCESSING ***")
```

```
Data appears to be NPY format, version 1.0
```

Next we need to determine how long the header is, and then read it in. The header is always ASCII in NPY version 1, but may be UTF-8 in version 3. Since ASCII is a subset of UTF-8, decoding does no harm even if we do not check the version:

```python
# Little-endian short int (tuple 0 element)
header_len = struct.unpack('<H', binfile.read(2))[0]
# Read specified number of bytes
header = binfile.read(header_len)
# Convert header bytes to a dictionary
# Use safer ast.literal_eval()
header_dict = ast.literal_eval(header.decode('utf-8'))
print(f"Read {header_len} bytes "
      f"into dictionary: \n{header_dict}")
```

```
Read 118 bytes into dictionary:
{'descr': '<f8', 'fortran_order': False, 'shape': (2, 2, 3)}
```

While this dictionary stored in the header gives a nice description of the dtype, value order, and the shape, the convention used by NumPy for value types is different from that used in the struct module. We can define a (partial) mapping to obtain the correct spelling of the data type for the reader. We only define this mapping for some data types encoded as little-endian, but the big-endian versions would simply have a greater-than sign instead.

The key for `'fortran_order'` indicates whether the fastest or slowest varying dimension is contiguous in memory. Most systems use "C order" instead.

We are not aiming for high efficiency here, but to minimize code. Therefore, I will expediently read the actual data into a simple list of values first, and then later convert that to a NumPy array:

```
# Define spelling of data types and find the struct code
dtype_map = {'<i2': '<i', '<i4': '<l', '<i8': '<q',
             '<f2': '<e', '<f4': '<f', '<f8': '<d'}
dtype = header_dict['descr']
fcode = dtype_map[dtype]
# Determine number of bytes from dtype spec
nbytes = int(dtype[2:])

# List to hold values
values = []

# Python 3.8+ "walrus operator"
while val_bytes := binfile.read(nbytes):
    values.append(struct.unpack(fcode, val_bytes)[0])

print("Values:", values)
```

```
Values: [0.0, 1.0, 2.0, 3.0, 4.0, 5.0, 6.0, 7.0, 8.0, 9.0, 10.0, 11.0]
```

Let us now convert the raw values into an actual NumPy array of appropriate shape and dtype. We will also look for whether to use Fortran- or C-order in memory:

```
shape = header_dict['shape']
order = 'F' if header_dict['fortran_order'] else 'C'
newarr = np.array(values, dtype=dtype, order=order)
newarr = newarr.reshape(shape)
print(newarr, '\n', newarr.shape, newarr.dtype)
print("\nMatched standard parser:", (arr == newarr).all())
```

```
[[[ 0.  1.  2.]
  [ 3.  4.  5.]]

 [[ 6.  7.  8.]
  [ 9. 10. 11.]]]
 (2, 2, 3) float64

Matched standard parser: True
```

Just as binary data can be oddball, so can text.

Custom Text Formats

Need we emphasize the similarity of these two sequences? Yes, for the resemblance we have in mind is not a simple collection of traits chosen only in order to delete their difference. And it would not be enough to retain those common traits at the expense of the others for the slightest truth to result. It is rather the intersubjectivity in which the two actions are motivated that we wish to bring into relief, as well as the three terms through which it structures them.

–Jacques Lacan

Concepts:

- Line-oriented and hierarchical structures
- Heuristics to identify data of interest
- Character encodings and mojibake
- Guessing with chardet (character detection)

In life as a data scientist, but especially if you occasionally wear the hat of a systems administrator or similar role, you will encounter textual data with unusual formats. Log files are one common source of these kinds of files. Many or most log files *do* stick to the record-per-line convention; if so, we are given an easy way to separate records. From there, a variety of rules or heuristics can be used to determine exactly what *kind* of record the line corresponds to.

Not all log files, however, stick to a line convention. Moreover, over time, you will likewise encounter other types of files produced by tools that store nested data and chose to create their own format rather than use some widely used standard. For hierarchical or other non-tabular structures, the motivation for eschewing strict record-per-line format is often compelling and obvious.

In many cases, the authors of the programs creating one-off formats are entirely free of blame. Standard formats for representing non-tabular data did not exist a decade prior to this writing in 2020, or at least were not widely adopted across a range of programming languages in that not-so-distant past. Depending on your exact domain, legacy data and formats are likely to dominate your work. For example, JSON was first standardized in 2013, as ECMA-404. YAML was created in 2001, but not widely used before approximately 2010. XML dates to 1996, but has remained unwieldy for human-readable formats since then. Hence many programmers have gone their own way, and left as traces the files you now need to import, analyze, and process.

A Structured Log

Scanning my own system, I found a good example of a reasonably human-readable log file that is not parsable in a line-oriented manner. The Perl package management tool cpan logs the installation actions of each library it manages. The format used for such logs varies per package (very much in a Perl style). The package *Archive::Zip* left the discussed log on my system (for its self-tests). This data file contains sections that are actual Perl code defining test classes, interspersed with unformatted output messages. Each of the classes has a variety of attributes, largely overlapping but not identical. A sensible memory data format for this is a data frame with missing values marked where a given attribute name does not exist for a class.

Obviously, we could use Perl itself to process those class definitions. However, that is unlikely to be the programming language we wish to actually use to work with the data extracted. We will use Python to read the format, and use only heuristics about what elements we expect. Notably, we *cannot* statically parse Perl, which task was shown to be strictly equivalent to solving the halting problem (https://en.wikipedia.org/wiki/Halting_problem) by Jeffrey Kegler in several 2008 essays for The Perl Review (http://www.jeffreykegler.com/Home/perl-and-undecidability). Nonetheless, the output in our example uses a friendly, but not formally defined, subset of the Perl language. Here is a bit of the file being processed:

```bash
%%bash
head -25 data/archive-zip.log
```

```
zipinfo output:
$ZIP = bless( {
  "versionNeededToExtract" => 0,
  "numberOfCentralDirectories" => 1,
  "centralDirectoryOffsetWRTStartingDiskNumber" => 360,
  "fileName" => "",
  "centralDirectorySize" => 76,
  "writeCentralDirectoryOffset" => 0,
  "diskNumber" => 0,
  "eocdOffset" => 0,
  "versionMadeBy" => 0,
  "diskNumberWithStartOfCentralDirectory" => 0,
  "desiredZip64Mode" => 0,
  "zip64" => 0,
  "zipfileComment" => "",
  "members" => [],
  "numberOfCentralDirectoriesOnThisDisk" => 1,
  "writeEOCDOffset" => 0
```

```
}, 'Archive::Zip::Archive' );

Found EOCD at 436 (0x1b4)

Found central directory for member #1 at 360
$CDMEMBER1 = bless( {
  "compressedSize" => 300,
```

Computer science theory to the side, we can notice some patterns in the file that will suffice for us. Every *record* that we care about starts a line with a dollar sign, which is the marker used for variable names in Perl and some other languages. That line also happens to follow with the class constructor bless(). We find the end of the record by a line ending with);. On that same last line, we also find the name of the class being defined, but we do not, in this example, wish to retain the common prefix Archive::Zip:: that they all use. Also stipulated for this example is that we will not try to process any additional data that is contained in the output lines.

Clearly it would be possible to create a valid construction of a Perl class that our heuristic rules will fail to capture accurately. However, our goal here is not to implement the Perl language, but only to parse the very small subset of it contained in this particular file (and hopefully cover a family of similar logs that may exist for other CPAN libraries). A small state machine is constructed to branch within a loop over lines of the file:

```python
def parse_cpan_log(fh):
    "Take a file-like object, produce a DF of classes generated"
    import pandas as pd
    # Python dictionaries are ordered in 3.6+
    classes = {}
    in_class = False

    for n, line in enumerate(fh):
        # Remove surrounding whitespace
        line = line.strip()
        # Is this a new definition?
        if line.startswith('$'):
            new_rec = {}
            in_class = True # One or more variables contain the "state"
```

```
        # Is this the end of the definition?
        elif line.endswith(');'):
            # Possibly fragile assumption of parts of line
            _, classname, _ = line.split()
            barename = classname.replace('Archive::Zip::', '')
            # Just removing extra quotes this way
            name = ast.literal_eval(barename)
            # Distinguish entries with same name by line number
            classes[f"{name}_{n}"] = new_rec
            in_class = False

        # We are still finding new key/val pairs
        elif in_class:
            # Split around Perl map operator
            key, val = [s.strip() for s in line.split('=>')]
            # No trailing comma, if it was present
            val = val.rstrip(',')
            # Special null value needs to be translated
            val = "None" if val == "undef" else val
            # Also, just quote variables in vals
            val = f'"{val}"' if val.startswith("$") else val
            # Safe evaluate strings to Python objects
            key = ast.literal_eval(key)
            val = ast.literal_eval(val)
            # Add to record dictionary
            new_rec[key] = val

    return pd.DataFrame(classes).T
```

The function defined is a bit longer than most examples in this book, but is typical of a small text processing function. The use of the state variable in_class is common when various lines may belong to one domain of parsing or another. This pattern of looking for a start state based on something about a line, accumulating contents, then looking for a stop state based on a different line property is very common in these kinds of tasks. Beyond the state maintenance, the rest of the lines are, in the main, merely some minor string manipulation.

Let us now read and parse the data file:

```
df = parse_cpan_log(open('data/archive-zip.log'))
df.iloc[:, [4, 11, 26, 35]]  # Show only a few columns
```

	centralDirectorySize	zip64	crc32
Archive_18	76	0	NaN
ZipFileMember_53	NaN	0	2889301810
ZipFileMember_86	NaN	0	2889301810
Archive_113	72	1	NaN
...	...	...	...
ZipFileMember_466	NaN	0	3632233996
Archive_493	62	1	NaN
ZipFileMember_528	NaN	1	3632233996
ZipFileMember_561	NaN	1	3632233996

	lastModFileDateTime
Archive_18	NaN
ZipFileMember_53	1345061049
ZipFileMember_86	1345061049
Archive_113	NaN
...	...
ZipFileMember_466	1325883762
Archive_493	NaN
ZipFileMember_528	1325883770
ZipFileMember_561	1325883770

```
18 rows × 4 columns
```

In this case, the DataFrame might better be utilized as a Series with a hierarchical index:

```
with show_more_rows(25):
    print(df.unstack())
```

```
versionNeededToExtract  Archive_18            0
                        ZipFileMember_53      20
                        ZipFileMember_86      20
                        Archive_113           45
                        ZipFileMember_148     45
                        ZipFileMember_181     20
                        Archive_208           45
                        ZipFileMember_243     45
                        ZipFileMember_276     45
```

```
                          Archive_303            813
                          ZipFileMember_338       45
                          ZipFileMember_371       45
                                                 ...
fileAttributeFormat       Archive_208            NaN
                          ZipFileMember_243        3
                          ZipFileMember_276        3
                          Archive_303            NaN
                          ZipFileMember_338        3
                          ZipFileMember_371        3
                          Archive_398            NaN
                          ZipFileMember_433        3
                          ZipFileMember_466        3
                          Archive_493            NaN
                          ZipFileMember_528        3
                          ZipFileMember_561        3
Length: 720, dtype: object
```

Character Encodings

The question of character encodings of text formats is somewhat orthogonal to the data issues the bulk of this book addresses. However, being able to read the content of a text file is an essential step in processing the data within it, so we should look at possible problems. The problems that occur are an issue for "legacy encodings," but should be solved as text formats standardized on Unicode. That said, it is not uncommon that you need to deal with files that are decades old, either preceding Unicode altogether, or created before organizations and software (such as operating systems) fully standardized their text formats to Unicode. We will look both at the problems that arise and heuristic tools to solve them.

The American Standard Code for Information Interchange (ASCII) was created in the 1960s as a standard for encoding text data. However, at the time, in the United States, consideration was only made to encode the characters used in English text. This included upper and lowercase characters, some basic punctuation, numerals, and a few other special or control characters (such as newline and the terminal bell). To accommodate this collection of symbols, 128 positions were sufficient, so the ASCII standard defines only values for 8-bit bytes where the *high-order bit* is a zero. Any byte with a high-order bit set to 1 is not an ASCII character.

Extending the ASCII standard in a "compatible" way are the ISO-8859 character encodings. These were developed to cover the characters in (approximately) phonemic alphabets, primarily those originating in Europe. Many alphabetic languages are based on Roman letters, but add a variety of diacritics that are not used in English.

Other alphabets are of moderate size, but unrelated to English in letter forms, such as Cyrillic, Greek, and Hebrew. All of the encodings that make up the ISO-8859 family preserve the low-order values of ASCII, but encode additional characters using the high-order bits of each byte. The problem is that 128 additional values (in a byte with 256 total values) is not large enough to accommodate all of those different extra characters, so particular members of the family (e.g. ISO-8859-6 for Arabic) use the high-order bit values in incompatible ways. This allows English text to be represented in all encodings in this family, but each sibling is mutually incompatible.

For CJK languages (Chinese-Japanese-Korean), the number of characters needed is vastly larger than 256, so any single byte encoding is not suitable to represent these languages. Most encodings that were created for these languages use 2 bytes for each character, but some are of variable length. However, a great many incompatible encodings were created, not only for the different languages, but also within a particular language. For example, EUC-JP, SHIFT_JIS, and ISO-2022-JP are all encodings used to represent Japanese text, in mutually incompatible ways. Abugida writing systems, such as Devanagari, Telugu, or Ge'ez, represent syllables, and hence have larger character sets than alphabetic systems; however, most do not utilize letter case, hence roughly halving the code points needed.

Adding to the historical confusion, not only do other encodings outside of the ISO-8859 family exist for alphabetic languages (including some also covered by an ISO-8859 member), but Microsoft, in the 1980s, fervently pursued its "embrace-extend-extinguish" strategy to try to kill open standards. In particular, the windows-12NN character encodings are deliberately "almost-but-not-quite" the same as corresponding ISO-8859 encodings. For example, windows-1252 uses most of the same code points as ISO-8859-1, but is just different enough as not to be entirely compatible.

The sometimes amusing, but usually frustrating, result of trying to decode a byte sequence using the wrong encoding is called mojibake (meaning "character transformation" in Japanese, or, more holistically, "corrupted text"). Depending on the pairs of encoding used for writing and reading, the text may superficially resemble genuine text, or it might have displayed markers for unavailable characters and/or punctuation symbols that are clearly misplaced.

Unicode is a specification of code points for all characters in all human languages. It may be *encoded* as bytes in multiple ways. However, if a format other than the default and prevalent UTF-8 is used, the file will always have a "magic number" at its start, and the first few bytes will unambiguously encode the byte length and endianness of the encoding. UTF-8 files are neither required nor encouraged to use a byte-order mark (BOM), but one exists that is not ambiguous with any code points. UTF-8 itself is a variable length encoding; all ASCII characters remain encoded as a single byte, but for other characters, special values that use the high-order bit trigger an expectation to read additional bytes to decide what Unicode character is encoded. For the data scientist, it is enough to know that all modern programming languages and tools handle Unicode files seamlessly.

The next few short texts are snippets of Wikipedia articles on character encoding written for various languages:

```
for fname in glob('data/character-encoding-*.txt'):
    bname = os.path.basename(fname)
    try:
        open(fname).read()
        print("Read 'successfully':", bname, "\n")
    except Exception as err:
        print("Error in", bname)
        print(err, "\n")
```

```
Error in character-encoding-nb.txt
'utf-8' codec can't decode byte 0xc4 in position 171: invalid
continuation byte

Error in character-encoding-el.txt
'utf-8' codec can't decode byte 0xcc in position 0: invalid
continuation byte

Error in character-encoding-ru.txt
'utf-8' codec can't decode byte 0xbd in position 0: invalid start byte

Error in character-encoding-zh.txt
'utf-8' codec can't decode byte 0xd7 in position 0: invalid
continuation byte
```

Something goes wrong with trying to read the text in these files. If we are so fortunate as to know the encoding used, it is easy to remedy the issue. However, the files themselves do not record their encoding. In addition, depending on what fonts you are using for display, some characters may show as boxes or question marks on your screen, which makes identification of the problems harder:

```
zh_file = 'data/character-encoding-zh.txt'
print(open(zh_file, encoding='GB18030').read())
```

字符编码（英語：Character encoding）、字集碼是把字符集中的字符编码为指定集合中某一对象（例如：比特模式、自然数序列、8位元组或者电脉冲），以便文本在计算机中存储和通过通信网络的传递。常见的例子包括将拉丁字母表编码成摩斯电码和ASCII。

Even if we take a hint from the filename that the encoding represents Chinese text, we will either fail or get mojibake as a result if we use the wrong encoding in our attempt:

```
try:
    # Wrong Chinese encoding
    open(zh_file, encoding='GB2312').read()
except Exception as err:
    print("Error in", os.path.basename(zh_file))
    print(err)
```

```
Error in character-encoding-zh.txt
'gb2312' codec can't decode byte 0xd5 in position 12: illegal multibyte
sequence
```

Note that we did not see the error immediately. If we had only read 11 bytes, it would have been "valid" (but the wrong characters). Likewise, the `character-encoding-nb.txt` file above would have succeeded for an entire 170 bytes without encountering an issue. We can see a wrong guess going wrong in these files. For example:

```
ru_file = 'data/character-encoding-ru.txt'
print(open(ru_file, encoding='iso-8859-10').read())
```

```
—ÐŊÞā áØÜÔÞÛÞÕ (ÐÝÓÛ. character set) - âÐŊÛÕØæÐ,
ŪÐÔÐîéÐï ÚÞÔØāÞÕúā ÚÞÝÕ¡ÝÞÓ ÜÝÞÖÕÕãâÐ áØÜÔÞÛÞ ÐÛäÐÔÕØâÐ
(ÞŊë¡ÝÞ íÛÕŪÕŪŌÝâÐ âÕÚÚáâÐ: ŊāÚÕ, æÞää, ÚÝÞÛÕ ßāÕßØÝÐÝÕï).
ÂÐÚÐÏ âÐÐŊÛÕÖæÐ áÞßÞáāâÐÐÕÛÕïÕÕâ ÚÞÔÕÕÐÛÕ áØÜÔÞÛÕā ßÞáÛÕÕÐÐÞÔÔÔãÔãâÕÝÞáÝÕÝ ÞÛÕ ÔÞÔÔ ÞÛÞ ÝÞáÛÕÛÕÛÕÛ áØÜÔÞÛÞ ÞāāÞÞÛÕ ÐÛÕÔÞÔæÐÐ
(âÞ¡ÞÛ Ø âÐÐÐ Õ ÚÞÕÕ MÞāÚÞ, áÐÞÛÕÝÐÕëä äÚÔÞÛÕ ÝÐ äÚÞÐÕ,
ÝāÚÕŪÕ Ø ÕÕÞÞÛÕ æ (ŊÕâÞÚ) Õ ÚÞÜßâÔÕÝÐÞÐÞ).
```

Here we read *something*, but even without necessarily knowing any of the languages at issue, it is fairly clearly gibberish. As readers of English, we can at least recognize the base letters that these mostly diacritic forms derive from. They are jumbled together in a manner that doesn't follow any real sensible phonetic rules, such as vowels and consonants roughly alternating, or a meaningful capitalization pattern. Included here is the brief English phrase "character set."

In this particular case, the text genuinely is in the ISO-8859 family, but we chose the wrong sibling among them. This gives us one type of mojibake. As the filename hints at, this happens to be in Russian, and uses the Cyrillic member of the ISO-8859 family. Readers may not know the Cyrillic letters, but if you have seen any signage or text incidentally, this text will not look *obviously wrong*:

```
print(open(ru_file, encoding='iso-8859-5').read())
```

```
Набор символов (англ. character set) - таблица,
задающая кодировку конечного множества символов алфавита
(обычно элементов текста: букв, цифр, знаков препинания).
Такая таблица сопоставляет каждому символу последовательность
длиной в один или несколько символов другого алфавита
(точек и тире в коде Морзе, сигнальных флагов на флоте,
нулей и единиц (битов) в компьютере).
```

Similarly, if you have seen writing in Greek, this version will perhaps not look obviously wrong:

```
el_file = 'data/character-encoding-el.txt'
print(open(el_file, encoding='iso-8859-7').read())
```

```
Μια κωδικοποίηση χαρακτήρων αποτελείται από έναν κώδικα που
συσχετίζει ένα σύνολο χαρακτήρων όπως πχ οι χαρακτήρες που
χρησιμοποιούμε σε ένα αλφάβητο με ένα διαφορετικό σύνολο
πχ αριθμών, ή ηλεκτρικών σημάτων, προκειμένου να
διευκολυνθεί η αποθήκευση, διαχείριση κειμένου σε
υπολογιστικά συστήματα καθώς και η μεταφορά κειμένου μέσω
τηλεπικοινωνιακών δικτύων.
```

Merely being not obviously wrong in a language you are not familiar with is a weak standard to meet. Having native, or at least modestly proficient, readers of the languages in question will help, if that is possible. If this is not possible—which often it will not be if you are processing many files with many encodings—automated tools can make reasonable heuristic guesses. This does not guarantee correctness, but it is suggestive.

The way the Python chardet module works is similar to the code in all modern web browsers. HTML pages can declare their encoding in their headers, but this declaration is often wrong, for various reasons. Browsers do some hand-holding and try to make better guesses when the data clearly does not match declared encoding. The general idea in this detection is threefold. A detector will scan through multiple candidate encodings to reach a best guess:

- Under the candidate encoding, are any of the byte values or sequences simply invalid?
- Under the candidate encoding, is the character frequency similar to that typically encountered in the language(s) often encoded using that encoding?
- Under the candidate encoding, are digraph frequencies similar to those typically encountered?

We do not need to worry about the exact details of the probability ranking, just the API to use. Implementations of the same algorithm are available in a variety of programming languages. Let us look at the guesses chardet makes for some of our text files:

```python
import chardet

for fname in glob('data/character-encoding-*.txt'):
    # Read the file in binary mode
    bname = os.path.basename(fname)
    raw =  open(fname, 'rb').read()
    print(f"{bname} (best guess):")
    guess = chardet.detect(raw)
    print(f"    encoding: {guess['encoding']}")
    print(f"  confidence: {guess['confidence']}")
    print(f"    language: {guess['language']}")
    print()
```

```
character-encoding-nb.txt (best guess):
    encoding: ISO-8859-9
  confidence: 0.6275904603111617
    language: Turkish

character-encoding-el.txt (best guess):
    encoding: ISO-8859-7
  confidence: 0.9900553828371981
    language: Greek
```

```
character-encoding-ru.txt (best guess):
    encoding: ISO-8859-5
  confidence: 0.9621526092949461
    language: Russian


character-encoding-zh.txt (best guess):
    encoding: GB2312
  confidence: 0.99
    language: Chinese
```

These guesses are only partially correct. The language code nb is actually Norwegian Bokmål, not Turkish. This guess has a notably lower probability than others. Moreover, it was actually encoded using ISO-8859-10. However, in this particular text, all characters are identical between ISO-8859-9 and ISO-8859-10, so that aspect is not really wrong. A larger text would more reliably guess between Bokmål and Turkish by letter and digram frequency; it does not make much difference if that is correct for most purposes, since our concern as data scientists is to get the *data* correct:

```
print(open('data/character-encoding-nb.txt',
          encoding='iso-8859-9').read())
```

```
Tegnsett eller tegnkoding er det som i datamaskiner
definerer hvilket lesbart symbol som representeres av et gitt
heltall. Foruten Unicode finnes de nordiske bokstavene ÄÅÆÖØ
og äåæöø (i den rekkefølgen) i følgende tegnsett: ISO-8859-1,
ISO-8859-4, ISO-8859-9, ISO-8859-10, ISO-8859-14, ISO-8859-15
og ISO-8859-16.
```

The guess about the zh text is wrong as well. We have already tried reading that file as GB2312 and reached an explicit failure in doing so. This is where domain knowledge becomes relevant. GB18030 is strictly a superset of GB2312. In principle, the Python chardet module is aware of GB18030, so the problem is not a missing feature per se. Nonetheless, in this case, unfortunately, chardet guesses an impossible encoding, in which one or more encoded characters do not exist in the subset encoding.

The errors in encoding inference are illustrative, even if not too serious in these particular cases. Adding more text than 2-3 sentences would make guesses more reliable, and most text documents will be much longer. However, text formats for non-text data will typically only have short snippets of text, often just single words in a categorical feature.

The specific strings "blue", "mavi", "blå", "blau", and "sininen" are all plausible words in English, Turkish, Norwegian, German, and Finnish. The a-ring character does not occur in Turkish or English, but other than that, the distinction is strictly in vocabulary, not letter or digraph plausibility.

For example, a CSV file with personal names will only have clusters of 5-10 letters for each name, not full paragraphs. The number of letters and digraphs is small, and even if uncommon ones occur in isolation, that is hardly definitive. If you have some domain knowledge or guidance on the problem, you could write more custom code to validate candidate encodings against language-specific wordlists (including common names); even there, you would have to allow a certain rate of non-matches for misspellings and rare words.

Exercises

We present here two exercises. One of them deals with a custom binary format, the other with web scraping. Not every topic of this chapter is addressed in the exercises, but these two are important domains for practical data science.

Enhancing the NPY Parser

The binary data we read from the NPY was in the simplest format we could choose. For this exercise you want to process a somewhat more complex binary file using your own code. Write a custom function that reads a file into a NumPy array, and test it against several arrays you have serialized using `numpy.save()` or `numpy.savez()`.

The test cases for your function are at the URLs:

```
https://www.gnosis.cx/cleaning/students.npy
```

```
https://www.gnosis.cx/cleaning/students.npz
```

We have not previously looked at the NPZ format, but it is a zip archive of one or more NPY files, allowing both compression and storage of multiple arrays. Ideally, your function will handle both formats, and will determine which type of file you are reading based on the magic string in the first few bytes. As a first pass, only try to parse the NPY version, then enhance from there.

Using the official readers, we can see that this array adds something the earlier example had not. Specifically, it stores a `recarray` that combines several data types into each value in the array, as shown in the output below. The rules we described earlier in this chapter will actually still suffice, but you have to think about them carefully.

The data we want to match in your reader will be exactly the same as using the official reader:

```
students = np.load(open('data/students.npy', 'rb'))
print(students)
print("\nDtype:", students.dtype)
```

```
[[('Mia', 12, 1.3) ('Liam', 13, 0.6) ('Isabélla', 11, 2.1)]
 [('Mason', 12, 1.6) ('Olivia', 11, 2.3) ('Sophia', 12, 0.7)]]

Dtype: [('first', '<U8'), ('age', '<i2'), ('distance', '>f4')]
```

When you move on to processing the NPZ format, you can compare again with the official reader. As mentioned, this might have several arrays inside it, although only one is stored in the example:

```
arrs = np.load(open('data/students.npz', 'rb'))
print(arrs)
arrs.files
```

```
<numpy.lib.npyio.NpzFile object at 0x7f5e12d8d070>
['arr_0']
```

The contents of arr_0 within the NPZ file are identical to the single array in the NPY. However, after you have successfully parsed this NPZ file, try creating one or more others that actually do store multiple arrays, and parse those using custom code. Decide on the best API to use for a function that may need to return either one or several arrays. For this part of the task, the Python standard library module zipfile will be very helpful for you.

There is no reason this exercise has to be performed in Python. Other programming languages are perfectly well able to read binary data, and the general steps involved will be very similar to those performed in this chapter in the *Binary Serialized Data Structures* section. You could, for example, read the data within an NPY file into an R array instead.

Scraping Web Traffic

The author's web domain, gnosis.cx, has been operating for more than two decades, and retains most of the "Web 0.5" technology and visual style it was first authored with. One thing the web host provides, as do most others, is reports on traffic at the site (using nearly as ancient styling as that of the domain itself).

You can find the most current reports at:

https://www.gnosis.cx/stats/

A snapshot of the reports current at the time of this writing are also copied to:

https://www.gnosis.cx/cleaning/stats/

An image of the report page at the time of writing follows:

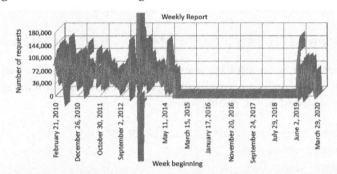

Report Navigation

- Executive Summary
- General Overview
- Yearly Report
- Quarterly Report
- Monthly Report
- Weekly Report
- Daily Report
- Daily Summary
- Hourly Report
- Hourly Summary
- Quarter-Hour Report
- Quarter-Hour Summary
- Five-Minute Report
- Five-Minute Summary
- Domain Report
- Organization Report
- Directory Report
- Request Report
- File Type Report
- File Size Report
- Status Code Report
- Failure Report
- Redirection Report

	Week beginning	Number of requests	Percentage of the requests
1.	March 29, 2020	5,932	0.04%
2.	March 22, 2020	5,764	0.03%
3.	March 15, 2020	6,723	0.04%
4.	March 8, 2020	7,912	0.05%
5.	March 1, 2020	5,842	0.03%
6.	February 23, 2020	11,223	0.07%
7.	February 16, 2020	59,701	0.35%
8.	February 9, 2020	58,200	0.34%
9.	February 2, 2020	44,511	0.26%
10.	January 26, 2020	39,916	0.23%
11.	January 19, 2020	36,728	0.21%
12.	January 12, 2020	38,820	0.23%
13.	January 5, 2020	35,549	0.21%
14.	December 29, 2019	31,319	0.18%
15.	December 22, 2019	31,822	0.19%

Figure 3.10: Traffic report for gnosis.cx

The weekly table shown is quite long since it goes back to February 2010. The actual site is a decade older than that, but servers and logging databases were modified, losing older data. There is also a rather large glitch of almost 5 years in the middle where traffic shows as zero. The rather dramatic fall in traffic over the 6 weeks up to the snapshot reflects a change to using a CDN proxy for DNS and SSL (hence hiding traffic from the actual web host).

Your goal in this exercise is to write a tool to dynamically scrape the data made available in the various tables listing traffic sliced by different time increments and recurring periods (which day of the week, which month of the year, and so on). As part of this exercise, have your scripts generate less terrible graphs than the one shown in the screen picture (meaningless false perspective in a line graph offends good sensibility, and the apparent negative spike to negative traffic around the start of 2013 is merely inexplicable).

It is a common need to scrape a website similar to these reports. The pattern of having a regular and infrequently changed structure but updated contents on a daily basis often reflects a data acquisition requirement. A script like the one you will write in this exercise could run on a cronjob or under a similar mechanism, to maintain local copies and revisions of such rolling reports.

Denouement

They invaded the hexagons, showed credentials which were not always false, leafed through a volume with displeasure and condemned whole shelves: their hygienic, ascetic furor caused the senseless perdition of millions of books.

–Jorge Luis Borges (The Library of Babel)

Topics covered in this chapter: Web Scraping; Portable Document Format; Image Formats; Binary Formats; Custom Text Formats.

This chapter contemplated data sources that you may not, in your first thought, think of as *data* per se. Within web pages and PDF documents, the intention is usually to present human-readable content that only contains analyzable data as a secondary concern. In the ideal situation, whoever produced those less structured documents will also provide structured versions of the same data; however, that ideal situation is only occasionally realized. A few nicely written Free Software libraries let us do a reasonable job of extracting meaningful data from these sources, albeit always in a way that is somewhat specific to the particular document, or at least to the family or revisions of a particular document.

Images are a very common interest in machine learning. Drawing various conclusions about, or characterizations of, the content portrayed in images is a key application of deep neural networks, for example. While those actual machine learning techniques are outside the scope of this particular book, this chapter introduced you to the basic APIs for acquiring an array/tensor representation of images, and performing some basic correction or normalization that will aid in those later machine learning models.

There are formats as well that, while directly intended as a means of recording and communicating data as such, are not widely used and tooling to read them directly may not be available to you. The specific examples we present, for both binary and textual custom formats, are ones that library support exists for (less so for the text format this chapter examines), but the general kinds of reasoning and approach to creating custom ingestion tools presented resemble those you will need to use when you encounter an antiquated, in-house, or merely idiosyncratic format.

The next chapter begins the next saga of this book. These early chapters paid special attention to data formats you need to work with. The next two chapters look at problems characteristic of data elements per se, not only their representation. We begin by looking for anomalies in data.

PART II

The Vicissitudes of Error

4

Anomaly Detection

The map is not the territory and data is not the world observed. Data is messy, inconsistent, and unreliable. The world is messier, less consistent, and less reliable.

–cf. Alfred Korzybski

When we think about anomaly detection, there are two distinct, and mostly independent, concepts that go by the name. The topic of this chapter is perhaps the less exciting of the two. Security and cryptography researchers, importantly, look for anomalies that can represent fraud, forgery, and system intrusion attempts. By the intention of perpetrators, these outliers in the normal patterns of data are subtle and hard to detect, and a conflict exists between those wishing to falsify data and those wishing to detect that falsification.

The concept of interest to us in this book is more quotidian. We wish to detect those cases where data goes bad in the ordinary course of its collection, collation, transmission, and transcription. Perhaps an instrument gives a bad reading some or all of the time. Perhaps some values are systematically altered in the course of reencoding to a different data format. Perhaps the wrong units of measure were used for a subset of the data. And so on. By accident, these broader checks may occasionally identify changes that reflect actual malice, but more often they will simply detect errors, and *perhaps* bias (but less often, since bias still is usually toward *plausible* values).

Anomaly detection has an especially close connection to *Chapter 5, Data Quality*, and often to the topic of *Chapter 6, Value Imputation*. The loose contrast between this chapter and the next one on data quality is that anomalies are individual data values that can be diagnosed as probably wrong, whereas data quality more broadly looks at *patterns* of the dataset as a whole that can present or identify problems.

When anomalies *are* detected it sometimes makes sense to impute more likely values rather than to discard those observations altogether. In terms of the structure of this book, the lessons of this chapter will allow you to identify and mark anomalies as "missing" while *Chapter 6, Value Imputation*, will pick up with filling in those better-imputed values (imputation is simply replacing mising data points with values that are likely, or at least plausible).

These connected chapters—4, 5, and 6—form a broader unit, and roughly describe a pipeline or series of steps. That is, given your inevitably flawed data you might first look for anomalies and mark them missing. Next you might look for more systematic attributes of your dataset, and remediate them in various ways. Finally, you might impute (or drop) data that was either missing to start with or marked so because of properties this chapter will help you detect. The step past the final step of this sequence is the actual modeling or analysis you perform, and is the subject of many excellent books, but not of this one.^{clean code}

clean code

My mention of these steps is a good opportunity to repeat an admonishment that has occurred elsewhere herein. The steps of your data processing pipeline should be coded and documented carefully and reproducibly. It is often easy and tempting to make changes to datasets in an exploratory way—as this book does—but in the process lose a good record of exactly what steps were taken. The exploration is an integral part of data science, but reproducibility should not be lost in that process. Good practice is to retain your original dataset—in whatever data format it originally presents itself—and generate the final version via scripts (maintained in version control) rather than within notebooks or interactive shells. Care must always be taken to allow someone else to repeatably move from the raw original dataset to the version that is fed into a machine learning model or other analytic tool. Keeping an audit trail of what tool or function produced what change is hygienic practice.

***

Before we get to the sections of this chapter, let us run our standard setup code:

```
from src.setup import *
%load_ext rpy2.ipython
```

```
%%R
library(tidyverse)
require("RPostgreSQL")
```

Missing Data

Gregory: Is there any other point to which you would wish to draw my attention?
Holmes: To the curious incident of the dog in the night-time.
Gregory: The dog did nothing in the night-time.
Holmes: That was the curious incident.

–Arthur Conan Doyle

Concepts:

- Sentinels versus explicit absence
- Semantics of NULL, NaN, and N/A
- Nullable columns in SQL
- Absence in hierarchies
- Pitfalls of sentinels

Some data formats explicitly support missing data while other formats use a special value, known as a **sentinel value**, of one sort or another to indicate missingness. Non-tabular formats may indicate missing data simply by not including any value in a position where it might otherwise occur. However, sentinel values are sometimes ambiguous, unfortunately.

In particular, within many data formats, and within most data frame libraries, missing numeric values are represented by the special IEEE-754 floating-point value NaN (Not-a-Number). The problem here is that NaN, by design and intention, can arise as the result of some attempts at computation that are not obviously unreasonable. While such an unrepresentable value is indeed *unavailable*, this is potentially semantically different from data that was simply never collected in the first place. As a small digression, let us look at coaxing a NaN to arise in an "ordinary" computation (albeit a contrived one).

```
for n in range(7, 10):
    exp1 = 2**n
    a = (22/7) ** exp1
    b = π ** exp1
    # Compute answer in two "equivalent" ways
    res1 = (a * a) / (b * b)
    res2 = (a / b) * (a / b)
    print(f"n={n}:\n   "
          f"method1: {res1:.3f}\n   "
          f"method2: {res2:.3f}")
```

```
n=7:
  method1: 1.109
  method2: 1.109
n=8:
  method1: 1.229
  method2: 1.229
n=9:
  method1: nan
  method2: 1.510
```

Parallel to the pitfall of missing floats being represented as NaNs, missing strings are almost always represented as *strings*. Generally, one or more reserved values such as "N/A" or the empty string are used when a string value is missing. However, those sentinels do not clearly distinguish between "not applicable" and "not available," which are subtly different.

As a toy example, we might have collected names of people, including "middle name." Having a sentinel value for "middle name" would not distinguish between survey subjects who have no middle name and those who merely had not provided it. Reaching just slightly for a data science purpose: perhaps we wish to find the correlation between certain middle names and demographic characteristics. In the United States, for example, the middle name "Santiago" would be strongly associated with Hispanic family origin; a survey subject who provided no middle name might nonetheless have that middle name. In principle, a string field could contain different sentinels for, e.g. "No middle name" and "No response," but datasets are *very rarely* careful in those distinctions.

SQL

In SQL databases, an explicit NULL is available for all column types. Whether a particular column is "nullable" is determined by the database administrator (or whoever had that functional role, however much or little qualified). This allows a distinction in principle between an explicit NaN for a numeric field and a NULL for missing values.

Unfortunately, many or most actual database tables fail to utilize these available distinctions (i.e. the specific configured and populated tables). In practice, you are likely to see many combinations of empty strings, NaNs, actual NULLs, or other sentinels, even within SQL databases. This is not because any widely used RDBMS fails to support these different values and types; it is rather that in the history of various clients putting data into them, using various codebases, non-optimal choices were made.

To run the code in the next cells, you need to obtain access to an RDBMS. The PostgreSQL server running on my local system, in particular, has a database called `dirty`, and that in turn contains a table called `missing`. If you use a different RDBMS, your driver will have a different name, and your engine will use a different scheme in its connection URL. The particular user, password, host, and port will also vary. Database servers also often use authentication methods other than a password to grant access. However, the Python DB-API (*database API*) is quite consistent, and you will work with the connection object and engine in identical ways when you access other RDBMSs. For illustrative purposes, we show our PostgreSQL configuration function `connect_local()`, which is contained in `setup.py`.

```python
# PostgreSQL configuration
def connect_local():
    user = 'cleaning'
    pwd = 'data'
    host = 'localhost'
    port = '5432'
    db = 'dirty'
    con = psycopg2.connect(database=db, host=host, user=user,
password=pwd)
    engine = create_engine(f'postgresql://{user}:{pwd}@{host}:{port}/
{db}')
    return con, engine
```

With the connection established, we can examine some of our data in Python.

```python
con, engine = connect_local()
cur = con.cursor()
# Look at table named "missing"
cur.execute("SELECT * FROM missing")
for n, (a, b) in enumerate(cur):
    print(f"{n+1} | {str(a):>4s} | {b}")
```

```
1 |  nan | Not number
2 | 1.23 | A number
3 | None | A null
4 | 3.45 | Santiago
5 | 6.78 |
6 | 9.01 | None
```

As Python objects, an SQL NULL is represented as the singleton None, which is a reasonable choice. Let us review this friendly data representation.

- Row 1 contains a NaN (not computable) and a string describing the row
- Row 2 contains a regular float value and a string describing it
- Row 3 contains an SQL NULL (not available) and a string
- Row 4 contains a regular float value and a regular string
- Row 5 contains a regular float value and an empty string ("not applicable")
- Row 6 contains a regular float value and a NULL ("not available")

In terms of actually supporting the distinction between a true NULL and a sentinel value like NaN, libraries are of mixed quality. Pandas has made some strides with version 1.0 by introducing the special singleton pd.NA to be used as a "missing" indicator across data types, instead of np.nan, None, and pd.NaT (Not a Time). However, as of this writing, the singleton is not utilized in any of the standard data readers, and getting the value into data requires special efforts. I hope this will have improved by the time you read this.

R's Tidyverse does better because R itself has an NA special value. Slightly confusingly, R also contains an *even more special* pseudo-value NULL, which is used to indicate that something is undefined (as opposed to simply missing). R's NULL can result from some expressions and function calls, but it cannot be an element in arrays or data frames.

```
%%R
# Notice NULL is simply ignored in the construction
tibble(val = c(NULL, NA, NaN, 0),
       str = c("this", "that", NA))
```

```
# A tibble: 3 x 2
     val   str
   <dbl>  <chr>
1     NA  this
2    NaN  that
3      0  NA
```

What SQL calls NULL, R calls NA; NaN remains a separate value indicating "not computable." [NaN] This allows R to interface correctly and unambiguously with SQL, or with the occasional other formats which also explicitly mark "missing" in a non-sentinel manner.

NaN

The IEEE-754 standard, in fact, reserves a large number of bit patterns as NaNs: 16 million of them for 32-bit floats, and vastly more for 64-bit floats. Moreover, these many NaNs are divided into a generous number each for **signaling** versus **quiet** NaNs. In concept, when the standard was developed, the choice of which of the millions of NaNs available (the "payload") could be used to record information about exactly what kind of operation led to the NaN occurring. That said, no software used in data science—and nearly no software used in array and numeric computation—actually utilizes the distinction among the many NaNs. In practical terms, NaN is equivalent to a singleton, like R's NA, Python's None, or JavaScript's null.

This R code assumes the same PostgreSQL database is available as that used in the Python example. As with the Python code, a different RDBMS will require a different driver name, and user, password, host, and port will vary in your configuration:

```
%%R
drv <- dbDriver("PostgreSQL")
con <- dbConnect(drv, dbname = "dirty",
                 host = "localhost", port = 5432,
                 user = "cleaning", password = "data")
sql <- "SELECT * FROM missing"
data <- tibble(dbGetQuery(con, sql))
data
```

```
# A tibble: 6 x 2
        a  b
    <dbl>  <chr>
1   NaN    "Not number"
2   1.23   "A number   "
3   NA     "A null     "
4   3.45   "Santiago   "
5   6.78   "           "
6   9.01    NA
```

In contrast, Pandas 1.0 produces the less correct data frame. The `engine` object was configured and discussed above with the `connect_local()` function:

```
pd.read_sql("SELECT * FROM missing", engine)
```

```
         A            b
0      NaN   Not number
1     1.23     A number
2      NaN       A null
3     3.45     Santiago
4     6.78
5     9.01         None
```

Hierarchical Formats

In formats like JSON that nest data flexibly, there is an obvious way of representing missing data: by not representing it at all. If you perform hierarchical processing, you will need to check for the presence or absence of a given dictionary key at a given level. The JSON specification itself does not address `NaN` values, which means that some systems producing data may choose to use the JavaScript `null` value in its place, producing the ambiguity we have discussed above. However, many specific libraries extend the definition to recognize `NaN` (and sometimes `inf`, which is also a floating-point number) as a value. To illustrate:

```
json.loads('[NaN, null, Infinity]')  # null becomes Python None

[nan, None, inf]
```

Let us represent the same data of the SQL table illustrated above in a (relatively) compact way. Notice, however, that since in the Python `json` library `NaN` is a recognized value, we *could* explicitly represent all missing keys and match them with `null` as needed. Obviously, we data scientists do not usually generate the data we need to consume; so the format we get is the one we need to process.

We can read this particular data into a Pandas DataFrame easily, subject to the sentinel limitation. Since a data frame imposes a tabular format, the missing row/column positions must be filled with some value, in this case with a `NaN` as sentinel. Of course, as discussed in *Chapter 2, Hierarchical Formats*, nested data may simply not be amenable to being represented in a tabular way.

```
json_data = '''
{"a": {"1": NaN, "2": 1.23, "4": 3.45, "5": 6.78, "6": 9.01},
 "b": {"1": "Not number", "2": "A number", "3": "A null",
       "4": "Santiago", "5": ""}
```

```
}'''
pd.read_json(json_data).sort_index()
```

```
          A            b
1       NaN    Not number
2      1.23      A number
3       NaN        A null
4      3.45      Santiago
5      6.78
6      9.01           NaN
```

Let us also process this JSON data in a more hierarchical and procedural way for illustration, classifying special/missing values as we encounter them. For the example, we assume that the top level is a dictionary of dictionaries, but obviously we could walk other structures as well if needed:

```
data = json.loads(json_data)
rows = {row for dct in data.values()
            for row in dct.keys()}

for row in sorted(rows):
    for col in data.keys():
        val = data[col].get(row)
        if val is None:
            print(f"Row {row}, Col {col}: Missing")
        elif isinstance(val, float) and math.isnan(val):
            print(f"Row {row}, Col {col}: Not a Number")
        elif not val:
            print(f"Row {row}, Col {col}: Empty value {repr(val)}")
```

```
Row 1, Col a: Not a Number
Row 3, Col a: Missing
Row 5, Col b: Empty value ''
Row 6, Col b: Missing
```

Sentinels

In textual data formats, mainly delimited and fixed-width files, missing data is indicated either by absence or by a sentinel. Both delimited and fixed-width formats are able to omit a certain field in a row—albeit, in fixed-width, this does not distinguish among an empty string, a string of spaces, and a missing value. Two commas next to each other in CSV should be unambiguous for "no value."

Ideally, this absence should be used to indicate missingness, and potentially allow some other sentinel to indicate "Not Applicable," "Not Calculable," "No Middle Name," or other specific markers for known values that fall outside the domain of a variable. In practice, however, the "best practice" I recommend here is often not what is used in the datasets you will actually need to work with.

The use of sentinels is not limited to text formats. Often in SQL, for example, TEXT or CHAR columns that could, in principle, be made nullable and use NULL to indicate missing values instead use sentinels (and not always single sentinels; in practice they often acquire multiple markers over multiple generations of software changes). Sometimes formats such as JSON that can hold text values likewise use sentinels rather than omitting keys. Even in formats like HDF5 that enforce data typing, sometimes sentinel numeric values are used to indicate missing values rather than relying on NaN as a special marker (which has its own problems, discussed above).

In Pandas, in particular, as of version 1.0, the following sentinel values are recognized by default as meaning "missing" when reading delimited or fixed-width files: `' '`, `'#N/A'`, `'#N/A N/A'`, `'#NA'`, `'-1.#IND'`, `'-1.#QNAN'`, `'-NaN'`, `'-nan'`, `'1.#IND'`, `'1.#QNAN'`, `'N/A'`, `'NA'`, `'NULL'`, `'NaN'`, `'n/a'`, `'nan'`, and `'null'`. Some of these must arise in domains or from tools I am personally unfamiliar with, but many I have seen. However, I have also encountered numerous sentinels not in that list. You will need to consider sentinels for your specific dataset, and such defaults are only some first guesses the tool provides. Other tools will have different defaults.

Libraries for working with datasets, often as data frames, will have mechanisms to specify the particular values to treat as sentinels for missing data. Let us look at an example that is closely based on real-world data obtained from the United States National Oceanic and Atmospheric Administration (NOAA). This data was, in fact, provided as CSV files; a more descriptive filename is used here, and many of the columns are omitted. But only one data value is changed in the example. In other words, this is a dataset I actually had to work with outside of writing this book, and the issues discussed were not ones I knew about in advance of doing that.

The dataset we read below concerns weather measurements at a particular weather station. The station at Sorstokken, Norway, is chosen here more-or-less at random from thousands available. Other stations employ the same encoding, which is nowhere obviously documented. Unfortunately, undocumented or underdocumented field constraints are the rule in published data, not the exception. The column names are somewhat abbreviated, but not too hard to guess the meaning of: temperature (°F), maximum wind gust speed (mph), etc:

```
sorstokken = pd.read_csv('data/sorstokken-no.csv.gz')
sorstokken
```

	STATION	DATE	TEMP	VISIB	GUST	DEWP
0	1001499999	2019-01-01	39.7	6.2	52.1	30.4
1	1001499999	2019-01-02	36.4	6.2	999.9	29.8
2	1001499999	2019-01-03	36.5	3.3	999.9	35.6
3	1001499999	UNKNOWN	45.6	2.2	22.0	44.8
...	...	...	...	...	...	...
295	1001499999	2019-12-17	40.5	6.2	999.9	39.2
296	1001499999	2019-12-18	38.8	6.2	999.9	38.2
297	1001499999	2019-12-19	45.5	6.1	999.9	42.7
298	1001499999	2019-12-20	51.8	6.2	35.0	41.2

299 rows × 6 columns

We notice a few things in the view of a selection of the table. The DATE value UNKNOWN is included (by my construction). Also, some GUST values are 999.9 (in the original data). The use of several 9 digits as a sentinel is a common convention. The number of 9s used varies, however, as does the position of a decimal point if any is used. Another common convention is using a -1 as a sentinel for numeric values that semantically must be positive for legitimate values. For example, the -1 convention might sensibly be used for wind gust speed, but it could not be for degrees Fahrenheit or Celsius, which can perfectly well have the value -1 for ordinary Earth surface temperatures. On the other hand, if we were using the same units to measure the temperatures inside an iron forge (the melting point of iron is 2,800°F/1,538°C), -1 would be safely outside the possible operating range.

Looking at the minimum and maximum values of a given variable is often a clue about the sentinels used. For numbers—and also for dates—a value that is *unreasonably large* or *unreasonably small* is generally used for a sentinel. This can go wrong where legitimate measurements later exceed their initially anticipated range:

```
pd.DataFrame([sorstokken.min(), sorstokken.max()])
```

	STATION	DATE	TEMP	VISIB	GUST	DEWP
0	1001499999	2019-01-01	27.2	1.2	17.1	16.5
1	1001499999	UNKNOWN	88.1	999.9	999.9	63.5

Here we see that TEMP and DEWP seem always to fall within a "reasonable" range. DATE alerts us to a problem value this way; it might also do so, but possibly more subtly, if the sentinel had been for example 1900-01-01, which is an actual date but one from before NOAA measurements were taken. Likewise, VISIB and GUST have unreasonably high and *special*-looking values. For string values, sentinels are quite likely to occur right in the middle of valid values. "No Middle Name" is alphabetically between "Naomi" and "Nykko." Let us look more closely at these variables with sentinels.

Outliers and standard deviation (σ) are discussed more in a later section:

```
print("Normal max:")
for col in ['VISIB', 'GUST']:
        s = sorstokken[col]
        print(col, s[s < 999.9].max(),
                "...standard deviation w/ & w/o sentinel:",
                f"{s.std():.1f} / {s[s < 999.9].std():.1f}")
```

```
Normal max:
VISIB 6.8 ...standard deviation w/ & w/o sentinel: 254.4 / 0.7
GUST 62.2 ...standard deviation w/ & w/o sentinel: 452.4 / 8.1
```

I believe VISIB is measured in miles, and seeing a thousand miles is unreasonable. GUST wind speed is in mph, and likewise 999.9 is not something that will occur on Earth. However, one should worry when sentinels are within three orders of magnitude of actual values, as here. For power law distributed values, even that rule of thumb about orders of magnitude is of little help.

In Pandas and other tools, we can instruct the tool to look for specific sentinels, and substitute specific values. Of course, we could do so after data is read into a data structure using regular data frame filtering and manipulation techniques. If we can do so at read time, so much the better. Here we look for sentinels on a column-specific basis:

```
sorstokken = pd.read_csv('data/sorstokken-no.csv.gz',
                        na_values={'DATE': 'UNKNOWN',
                                    'VISIB': '999.9',
                                    'GUST': '999.9'},
                        parse_dates=['DATE'])
sorstokken.head()
```

	STATION	DATE	TEMP	VISIB	GUST	DEWP
0	1001499999	2019-01-01	39.7	6.2	52.1	30.4
1	1001499999	2019-01-02	36.4	6.2	NaN	29.8
2	1001499999	2019-01-03	36.5	3.3	NaN	35.6
3	1001499999	NaT	45.6	2.2	22.0	44.8
4	1001499999	2019-01-06	42.5	1.9	NaN	42.5

The topics in this section are largely driven by data formats themselves. Let us turn to anomalies caused more often by collection processes.

Miscoded Data

"When I use a word," Humpty Dumpty said, in rather a scornful tone, "it means just what I choose it to mean – neither more nor less."

–Lewis Carroll

Concepts:

- Categorical and ordinal constraints
- Encoded values and metadata definitions
- Rare categories

When I discuss miscoded data in this section, I am primarily addressing categorical data, also called "factors" in R (and sometimes elsewhere). Ordinal data might be included too inasmuch as it has known bounds. For example, if a ranking scale is specified as ranging from 1 to 10, any values outside of that numeric range—or if genuinely ordinal, any values that are not integral—must be miscoded in some manner.

Quantitative data can obviously be miscoded as well, in some sense. A data entry intending a value of 55 might be carelessly entered as 555. But equally, a value intended as 55 might be mis-entered as 54, which is less likely to be caught as obviously wrong. In any event, the examination of quantitative features for errors is addressed in the later sections of this chapter. Numbers, especially real numbers (or complex numbers, integers, fractions, etc.), do not present as immediately wrong, but only in their distribution or domain constraints.

For an ordinal value, verifying its type and range should assure the validity of the coding, in most cases (ordinals with non-contiguous integers as valid values do occur sometimes, but less common). In the Dermatology Data Set (`https://archive.ics.uci.edu/ml/datasets/Dermatology`) available from the UCI Machine Learning Repository, most fields are coded as 0, 1, 2, or 3. One field is only 0 or 1; the age and target (the skin condition) are continuous and factor variables, respectively.

In this example, nothing is miscoded; note that verifying that is *not* the same as knowing all values are *correct*:

```
from src.dermatology import *
(pd.DataFrame(
    [derm.min(), derm.max(), derm.dtypes])
    .T
    .rename(columns={0:'min', 1:'max', 2:'dtype'})
)
```

	Min	max	dtype
erythema	0	3	int64
scaling	0	3	int64
definite borders	0	3	int64
itching	0	3	int64
...	...	...	...
inflammatory monoluclear infiltrate	0	3	int64
band-like infiltrate	0	3	int64
Age	0	75	float64
TARGET	cronic dermatitis	seboreic dermatitis	object

35 rows × 3 columns

Minimum, maximum, and verifying the use of the integer data type is sufficient to assure ordinals are not miscoded. Categorical variables are *sometimes* encoded in an ordinal fashion, but often consist of words naming their values. For example, the below dataset is very similar to the one used in an exercise of *Chapter 6, Value Imputation*. However, in this version, some errors exist that we will look at in the next several sections. This data contains the (hypothetical) height, weight, hair length, and favorite color of 25,000 survey subjects:

```
humans = pd.read_csv('data/humans-err.csv')
# random_state for deterministic sample
humans.sample(5, random_state=1)
```

	Height	Weight	Hair_Length	Favorite
21492	176.958650	72.604585	14.0	red
9488	169.000221	79.559843	0.0	blue
16933	171.104306	71.125528	5.5	red
12604	174.481084	79.496237	8.1	blue
8222	171.275578	77.094118	14.6	green

As one would expect semantically, `Favorite` is a categorical value, with a small number of legitimate values. Generally, the way to examine such a feature for miscoding starts with examining the unique values it takes. Obviously, if documentation exists as to the expected values that can help us. However, keep in mind a software developers' motto that "documentation" is a synonym for "*lies*." It may not accurately reflect the data itself:

```
humans.Favorite.unique()
```

```
array(['red', 'green', 'blue', 'Red', ' red', 'green', 'blüe',
       'chartreuse'], dtype=object)
```

At an initial look at unique values, we already see several likely problems. For example, ' red' with a space at the beginning is a common kind of data entry error, and we can most likely assume it was intended simply as 'red'. On the other hand, 'Red' capitalized versus in lowercase is not necessarily self-evident as to which is correct. The string 'blüe' looks like another misspelling of the English word. Something strange is happening with 'green' still; we will return to that.

To get a sense of the intention of the data, we can check whether some variations are rare with others common. This is often a strong hint:

```
humans.Favorite.value_counts()
```

```
red           9576
blue          7961
green         7458
Red              1
chartreuse       1
 red             1
green            1
blüe             1
Name: Favorite, dtype: int64
```

These counts tell us a lot. The color 'chartreuse' is a perfectly good color name, albeit a less commonly used word. It *could* be a legitimate value, but most likely its rarity indicates some sort of improper entry, given that only three colors (modulo some spelling issues we are working on) seem to be otherwise available. Most likely, we will want to mark this value as missing for later processing. But *only* most likely; there may be domain knowledge that indicates that despite its rarity, it is a value we wish to consider. If documentation exists describing it, that lends weight to the option of simply keeping it.

The rare occurrence of ' red' with a leading space and 'Red' capitalized give us strong support for the assumption that they are simply miscoded versions of 'red'. However, if we were roughly evenly split on capitalized and lowercase versions, or even if neither was *rare*, the correct action would be less clear. Nonetheless, in many cases, canonicalization or normalization to one particular case (case folding) would be good practice, and data frame tools make this easy to vectorize on large datasets. However, sometimes capitalization represents intended differences, for example in otherwise identical last names that have distinct capitalization among different families. Likewise, in many scientific fields, short names or formulae can be case-sensitive and should not be case-folded. Having a sense of the content domain remains important.

We are left with the curious case of the two greens. They look identical; likewise, for example, a trailing space in the above categorical values would not be visible on screen. Manually looking closer at those values is needed here:

```
for color in sorted(humans.Favorite.unique()):
    print(f"{color:>10s}", [ord(c) for c in color])

       red [32, 114, 101, 100]
       Red [82, 101, 100]
      blue [98, 108, 117, 101]
      blüe [98, 108, 252, 101]
chartreuse [99, 104, 97, 114, 116, 114, 101, 117, 115, 101]
     green [103, 114, 101, 101, 110]
     green [103, 114, 1077, 1077, 110]
       red [114, 101, 100]
```

What we find here from the Unicode code points is that one of our greens in fact has two Cyrillic "ye" characters rather than Roman "e" characters. This substitution of near-identical glyphs is often—as in this instance of a sneaky book author—a result of malice or deception. However, in the large world of human languages, it genuinely can occur that a particular string of characters innocently resembles some other string that it is not. Other than perhaps making it more difficult to type some strings at the particular keyboard with which you are familiar, this visual similarity is not per se a data integrity issue. However, here, with the one mixed-language version also being rare, clearly it is something to correct to the regular English word in Roman letters.

Once we have made decisions about the remediations desired—in a manner sensitive to domain knowledge—we can translate troublesome values. For example:

```
humans.loc[humans.Favorite.isin(['Red', ' red']), 'Favorite'] = 'red'
humans.loc[humans.Favorite == 'chartreuse', 'Favorite'] = None
```

```
humans.loc[humans.Favorite == 'blüe', 'Favorite'] = 'blue'
humans.loc[humans.Favorite == 'green', 'Favorite'] = 'green'
humans.Favorite.value_counts()
```

```
red        9578
blue       7962
green      7459
Name: Favorite, dtype: int64
```

Let us turn to areas where domain knowledge can inform anomaly detection.

Fixed Bounds

"Cricket is an art. Like all arts it has a technical foundation. To enjoy it does not require technical knowledge, but analysis that is not technically based is mere impressionism."

–C.L.R. James, Beyond A Boundary

Concepts:

- Domain versus measurement limits
- Imputation and clipping
- Improbability versus impossibility
- Exploring hypotheses for data errors

Based on our domain knowledge of the problem and dataset at hand, we may know of fixed bounds for particular variables. For example, we might know that the tallest human who has lived was Robert Pershing Wadlow at 271cm, and that the shortest adult was Chandra Bahadur Dangi at 55cm. Values outside this range are probably unreasonable to allow in our dataset. In fact, we may perhaps wish to assume much stricter bounds; as an example, let us choose between 92cm and 213cm (which will include the *vast* majority of all adult humans). Let us check whether our humans dataset conforms with these bounds:

```
((humans.Height < 92) | (humans.Height > 213)).any()
```

```
False
```

For height, then, our domain-specific fixed bounds are not exceeded in the dataset. What about the variable Hair_Length? From the actual physical meaning of the measurement, hair cannot be negative length.

However, let us stipulate as well that the measuring tape used for our observations was 120cm long (i.e. hypothetical domain knowledge), and that, therefore, a length more than that cannot be completely legitimate (such a length is rare, but not impossible among humans). First, let us look at the hair lengths that exceed the measuring instrument:

```
humans.query('Hair_Length > 120')
```

	Height	Weight	Hair_Length	Favorite
1984	165.634695	62.979993	127.0	red
8929	175.186061	73.899992	120.6	blue
14673	174.948037	77.644434	130.1	blue
14735	176.385525	68.735397	121.7	green
16672	173.172298	71.814699	121.4	red
17093	169.771111	77.958278	133.2	blue

There are just a few samples with a hair length longer than a possible measurement. However, all of these numbers are only modestly longer than the measuring instrument or scale. Without more information on the collection procedure, it is not possible to be confident of the source of the error. Perhaps some subjects made their own estimates of their very long hair length rather than using the instrument. Perhaps one data collection site actually had a longer measuring tape that was not documented in our metadata or data description. Or perhaps there is a transcription error, such as adding a decimal point; e.g. maybe the 124.1cm hair was 24.1cm in reality. Or perhaps the unit was confused, and millimeters were actually measured rather than centimeters (as is standard in hair clippers and other barbering equipment).

In any case, this problem affects only 6 of the 25,000 observations. Dropping those rows would not lose us a large amount of data, so that is a possibility. Imputing values would perhaps be reasonable (for example, stipulating that these 6 subjects had average hair length). Value imputation is the subject of *Chapter 6*, and options are discussed there in more detail; at this stage, the first pass might be marking those values as missing.

However, for these out-of-range values that cluster relatively close to legitimate values, clipping the values to the documented maximum might also be a reasonable approach. The operation "clip" is also sometimes called "clamp," "crop," or "trim" depending on the library you are working with. The general idea is simply that a value outside of a certain bound is treated as if it is that bound itself. We can version our data as we modify it:

```
humans2 = humans.copy()  # Retain prior versions of dataset
humans2['Hair_Length'] = humans2.Hair_Length.clip(upper=120)
humans2[humans2.Hair_Length > 119]
```

	Height	Weight	Hair_Length	Favorite
1984	165.634695	62.979993	120.0	red
4146	173.930107	72.701456	119.6	red
8929	175.186061	73.899992	120.0	blue
9259	179.215974	82.538890	119.4	green
14673	174.948037	77.644434	120.0	blue
14735	176.385525	68.735397	120.0	green
16672	173.172298	71.814699	120.0	red
17093	169.771111	77.958278	120.0	blue

A slightly lower threshold for a filter shows that 119.6 was left unchanged, but the values over 120.0 were all set to 120 exactly.

The too-big values were not difficult to massage. Let us look at the physical lower bound of zero next. A value of exactly zero is perfectly reasonable. Many people shave their heads or are otherwise bald. This is invented data, pulled from a distribution that feels vaguely reasonable to this author, so do not put too much weight in the exact distributions of lengths. Just note that zero length is a relatively common occurrence in actual humans:

```
humans2[humans2.Hair_Length == 0]
```

	Height	Weight	Hair_Length	Favorite
6	177.297182	81.153493	0.0	blue
217	171.893967	68.553526	0.0	blue
240	161.862237	76.914599	0.0	blue
354	172.972247	73.175032	0.0	red
...	...	...	...	...
24834	170.991301	67.652660	0.0	green
24892	177.002643	77.286141	0.0	green
24919	169.012286	74.593809	0.0	blue
24967	169.061308	65.985481	0.0	green

517 rows × 4 columns

However, what about the impossible negative lengths? We can easily create a filter to look at those also:

```
neg_hair = humans2[humans2.Hair_Length < 0]
neg_hair
```

	Height	Weight	Hair_Length	Favorite
493	167.703398	72.567763	-1.0	blue
528	167.355393	60.276190	-20.7	green
562	172.416114	60.867457	-68.1	green
569	177.644146	74.027147	-5.9	green
...	...	...	...	...
24055	172.831608	74.096660	-13.3	red
24063	172.687488	69.466838	-14.2	green
24386	176.668430	62.984811	-1.0	green
24944	172.300925	72.067862	-24.4	red

118 rows × 4 columns

There are a moderate number of these obviously miscoded rows. As elsewhere, simply dropping the problem rows is often a reasonable approach. However, a quick glance at the tabular data, as well as some slight forensics, suggests that quite likely a negative sign snuck into many reasonable values. It is at least *plausible* that these quantities are right, but simply with an inverted sign. Let us look at some statistics of the problem values. Just for fun, we will look at very similar summaries using both R and Pandas:

```
%%R -i neg_hair
summary(neg_hair$Hair_Length)
```

Min.	1st Qu.	Median	Mean	3rd Qu.	Max.
-95.70	-38.08	-20.65	-24.35	-5.60	-0.70

```
neg_hair.Hair_Length.describe()
```

```
count    118.000000
mean     -24.348305
std       22.484691
min      -95.700000
25%      -38.075000
50%      -20.650000
75%       -5.600000
max       -0.700000
Name: Hair_Length, dtype: float64
```

The general statistics do not contradict this sign-inversion hypothesis. However, before we draw a conclusion, let us continue to look at these bad values more closely for this exercise. There might be additional patterns:

```
plt.hist(neg_hair.Hair_Length, bins=30)
plt.title("Distribution of invalid negative hair length");
```

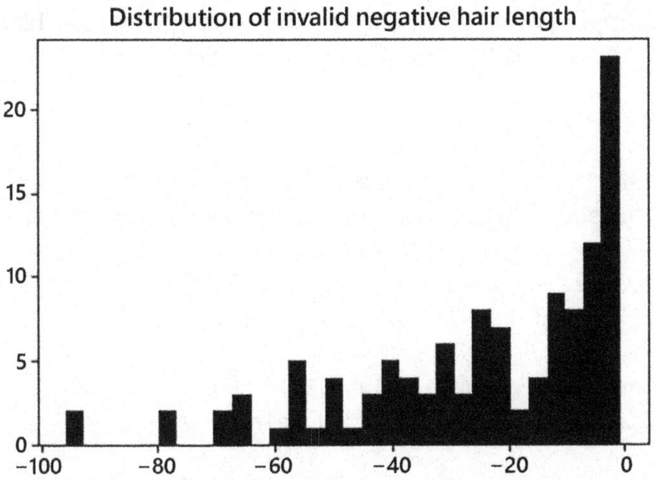

Figure 4.1: Histogram showing distribution of negative hair length values

This distribution of negative values roughly matches the distribution of positive ones. There are a larger number of people with short hair of varying short lengths, and a tail of fewer people at longer lengths. However, at a glance, the region close to zero seems to be a bit *too much* of a peak. For the one hundred or so rows of data in the example, you could eyeball them all manually, but for larger datasets, or larger bounds-violation sets, honing in on nuances programmatically is more general:

```
neg_hair.Hair_Length.value_counts()
```

```
-1.0      19
-41.6      2
-6.8       2
-30.1      2
          ..
-3.3       1
-51.4      1
-25.1      1
-4.8       1
Name: Hair_Length, Length: 93, dtype: int64
```

Indeed there is a pattern here. There are 19 values of *exactly* -1, and only one or two occurrences of each other invalid negative value. It seems very likely that something different is happening between the -1 error and the other negative value errors. Perhaps -1 was used as a sentinel, for example. Of course, it is also possible that -1 could result from the stipulated sign-inversion error; we cannot entirely separate those two possibilities.

The working hypothesis I would probably use to handle this problem in the dataset (if not simply dropping everything questionable outright) would be to mark the -1 values as *missing* but invert the sign of other negative values:

```
humans3 = humans2.copy()      # Versioned changes to data

# The "sentinel" negative value means missing
humans3.loc[humans3.Hair_Length == -1, 'Hair_Length'] = None

# All other values simply become non-negative
humans3['Hair_Length'] = humans3.Hair_Length.abs()

plt.hist(humans3.Hair_Length, bins=30)
plt.title("Distribution of corrected hair lengths");
```

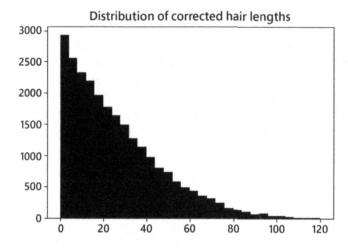

Figure 4.2: Histogram showing corrected hair lengths

We have performed a typical cleaning of bounded values. Let us turn to values without sharp bounds, but with general distribution statistics.

Outliers

If Congress had meant to so limit the Act, it surely would have used words to that effect.

–*Tennessee Valley Auth. v. Hill, 437 U.S. 153 (1978)*

Concepts:

- Z-score and unexpected values
- Interquartile range
- Standard deviation and frequency of occurrence

In continuous data, values that fall within normative ranges might still be strongly uncharacteristic within those bounded expectations. In the simplest case, this occurs when a value is very different from other values of the same variable. The standard way to characterize the expectedness of a value is a measure called a z-score. This value is simply the distance of each point from the mean of the variable, divided by the standard deviation of the variable.

$$Z = \frac{x - \mu}{\sigma}$$

Where μ is the sample mean, and σ is the standard deviation.

This measure is most precise for data that follows a normal distribution, but generally it is useful for any data that is unimodal (having one peak), somewhat symmetric, and scale-dependent. In more ordinary language, we just want to look for the histogram of a data variable having one peak, and tapering off at roughly the same rate on both sides. Completely normal distribution is unusual in real-world data.

A slightly different way of identifying outliers is often used as well. Box and whisker plots (usually simply called boxplots) will often include outliers as separate visual elements. While it is possible to use a z-score in such a visualization, more often these plots utilize **interquartile range (IQR)** and a fixed multiplier to define outliers. The different techniques will produce similar, but not identical, answers.

Z-Score

We can see that height and weight in our dataset follow a generally normal-like distribution by visualizing them. We have seen just above that hair length, after correction, is strictly single tailed. However, the one-sided drop-off from a mode at 0 is close enough to one tail of a normal distribution that the z-score is still reasonable to consider.

```
fig, (ax1, ax2) = plt.subplots(1, 2, figsize=(12, 4))
ax1.hist(humans3.Height, bins=50)
ax2.hist(humans3.Weight, bins=50)
ax1.set_title("Distribution of Height")
ax2.set_title("Distribution of Weight");
```

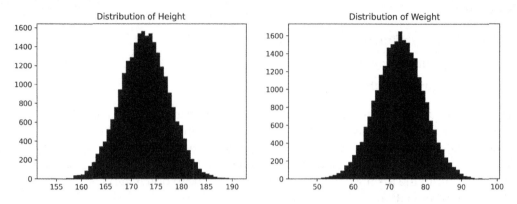

Figure 4.3: Histograms showing distributions of height and weight

If we wish to be more precise in quantifying the normality of variables, we can use statistical tests such and Anderson-Darling, Shapiro-Wilk, or Skewness-Kurtosis All. Each of these techniques tries to reject the hypothesis that a distribution is normal. For different p-values (probabilities), different test statistics determine a threshold for this rejection (although for large samples, even small deviations from normality will reject the hypothesis, but do not matter from the point of view of the z-score being useful). In Anderson-Darling, if the test statistic is not much more than 1.0 the curve is definitely normal enough to measure outliers with a z-score. The inverse does not hold, however; many non-normal curves are still reasonable to use the z-score with. Essentially, we just need to avoid this measure for power law or exponential distributions, and for curves that are strongly multi-modal. Let us perform Anderson-Darling tests on our height, weight, and hair length variables:

```
from scipy.stats import anderson

for var in ('Height', 'Weight', 'Hair_Length'):
    data = humans3[var][humans3[var].notnull()]
    stat = anderson(data, 'norm').statistic
    print(f"Anderson-Darling statistic for {var:<12s}: {stat:6.2f}")
```

```
Anderson-Darling statistic for Height      :   0.24
Anderson-Darling statistic for Weight      :   0.54
Anderson-Darling statistic for Hair_Length : 578.19
```

Having recognized that hair length is not normal, but that it shows a one-sided decay along a linear scale nonetheless, we can add z-scores for all of our quantitative variables to the working data frame. As before, as good practice of keeping versions of our modifications, we copy the data to a new data frame before the next transformations.

We ignore the delta degrees of freedom parameter in our calculation of standard deviation because it is trivial with 25,000 samples (if we had only 10 or 20 samples, it could matter). The degrees of freedom concerns the anticipated variance within a total population based on a sample; but these only vary significantly when samples are tens of observations, not tens of thousands:

```
humans4 = humans3.copy()

for var in ('Height', 'Weight', 'Hair_Length'):
    zscore = (humans4[var] - humans4[var].mean()) / humans4[var].std()
    humans4[f"zscore_{var}"] = zscore

humans4.sample(5, random_state=1)
```

	Height	Weight	Hair_Length	Favorite	zscore_Height
21492	176.958650	72.604585	14.0	red	0.880831
9488	169.000221	79.559843	0.0	blue	-0.766210
16933	171.104306	71.125528	5.5	red	-0.330758
12604	174.481084	79.496237	8.1	blue	0.368085
8222	171.275578	77.094118	14.6	green	-0.295312

	zscore_Weight	zscore_Hair_Length
21492	-0.042032	-0.568786
9488	0.997585	-1.225152
16933	-0.263109	-0.967294
12604	0.988078	-0.845397
8222	0.629028	-0.540656

The choice of a z-score threshold is very domain- and problem-dependent. A rule of thumb is often to use a z-score of an absolute value more than 3 as a cut-off to define outliers. But what is *expected* very much depends on the size of a dataset.

 In statistics, we sometimes recall the *68–95–99.7 rule*, which lists the percentage of observations that fall within one, two, or three standard deviations in a normal distribution.

At any distance from the mean, *some* observations would be expected if they are numerous enough, but the number diminishes rapidly with more standard deviations' distance.

Let us look at that common z-score threshold of 3. Remember that we are working with 25,000 samples here, so generally we expect to find roughly 75 of them outside of 3 standard deviations, under the *68–95–99.7 rule* discussed above. Let us look at the table for height, but just check the number of rows outside this bound for the other variables:

```
humans4[humans4.zscore_Height.abs() > 3]
```

	Height	Weight	Hair_Length	Favorite	zscore_Height
138	187.708718	86.829633	19.3	green	3.105616
174	187.537446	79.893761	37.5	blue	3.070170
412	157.522316	62.564977	6.8	blue	-3.141625
1162	188.592435	86.155948	53.1	red	3.288506
...	...	...	...	...	...
22945	157.293031	44.744929	18.4	red	-3.189077
23039	187.845548	88.554510	6.9	blue	3.133934
24244	158.153049	59.725932	13.8	green	-3.011091
24801	189.310696	85.406727	2.3	green	3.437154

	zscore_Weight	zscore_Hair_Length
138	2.084216	-0.320304
174	1.047496	0.532971
412	-1.542673	-0.906345
1162	1.983518	1.264351
...	...	...
22945	-4.206272	-0.362499
23039	2.342037	-0.901657
24244	-1.967031	-0.578162
24801	1.871531	-1.117320

51 rows × 7 columns

```
print("Outlier weight:", (humans4.zscore_Weight.abs() > 3).sum())
print("Outlier hair length:", (humans4.zscore_Hair_Length.abs() >
3).sum())
```

```
Outlier weight: 67
Outlier hair length: 285
```

We have already noted that hair length is single-tailed, so we might expect approximately twice as many outliers. The actual number is somewhat more than twice that many, but that is not itself an extreme divergence of values. Height and weight actually have modestly lower kurtosis than we would expect from the normal distribution (the tails thin out slightly faster).

In any case, a z-score of 3 is probably too small to be useful for our sample size. 4 sigma is probably more relevant for our purpose of distinguishing merely unusual from probably wrong observations, and maybe 4.5 for the one-tailed hair length.

A table of the frequency of once-a-day observations falling outside of a given standard deviation (σ) provides a helpful intuition. A shorthand trick to remember the effect of sigma is the *68–95–99.7 rule* mentioned earlier; that is, the percentage of things falling within one, two, and three standard deviations:

Range	Proportion of observations	Frequency for daily event
± 1σ	1 in 3	Twice a week
± 2σ	1 in 22	Every three weeks
± 3σ	1 in 370	Yearly
± 4σ	1 in 15,787	Every 43 years (twice in a lifetime)
± 5σ	1 in 1,744,278	Every 5,000 years (once in recorded history)
± 6σ	1 in 506,797,346	Every 1.4 million years (twice in history of humankind)
± 7σ	1 in 390,682,215,445	Every 1 billion years (four times in history of Earth)

Let us see the outliers given the broader z-score bounds:

```
cond = (
    (humans4.zscore_Height.abs() > 4) |
    (humans4.zscore_Weight.abs() > 4) |
    (humans4.zscore_Hair_Length.abs() > 4.5))
humans4[cond]
```

```
          Height      Weight  Hair_Length  Favorite  zscore_Height
13971  153.107034   63.155154         4.4     green      -4.055392
14106  157.244415   45.062151        70.7       red      -3.199138
22945  157.293031   44.744929        18.4       red      -3.189077

       zscore_Weight   zscore_Hair_Length
13971      -1.454458            -1.018865
14106      -4.158856             2.089496
22945      -4.206272            -0.362499
```

Using modest domain knowledge of human physical characteristics, even though they are outside the "norm," persons of 153cm or 45kg are small, but not outside of bounds we would expect. The small number of 4 sigma outliers are both short and light according to the data, which we would expect to be correlated to a relatively high degree, lending plausibility to the measurements.

Moreover, the height bounds we discussed in the above section on fixed bounds were considerably wider than this 4 sigma (or even 5 sigma) detects. Therefore, while we *could* discard or mark missing values in these outliers rows, the analysis does not seem to motivate doing so.

Interquartile Range

Using the IQR rather than the z-score makes less of an assumption of normality of a distribution. However, this technique will also fail to produce meaningful answers for power law or exponential data distributions. If you can identify a distribution as one that ranges over many orders of magnitude like those, looking at the quartiles of either an Nth root or a logarithm of the raw data might still produce reasonable results. The same transformation, in fact, can be equally relevant if you use z-score analysis.

The idea of the IQR is simply to look at the quartile cut-offs in a variable and measure the numeric distance between the first and third quartile, i.e. between the 25% and 75% percentiles. Exactly half the data is in that range, but we often also expect that most data will be within some distance beyond those cut-offs, defined as a multiplier of the range between cut-offs. Most commonly, a multiplier of 1.5 is chosen; this is merely a convention that is often useful but lacks any deeper meaning.

I include in this text a brief function to visualize boxplots that show the IQR defined outliers. Normally, this functionality is only included in the source code repository for the book, but here I think it is worthwhile for readers to see the configuration that goes into these few lines in Matplotlib (other visualization libraries have similar capabilities; often higher-level abstractions with more visual pizzazz, in fact):

```
# Function defined but not run in this cell
def show_boxplots(df, cols, whis=1.5):
    # Create as many horizontal plots as we have columns
    fig, axes = plt.subplots(len(cols), 1, figsize=(10, 2*len(cols)))
    # For each one, plot the non-null data inside it
    for n, col in enumerate(cols):
        data = df[col][df[col].notnull()]
        axes[n].set_title(f'{col} Distribution')
        # Extend whiskers to specified IQR multiplier
        axes[n].boxplot(data, whis=whis, vert=False, sym='x')
        axes[n].set_yticks([])
    # Fix spacing of subplots at the end
    fig.tight_layout()
```

While the default multiplier (the "whisker" width) is 1.5, we have already seen that the human data is large enough that values have to be relatively extreme to appear as genuinely *unlikely* to be genuine. We choose, therefore, a whisker width of 2.5 instead:

```
show_boxplots(humans4, ["Height", "Weight", "Hair_Length"], 2.5)
```

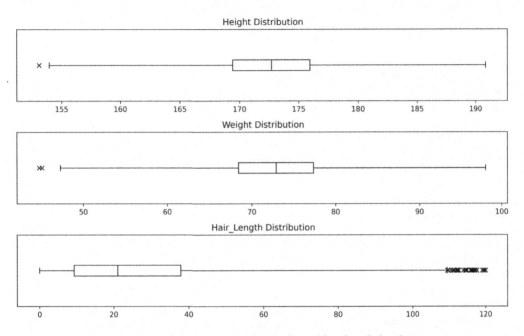

Figure 4.4: Boxplots showing height, weight, and hair length distribution

The central boxes represent the IQR, from 25% to 75% percentile. The whiskers extend to multiplier times IQR above/below the box. An *x* marks outliers past the whiskers.

Only one outlier appears at this threshold for height, at the short end. Likewise, only two appear for weight, both at the light end. This was the same pattern we found with the z-score. Rather more "outlier" long hair lengths occur, but we already had used a larger z-score to filter that more restrictively. We could similarly use a larger *whisker* width to filter more hair lengths out, if we wished.

While the visualization is handy, we want to find the actual data rows that are marked with *x*'s in the plots. Let us code that. We find the quartiles, compute the IQR, then display the inlier ranges:

```
quartiles = (
    humans4[['Height', 'Weight']]
    .quantile(q=[0.25, 0.50, 0.75, 1.0]))
quartiles
```

```
          Height      Weight
0.25    169.428884   68.428823
0.50    172.709078   72.930616
0.75    175.953541   77.367039
1.00    190.888112   98.032504
```

```
IQR = quartiles.loc[0.75] - quartiles.loc[0.25]
IQR
```

```
Height    6.524657
Weight    8.938216
dtype: float64
```

```
for col, length in IQR.iteritems():
    high = quartiles.loc[0.75, col] + 2.5*IQR[col]
    low = quartiles.loc[0.25, col] - 2.5*IQR[col]
    print(f"Inliers for {col}: [{low:.3f}, {high:.3f}]")
```

```
Inliers for Height: [153.117, 192.265]
Inliers for Weight: [46.083, 99.713]
```

Actually, filtering using the inlier range in this case gives us the same answer as the z-score approach. Of necessity, the very shortest person is the shortest regardless of which outlier detection technique we use. But selecting a domain-motivated IQR multiplier may identify more or fewer outliers than using a domain-motivated z-score, depending on actual data distributions:

```
cond = (
    (humans4.Height > 192.265) |
    (humans4.Height < 153.117) |
    (humans4.Weight > 99.713)  |
    (humans4.Weight < 46.083))
humans4[cond]
```

	Height	Weight	Hair_Length	Favorite	zscore_Height
13971	153.107034	63.155154	4.4	green	-4.055392
14106	157.244415	45.062151	70.7	red	-3.199138
22945	157.293031	44.744929	18.4	red	-3.189077

	zscore_Weight	zscore_Hair_Length
13971	-1.454458	-1.018865
14106	-4.158856	2.089496
22945	-4.206272	-0.362499

Univariate outliers can be important to detect, but sometimes it is a combination of features that becomes anomalous.

Multivariate Outliers

If you are not part of the solution, you are part of the precipitate.

–Anonymous

Concepts:

- Variance in deterministic synthetic features
- Expectations of relative rarity

Sometimes univariate features can fall within relatively moderate z-score boundaries, and yet combinations of those features are unlikely or unreasonable. Perhaps an actual machine learning model might predict that combinations of features are likely to be wrong. In this section we only look at simpler combinations of features to identify problematic samples.

In *Chapter 7, Feature Engineering* we discuss polynomial features. That technique multiplies together the values of two or more variables pertaining to the same observation and treats the result as a new feature. For example, perhaps neither height nor weight in our working example are outside a reasonable bound, and yet the multiplicative product of them is. While this is definitely possible, we generally expect these features to be positively correlated to start with, so multiplication would probably only produce something new *slightly* outside the bounds already detected by univariate outlier detection.

However, let us consider a derived feature that is well-motivated by the specific domain. Body Mass Index (BMI) is a measure often used to measure healthy weights for people, and is defined as:

$$BMI = \frac{kg}{m^2}$$

That is, weight and height are in an inverse relationship in this derived quantity rather than multiplicatively combined. Perhaps this multivariate derived feature shows some problem outliers. Let us construct another data frame version that discards previous calculated columns, but adds BMI and its z-score:

```
humans5 = humans4[['Height', 'Weight']].copy()
# Convert weight from cm to m
humans5['BMI'] = humans5.Weight / (humans5.Height/100)**2
humans5["zscore_BMI"] = (
    (humans5.BMI - humans5.BMI.mean()) /
     humans5.BMI.std()
)
humans5
```

	Height	Weight	BMI	zscore_BMI
0	167.089607	64.806216	23.212279	-0.620410
1	181.648633	78.281527	23.724388	-0.359761
2	176.272800	87.767722	28.246473	1.941852
3	173.270164	81.635672	27.191452	1.404877
...	...	...	...	...
24996	163.952580	68.936137	25.645456	0.618008
24997	164.334317	67.830516	25.117048	0.349063
24998	171.524117	75.861686	25.785295	0.689182
24999	174.949129	71.620899	23.400018	-0.524856

25000 rows × 4 columns

Looking for outliers in the derived feature, we see strong signals. As was discussed, at a z-score of 4 and a dataset of 25,000 records, we expect to see slightly more than one record appearing as an outlier by natural random distribution. Indeed, the two z-scores we see below that are only slightly more than 4 in absolute value occurred in the dataset before it was engineered to highlight the lesson of this section:

```
humans5[humans5.zscore_BMI.abs() > 4]
```

	Height	Weight	BMI	zscore_BMI
21388	165.912597	90.579409	32.905672	4.313253
23456	187.110000	52.920000	15.115616	-4.741383
23457	158.330000	92.780000	37.010755	6.402625
24610	169.082822	47.250297	16.527439	-4.022805

As well as one example of a moderate outlier for high BMI and one for low BMI, we also have two more extreme values on each side. In this case, these were constructed for the section, but similar multivariate outliers will occur in the wild. The -4.74 z-score is not an extreme we would expect in 25,000 samples, but is perhaps not completely implausible. However, the +6.4 z-score is astronomically unlikely to occur without a data error (or a construction by a book author). Since BMI is a derived feature that combines height and weight—and moreover since each of those is within reasonable bounds on its own—the correct approach is almost surely simply to discard these problem rows. Nothing in the data themselves guides us toward knowing whether weight or height is the problem value, and no remediation is sensible.

Fortunately for this particular dataset, only 2 (or *maybe* 4) samples display the problem under discussion. We have plentiful data here, and no real harm is done by discarding those rows. Obviously, the particular decisions made about z-score thresholds and disposition of particular data rows that are illustrated in this section and the last several are only examples. You will need to decide within your problem and domain what the most relevant levels and tests are, and what remediations to perform.

Exercises

The two exercises in this chapter ask you to look for anomalies first in quantitative data, then in categorical data.

A Famous Experiment

The Michelson–Morley experiment was an attempt in the late 19th century to detect the existence of the *luminiferous aether*, a widely assumed medium that would carry light waves. This was the most famous "failed experiment" in the history of physics in that it did not detect what it was looking for—something we now know not to exist at all.

The general idea was to measure the speed of light under different orientations of the equipment relative to the direction of movement of the Earth, since relative movement of the ether medium would add or subtract from the speed of the wave. Yes, it does not work that way under the theory of relativity, but it was a reasonable guess 150 years ago.

Apart from the physics questions, the dataset derived by the Michelson–Morley experiment is widely available, including as a sample built into R. The same data is available at:

```
https://www.gnosis.cx/cleaning/morley.dat
```

Figuring out the format, which is not complex, is a good first step of this exercise (and typical of real data science work).

The specific numbers in this data are measurements of the speed of light in km/s with a zero point of 299,000. So, for example, the mean measurement in experiment 1 was 299,909 km/s. Let us look at the data in the R bundle:

```
%%R -o morley
data(morley)
morley %>%
    group_by('Expt') %>%
    summarize(Mean = mean(Speed), Count = max(Run))

'summarise()' ungrouping output (override with '.groups' argument)
# A tibble: 5 x 3
   Expt  Mean Count
  <int> <dbl> <int>
1     1   909    20
2     2   856    20
3     3   845    20
4     4   820.   20
5     5   832.   20
```

In the summary, we just look at the number of runs of each experimental setup, and the mean across that setup. The raw data has 20 measurements within each setup.

Using whatever programming language and tools you prefer, identify the outliers first within each setup (defined by an Expt number) and then within the data collection as a whole. The hope in the original experiment was that each setup would show a significant difference in central tendency, and indeed their means are somewhat different.

This book and chapter does not explore confidence levels and null hypotheses in any detail, but create a visualization that aids you in gaining visual insight into how much apparent difference exists between the several setups.

If you discard the outliers within each setup, are the differences between setups increased or decreased? Answer with either a visualization or by looking at statistics on the reduced groups.

Misspelled Words

For this exercise we return to the 25,000 human measurements we have used to illustrate a number of concepts. However, in this variation of the dataset, each row has a person's first name (pulled from the US Social Security Agency list of common first names over the last century; apologies that the names lean Anglocentric because of the past history of US population and immigration trends).

The dataset for this exercise can be found at:

```
https://www.gnosis.cx/cleaning/humans-names.csv
```

Unfortunately, our hypothetical data collectors for this dataset are simply terrible typists, and they make typos when entering names with alarming frequency. There are some number of intended names in this dataset, but quite a few simple miscodings of those names as well. The problem is: how do we tell a real name from a typo?

There are a number of ways to measure the similarity of strings and that provide a clue as to likely typos. One general class of approach is in terms of *edit distance* between strings. The R package **stringdist**, for example, provides Damerau–Levenshtein, Hamming, Levenshtein, and optimal string alignment as measures of edit distance. Less edit-specific fuzzy matching techniques utilize a "bag of n-grams" approach, and include q-gram, cosine distance, and Jaccard distance. Some heuristic metrics like Jaro and Jaro-Winkler are also included in `stringdist` along with the other measures mentioned. Soundex, soundex variants, and metaphone look for similarity of the sounds of words as pronounced, but are therefore specific to languages and even regional dialects.

In a reversal of the more common pattern of Python versus R libraries, Python is the one that scatters string similarity measures over numerous libraries, each including just a few measures. However, **python-Levenshtein** is a very nice package including most of these measures. If you want cosine similarity, you may have to use `sklearn.metrics.pairwise` or another module. For phonetic comparisons, **fonetika** and **soundex** both support multiple languages (but different languages for each; English is in common for almost all packages).

On my personal system, I have a command-line utility called `similarity` that I use to measure how close strings are to each other. This particular few-line script measures Levenshtein distance, but also normalizes it to the length of the longer string. A short name will have a small numeric measure of distance, even between dissimilar strings, while long strings that are close overall can have a larger measure before normalization (depending on what measure is chosen, but for most of them). A few examples show this:

String 1	String 2	Levenshtein distance	Similarity ratio
David	Davin	1	0.8
David	Maven	3	0.4
the quick brown fox jumped	thee quikc brown fax jumbed	5	0.814814814815

For this exercise, your goal is to identify every *genuine* name and correct all the misspelled ones to the correct canonical spelling. Keep in mind that sometimes multiple legitimate names are actually close to each other in terms of similarity measures. However, it is probably reasonable to assume that *rare* spellings are typos, at least if they are also relatively similar to common spellings. You may use whatever programming language, library, and metric you feel is the most useful for the task.

Reading in the data, we see it is similar to the human measures we have seen before:

```
names = pd.read_csv('data/humans-names.csv')
names.head()
```

```
        Name       Height      Weight
0      James    167.089607   64.806216
1      David    181.648633   78.281527
2    Barbara    176.272800   87.767722
3       John    173.270164   81.635672
4    Michael    172.181037   82.760794
```

It is easy to see that some "names" occur very frequently and others only rarely. Look at the middling values as well when working on this exercise:

```
names.Name.value_counts()
```

```
Elizabeth    1581
Barbara      1568
Jessica      1547
Jennifer     1534
    ...
```

```
ichael          1
Wlliam          1
Richrad         1
Mray            1
Name: Name, Length: 249, dtype: int64
```

Denouement

When you have eliminated the impossible, whatever remains, however improbable, must be the truth.

–Arthur Conan Doyle

Topics covered in this chapter: Missing Data; Sentinels; Miscoded Data; Fixed Bounds; Outliers.

The anomalies that we have discussed in this chapter fall into a few relatively distinct categories. For the first kind, there are the special values that explicitly mark missing data, although those markers are sometimes subject to pitfalls. However, an explicit indication of missingness is probably the most straightforward kind of anomaly. A second kind of anomaly is categorical values that are miscoded; some finite number of values are proper (although not always clearly documented), and anything that isn't one of those few values is an anomaly.

The third kind of anomaly is in continuous—or at least ranged—data values that fall outside of the bounds of our expectations. These are also called *outliers*, although exactly how much a value has to lie outside typical values to be a problem is very domain- and problem-dependent. Expectations may take the form of a priori assumptions that arise from domain knowledge of the measurement. They may also arise from the distribution of data within a variable overall, and the deviation of one particular value from others measured as that variable. At times, our expectations about bounds can even be multivariate, and some numeric combination of multiple variables produces a value outside of expectation bounds.

For all of these kinds of anomalies, there are essentially two actions we might take. We may decide to discard an observation or sample altogether if it has one of these problems. Or alternately, we may simply more explicitly mark one feature within an observation as missing based on its value not being reliable. When we modify values to the "missing" special value, keeping track of our changes and data versions is extremely important practice. What we choose to do with those values marked as explicitly missing is a downstream decision that is discussed at more length in later chapters.

In the next chapter, we move from looking for problems with particular data points and on to looking for problems with the overall "shape" of a dataset.

5
Data Quality

All data is dirty, some data is useful.

–cf. George Box

Welcome to the mid-point of the book. In something like the loose way in which a rock *"concept album"* tells an overarching story through its individual songs, this book is meant, to a certain degree, to follow the process a data scientist goes through from acquiring raw data to feeding suitable data into a machine learning model or data analysis. Up until this point, we have looked at how one goes about getting data into a program or analysis system (e.g. a notebook), and we touched on identifying data that has clearly "gone bad" at the level of individual data points in *Chapter 4, Anomaly Detection*. In the chapters after this one, we will look at remediation of that messy and marked data that earlier chapters delivered in stages.

Now, however, is the time to look for ways in which your data may have problems, not in its individual details, but in its overall "shape" and character. In some cases, these problems will pertain to the general collection techniques used, and in particular to systematic bias that might be introduced during collection. In other cases, problems are not the fault of data collectors, but simply of units and scales, and correction can be quite mechanical and routine. At this point, we gradually ease into active interventions that do not simply detect dirt as we have done hitherto, but also go about cleaning it. One such cleanup might involve handling the inherent biases that cyclicities in data often create (often over time periods, but not exclusively).

In the last section of this chapter, we look at the idea of performing validation that is domain-specific and utilizes rules that are practical, beyond being simply numeric. Of course, every domain might have its own such rules, and an example in this chapter is meant to inspire thought, not provide a blueprint for your specific tasks. In fact, it can hardly be said often enough that everything within this book is meant to provide inspiration for ways of thinking about data science problems, and never merely recipes to copy directly to the task you have in front of you.

***

Before we get to the sections of this chapter, let us run our standard setup code.

```
from src.setup import *
%load_ext rpy2.ipython
```

```
%%R
library(gridExtra)
library(tidyverse)
```

Missing Data

> *Absence of evidence is not evidence of absence.*
>
> *–Martin Rees*

Concepts:

- Aspects of missing data
- Distribution of records in parameter space
- Bias in missing data

The story of missing data forms a trilogy in this book. The prior chapter, *Chapter 4, Anomaly Detection*, led with a section on missing data. In that case, our concern was to identify "missingness," which can be marked in various ways by various datasets in various data formats. The next chapter, *Chapter 6, Value Imputation*, is primarily about what we might do to fill missing values with reasonable guesses.

This chapter falls between the previous and the next one. We have already taken mechanical or statistical tests to identify some data as missing (or as unreliable enough that it is better to pretend it is missing). But we have not yet decided whether to keep or drop the observations to which those missing data points belong. For this section, we need to assess the significance of that missing data to our overall dataset.

When we have a record with missing data, we essentially have two choices about its disposition. On the one hand, we can discard that particular record. On the other hand, we can impute some value for the missing value, as will be discussed in *Chapter 6*. Actually, in some sense there is a third option as well: we may decide that because of the amount or distribution of missing data in our dataset, the data is simply not usable for the purpose at hand. While, as data scientists, we never want to declare a task hopeless, as responsible researchers we need to consider the possibility that particular data simply cannot support any conclusions. Missing data is not the *only* thing that could lead us to this conclusion, but it is certainly one common fatal deficit.

If we wish to discard records — but also to a large extent if we wish to impute values — we need to think about whether what remains will be a fair representation of the parameter space of the data. Sample bias can exist not only in the overall composition of a dataset, but also more subtly in the distribution of missing values. Keep in mind that "missing" here might result from the processing in *Chapter 4*, in which some values may have been marked missing because we determined they were unreliable, even if they were not per se absent in the raw data.

For example, I created a hypothetical dataset of persons with names, ages, genders, and favorite colors and flowers. The ages, genders, and names are modeled on the actual distribution of popular names over time reported by the United States Social Security Administration. I assigned favorite colors and flowers to the people for this illustration.

```
df = pd.read_parquet('data/usa_names.parq')
df
```

	Age	Gender	Name	Favorite_Color	Favorite_Flower
0	48	F	Lisa	Yellow	Daisy
1	62	F	Karen	Green	Rose
2	26	M	Michael	Purple	None
3	73	F	Patricia	Red	Orchid
...	...	...	...	...	...
6338	11	M	Jacob	Red	Lily
6339	20	M	Jacob	Green	Rose
6340	72	M	Robert	Blue	Lily
6341	64	F	Debra	Purple	Rose

6342 rows × 5 columns

In general, this is an ordinary-looking dataset, with a moderately large collection of records. We can notice in the data frame summary that at least some data is missing. This is worth investigating more carefully.

```
with show_more_rows():
    print(df.describe(include='all'))
```

	Age	Gender	Name	Favorite_Color	Favorite_Flower
count	6342.000000	6342	6342	5599	5574
unique	NaN	2	69	6	5
top	NaN	F	Michael	Yellow	Orchid
freq	NaN	3190	535	965	1356
mean	42.458846	NaN	NaN	NaN	NaN
std	27.312662	NaN	NaN	NaN	NaN
min	2.000000	NaN	NaN	NaN	NaN
25%	19.000000	NaN	NaN	NaN	NaN
50%	39.000000	NaN	NaN	NaN	NaN
75%	63.000000	NaN	NaN	NaN	NaN
max	101.000000	NaN	NaN	NaN	NaN

Using Pandas' .describe() method or similar summaries by other tools allows us to see that Age, Gender, and Name have values for all 6,342 records. However, Favorite_Color and Favorite_Flower are missing for approximately 750 records each. In itself, missing data in 10-15% of the rows is quite likely not to be a huge problem. This statement assumes that missingness is not itself biased. Even if we need to discard those records altogether, that is a relatively small fraction of a relatively large dataset. Likewise, imputing values would *probably* not introduce too much bias, and other features could be utilized within those records. In the below section and in *Chapter 6, Value Imputation*, in relation to undersampling and oversampling, we discuss the dangers of exclusion resulting in class imbalance.

While uniformly randomly missing data can be worked around relatively easily, data that is missing in a biased way can present a more significant problem. To figure out which category we are in with this dataset, let us compare those missing flower preferences to the ages of the people. Looking at every individual age up to 101 years old is hard to visualize; for this purpose, we will group people into 10-year age groups. The graph below uses a statistical graphing library called Seaborn, which is built on top of Matplotlib.

```
df['Age Group'] = df.Age//10 * 10
fig, ax = plt.subplots(figsize=(12, 4.5))
sns.countplot(x="Age Group", hue="Favorite_Flower",
              ax=ax, palette='gray', data=df)
ax.set_title("Distribution of flower preference by age");
```

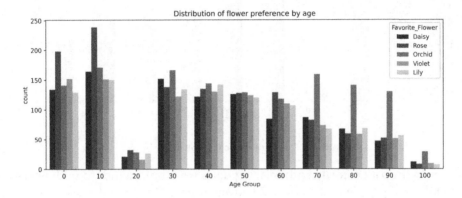

Figure 5.1: Distribution of flower preference by age

A few patterns jump out in this visualization. It appears that older people tend to have a strong preference for orchids, and young people a moderate preference for roses. This is perhaps a property of the data meriting analysis. More significantly for this section, there are few data points for favorite flower at all in the 20-30 age group. One might imagine several explanations, but the true answer would depend on problem and domain knowledge. For example, perhaps the data corresponding to these ages was not collected during a certain time period. Or perhaps people in that age group reported a different favorite flower but its name was lost in some prior inaccurate data validation/cleaning step.

If we look at the records with missing color preference, we see a similar pattern in relation to age. The drop in frequency of available values occurs instead in the 30-40 age group though.

```
fig, ax = plt.subplots(figsize=(12, 4.5))
sns.countplot(x="Age Group", hue="Favorite_Color",
              ax=ax, palette='gray', data=df)
ax.set_title("Distribution of color preference by age");
```

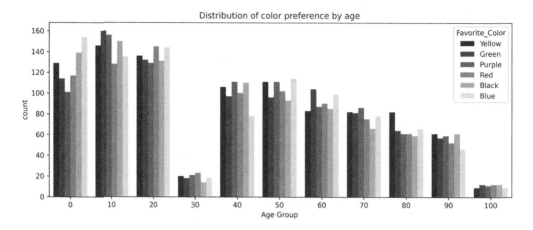

Figure 5.2: Distribution of color preference by age

If we were to drop *all* records with missing data, we would wind up with nearly no representation of people in the entire 20-40 age range. This biased unavailability of data would be likely to weaken the analysis generally. The number of records would remain fairly large, but the parameter space, as mentioned, would have an empty (or at least much less densely occupied) region. Obviously, these statements depend both on the purpose of our data analysis and our assumptions about the underlying domain. If age is not an important aspect of the problem in general, our approach may not matter much. But if we think age is a significant independent variable, dropping this data would probably not be a workable approach.

This section, like many others, shows the kinds of exploration one should typically perform of a dataset. It does not provide one simple answer for the best remediation of bias in missing data. That decision will be greatly dependent upon the purpose for which the data is being used and also on background domain knowledge that may clarify the reasons for the data being missing. Remediation is inevitably a per-problem decision.

Let us turn to ways that bias might occur in relation to other features rather than simply globally in a dataset.

Biasing Trends

It is not the slumber of reason that engenders monsters, but vigilant and insomniac rationality.

–Gilles Deleuze

Concepts:

- Collection bias versus trends in underlying domain
- Perspective as source of bias
- Artifact of collection methods
- Visualization to identify bias
- Variance by group
- Externally identifying base rates
- Benford's law

At times, you may be able to detect sample bias within your data, and will need to make a domain area judgment about the significance of that bias. There are at least two kinds of sample bias that you should be on the lookout for. On the one hand, the distribution of observations may not match the distribution in the underlying domain. Quite likely, you will need to consult other data sources—or simply use your own domain area knowledge—to detect such a skew in the samples. On the other hand, the data themselves may reveal a bias by trends that exist between multiple variables. In this latter case, it is important to think about whether the detected "trend" could be a phenomenon you have detected in the data, or is a collection or curation artifact.

Understanding Bias

Bias is an important term in both statistics and human sciences, with a meaning that is strongly related, but that assumes a different valence across fields. In the most neutral statistical sense, bias is simply the fact, more commonly true than not, that a dataset does not accurately represent its underlying population of possible observations. This bare statement hides more nuance than is evident, even outside of observations about humans and politically laden matters. More often than not, neither we data scientists, who analyze data, nor the people or instruments that collected the raw data in the first place can provide an unambiguous delineation of exactly what belongs to the underlying population. In fact, the population is often somewhat circularly defined in terms of data collection techniques.

An old joke observes someone looking for their lost keys at night in the area under a street light. Asked why they do not also look elsewhere, they answer that it is because the visibility is better where they are looking. This is a children's joke, not told particularly engagingly, but it also lays the pattern for *most* data collection of *most* datasets.

Observers make observations of what they can *see* (metaphorically, most are probably voltages in an instrument, or bits on a wire, rather than actual human eyes), and not what they cannot. Survivorship bias is a term for the cognitive error of assuming those observations we have available are representative of the underlying population.

It is easy not to be conscious of bias that exists in data, and probably that much easier when it indeed *does* concern human or social subjects and human observers bring in psychological and social biases. But it is humans, in the end, even if aided by instruments we set up, who make observations of everything else too. For example, the history of ethology (the study of animal behavior) is largely a history of scientists seeing the behaviors in animals that exist—or that they believe should exist—in the humans around them, that they impose by metaphor and blindness. If you make a survey of books in your local library to determine the range of human literature or music, you will discover the predominance of writers and musicians who use your local language and play your local musical style. Even in areas that seem most obviously *not about* humans, our vantage point may create a perspectival bias. For example, if we catalog the types of stars that exist in the universe, and the prevalence of different types, we are always observing those within our cosmological horizon, which not only expresses an interaction of space and time, but also may not uniformly describe the entire universe. Cosmologists know this, of course, but they know it as an inherent bias to their observations.

In most of this section, we will look at a version of the synthetic United States name/age data to detect both of these patterns. As in the last section, this data approximately accurately represents the frequency of different names across different age groups, based on Social Security Administration data. We can see that within the actual domain, the popularity of various names authentically changed over time. As in the last section, it is useful to aggregate people into coarser age groups for visualization.

Throughout this book I have attempted to avoid social bias in the datasets I select or create as examples. For the imagined people in the rows of the name tables, I added features like favorite color or flower, rather than more obviously ethnically or culturally marked features like eye color, favorite food, or musical preference. Even those invented features I use are not entirely independent of culture though, and perhaps my position in the social world leads me to choose different factor values than would someone located elsewhere.

Moreover, by choosing the *top 5* most popular names in the United States each year, I impose a kind of majority bias: all are roughly Anglo names, and none, for example, are characteristically African-American, Latino, Chinese, or Polish, though such are all common outside of that top-5-by-year collation methodology.

```
names = pd.read_parquet('data/usa_names_states.parq')
names['Age Group'] = names.Age//10 * 10
names
```

	Age	Birth_Month	Name	Gender	Home	Age Group
0	17	June	Matthew	M	Hawaii	10
1	5	September	Emma	F	West Virginia	0
2	4	January	Liam	M	Alaska	0
3	96	March	William	M	Arkansas	90
...	...	...	...	...	...	...
6338	29	August	Jessica	F	Massachusetts	20
6339	51	April	Michael	M	Wyoming	50
6340	29	May	Christopher	M	North Carolina	20
6341	62	November	James	M	Texas	60

6342 rows × 6 columns

The fields Birth_Month and Home are added to this dataset, and let us stipulate that we suspect they may indicate some bias in the observations. Before we look at that, let us take a look at a more-or-less expected trend. Note that this dataset was artificially constructed only based on the most popular male and female names for each birth year. A particular name may not be in this top 5 (per gender) for a particular year, or even a particular decade, but nonetheless, a certain number of people in the United States were probably given that name (and would be likely to show up in non-synthetic data).

```
fig, ax = plt.subplots(figsize=(12, 4.5))
somenames = ['Michael', 'James', 'Mary', 'Ashley']
popular = names[names.Name.isin(somenames)]
sns.countplot(x="Age Group", hue="Name",
              ax=ax, palette='gray', data=popular)
ax.set_title("Distribution of name frequency by age");
```

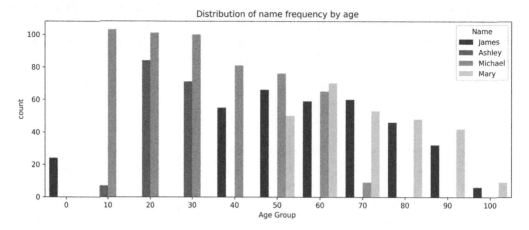

Figure 5.3: Distribution of name frequency by age

We can see trends in this data. Mary is a popular name among the older people in the dataset, but no longer shows up in the most popular names for younger people. Ashley is very popular among 20-40-year-olds, but we do not see it present outside that age group. James seems to have been used over most age ranges, although it fell out of the top-5 spot among 10-40-year-olds, resurging among children under 10. Michael, similarly, seems especially represented from 10-60 years of age.

The top-5 threshold used in the generation of the data has definitely created a few artifacts in the visualization, but a general pattern of some names becoming popular and others waning is exactly a phenomenon we would expect with a bare minimum of domain knowledge. Moreover, if we know only a little bit more about popular baby names in the United States, the specific distribution of names will seem plausible; both for the 4 shown and for the remaining 65 names that you can investigate within the dataset if you download it.

Detecting Bias

Let us apply a similar analysis to birth month as we did to name frequency. A minimum of domain knowledge will tell you that while there are small annual cyclicities in birth month, there should not be a general trend over ages. Even if some world-historical event had dramatically affected births in one particular month of one particular year, this should create little overall trend when we aggregate over decades of age.

```
fig, ax = plt.subplots(figsize=(12, 4.5))
months = ['January', 'February', 'March', 'April']
popular = names[names.Birth_Month.isin(months)]
sns.countplot(x="Age Group", hue="Birth_Month",
              ax=ax, palette='gray', data=popular)
ax.set_title("Distribution of birth month frequency by age");
```

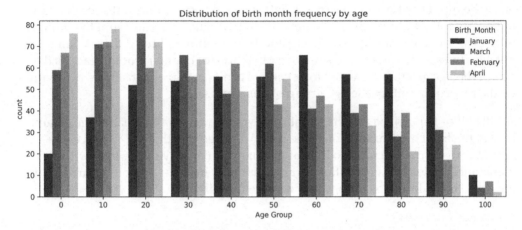

Figure 5.4: Distribution of birth month frequency by age

Contrary to our hope of excluding a biasing trend, we have discovered that—for unknown reasons—January births are dramatically underrepresented among the youngest people and dramatically overrepresented among the oldest people. This is overlain on an age trend of there being more young people, in general, but the pattern nonetheless appears strong. We have not looked at months beyond April, but of course we could in a similar fashion.

A certain amount of random fluctuation occurs in the dataset simply because of sampling issues. The fact that April is a somewhat more common birth month for 50-something people than for 40-something people in the dataset is quite likely meaningless since there are relatively few data points (on the order of 50) once we have cross-cut by both age and birth month. Distinguishing genuine data bias from randomness can require additional analysis (albeit, by construction, the January pattern jumps out strongly even in this simple visualization).

There are numerous ways we might analyze it, but looking for notable differences in the spread of one variable in relation to another can be a good hint. For example, we think we see an oddness in the pattern of January birth months, but is there a general irregularity in the distribution per age? We *could* attempt to analyze this using exact age, but that probably makes the distinction too fine-grained to have good subsample sizes. The decade of age is an appropriate resolution for this test. As always, think about your subject matter in making such judgments.

Since the number of people decreases with age, we need to find statistics that are not overly influenced by the raw numbers. In particular, we can count the number of records we have for each age group and birth month and see if those counts are notably divergent. Variance or standard deviation (of counts) will increase as the size of the age group increases. However, we can normalize that simply by dividing by the raw count within the age group of all months.

A little bit of Pandas magic gets us this. We want to group the data by age group, look at the birth month, and count the number of records that fall within each Age × Birth_Month. We wish to look at this in a tabular way rather than with a hierarchical index. This operation arranges months in order of their occurrence in the data, but ordering by chronology is more friendly.

```
by_month = (names
    .groupby('Age Group')
    .Birth_Month
    .value_counts()
    .unstack())

by_month = by_month[month_names]
by_month
```

Birth_Month Age Group	January	February	March	April	May	June	July	August
0	20	67	59	76	66	77	71	65
10	37	72	71	78	70	73	82	81
20	52	60	76	72	65	65	71	66
30	54	56	66	64	73	58	87	82
...	...	...	...	...	...	...	...	...
70	57	43	39	33	39	36	45	34
80	57	39	28	21	31	37	23	28
90	55	17	31	24	21	23	30	29
100	10	7	4	2	6	2	4	6

Birth_Month Age Group	September	October	November	December
0	67	67	56	63
10	83	79	70	79
20	68	75	76	71
30	66	65	57	58
...	...	...	...	...
70	38	30	37	37
80	27	31	34	37
90	33	25	28	20
100	5	5	7	7

11 rows × 12 columns

That data grid remains a bit too much to immediately draw a conclusion about, so as described, let us look at the normalized variance across age groups.

```
with show_more_rows():
    print(by_month.var(axis=1) / by_month.sum(axis=1))

Age Group
0            0.289808
10           0.172563
20           0.061524
30           0.138908
40           0.077120
50           0.059772
60           0.169321
70           0.104118
80           0.227215
90           0.284632
100          0.079604
dtype: float64
```

The over-100-years-old group shows a low normalized variance, but it is a small subset. Among the other age groups, the middle ages show a notably lower normalized variance across months than do the older or younger people. This difference is quite striking for those under 10 and those over 80 years old. We can reasonably conclude at this point that *some kind* of sample bias occurred in the collection of the birth month; specifically, there is a different bias in effect based on the age group of persons sampled. Whether or not this bias *matters* for the purpose at hand, *the fact should be documented clearly* in any work products of your analyses or models. In principle, some sampling technique that will be discussed in *Chapter 6, Value Imputation*, might be relevant to adjust for this.

Comparison to Baselines

The setup of this synthetic dataset is a giveaway, of course. As well as introducing birth month, I also added Home in the sense of state or territory of residence and/or birth. While there is no documented metadata that definitively clarifies the meaning of the column, let us take it as the state of current residence. If we had chosen to interpret it as birthplace, we might need to find historical data on populations at the times people of various ages were born; clearly that is possible, but the current assumption simplifies our task.

Let us take a look at the current population of the various US states. This will provide an external baseline relative to which we can look for sample bias in the dataset under consideration.

```
states = pd.read_fwf('data/state-population.fwf')
states
```

	State	Population_2019	Population_2010	House_Seats
0	California	39512223	37254523	53.0
1	Texas	28995881	25145561	36.0
2	Florida	21477737	18801310	27.0
3	New York	19453561	19378102	27.0
...	...	...	...	...
52	Guam	165718	159358	0.5
53	U.S. Virgin Isl	104914	106405	0.5
54	American Samoa	55641	55519	0.5
55	N. Mariana Isl	55194	53883	0.5

56 rows × 4 columns

As most readers will know, the range of population sizes across different US states and territories is quite large. In this particular dataset, representation of states in the House of Representatives is given as a whole number, but in order to indicate the special status of some entities that have non-voting representation, the special value of 0.5 is used (this is not germane to this section, just as a note).

Let us take a look at the distribution of home states of persons in the dataset. The step of sorting the index is used to assure that states are listed in alphabetical order, rather than by count or something else.

```
(names
    .Home
    .value_counts()
    .sort_index()
    .plot(kind='bar', figsize=(12, 3),
        title="Distribution of sample by home state")
);
```

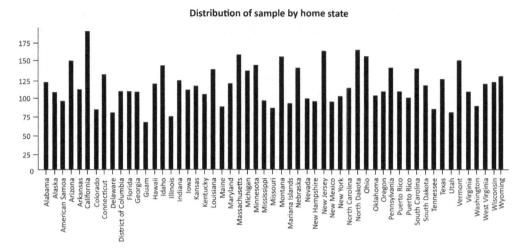

Figure 5.5: Distribution of sample by home state

There is clearly variation in the number of samples drawn from residents of each state. However, the largest state represented, California, has only about 3x the number of samples as the smallest. In comparison, a similar view of the underlying populations emphasizes the different distribution.

```
(states
    .sort_values('State')
    [['State', 'Population_2019']]
    .set_index('State')
    .plot(kind='bar', figsize=(12, 3),
        title="2019 Population of U.S. states and territories")
);
```

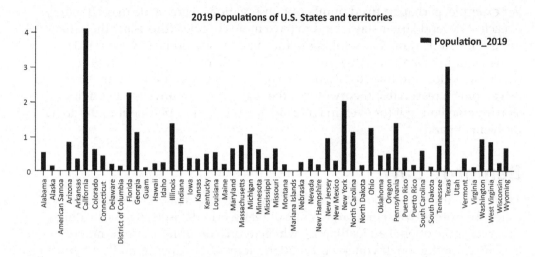

Figure 5.6: 2019 population of United States states and territories

While California provides the most samples for this dataset, Californians are simultaneously the *most underrepresented* relative to the baseline population of the states. As a general pattern, smaller states tend to be overrepresented generally. We can, and probably should, think of this as selection bias based on the size of the various states. As before, unless we have accurate documentation or metadata that describes the collection and curation procedures, we cannot be sure of the cause of the imbalance. But a strong trend exists in this inverse relationship of population to relative sample frequency.

A note here is that sometimes sampling approaches deliberately introduce similar imbalances. If the actual samples were precisely balanced, with some fixed N collected per state, this would fairly clearly point to such a deliberate categorical sampling as opposed to a sampling based on an underlying rate. The pattern we actually have is less obvious than that. We might form a hypothesis that the sampling rate is based on some other underlying feature not directly present in this data.

For example, perhaps a fixed number of observations were made in each *county* of each state, and larger states tend to have more counties (this is *not* the actual underlying derivation, but thinking in this manner should be in your mind). Understanding data integrity issues resembles either a scientific process of experimentation and hypothesis, or perhaps even more so a murder mystery. Developing a reasonable theory of *why* the data is dirty is always a good first step in remediating it (or even in ignoring the issue as not pertinent to the actual problem at hand).

Benford's Law

There is a curious fact about the distribution of *digits* in many observed numbers called **Benford's Law**. For a large range of real-world datasets, we see leading *1* digits far more often than leading 2s, which in turn occur far more commonly than leading 3s, and so on. If you see this pattern, it probably does not reflect harmful bias; in fact, for many kinds of observations, if you *fail* to see it, that might itself reflect bias (or even fraud).

If a distribution precisely follows Benford's law, it will specifically have digits distributed as:

$$P(d) = \log_{10}\left(1 + \frac{1}{d}\right)$$

However, this distribution is often only approximate for real-world data.

When data is distributed according to a power law or a scaling factor, it becomes relatively intuitive to understand what leading digits will be distributed in a "biased" way. However, much observational data that is not obviously scaling in nature still follows Benford's law (at least approximately). Let us pick an example to check; I scraped and cleaned up formatting for the populations and areas of the most populous US cities.

```
cities = pd.read_fwf('data/us-cities.fwf')
cities
```

	NAME	POP2019	AREA_KM2
0	New York City	8336817	780.9
1	Los Angeles	3979576	1213.9
2	Chicago	2693976	588.7
3	Houston	2320268	1651.1
...	...	...	...
313	Vacaville	100670	75.1
314	Clinton	100471	72.8

```
315              Bend     100421        85.7
316      Woodbridge       100145        60.3
317 rows × 3 columns
```

Let us first count the leading digits of populations.

```
pop_digits = cities.POP2019.astype(str).str[0].value_counts()
with show_more_rows():
    print(pop_digits)
```

```
1     206
2      53
3      20
4      10
6       9
5       8
8       5
7       3
9       3
Name: POP2019, dtype: int64
```

Now we ask the same question of area in square kilometers.

```
area_digits = cities.AREA_KM2.astype(str).str[0].value_counts()
with show_more_rows():
    print(area_digits)
```

```
1     118
2      47
3      31
4      23
9      21
8      21
7      20
6      20
5      16
Name: AREA_KM2, dtype: int64
```

Neither collection of data *exactly* matches the Benford's law ideal distribution, but both show the general pattern of favoring leading digits in roughly ascending order.

Let us turn to evaluating the importance of the uneven distribution of categorical variables.

Class Imbalance

It seems to be correct to begin with the real and the concrete, with the real precondition, thus to begin [...] with the population. However, on closer examination this proves false. The population is an abstraction if I leave out, for example, the classes of which it is composed.

–Karl Marx

Concepts:

- Predicting rare events
- Imbalance in features versus in targets
- Domain versus data integrity imbalance
- Forensic analysis of sources of imbalance
- Stipulating the direction of causality

The data you receive will have imbalanced classes, if it has categorical data at all. The several distinct values that a categorical variable may have are also sometimes called *factor levels* ("factor" is synonymous with "feature" or "variable," as discussed in the *Preface* and *Glossary*). Moreover, as will be discussed in *Chapter 6, Value Imputation* in the section on *Sampling*, dividing a continuous variable into increments can often usefully form synthetic categories also. In principle, any variable might have a categorical aspect, depending on the purpose at hand. When these factor levels occur with notably different frequency, it may show selection bias or some other kind of bias; however, it very often simply represents the inherent nature of the data, and is an essential part of the observation.

A problem arises because many types of machine learning models have difficulty predicting rare events. Discussion of concretely rebalancing classes is deferred until the *Chapter 6* discussion of undersampling and oversampling, but here we at least want to reflect on identifying class imbalance. Moreover, while many machine learning techniques are highly sensitive to class imbalance, others are more or less indifferent to it. Documentation of the characteristics of particular models, and their contrast with others, is outside the scope of this particular book.

In particular, though, the main difference between when class imbalance poses a difficulty versus when it is central to the predictive value of the data is precisely the difference between a target and the features. Or equivalently, the difference between a dependent variable and independent variables. When we think of a rare event that might cause difficulty for a model, we usually mean a rare target value, and only occasionally are we concerned about a rare feature. When we wish to use sampling to rebalance classes, it is almost always in relation to target class values.

We will work with a simple example. Two weeks of Apache server logs from my web server are provided as sample data. Such a log file has a number of features encoded in it, but one particular value in each request is the HTTP status code returned. If we imagine trying to model the behavior of my web server, quite likely we would wish to treat this status code as a target that might be predicted by the other (independent) variables. Of course, the log file itself does not impose any such purpose; it simply contains data on numerous features of each request (including response).

The status codes returned from the actual requests to my web server are extremely unbalanced, which is generally a good thing. I want most requests to result in *200 OK* responses (or at least *some* 2xx code). When they do not, there is either a problem with the URLs that users have utilized or there is a problem with the web server itself. Perhaps the URLs were published in incorrect form, such as in links from other web pages; or perhaps deliberately wrong requests were used in attempts to hack my server. I never really *want* a status code outside of 2xx, but inevitably some arise. Let us look at their distribution:

```bash
%%bash
zcat data/gnosis/*.log.gz |
    cut -d' ' -f9 |
    sort |
    uniq -c

  10280 200
      2 206
    398 301
   1680 304
    181 403
    901 404
      9 500
```

The 200 status dominates here. The next highest occurrence is *304 Not Modified*, which is actually fine as well. It simply indicates that a cached copy on a client remains current. Those 4xx and 5xx (and perhaps 301) status codes are generally undesirable events, and I may want to model the patterns that cause them. Let us remind ourselves what is inside an Apache `access.log` file (the name varies by installation, as can the exact fields).

```bash
%%bash
zcat data/gnosis/20200330.log.gz | head -1 | fmt -w50

162.158.238.207 - - [30/Mar/2020:00:00:00 -0400]
"GET /TPiP/024.code HTTP/1.1" 200 75
```

There is a variety of data in this line, but notably it is easy to think of pretty much all of it as categorical. The IP address is a *dotted quad*, and the first (and often second) quad tends to be correlated with the organization or region where the address originates. Allocation of IPv4 addresses is more complex than we can detail here, but it may be that requests originating from a particular /8 or /16 origin tend to get non-200 responses. Likewise, the date—while unfortunately not encoded in ISO 8601 format—can be thought of as categorical fields for month, hour, minute, and so on.

Let us show a bit of Pandas code to read and massage these records into a data frame. The particular manipulations done are not the main purpose of this section, but gaining familiarity with some of these methods is worthwhile.

One thing to notice, however, is that I have decided that I am not really concerned with the pattern where, for example, my web server became erratic for a day. That has not occurred in this particular data, but if it had I would assume that was a one-off occurrence not subject to analysis. The separate cyclical elements of hour and minute might detect recurrent issues (which are discussed more in later sections of this chapter). Perhaps, for example, my web server gives many 404 responses around 3 a.m., and that would be a pattern/problem worth identifying.

```python
def apache_log_to_df(fname):
    # Read one log file.  Treat is as a space separated file
    # There is no explicit header, so we assign columns
    cols = ['ip_address', 'ident', 'userid', 'timestamp',
            'tz', 'request', 'status', 'size']
    df = pd.read_csv(fname, sep=' ', header=None, names=cols)

    # The first pass gets something workable, but refine it
    # Datetime has superfluous '[', but fmt matches that
    fmt = "[%d/%b/%Y:%H:%M:%S"
    df['timestamp'] = pd.to_datetime(df.timestamp, format=fmt)

    # Convert timezone to an integer
    # Not general, I know these logs use integral timezone
    # E.g. India Standard Time (GMT+5:30) would break this
    df['tz'] = df.tz.str[:3].astype(int)
```

```
# Break up the quoted request into sub-components
df[['method', 'resource', 'protocol']] = (
        df.request.str.split(' ', expand=True))

# Break the IP address into each quad
df[['quad1', 'quad2', 'quad3', 'quad4']] = (
        df.ip_address.str.split('.', expand=True))

# Pandas lets us pull components from datetime
df['hour'] = df.timestamp.dt.hour
df['minute'] = df.timestamp.dt.minute

# Split resource into the path/directory vs. actual page
df[['path', 'page']] = (
        df.resource.str.rsplit('/', n=1, expand=True))
# Only care about some fields for current purposes
cols = ['hour', 'minute',
        'quad1', 'quad2', 'quad3', 'quad4',
        'method', 'path', 'page', 'status']
return df[cols]
```

This function allows us to read all of the daily log files into a single Pandas DataFrame simply by mapping over the collection of file names and concatenating data frames. Everything except perhaps page in the resulting data frame is reasonable to think of as a categorical variable.

```
reqs = pd.concat(map(apache_log_to_df,
                 glob('data/gnosis/*.log.gz')))
# Each file has index from 0, so dups occur in raw version
reqs = reqs.reset_index().drop('index', axis=1)
# The /16 subnetwork is too random for this purpose
reqs.drop(['quad3', 'quad4'], axis=1, inplace=True)
reqs
```

	hour	minute	quad1	quad2	method	path
0	0	0	162	158	GET	/download/pywikipedia/cache
1	0	3	172	68	GET	/TPiP
2	0	7	162	158	GET	download/pywikipedia/archive
3	0	7	162	158	GET	/juvenilia
...	...	...	...	...	...	...
13447	23	52	162	158	GET	/download/gnosis/util
13448	23	52	172	69	GET	
13449	23	52	162	158	GET	/publish/resumes
13450	23	56	162	158	GET	/download/pywikipedia/cache

	page	status
0	DuMont%20Television%20Network	200
1	053.code	200
2	?C=N;O=A	200
3	History%20of%20Mathematics.pdf	200
...	...	...
13447	hashcash.py	200
13448	favicon.ico	304
13449		200
13450	Joan%20of%20Lancaster	200

13451 rows × 8 columns

Within my web server, I have relatively few directories where content lives, but relatively many different concrete pages within many of those directories. In fact, the path /download/pywikipedia/cache is actually a robot that performs some formatting cleanup of Wikipedia pages that I had forgotten that I left running 15+ years ago. Given that it may be pointed to any Wikipedia page, there is effectively an infinite space of possible pages my server will reply to. There are also a small number of long path components because URL parameters are sometimes passed in to a few resources. Let us visualize the distribution of the other features in this dataset, with an eye to the places where class imbalance occurs.

```
fig, axes = plt.subplots(3, 2, figsize=(12, 9))

# Which factors should we analyze for class balance?
factors = ['hour', 'minute', 'quad1', 'quad2', 'method', 'status']

# Loop through the axis subplots and the factors
for col, ax in zip(factors, axes.flatten()):
    # Minute is categorical but too many so quantize
```

```
if col == 'minute':
    data = (reqs[col] // 5 * 5).value_counts()
else:
    data = reqs[col].value_counts()
data.plot(kind='bar', ax=ax)
ax.set_title(f"{col} distibution")


# Matplotlib trick to improve spacing of subplots
fig.tight_layout()
```

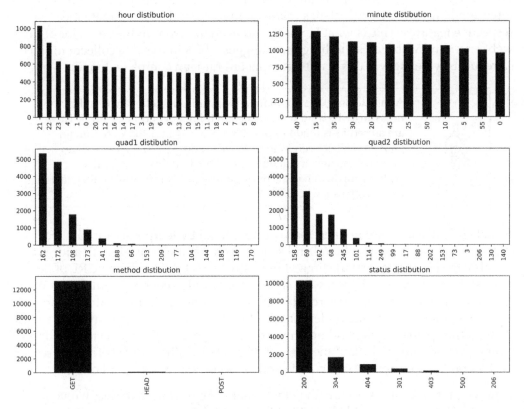

Figure 5.7: Distributions of different features

In these plots, we see some highly imbalanced classes and some mostly balanced ones. The hours show a minor imbalance, but with a fairly strong pattern of more requests around 21:00–24:00 in Atlantic Daylight Time. Why my hosted server is in that timezone is unclear to me, but this is around 6 p.m. US Pacific Time, so perhaps users in California and British Columbia tend to read my pages after work. The distribution of 5-minute increments within an hour is generally uniform, although the slight elevation of a few increments could possibly be more than random fluctuation.

The imbalance in the initial quads of IP address seems striking, and might initially suggest an important bias or error. However, after probing only slightly deeper, we can determine using online "whois" databases that (at the time of writing) both `162.158.0.0/16` and `172.69.0.0/16` are assigned to the CDN (content delivery network) that I use to proxy traffic. So the imbalance in these features has simply provided a clue that almost all requests are proxied through a known entity. In particular, it means that we are unlikely to be able to use these features usefully in any kind of predictive model. At most, we might perform feature engineering—as will be discussed in *Chapter 7, Feature Engineering*—to create a derived feature such as `is_proxied`.

The class imbalances that remain are in the HTTP method and in the status code returned. In neither case is it at all surprising that GET and 200 dominate the respective features. This is what I expect, and even hope for, in the behavior of my web server and website. So nothing there suggests bias in the data collection; since *all* requests were logged, this is not a sample but rather a complete domain.

As a side note, the population is specifically delineated, and cannot necessarily be used to describe anything beyond those lines. These are all requests made to port 80 or port 443 for the web domain gnosis.cx between March 29, 2020, and April 11, 2020; we can draw no conclusions about other web domains or other dates without further analysis or reasoning about how typical this data is of the web as a whole.

As data scientists, we are not necessarily constrained by temporal causality. For example, it is clear that in a literal and sequential way, the requesting IP address, possibly the userid, maybe the time of the request, and definitely the URL of the request, both method and path, will *cause* a certain status code and number of bytes to be returned. In many cases (probably all of them on my simple, static website), the size is simply that of the underlying HTML page. But in concept, a server might do something different depending on the date and time, or the requester's address. In any case, certain *facts* about the request exist a few milliseconds before the server decides on the appropriate status code and response size and logs all of that.

However, for an analysis, we might want to make predictions that exactly reverse causality. Perhaps we would like to treat the size of the response as an independent variable in our effort to predict the time of day. For example, it could be that large files are always requested around 7 p.m. rather than at other times. Our *model* might try to predict a cause from its effect—and that is perfectly legitimate in data science, as long as we are aware of it. In fact, we may only look for correlations, entirely ignoring for a particular task the potential hidden cause of multiple features. Data science is something different from other sciences; the endeavors are, hopefully, complementary.

***

In this section, we focused merely on recognizing, and to a limited extent analyzing, class imbalance. What it means for the actual task to which we wish to put this data is another matter. A significant distinction to keep in mind is that between independent and dependent variables. Generally, imbalance in a dependent variable will skew classification models in a more important way than imbalance in an independent variable. So, for example, if we wish to predict the likely status code that will be produced by a request based on other features of the request, we would be likely to use sampling techniques that will be discussed in *Chapter 6, Value Imputation*, to *balance the dataset* synthetically.

On the other hand, class imbalance is not completely irrelevant in independent variables, at least not for all kinds of models. This very much depends on the kind of model. If we use something in the family of decision trees, for example, it makes little difference that HEAD requests are rare if we wish to detect the (hypothetical) fact that HEAD is strongly associated with 500 status codes. However, if we use a K-nearest neighbors family of algorithm, the actual distance in parameter space can be important. Neural networks fall somewhere in the middle in terms of sensitivity to class imbalance in independent variables. If we encode the HTTP method either as an ordinal value or using one-hot encoding, we may naïvely *underweight* that strong but rare feature. One-hot encoding is discussed in *Chapter 7, Feature Engineering*. For an independent variable, we would not generally wish to *oversample* a rare factor level; but we might wish to artificially *overweight* it.

We also should think about the numeric ranges of data, which might reflect very different underlying units.

Normalization and Scaling

Measure with a micrometer. Mark with chalk. Cut with an axe.

–Rule for precision

Concepts:

- The effect of numeric ranges in variables
- Univariate and multivariate effects
- Numeric forms of various scalers
- Factor and sample weighting

The idea behind normalization of data is simply bringing all the features being utilized in a dataset into a comparable numeric range. When starkly different units are used for different features — that is, for dimensions of a parameter space — some machine learning models will disproportionately utilize those features which simply have a larger numeric range. Special cases of differently scaled numeric ranges occur when one feature has outliers that have not been removed, or when one feature is normally distributed but another feature is exponentially distributed.

This book generally steers away from showing machine learning examples or code. There are many wonderful libraries that address that 20% of your work, as a data scientist, that you will do after you have done the 80% that this book teaches you. However, to emphasize the motivation for normalization, we will create a very simple machine learning model on some overly neat data that illustrates an overwhelming benefit of scaling. For this example, a small amount of code in scikit-learn is used. Notably, however, the scaler classes in scikit-learn are extremely useful even if you do not wish to use that library for modeling. It is certainly reasonable — and perhaps even best practice within Python — to use scikit-learn even if you only ever perform normalization with it.

The synthetic dataset here has two features and one target; all are continuous variables.

```
unscaled = make_unscaled_features()
unscaled
```

	Feature_1	Feature_2	Target
0	0.112999	19247.756104	11.407035
1	0.204178	23432.270613	20.000000
2	0.173678	19179.445753	17.336683
3	0.161411	17579.625264	16.633166
...	...	...	...
196	0.137692	20934.654450	13.316583
197	0.184393	18855.241195	18.241206
198	0.177846	19760.314890	17.839196
199	0.145229	20497.722353	14.371859

200 rows × 3 columns

At a glance, we can see that the `Target` values are on the order of 15, while `Feature_1` is on the order of 0.1 and `Feature_2` is on the order of 20,000. The invented example does not assign any specific units for these measures, but there are many quantities you might measure whose units produce numeric values in those ranges. As an initial question, we might ask whether any of the features have a univariate correlation with the target. A machine learning model will find more than just this, but it is a useful first question.

```
unscaled.corr()
```

	Feature_1	Feature_2	Target
Feature_1	1.000000	-0.272963	0.992514
Feature_2	-0.272963	1.000000	-0.269406
Target	0.992514	-0.269406	1.000000

We see that `Feature_1` has a very strong positive correlation with the `Target`, and `Feature_2` has a moderate negative correlation. So on the face of it, a model should have plenty to work with. Indeed, we can tell from the correlation matrix that linear models would do extremely well, with or without normalization; but that is the topic of a different book. This point can be made visually by plotting `Target` against each feature.

```
plot_univariate_trends(unscaled)
```

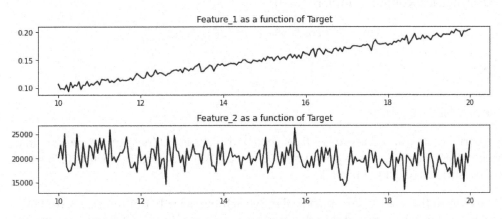

Figure 5.8: Feature_1 and Feature_2 as functions of Target

`Feature_1` has a visually obvious correlation; `Feature_2` reveals at most a very weak one to a human eye.

Applying a Machine Learning Model

As promised, let us apply a machine learning model against this data, trying to predict the target based on the features. In ML, we conventionally use the names X and y for features and target, respectively. This follows the common pattern, from high school algebra, of naming an independent variable x and a dependent variable y. Since we generally have multiple features, a capital X is used. While we cannot discuss the motivation in any depth, good practice in machine learning is to always reserve a portion of your training data for testing, so that you do not overfit your model. That is done with the function `train_test_split()`.

```
from sklearn.model_selection import train_test_split

X = unscaled.drop('Target', axis=1)
y = unscaled['Target']

X_train, X_test, y_train, y_test = (
    train_test_split(X, y, random_state=1))
```

For this example, we use a K-neighbors regressor to try to model our data. For many kinds of problems, this is a very effective algorithm, but it is also one that looks directly at distances in parameter space, and is hence very sensitive to scaling. If we naïvely apply this model to our raw data, the R-squared score is very low (other metrics would be similarly bad).

```
from sklearn.neighbors import KNeighborsRegressor

knn = KNeighborsRegressor()
knn.fit(X_train, y_train).score(X_test, y_test)
```

```
0.027756186064182953
```

A "perfect" R-squared score is 1.0. A very bad score is 0.0 (negative scores are also sometimes possible, and even worse in a sense). But for anything below 0.25 or so, we essentially reject the model.

By using, in this case, a min-max scaler, we achieve a far better metric score. The scaler we use here simply takes the minimum value of the raw feature, and shifts all values by that amount toward zero by subtraction, then divides all values by the shifted maximum value. The effect is to produce a range that is always [0, 1], for every feature. This synthetic feature does not have any physical meaning per se, as the original measure presumably did.

But by applying this scaler, all features are guaranteed to occupy the same numeric range (with the specific values distributed differently within their ranges). Let us apply this min-max scaling to our features before fitting the model again.

```
from sklearn.preprocessing import MinMaxScaler
X_new = MinMaxScaler().fit_transform(X)


X_train, X_test, y_train, y_test = (
    train_test_split(X_new, y, random_state=1))


knn2 = KNeighborsRegressor()
knn2.fit(X_train, y_train).score(X_test, y_test)
```

```
0.9743878175626131
```

Notice that I did not bother to scale the target in the above code. There would be no harm in doing so for the model, but there is no benefit either since the target is not part of the parameter space of the features. Moreover, if we scaled the target, we would have to remember to unscale it correspondingly to get a meaningful number in the desired units.

Scaling Techniques

The scaling technique we used above utilized scikit-learn's `MinMaxScaler`. All of the scalers in scikit-learn use the same API, and are implemented in an efficient and correct manner. There is certainly a good argument for using those within Python, even if scikit-learn is not otherwise part of your overall modeling pipeline. However, it is not difficult to do the same scaling "by hand" using lower-level vectorized operations. For example, this would be simple in NumPy; here we show an example in R, and focus only on the algorithm. One nice detail of the scikit-learn API is that it knows to normalize column-by-column. In the comparison, we only do one column.

```
%%R -i X,X_new
# Import the data frame/array from Python
py_raw_data <- X$Feature_1   # only feature 1
py_scaled <- X_new[,1]       # scaled column 1

# Utility function to scale as [0, 1]
normalize <- function(x) {
    floor <- min(x)   # Only find min once
    return ((x - floor) / (max(x) - floor))
}

# Scale the raw data
```

```
r_scaled <- normalize(py_raw_data)

# Near equality of elements from normalize() and MinMaxScaler
all.equal(py_scaled, r_scaled)
```

```
[1] TRUE
```

Notice that even for a straightforward operation like this, the different implementations, across libraries and languages, do not perform identical operations in an identical order. This allows some floating-point rounding differences to creep in. Comparing for strict equality of floating-point values is almost always the wrong thing to do; measurements have finite precision and operations introduce 1-ULP (unit in the last place) errors frequently. On the other hand, these slight numeric differences make no practical difference for actual models, only for equality checks.

```
%%R
print("A few 'equalities':")
print(py_scaled[1:5])
print(r_scaled[1:5])

print("Exactly equal?")
print((py_scaled == r_scaled)[1:10])

print("Mean absolute difference:")
print(mean(abs(py_scaled - r_scaled)))
```

```
[1] "A few 'equalities':"
[1] 0.1776148 1.0000000 0.7249096 0.6142706 0.8920478
[1] 0.1776148 1.0000000 0.7249096 0.6142706 0.8920478
[1] "Exactly equal?"
[1] TRUE FALSE FALSE FALSE FALSE TRUE FALSE TRUE TRUE TRUE
[1] "Mean absolute difference:"
[1] 6.130513e-17
```

Another very common scaling technique is called `StandardScaler` in scikit-learn. It sets the mean of a feature to 0 and the standard deviation to 1. This scaling is particularly relevant when a variable is (very roughly) normally distributed. The name hints that this approach is usually the default scaler to choose (although probably it was derived from "standard deviation" when the name was chosen). Let us implement it to illustrate the simple transformation. Here we display the values from `Feature_2`, which are around 20,000 in the raw data.

```
from sklearn.preprocessing import StandardScaler
X_new2 = StandardScaler().fit_transform(X)
```

```
# Second column for example (both were scaled)
plt.hist(X_new2[:, 1], bins=30)
plt.title("Value distribution after StandardScaler");
```

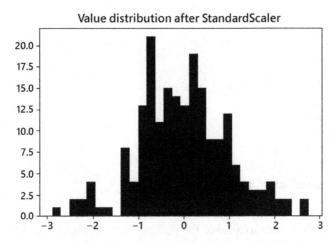

Figure 5.9: Feature_2 value distribution after the StandardScaler transformation

StandardScaler uses more numeric operations than MinMaxScaler, since it involves standard deviation, and that gives the calculation more opportunity for introducing numeric errors. The code in scikit-learn performs tricks to minimize this error better than the simple version we present, although again the magnitude is unlikely to be genuinely important. Let us manually reproduce the basic operation of StandardScaler.

```
%%R -i X,X_new2
# Import the data frame/array from Python
py_raw_data <- X$Feature_2  # Only feature 2
py_scaled <- X_new2[, 2]    # scaled column 2

r_scaled = (py_raw_data - mean(py_raw_data)) /
            sd(py_raw_data)

all.equal(py_scaled, r_scaled)
```

```
[1] "Mean relative difference: 0.002503133"
```

In this calculation, we do not pass the all.equal() test. R characterizes the failure beyond only a boolean FALSE. We can make the comparison with a bit more laxness by setting the tolerance parameter. Let us also verify the characteristics of the scaled data.

```
%%R
print("Mean from R scaling:")
print(mean(r_scaled))

print("Standard deviation:")
print(sd(r_scaled))

print("Almost equal with tolerance 0.005")
all.equal(py_scaled, r_scaled, tolerance = 0.005)
```

```
[1] "Mean from R scaling:"
[1] 6.591949e-17
[1] "Standard deviation:"
[1] 1
[1] "Almost equal with tolerance 0.005"
[1] TRUE
```

A number of variations are available for scaling through basic multiplication and subtraction operations. For example, rather than normalize on standard deviation, we could normalize using inter-quartile range (IQR). The scikit-learn class RobustScaler does this, for example. To some degree, IQR — or generally quantile-based approaches — are more robust against outliers. However, the degree to which IQR range scaling normalizes is limited, and a stricter quantile approach can be more aggressive.

Let us replicate Feature_1 in the sample dataset we are presenting, but make just one value (out of 200) an *extreme* outlier. Recall that Feature_1 has values on the order of 0.1. We will introduce a single value of 100 into the variable. Arguably, this is an extreme-enough outlier that we should have removed it already, using the techniques discussed in *Chapter 4, Anomaly Detection*, but for whatever reason we did not.

```
X['Feature_3'] = X.Feature_1
X.loc[0, 'Feature_3'] = 100
```

When we attempt to utilize RobustScaler, the transformed data still has one data point at an extreme value. In fact, that extreme is worse than the out-of-bounds value, 100, that we selected; moreover, the outlier is even farther out than under a StandardScaler transformation. RobustScaler is really only productive under a collection including a moderate number of moderate outliers (of the sort that might have escaped anomaly detection).

```
from sklearn.preprocessing import RobustScaler
X_new3 = RobustScaler().fit_transform(X)

# Third column for example (all were scaled)
plt.hist(X_new3[:, 2], bins=30)
plt.title("Value distribution after RobustScaler");
```

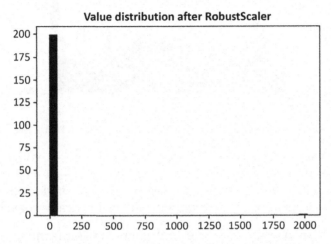

Figure 5.10: Feature_1 value distribution after RobustScaler

A stronger approach we can use is to rigorously scale values so that they fall *exclusively* within quantiles. In essence, this scales the data within each quantile range separately, and hence imposes both a reasonable distribution overall and strict bounds on values.

```
from sklearn.preprocessing import QuantileTransformer
# Ten quantiles is also called "decile"
deciles = QuantileTransformer(n_quantiles=10)
X_new4 = deciles.fit_transform(X)

# Third column for example (all were scaled)
plt.hist(X_new4[:, 2], bins=30)
plt.title("Value distribution after QuantileTransformer");
```

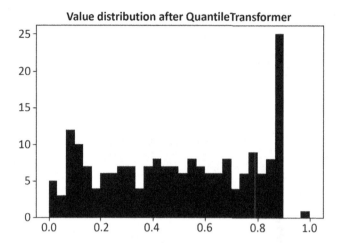

Figure 5.11: Feature_1 value distribution after QuantileTransformer

Obviously, this transformed data is not completely uniform — it would have little value if there was not *some* variability beyond ordinal order — but it is bounded and reasonably evenly distributed across the range [0, 1]. The single outlier point remains as a minor outlier from the main distribution, but is numerically not very distant.

In principle, even though the specific transformers in scikit-learn operate in a column-wise fashion, we might wish to apply a different scaling technique to each column or feature. As long as the particular transformation generates numeric ranges among the transformed values on roughly the same scale (i.e. usually of about distance one or two between maximum and minimum value, at least for the majority of data), all machine learning techniques that utilize distance in parameter space as part of their algorithm will be satisfied. Examples of such algorithms include linear models, support vector machines, and K-nearest neighbors. As was mentioned, algorithms in the family of decision trees simply do not care about specific distance in a dimension, and neural networks can perform a kind of scaling by allowing what we can informally call a "**scaling layer**" that at least *might* act as a multiplier of each input feature (exactly what a trained network "decides" to use neurons and layers for is always somewhat opaque to our intentions or understanding).

Factor and Sample Weighting

There are times when you will wish to give a particular feature more significance than *fair scaling* across features allows. This is a slightly different issue than the one that is addressed by sampling in *Chapter 6, Value Imputation*. In that later chapter, I discuss either undersampling or oversampling to produce more witnesses of minority target classes. That is certainly a possible approach to balancing classes within a feature rather than a target, but is not usually the best approach.

If nothing else, oversampling across two distinct unbalanced classes has the potential to explode the number of synthetic samples.

In the case of unbalanced feature classes, another approach is available. We can simply *overweight* minority classes rather than oversample them. Many machine learning models contain an explicit hyperparameter called something like `sample_weight` (the scikit-learn spelling). Separately from the sample weights, however, these same model classes will also sometimes have something like `class_weight` as a separate hyperparameter. The distinction here is exactly the one we have been making: sample weight allows you to overweight (or underweight) specific rows of input data, while class weight allows you to over/underweight specific target class values.

To add more nuance to this matter, we are not restricted to over/underweighting only to address class imbalance. We can, in fact, apply it for any reason we like. For example, we may know that certain measurements in our dataset are more reliable than others, and wish to overweight those. Or we may know that getting predictions right for samples with a certain characteristic is more important for task-specific reasons, even while not wishing entirely to discard those samples lacking that characteristic.

Let us return to the Apache log file example to illustrate all of these concerns. Recall that the processed data looks something like this:

```
reqs.sample(8, random_state=72).drop('page', axis=1)
```

	hour	minute	quad1	quad2	method
3347	0	4	172	69	GET
2729	9	43	172	69	GET
8102	4	16	172	69	GET
9347	0	48	162	158	GET
6323	21	30	162	158	GET
2352	0	35	162	158	GET
12728	9	0	162	158	GET
12235	19	3	172	69	GET

	path	status
3347	/publish/programming	200
2729	/TPiP	200
8102	/member/images	404
9347	/publish/images	304
6323	/download/pywikipedia/cache	200
2352	/download/gnosis/xml/pickle/test	200
12728	/download/relax	200
12235	/dede2	404

We noted that both `method` and `status` are highly imbalanced in pretty much the way we expect them to be in a working web server. The method data specifically has this imbalance that we saw plotted above, in *Figure 5.7*. The hypothetical task we have in mind is to predict status codes based on the other features of the dataset (without actually issuing an HTTP request, which might change based on the current time, for example).

```
reqs.method.value_counts()
```

```
GET      13294
HEAD       109
POST        48
Name: method, dtype: int64
```

In other words, GET requests are 122 times more common than HEAD requests, and 277 times more common than POST requests. We may be concerned that this limits our ability to make predictions on the rare class values for the method. Often our models will simply figure this out for us, but sometimes they will not. Moreover, although it is a frequently occurring path, we have decided that we need our model to be more sensitive to paths of /TPiP and so will artificially overweight that by 5x as well. Notice that in this stipulation, the overweighting has nothing whatsoever to do with the underlying distribution of the feature, but rather is a domain requirement of the underlying purpose of our modeling.

Likewise, we are especially concerned about predicting 404 status codes (i.e. enhance the recall of this label), but are not necessarily interested in the overall balance of the target. Instead, we will weight all other outcomes as 1, but weight 404s as 10, for task purposes we have determined before performing modeling. Let us do all of that in code, in this case using a random forest model from scikit-learn. Should some row match both the overweighted `path` and an underrepresented `method`, the larger multiplier for the `method` will take precedence.

```
# The row index positions for rows to overweight
tpip_rows = reqs[reqs.path == '/TPiP'].index
head_rows = reqs[reqs.method == 'HEAD'].index
post_rows = reqs[reqs.method == 'POST'].index

# Configure the weights in a copy of data frame
reqs_weighted = reqs.copy()
reqs_weighted['weight'] = 1  # Default weight of one
```

```
reqs_weighted.loc[tpip_rows, 'weight'] = 5
reqs_weighted.loc[head_rows, 'weight'] = 122
reqs_weighted.loc[post_rows, 'weight'] = 277

# Do not use column page in the model
reqs_weighted.drop('page', axis=1, inplace=True)

# View the configured weights
reqs_weighted.sample(4, random_state=72)
```

	hour	minute	quad1	quad2	method	path	status
3347	0	4	172	69	GET	/publish/programming	200
2729	9	43	172	69	GET	/TPiP	200
8102	4	16	172	69	GET	/member/images	404
9347	0	48	162	158	GET	/publish/images	304

	weight
3347	1
2729	5
8102	1
9347	1

These sample weights are stored on a per-row basis; in other words, we have 13,451 of them. For this example, most are simply weight 1, but they could all be distinct numbers, in concept. Configuring the weights we wish to use with the target is different. We *could* leverage the sample weight itself to choose rows with a certain target label; however, that approach is unnecessarily clunky and is not usually our preferred approach. Instead, we simply wish to create a small mapping from label to weight.

```
target_weight = {code:1 for code in reqs.status.unique()}
target_weight[404] = 10
target_weight
```

```
{200: 1, 304: 1, 403: 1, 404: 10, 301: 1, 500: 1, 206: 1}
```

Here we will create, fit, train, and score a scikit-learn model. The API will vary if you use some other library, but the concepts will remain the same. It only takes a line to perform a train/test split, as is good practice in real code. As a minor API detail, we need to encode our string categorical values for this model type, so we will use OrdinalEncoder.

```
from sklearn.ensemble import RandomForestClassifier
from sklearn.preprocessing import OrdinalEncoder

# Create the model object with target weights
rfc = RandomForestClassifier(class_weight=target_weight,
                             random_state=0)

# Select and encode the features and target
X = reqs_weighted[['hour', 'minute',
                   'quad1', 'quad2',
                   'method', 'path']]

# Encode strings as ordinal integers
X = OrdinalEncoder().fit_transform(X)
y = reqs_weighted['status']
weight = reqs_weighted.weight

# Perform the train/test split, including weights
X_train, X_test, y_train, y_test, weights_train, _ = (
    train_test_split(X, y, weight, random_state=1))

# Fit the model on the training data and score it
rfc.fit(X_train, y_train, sample_weight=weights_train)
rfc.score(X_test, y_test)
```

```
0.8183169788878977
```

As with R-squared used in the regression example, 1.0 represents perfect accuracy. Accuracy cannot be less than 0.0 though.

Without more context and analysis, I cannot say whether this model does well or poorly for the intended purpose. Quite possibly some other model class and/or some better-tuned weights would serve the hypothetical purpose better. The steps in trying those are straightforward, and mostly the same as the code shown.

We turn now to a difficult but important concept. Many times we wish to remove expected trends from data to reveal the exceptions to those trends.

Cyclicity and Autocorrelation

Do I contradict myself?
Very well then I contradict myself,
(I am large, I contain multitudes.)

–Walt Whitman

Concepts:

- Detrending sequential data
- Detected cycles versus a priori domain knowledge
- Expected versus distinctive variability
- Multiple cyclicities
- Autocorrelation

There are times when you expect your data to have periodic behavior within it. In such cases—especially when multiple overlapping cyclicities exist within sequential data—the deviations from the cyclical patterns can be more informative than the raw values. Most frequently we see this in association with time series data, of course. To some degree, this concern falls under the purview of *Chapter 7, Feature Engineering*, and indeed we return there to some of the same concerns, and even to the same dataset we discuss here.

As a first step, we would like to be able to recognize and analyze periodicities or cyclicities in our data. Some of these are intuitively obvious once we have some domain knowledge, but others lurk in the data themselves and not necessarily in our initial intuitions. For this section, I will utilize a dataset collected many years ago by my friend, and occasional co-author, Brad Huntting. For a period in the past, Brad collected temperatures in and outside his house in Colorado (USA), generally every 3 minutes. The data presented here covers a few days less than a year.

Rooms inside the house were regulated by thermostats; the outdoors naturally shows seasonal variation. Moreover, the data itself is imperfect. When we return to this data in *Chapter 7, Feature Engineering*, we will look at gaps, recording errors, and other problems in the data collection. For the purpose of this section, a minor degree of data cleanup and value imputation was performed in the code that loads the dataset. See also *Chapter 6, Value Imputation*, for additional discussion of imputation generally, with different examples.

First, let us read in the data using a Python function that loads a Pandas DataFrame. However, beyond the loading step, we will perform the analysis and visualization in R and its Tidyverse. Very similar capabilities exist in other libraries and languages, including Pandas. The underlying concepts are important here, not the specific APIs and languages used. Brad uses a web domain name of "glarp" so we use that same invented word for some variable names referring to this data about his house temperatures.

```python
thermo = read_glarp()
start, end = thermo.timestamp.min(), thermo.timestamp.max()
print("Start:", start)
print("  End:", end)
# Fencepost counting includes ends
print(" Days:", 1 + (end.date() - start.date()).days)
```

```
Start: 2003-07-25 16:04:00
  End: 2004-07-16 15:28:00
 Days: 358
```

Let us look at a few rows of the dataset to have a feeling for its nature. We can see that one row exists every 3 minutes during the interval of recording. For this section, the interval is completely regular at 3 minutes, and no missing values are present. Moreover, a few obvious recording errors in the raw data are cleaned up here with imputed values.

```r
%%R -i thermo
glarp <- as.tibble(thermo)
glarp
```

```
# A tibble: 171,349 x 5
   timestamp           basement   lab livingroom outside
   <dttm>                 <dbl> <dbl>      <dbl>   <dbl>
 1 2003-07-25 16:04:00       24  25.2       29.8    27.5
 2 2003-07-25 16:07:00       24  25.2       29.8    27.3
 3 2003-07-25 16:10:00       24  25.2       29.8    27.3
 4 2003-07-25 16:13:00     24.1  25.2       29.8    27.4
 5 2003-07-25 16:16:00     24.1  25.2       29.8    27.8
 6 2003-07-25 16:19:00     24.1  25.2       29.8    27.5
 7 2003-07-25 16:22:00     24.1  25.2       29.8    27.6
 8 2003-07-25 16:25:00     24.1  25.2       29.8    27.6
 9 2003-07-25 16:28:00     24.1  25.2       29.8    27.7
10 2003-07-25 16:31:00     24.1  25.2       29.8    27.6
# ... with 171,339 more rows
```

We can visualize this data as a first step to removing cyclicities with the goal of focusing on the ways in which individual measurements vary from *expectations*. These operations are also called "**detrending**" the data. Let us look first at outside temperatures, plotting their pattern using ggplot2.

```
%%R
ggplot(glarp, aes(x=timestamp, y=outside)) +
  geom_line() + clean_theme +
  ggtitle("Outside temperature over recording interval")
```

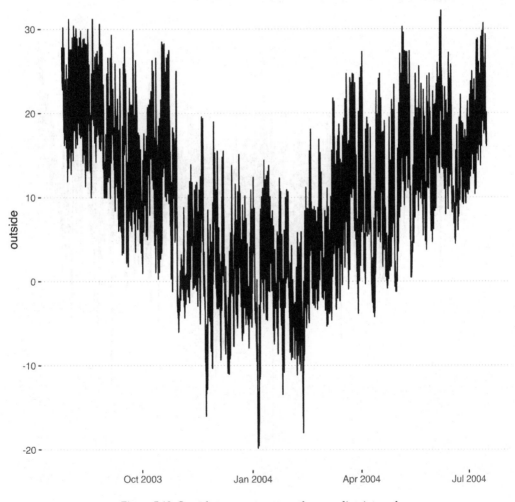

Figure 5.12: Outside temperature over the recording interval

As is easy to guess, there is a general pattern of northern hemisphere temperatures being warmer in July than in January, with a great deal of jitter within the global trend. Even though only 1 year of data is available, we know from very basic domain knowledge to expect similar annual cycles for other years. In contrast, as we can also anticipate, indoor temperatures both fall within a narrower range and show less of a clear pattern.

```
%%R
ggplot(glarp, aes(x=timestamp, y=basement)) +
  geom_line() + clean_theme +
  ggtitle("Basement temperature over recording interval")
```

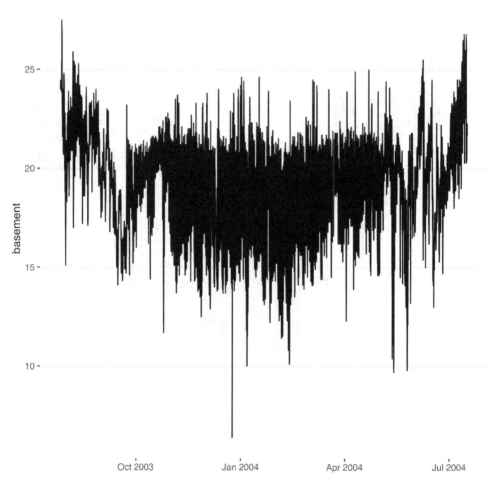

Figure 5.13: Basement temperature over the recording interval

Overall, indoor temperatures in the basement are relatively narrowly bound between about 14°C and 23°C. Some points fall outside of this range, both some high summer temperatures indicating that the house had a heating system but no air conditioner, and some low winter temperatures in sharp spikes, perhaps reflecting periods when windows were opened. However, the outside lows reached about -20°C while these indoor lows are generally above 10°C. Something somewhat odd seems to have happened around September and October of 2003 as well; perhaps this reflects some change in the heating system during that period.

Domain Knowledge Trends

As a first task, let us think about outdoor temperatures that are presumably little affected by the house heating system. We would like to identify unexpectedly warm or unexpectedly cold measurements as inputs to our downstream model. For example, a temperature of 10°C might either be a surprisingly cold summer temperature or a surprisingly warm winter temperature, but in itself it is merely globally typical and does not carry very much information about the observation without additional context.

Given that yearly temperatures will continue to repeat from year to year, it might make sense to model this yearly pattern as a portion of a sine wave. However, in shape, it certainly resembles a parabola for this period from roughly the warmest day of 2003 until roughly the warmest day of 2004. Since we are merely detrending a year-scale pattern, not *modeling* the behavior, let us fit a second-order polynomial to the data, which will account for *most* of the variation that exists in the measurements.

```
%%R
# Model the data as a second order polynomial
year.model <- lm(outside ~ poly(timestamp, 2), data = glarp)

# Display the regression and the data
ggplot(glarp, aes(x=timestamp)) + clean_theme +
  geom_line(aes(y = outside), color = "gray") +
  geom_line(aes(y = predict(year.model)),
            color = "darkred", size = 2) +
  ggtitle("Outside temperature versus polynomial fit")
```

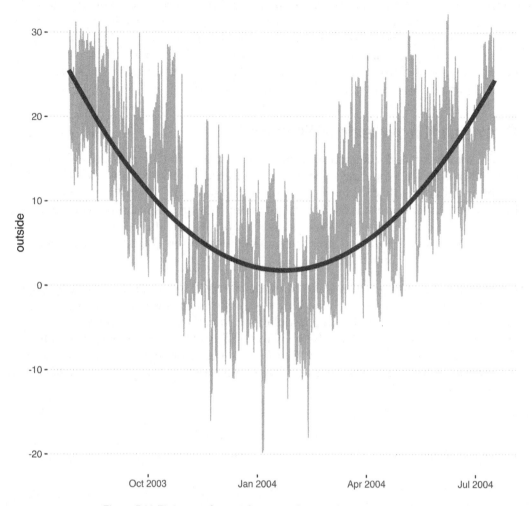

Figure 5.14: Fitting a polynomial curve to the outside temperature data

We can see in the plot that our annual detrending accounts for most of the data variation, so we can simply subtract the trend from the underlying points to get, as a first pass, the degree to which a measurement is unexpected. A new tibble named outside will hold the data for this narrower focus.

```
%%R
outside <- glarp[, c("timestamp", "outside")] %>%
    add_column(no_seasonal = glarp$outside - predict(year.model))
outside
```

```
# A tibble: 171,349 x 3
   timestamp           outside no_seasonal
   <dttm>                <dbl>       <dbl>
 1 2003-07-25 16:04:00    27.5        1.99
 2 2003-07-25 16:07:00    27.3        1.79
 3 2003-07-25 16:10:00    27.3        1.79
 4 2003-07-25 16:13:00    27.4        1.89
 5 2003-07-25 16:16:00    27.8        2.29
 6 2003-07-25 16:19:00    27.5        1.99
 7 2003-07-25 16:22:00    27.6        2.10
 8 2003-07-25 16:25:00    27.6        2.10
 9 2003-07-25 16:28:00    27.7        2.20
10 2003-07-25 16:31:00    27.6        2.07
# ... with 171,339 more rows
```

Visualizing the seasonally detrended temperatures, we see a remaining range from around -20°C to +20°C. This is somewhat less than the range of the raw temperatures, but only somewhat. Variability has decreased, but only modestly.

However, there is no obvious overall annual trend once we have performed this removal, and the synthetic value is centered at 0.

```
%%R
ggplot(outside, aes(x=timestamp)) +
  geom_line(aes(y = no_seasonal)) + clean_theme +
  ggtitle("Outside temperature with removed seasonal expectation")
```

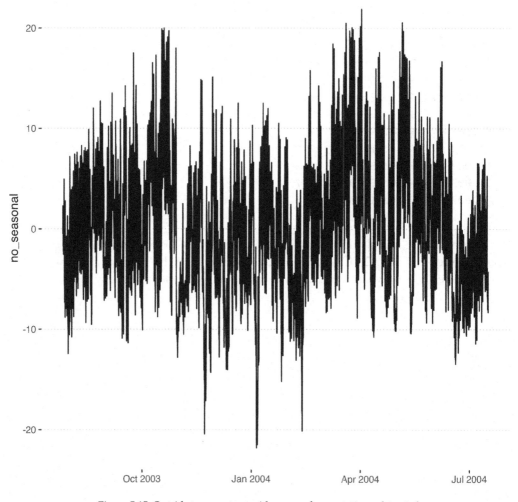

Figure 5.15: Outside temperature with seasonal expectation subtracted

The second obvious insight we might have into outdoor temperature cycles is that it is warmer during the day than at night. Given that there are 358 days of data, a polynomial will clearly not fit, but a trigonometric model is likely to fit to a better degree. We do not calculate a Fourier analysis here, but rather simply look for an expected daily cyclicity. Since we have observations every 3 minutes during each day, we wish to convert these 3,360 intervals into 2π radians for the regression to model. The model will simply consist of fitted sine and cosine terms, which can additively construct any sine-like curve on the specified periodicity.

```
%%R
# Make one day add up to 2*pi radians
x <- 1:nrow(outside) * 2*pi / (24*60/3)

# Model the data as a first order trigonometric regression
day_model <- lm(no_seasonal ~ sin(x) + cos(x),
                data = outside)
print(day_model)

# Create a new tibble the holds the regression
# and its removal from the annually detrended data
outside2 <- add_column(outside,
                day_model = predict(day_model),
                no_daily = outside$no_seasonal - day_model)
outside2
```

```
Call:
lm(formula = no_seasonal ~ sin(x) + cos(x), data = outside)

Coefficients:
(Intercept)        sin(x)         cos(x)
  0.0002343    -0.5914551      3.6214463

# A tibble: 171,349 x 5
    timestamp           outside no_seasonal day_model no_daily
    <dttm>                <dbl>       <dbl>     <dbl>    <dbl>
 1 2003-07-25 16:04:00     27.5        1.99      3.61    -1.62
 2 2003-07-25 16:07:00     27.3        1.79      3.60    -1.81
 3 2003-07-25 16:10:00     27.3        1.79      3.60    -1.80
 4 2003-07-25 16:13:00     27.4        1.89      3.59    -1.69
 5 2003-07-25 16:16:00     27.8        2.29      3.58    -1.28
 6 2003-07-25 16:19:00     27.5        1.99      3.56    -1.57
 7 2003-07-25 16:22:00     27.6        2.10      3.55    -1.46
 8 2003-07-25 16:25:00     27.6        2.10      3.54    -1.44
 9 2003-07-25 16:28:00     27.7        2.20      3.53    -1.33
10 2003-07-25 16:31:00     27.6        2.07      3.51    -1.44
# ... with 171,339 more rows
```

It is difficult to tell from just the first few rows of the data frame, but the daily detrending is typically closer to zero than the seasonal detrending alone. The regression consists mostly of a cosine factor, but is shifted a bit by a smaller negative sine factor. The intercept is very close to zero, as we would expect from the seasonal detrending. If we visualize the three lines, we can get some sense; in order to show it better, only one week in early August of 2003 is shown. Other time periods have a similar pattern; all will be centered at zero because of the detrending.

```R
%%R
week <- outside2[5000:8360,]
p1 <- ggplot(week, aes(x = timestamp)) +
  no_xlabel + ylim(-8, +8) +
  geom_line(aes(y = no_seasonal))
p2 <- ggplot(week, aes(x = timestamp)) +
  no_xlabel + ylim(-8, +8) +
  geom_line(aes(y = day_model), color = "lightblue", size = 3)
p3 <- ggplot(week, aes(x = timestamp)) +
   clean_theme + ylim(-8, +8) +
  geom_line(aes(y = no_daily), color = "darkred")
grid.arrange(p1, p2, p3,
            top = "Annual de-trended; daily regression; daily de-
trended")
```

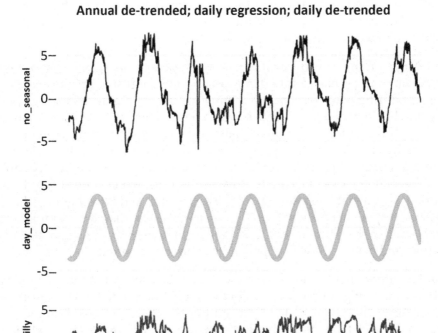

Figure 5.16: Annual detrended data; daily regression; daily detrended

The thicker, smooth line is the daily model of temperature. In electronic versions of this book, it will appear as light blue. At the top is the more widely varying seasonally detrended data. At the bottom, the daily detrended data has mostly lower magnitudes (in red if your reading format allows it). The third subplot is simply the subtraction of the middle subplot from the top one.

Around August 7 are some oddly low values. These look sharp enough to suggest data problems, but perhaps a thunderstorm brought August temperatures that much lower during one afternoon. One thing we can note in the date range plotted is that even the daily detrended data shows a weak daily cycle, albeit with much more noise. This would indicate that other weeks of the year have less temperature fluctuation than this one; in fact, some weeks will show an anti-cyclic pattern with the detrended data being an approximate inverse of the regression line. Notably, even on this plot, it looks like August 8 was anti-cyclic, while August 5 and 6 have a remaining signal matching the sign of the regression, and the other days have a less clear correspondence. By anti-cyclic, we do not mean that, for example, a night was warmer than the days around it, but rather that there was less than the expected fluctuation, and hence detrending produces an inverted pattern.

That said, while we have not removed every possible element of more complex cyclic trends, the range of most values in the doubly detrended data is approximately 8°C, whereas it was approximately 50°C for the raw data. Our goal is not to remove the underlying variability altogether but rather to emphasize the more extreme magnitude measurements, which this has done.

Discovered Cycles

We have good a priori beliefs about what outdoor temperatures are likely to do. Summers are warmer than winters, and nights are colder than days. However, no similarly obvious assumption presents itself for indoor temperatures. We saw earlier a plot for temperatures in Brad's basement. The data is interestingly noisy, but in particular we noticed that for about two summer months, the basement temperatures were pinned above about 21°C throughout the day and night. From this, we inferred that Brad's house had a heating system but no cooling system, and therefore the indoor temperature approximately followed the higher outdoor ones. We wish here to analyze only the heating system and its artificially maintained temperature, rather than the seasonal trend. Let us limit the data to non-summer days (here named according to the pattern in the data rather than the official season dates).

```r
%%R
not_summer <- filter(glarp,
                    timestamp >= as.Date("2003-08-15"),
                    timestamp <= as.Date("2004-06-15"))

# Plot only the non-summer days
ggplot(not_summer, aes(x=timestamp, y=basement)) +

  geom_line() + clean_theme +
  ggtitle("Basement temperature over non-summer days")
```

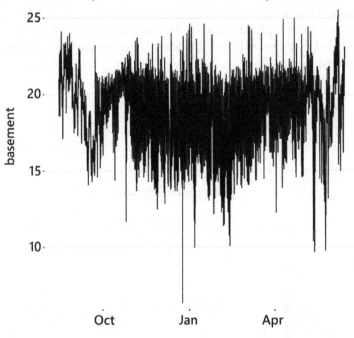

Figure 5.17: Basement temperature over non-summer days

Within the somewhat narrowed period, nearly every day of measurements has temperatures both above and below around 18-20°C, so most likely the heating system was operating for a portion of each day in almost all of these non-summer days. The question we would like to analyze—and perhaps to detrend—is whether cyclic patterns exist in indoor temperature data, among the considerable noisiness that is clearly present in the raw data.

A technique called **autocorrelation** lends itself well to this analysis. Autocorrelation is a mathematical technique that identifies repeating patterns, such as the presence of a periodic signal mixed with noise or non-periodic variation. In Pandas, the Series method .autocorr() looks for this. In R, the relevant function is called acf(). Other libraries or programming languages have similar capabilities. Let us take a look at what we discover. Note that we do not wish blindly to look for autocorrelations if our domain knowledge tells us that only certain periodicities "make sense" within the subject matter.

Although our data frame contains a timeseries column already, it is easier here simply to create one out of the basement column we will work with. The actual dates corresponding to data points are irrelevant for the operation; only their spacing in time is of interest. In particular, we can impose a frequency matching the number of observations in a day to get a plot labeled intuitively by the number of days. The acf() function generates a plot automatically, and returns an object with a number of values attached that you can utilize numerically. For the purpose of this section, the graph is sufficient.

```
%%R
per_day <- 24*60/3
basement.temps <- ts(not_summer$basement, frequency = per_day)
auto <- acf(basement.temps, lag.max = 10*per_day)
```

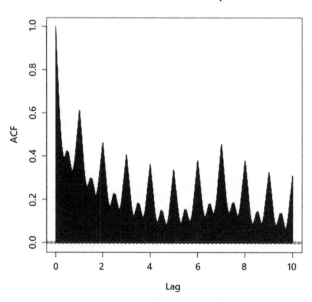

Figure 5.18: Density distribution of similarities at different increments

As the autocorrelation name suggests, this shows the correlation of the single data series with itself at each possible offset. Trivially, the zero increment is 100% correlated with itself. Everything other than that tells us something specific about the cyclicities within this particular data. There are strong spikes at each integral number of days. We limited the analysis to 10 days forward here. These spikes let us see that the thermostat in the basement had a setting to regulate the temperature to different levels at different times of each day, but in a way that was largely the same between one day and each of the next ten after it.

The spikes in this data are sloped rather than sharp (they are, at least, continuous rather than stepped). Any given 3-minute interval tends to have a similar temperature to those nearby it, diminishing fairly quickly, but not instantaneously, as measurements occur farther away. This is what we would expect in a house with a thermostat-controlled heating system, of course. Other systems might be different; for example, if a light was on a timer to come on for exactly 3 minutes then go out, on some schedule, the measurement of light levels would be suddenly, rather than gradually, different between adjacent measurements.

The pattern in the autocorrelation provides more information than only the daily cycle, however. We see also a lower correlation at approximately half-day intervals. This is also easily understood by thinking about the domain and the technology that produced it. To save energy, Brad set his thermostat timer to come on in the mornings when he'd wake up, then go to a lower level while he was at the office, then again to go up in the early evening when he returned home. I happen to know this was an automated setting, but the same effect might, for example, have occurred if it was simply a human pattern of manually adjusting the thermostat up and down at those times (the signal would probably be less strong than with a mechanical timer, but likely present).

Rising above the daily cyclicity, there is also a somewhat higher spike in the autocorrelation at 7 days. This indicates that days of the week are correlated with the temperature setting of the thermostat. Most likely, either because of a timer setting or human habit and comfort, a different temperature was set on weekdays versus weekends, for example. This secondary pattern is less strong than the general 24-hour cyclicity, but about as strong as the half-day cyclicity; examining the autocorrelation spikes more carefully could reveal exactly what duration Brad was at his office versus coming home, typically. The offset of the secondary spikes from the 24-hour spikes is probably not at exactly 12 hours, but is at some increment less than the full 24 hours.

We will not do these operations in this section, but think about using the autocorrelation as a detrending regression, much as we did with the trigonometric regression. This would effectively have separate periodicities of 12 and 24 hours, and at 7 days. Clearly, the raw data shown has a lot of additional noise, but it would presumably be reduced by subtracting out these known patterns. Some very atypical values would stand out even more strongly among this detrended data, and potentially thereby have even stronger analytic significance.

Sometimes the data validation that we need to perform is simply highly specific to the domain in question. For that, we tend to need more custom approaches and code.

Bespoke Validation

Explanations exist; they have existed for all time; there is always a well-known solution to every human problem – neat, plausible, and wrong.

–H. L. Mencken

Concepts:

- Leveraging domain knowledge beyond anomaly detection
- Example: evaluating duplicated data
- Validation as sanity check to further investigation

There are many times when domain knowledge informs the shape of data that is likely to be genuine versus data that is more likely to reflect some kind of recording or collation error. Even though general statistics on the data do not show anomalies, bias, imbalance, or other generic problems, we know something more about the domain or the specific problem that informs our expectations about "clean" data.

To illustrate, we might have an expectation that certain kinds of observations should occur with roughly a particular frequency compared to other observations; perhaps this would be specified further by the class values of a third categorical variable. For example, as background domain knowledge, we know that in the United States, family size is slightly less than 2 children, on average. If we had data that was meant to contain information about all the individual people in sampled households, we could use this as a guideline for the shape of the data. In fact, if we had auxiliary data on children per household by state, we might refine this reference expectation more when validating our data.

Obviously, we do not expect every household to have exactly 1.9 children in it. Given that humans come in integral units, we in fact could never have such a fractional number in any specific household at all. However, if we found that in our sampled households we averaged 0.5 children per household, or 4 children per household-with-children, we would have a strong indication that some kind of sample bias was occurring. Perhaps children are under- or overreported in the household data for individual households. Perhaps the selection of which households to sample biases the data toward those with children, or toward those without them. This scenario is largely similar to the issue addressed earlier in this chapter of comparisons to baselines. It adds only a minor wrinkle to the earlier examples in that we only identify households where we wish to validate our expectation of the number of children (i.e. under 18 years old) based on a shared address feature across several observations (that is, a household).

Collation Validation

Let us look at a completely different example that really cannot be formulated in terms of baseline expectations. In this section, we consider genomic data on ribosomal RNA (rRNA) that was downloaded from DNA Data Bank of Japan (DDBJ), specifically the 16S rRNA (Prokaryotes) in FASTA format (`ftp://ftp.ddbj.nig.ac.jp/ddbj_database/16S/`) dataset. You do not need to know anything about genomics or cellular biology for this example; we focus simply on the data formats used and an aggregation of records in this format.

Each sequence in this dataset contains a description of the organism in question and the nature of the sequence recorded. The FASTA format is widely used in genomics and is a simple textual format. Multiple entries in the line-oriented format can simply be concatenated in the same file or text. For example, a sequence entry might look like this:

```
FASTA
>AB000001_1|Sphingomonas sp.|16S ribosomal RNA
agctgctaatattagagccctatatatagaggggggccctatactagagatatatctatca
gctaatattagagccctatatatagaggggggccctatactagagatatatctatcaggct
attagagccctatatatagaggggggccctatactagagatataagtcgacgatattagca
agccctatatatagaggggggccctatactagagatatatctatcaggtgcacgatcgatc
cagctagctagc
```

The description published with this dataset indicates that each sequence contained is at least 300 base pairs, and the average length is 1,104 base pairs. There are 998,911 sequences contained as of this writing. Note that in DNA or RNA, every nucleobase uniquely determines which other base is paired in a double helix, so the format does not need to notate both. A variety of high-quality tools exist for working with genomic data; details of those are outside the scope of this book. However, as an example, let us use SeqKit to identify duplicated sequences. In this dataset, there are no pairs of sequences with the same name or ID, but quite a few contain the same base pairs. This is not an error, per se, since it reflects different observations. It may, however, be redundant data that is not useful for our analysis.

```
%%bash
cd data/prokaryotes
zcat 16S.fasta.gz |
    seqkit rmdup --by-seq --ignore-case \
                 -o clean.fasta.gz \
                 -d duplicated.fasta.gz \
                 -D duplicated.detail.txt
```

```
[INFO] 159688 duplicated records removed
```

Around 15% of all the sequences are duplicates. In general, these are multiple IDs that pertain to the same organism. We can see such in a quick examination of the duplication report produced by seqkit. As an exercise, you might think about how you would write a similar duplicate detection function in a general-purpose programming language; it is not particularly difficult, but SeqKit is certainly more optimized and better tested than would be a quick implementation you might produce yourself.

```
%%bash
cut -c-60 data/prokaryotes/duplicated.detail.txt | head
```

```
1384    JN175331_1|Lactobacillus, MN464257_1|Lactobacillus, MN4
1383    MN438326_1|Lactobacillus, MN438327_1|Lactobacillus, MN4
1330    AB100791_1|Lactococcus, AB100792_1|Lactococcus, AB10079
1004    CP014153_1|Bordetella, CP014153_2|Bordetella, CP014153_
934     MN439952_1|Lactobacillus, MN439953_1|Lactobacillus, MN43
912     CP003166_2|Staphylococcus, CP003166_3|Staphylococcus, CP
908     CP010838_1|Bordetella, CP010838_2|Bordetella, CP010838_3
793     MN434189_1|Enterococcus, MN434190_1|Enterococcus, MN4341
683     CP007266_3|Salmonella, CP007266_5|Salmonella, CP007266_6
609     MN440886_1|Leuconostoc, MN440887_1|Leuconostoc, MN440888
```

Horizontal transfer of rRNA between organisms is possible, but such an occurrence in the data might also represent a misclassification of an organism under examination. We can write some code to determine if such an event of multiple IDs for the same sequence are sometimes tagged as different bacteria (or perhaps archaea).

```python
def matched_rna(dupfile):
    """Count of distinct organisms per sequence match

    Return a mapping from line number in the duplicates
    to Counters of occurrences of species names
    """
    counts = dict()
    for line in open(dupfile):
        line = line.rstrip()
        _, match_line = line.split('\t')
        matches = match_line.split(', ')
        first_id = matches[0].split('|')[0]
        names = [match.split('|')[1] for match in matches]
        count = Counter(names)
        counts[first_id] = count
    return counts
```

It turns out that cataloging multiple organisms with apparently identical rRNA sequences is quite a common occurrence. But our analysis/validation may shed light on what is likely occurring with these duplicate records. Many lines in the duplication report show just one species with many observations. A significant minority show something else. Let us look at several examples.

```python
dupfile = 'data/prokaryotes/duplicated.detail.txt'
counts = matched_rna(dupfile)
```

In some examples, different observations have differing levels of specificity, but are not per se different organisms.

```python
print(counts['CP004752_1'])
print(counts['AB729796_1'])

Counter({'Mannheimia': 246, 'Pasteurellaceae': 1})
Counter({'Microbacterium': 62, 'Microbacteriaceae': 17})
```

Mannheimia is a genus of the family Pasteurellaceae, and Microbacterium is a genus of the family Microbacteriaceae. Whether these "discrepancies" need to be remediated in cleanup is very problem-specific, however. For example, we may wish to use the more general families in order to group matching sequences together. On the other hand, the problem may demand as much specificity in identifying organisms as is available. You have to decide how to process or handle different levels of specificity in your domain ontology.

A similar issue occurs in another record, but with what appears to be an additional, straightforward data error.

```
counts['AB851397_1']
```

```
Counter({'Proteobacteria': 1, 'proteobacterium': 2,
'Phyllobacteriaceae': 8})
```

Phyllobacteriaceae is a family in the broad phylum Proteobacteria, so either way we are dealing with rather non-specific classification. But "proteobacterium" appears to be a non-standard way of spelling the Linnaean family, both in being singular and in lacking of capitalization of the name.

Looking at another record, we might judge the classification as an observational error, but it is obviously difficult to be certain without deeper domain knowledge.

```
counts['CP020753_6']
```

```
Counter({'Shigella': 11, 'Escherichia': 153})
```

Both Shigella and Escherichia belong to the family Enterobacteriaceae. The identical sequence is characterized as belonging to different genera here. Whether this indicates a misidentification of the underlying organism or a horizontal transfer of rRNA between these organisms is not clear from this data alone. However, in your data science tasks, this is the sort of decision you are required to make, probably in consultation with domain experts.

One more record we can look at is very strange relative to this dataset. It shows many duplicates, but that is not really the surprising aspect.

```
counts['FJ537133_1']
```

```
Counter({'Aster': 1,
        "'Elaeis": 1,
        "'Tilia": 1,
        "'Prunus": 2,
        "'Brassica": 3,
        'Papaya': 1,
```

```
    "'Phalaris": 1,
    "'Eucalyptus": 1,
    "'Melochia": 1,
    'Chinaberry': 1,
    "'Catharanthus": 4,
    "'Sonchus": 1,
    "'Sesamum": 1,
    'Periwinkle': 1,
    'Candidatus': 1})
```

In this case, we have a number of genera of flowering plants — that is, eukaryotes — mixed with a dataset that is documented to catalog rRNA in prokaryotes. There is also a spelling inconsistency in that many of the genera listed have a spurious single-quote character at the beginning of their name. Whether or not it is plausible for these different plants, mostly trees, to share rRNA is a domain knowledge question, but it seems likely that these data do not belong within our hypothetical analysis of prokaryotic rRNA at all.

The examination of duplicated sequences in this dataset of rRNA sequences points to a number of likely problems in the collection. It also hints at problems that may lurk elsewhere within the collection. For example, even where identical sequences are not named by different levels of cladistic phylogeny, these differing levels may conflate the classification of other sequences. Perhaps, for example, this calls out for normalization of the data to a common phyletic level (which is a significantly large project, but it might be required for a task). Either way, this cursory validation suggests a need to filter the dataset to address only a well-defined collection of genera or families of organisms.

Transcription Validation

We discussed above, in this section, the possibility that the collection of records (i.e. sequences) may have problems in their annotation or aggregation. Perhaps records are inconsistent with each other or in some way present conflicting information. The examples we identified point to possible avenues for removal or remediation. In this second part of the section, we want to look at possible identifiable errors in the individual records.

This hypothetical is presented simply as a data example, not per se motivated by deep knowledge of RNA sequencing techniques. This is commonly the perspective of data scientists who work with domain experts. For example, I do not know how many of the measurements in the dataset utilized RNA-Seq versus older hybridization-based microarrays.

But for this purpose, let us suppose that a relatively common error in the sequencing technique causes inaccurate repetitions of short fragments of RNA base pairs that are not present in the actual measured rRNA. On the other hand, we also do know that microsatellites and minisatellites *do occur* in rRNA as well (although telomeres do not), so the mere presence of repeated sequences does not prove that a data collection error occurred; it is merely suggestive.

The purpose of this example is simply to present the idea that something as custom as what we do below *may* be relevant to your data validation for your specific domain. What we will look for is all the places where relatively long subsequences are repeated within a particular sequence. Whether this is an error or an interesting phenomenon is a matter for domain expertise. By default in the code below we look for repeated subsequences of 45 base pairs, but provide a configuration option to change that length. If each nucleotide were simply randomly chosen, each particular pattern of length 45 would occur with probability of about 10^{-27}, and repetitions — even with "birthday paradox" (https://en.wikipedia.org/wiki/Birthday_problem) considerations — would essentially never occur. But genetic processes are not so random as that.

As a first step, let us create a short function that iterates over a FASTA file, producing a more descriptive namedtuple for each sequence contained along with its metadata. Many libraries will do something similar, perhaps faster and more robustly than the code shown does, but the FASTA format is simple enough that such a function is simple to write.

```python
Sequence = namedtuple("FASTA", "recno ID name locus bp")

def get_sequence(fname):
    fasta = gzip.open(fname)
    pat = re.compile(r'n+')   # One or more 'n's
    sequence = []
    recno = 0
    for line in fasta:
        line = line.decode('ASCII').strip()
        if line.startswith('>'):
            # Modify base pairs to contain single '-'
            # rather than strings of 'n's
            bp = "".join(sequence)
            bp = re.sub(pat, '-', bp)   # Replace pat with a dash
            if recno > 0:
                yield Sequence(recno, ID, name, locus, bp)
            ID, name, locus = line[1:].split('|')
            sequence = []
```

```
        recno += 1
    else:
        sequence.append(line)
```

The get_sequence() function allows us to iterate lazily over all the sequences contained in a single gzipped file. Given that the total data is 1.1 GiB, not reading it all at once is an advantage. Beyond assuming such files are gzipped, it also makes an assumption that headers are formatted in the manner of the DDBJ rather than according to a different convention or lacking headers. As I say, other tools are more robust. Let us try reading just one record to see how the function works:

```
fname = 'data/prokaryotes/16S.fasta.gz'
prokaryotes = get_sequence(fname)
rec = next(prokaryotes)

print(rec.recno, rec.ID, rec.name, rec.locus)
print(fill(rec.bp, width=60))
```

```
1 AB000106_1 Sphingomonas sp. 16S ribosomal RNA
ggaatctgcccttgggttcggaataacgtctggaaacggacgctaataccggatgatgac
gtaagtccaaagatttatcgcccagggatgagcccgcgtaggattagctagttggtgagg
taaaggctcaccaaggcgacgatccttagctggtctgagaggatgatcagccacactggg
actgagacacggcccagactcctacgggaggcagcagtagggaatattggacaatgggcg
aaagcctgatccagcaatgccgcgtgagtgatgaaggccttagggttgtaaagctctttt
acccgggatgataatgacagtaccgggagaataagccccggctaactccgtgccagcagc
cgcggtaatacggagggggctagcgttgttcggaattactgggcgtaaagcgcacgtagg
cggcgatttaagtcagaggtgaaagcccggggctcaaccccggaatagcctttgagactg
gattgcttgaatccgggagaggtgagtggaattccgagtgtagaggtgaaattcgtagat
attcggaagaacaccagtggcgaaggcggatcactggaccggcattgacgctgaggtgcg
aaagcgtggggagcaaacaggattagataccctggtagtccacgccgtaaacgatgataa
ctagctgctggggctcatggagtttcagtggcgcagctaacgcattaagttatccgcctg
gggagtacggtcgcaagattaaaactcaaaggaattgacgggggcctgcacaagcggtgg
agcatgtggtttaattcgaagcaacgcgcagaaccttaccaacgtttgacatccctagta
tggttaccagagatggtttccttcagttcggctggctaggtgacaggtgctgcatggctg
tcgtcagctcgtgtcgtgagatgttgggttaagtcccgcaacgagcgcaacccctcgcctt
tagttgccatcattcagttgggtactctaaaggaaccgccggtgataagccggaggaagg
tggggatgacgtcaagtcctcatggcccttacgcgttgggctacacacgtgctacaatgg
cgactacagtgggcagctatctcgcgagagtgcgctaatctccaaaagtcgtctcagttc
ggatcgttctctgcaactcgagagcgtgaaggcggaatcgctagtaatcgcggatcagca
tgccgcggtgaatacgtccccaggtcttgtacacaccgcccgtcacaccatgggagttgg
tttcacccgaaggcgctgcgctaactcgcaagagaggcaggcgaccacggtgggatcagc
gactgggtgagtcgtacaggtgc
```

In order to check each sequence/record for the subsequence duplication we are concerned about, another short function can help us. This Python code uses a Counter again, as did the `matched_rna()` function earlier. It simply looks at every subsequence of a given length, many thereby overlapping, and returns only those counts that are greater than 1.

```
def find_dup_subseq(bp, minlen=45):
    count = Counter()
    for i in range(len(bp)-minlen):
        count[bp[i:i+minlen]] += 1
    return {seq: n for seq, n in count.items() if n > 1}
```

Putting it together, let us look at only the first 2,800 records to see if any have the potential problem we are addressing. Given that the full dataset contains close to 1 million sequences, many more such duplicates occur. An initial range was only chosen by trial and error to find exactly two examples. Duplicate subsequences are comparatively infrequent, but not so rare as not to occur numerous times among a million sequences.

```
for seq in islice(get_sequence(fname), 2800):
    dup = find_dup_subseq(seq.bp)
    if dup:
        print(seq.recno, seq.ID, seq.name)
        pprint(dup)
```

```
2180 AB051695_1 Pseudomonas sp. LAB-16
{'gtcgagctagagtatggtagagggtggtggaatttcctgtgtagc': 2,
 'tcgagctagagtatggtagagggtggtggaatttcctgtgtagcg': 2}
2534 AB062283_1 Acinetobacter sp. ST-550
{'aaaggcctaccaaggcgacgatctgtagcgggtctgagaggatga': 2,
 'aaggcctaccaaggcgacgatctgtagcgggtctgagaggatgat': 2,
 'accaaggcgacgatctgtagcgggtctgagaggatgatccgccac': 2,
 'aggcctaccaaggcgacgatctgtagcgggtctgagaggatgatc': 2,
 'ccaaggcgacgatctgtagcgggtctgagaggatgatccgccaca': 2,
 'cctaccaaggcgacgatctgtagcgggtctgagaggatgatccgc': 2,
 'ctaccaaggcgacgatctgtagcgggtctgagaggatgatccgcc': 2,
 'gcctaccaaggcgacgatctgtagcgggtctgagaggatgatccg': 2,
 'ggcctaccaaggcgacgatctgtagcgggtctgagaggatgatcc': 2,
 'ggggtaaaggcctaccaaggcgacgatctgtagcgggtctgagag': 2,
 'gggtaaaggcctaccaaggcgacgatctgtagcgggtctgagagg': 2,
```

```
'ggtaaaggcctaccaaggcgacgatctgtagcgggtctgagagga': 2,
'ggtggggtaaaggcctaccaaggcgacgatctgtagcgggtctga': 2,
'gtaaaggcctaccaaggcgacgatctgtagcgggtctgagaggat': 2,
'gtggggtaaaggcctaccaaggcgacgatctgtagcgggtctgag': 2,
'taaaggcctaccaaggcgacgatctgtagcgggtctgagaggatg': 2,
'taccaaggcgacgatctgtagcgggtctgagaggatgatccgcca': 2,
'tggggtaaaggcctaccaaggcgacgatctgtagcgggtctgaga': 2,
'tggtggggtaaaggcctaccaaggcgacgatctgtagcgggtctg': 2,
'ttggtggggtaaaggcctaccaaggcgacgatctgtagcgggtct': 2}
```

As before, this validation only points in the direction of asking domain- and problem-specific questions, and does not determine the correct action. Subsequence duplications may indicate errors in the sequencing process, but they might also reveal something relevant about the underlying domain, and genomic mechanisms. Collisions are far too unlikely to occur by mere chance, however.

Exercises

For the exercises of this chapter, we first ask you to perform a typical multi-step data cleanup using techniques you have learned. For the second exercise, you try to characterize sample bias in the provided dataset using analytic tools this book has addressed (or others of your choosing).

Data Characterization

For this exercise, you will need to perform a fairly complete set of data cleaning steps. The focus is on techniques discussed in this chapter, but concepts discussed in other chapters will be needed as well. Some of these tasks will require skills discussed in later chapters, so skip ahead briefly, as needed, to complete the tasks.

Here we return to the "Brad's House" temperature data, but in its raw form. The raw data consists of four files, corresponding to the four thermometers that were present. These files may be found at:

    https://www.gnosis.cx/cleaning/outside.gz

    https://www.gnosis.cx/cleaning/basement.gz

    https://www.gnosis.cx/cleaning/livingroom.gz

    https://www.gnosis.cx/cleaning/lab.gz

The format of these data files is a simple but custom textual format. You may want to refer back to *Chapter 1, Tabular Formats,* and to *Chapter 3, Repurposing Data Sources,* for inspiration on parsing the format. Let us look at a few rows:

```
%%bash
zcat data/glarp/lab.gz | head -5

2003 07 26 19 28 25.200000
2003 07 26 19 31 25.200000
2003 07 26 19 34 25.300000
2003 07 26 19 37 25.300000
2003 07 26 19 40 25.400000
```

As you can see, the space-separated fields represent the components of a datetime, followed by a temperature reading. The format itself is consistent for all the files. However, the specific timestamps recorded in each file are not consistent. All four data files end on 2004-07-16T15:28:00, and three of them begin on 2003-07-25T16:04:00. Various and different timestamps are missing in each file. For comparison, we can recall that the full data frame we read with a utility function that performs some cleanup has 171,346 rows. In contrast, the line counts of the several data files are:

```
%%bash
for f in data/glarp/*.gz; do
    echo -n "$f: "
    zcat $f | wc -l
done

data/glarp/basement.gz: 169516
data/glarp/lab.gz: 168965
data/glarp/livingroom.gz: 169516
data/glarp/outside.gz: 169513
```

All of the tasks in this exercise are agnostic to the particular programming languages and libraries you decide to use. The overall goal will be to characterize each of the 685k data points as one of several conceptual categories that we present below.

Task 1: Read all four data files into a common data frame. Moreover, we would like each record to be identified by a proper native timestamp rather than by separated components. You may wish to refer forward to *Chapter 7, Feature Engineering,* which discusses date/time fields.

Task 2: Fill in all missing data points with markers indicating they are explicitly missing. This will have two slightly different aspects. There are some implied timestamps that do not exist in any of the data files. Our goal is to have 3-minute increments over the entire duration of the data. In the second aspect, some timestamps are represented in some data files but not in others. You may wish to refer to the *Missing Data* section of this chapter and the same-named one in *Chapter 4, Anomaly Detection*; as well, the discussion of date/time fields in *Chapter 7* is likely relevant.

Task 3: Remove all regular trends and cycles from the data. The relevant techniques may vary between the different instruments. As we noted in the discussion in this chapter, three measurement series are of indoor temperatures regulated, at least in part, by a thermostat, and one is of outdoor temperatures. Whether or not the house in question had differences in thermostats or heating systems between rooms is left for readers to try to determine based on the data (at the very least though, heat circulation in any house is always imperfect and not uniform).

 Note: As a step in performing detrending, it may be useful to temporarily impute missing data, as is discussed in *Chapter 6, Value Imputation*.

Task 4: Characterize every data point (timestamp and location) according to these categories:

- A "regular" data point that falls within generally expected bounds.
- An "interesting" data point that is likely to indicate relevant deviation from trends.
- A "data error" that reflects an improbable value relative to expectations, and is more likely to be a recording or transcription error. Consider that a given value may be improbable based on its delta from nearby values and not exclusively because of absolute magnitude. *Chapter 4* is likely to be relevant here.
- A missing data point.

Task 5: Describe any patterns you find in the distribution of characterized data points. Are there temporal trends or intervals that show most or all data characterized in a certain way? Does this vary by which of four instruments we look at?

Oversampled Polls

Polling companies often deliberately utilize oversampling (overselection) in their data collection. This is a somewhat different issue than the overweighting discussed in a topic of this chapter, or than the mechanical oversampling that will be addressed in *Chapter 6, Value Imputation*. Rather, the idea here is that a particular class, or a value range, is known to be uncommon in the underlying population, and hence the overall parameter space is likely to be sparsely filled for that segment of the population. Alternately, the oversampled class may be common in the population but also represents a subpopulation about which the analytic purpose needs particularly high discernment.

The use of oversampling in data collection itself is not limited to human subjects surveyed by polling companies. There are times when it similarly makes sense for entirely unrelated subject domains, for example, the uncommon particles produced in cyclotrons or the uncommon plants in a studied forest. Responsible data collectors, such as the Pew Research Center that collected the data used in this exercise, will always explicitly document their oversampling methodology and expectations about the distribution of the underlying population. You can, in fact, read all of these details about the 2010 opinion survey we utilize at:

```
https://www.pewsocialtrends.org/2010/02/24/millennials-confident-
connected-open-to-change/
```

However, to complete this exercise, we prefer you skip initially consulting that documentation. For the work here, pretend that you received this data without adequate accompanying documentation and metadata (just to be clear: Pew is meticulous here). Such is all too often the case in the real world of messy data. The raw data, with no systematic alteration to introduce bias or oversampling, is available by itself at:

```
https://www.gnosis.cx/cleaning/pew-survey.csv
```

Task 1: Read in the data, and make a judgment about what ages were deliberately over- or undersampled, and to what degree. We may utilize this weighting in later synthetic sampling or weighting, but for now, simply add a new column called `sampling_multiplier` to each observation of the dataset matching your belief.

For this purpose, treat 1x as the "neutral" term. So, for example, if you believe 40-year-old subjects were overselected by 5x, assign the multiplier 5.0. Symmetrically, if you believe 50-year-olds were systematically underselected by 2x, assign the multiplier 0.5. Keep in mind that humans in the United States in 2010 were not uniformly distributed by age.

Moreover, with a sample size of about 2,000 and 75 different possible ages, we expect some non-uniformity of subgroup sizes simply from randomness. Merely random variation from the neutral selection rate should still be coded as 1.0.

Task 2: Some of the categorical fields seem to encode related but distinct binary values. For example, this question about technology is probably not ideally coded for data science goals:

```
pew = pd.read_csv('data/pew-survey.csv')
list(pew.q23a.unique())
```

```
['New technology makes people closer to their friends and family',
 'New technology makes people more isolated',
 '(VOL) Both equally',
 "(VOL) Don't know/Refused",
 '(VOL) Neither equally']
```

Since the first two descriptions may either be mutually believed or neither believed by a given surveyed person, encoding each as a separate boolean value makes sense. How to handle a refusal to answer is an additional decision for you to make in this re-encoding. Determine which categorical values should better be encoded as multiple booleans, and modify the dataset accordingly. Explain and justify your decisions about each field.

Task 3: Determine whether any other demographic fields than age were oversampled. While the names of the columns are largely cryptic, you can probably safely assume that a field with qualitative answers indicating degree of an opinion are dependent variables surveyed rather than demographic independent variables. For example:

```
list(pew.q1.unique())
```

```
['Very happy', 'Pretty happy', 'Not too happy', "(VOL) Don't know/
Refused"]
```

You may need to consult outside data sources to make judgments for this task. For example, you should be able to find the rough population distribution of US timezones (in 2010) to compare to the dataset distribution.

```
list(pew.timezone.unique())
```

```
['Eastern', 'Central', 'Mountain', 'Pacific']
```

Task 4: Some fields, such as q1 presented in *Task 3*, are clearly ordinally encoded. While it is not directly possible to assign relative ratios for (Very happy:Pretty happy) versus (Pretty happy:Not too happy), the ranking of those three values is evident, and calling them ordinal 1, 2, and 3 is reasonable and helpful. You will, of course, also have to encode refusal to answer in some fashion. Re-encode all relevant fields to take advantage of this intuitive domain knowledge you have.

Denouement

> *Quality is never an accident. It is always the result of intelligent effort.*
>
> *–John Ruskin*

Topics covered in this chapter: Missing Data (revisited); Bias; Class Imbalance; Normalization; Scaling; Overweighting; Cyclicity; Bespoke Validation.

In this chapter, we focused on the problem of bias in data. Datasets rarely, if ever, completely represent a population; rather they skew and select from that population to form a certain kind of picture. Sometimes this bias is intentional and well-founded as a way of filling parameter spaces. Other times it simply reflects the distribution of quantities or classes in the underlying reality. In this case, it is both the inherent virtue of our data and a pitfall in our analysis. But at other times still, elements of the data collection, collation, transcription, or aggregation can introduce biases that are more subtle and may need to be remediated in some manner for our analyses and modeling of the data. Detecting bias is the first step toward addressing it.

Related to bias, but somewhat parallel as a concern, are cyclicities in data. Very often a particular series of data—when the data is ordered in some manner, often as a time series—has components of "signal" and "variation" that can be usefully separated. A signal is, in some sense, a kind of bias, in that it provides an expectation that at time T there is a higher probability the measurement will be close to M. Identifying the signals is often an important aspect of data analysis—they are often not a priori—but identifying the deviations from the signal also provides an additional channel of interesting information.

The prior chapter on anomaly detection provided hints about identifying data that is generically statistically unlikely within a collection of values. But very often we want to look at problems that are more domain-specific. We are often able to take advantage of expectations we have about patterns in clean data that might be violated by the data we actually have. These patterns might only be represented by custom code that algorithmically expresses these expectations but that cannot be formulated in terms of generic statistical tests.

In the next chapter, we turn to the important and subtle question of imputing data.

PART III

Rectification and Creation

6

Value Imputation

I'm a substitute for another guy
I look pretty tall but my heels are high
The simple things you see are all complicated
I look pretty young, but I'm just back-dated, yeah

–Pete Townsend

Data can be missing or untrusted in a variety of ways, and for a variety of reasons. These ways are discussed especially in *Chapter 4, Anomaly Detection*, and *Chapter 5, Data Quality*. Sometimes your best option for dealing with bad data is simply to discard it. However, many times it is more useful to impute values in some manner, in order to retain the rest of the features within an observation. From the perspective of this chapter, let us assume that all data values identified as untrusted—even if initially present with *bad* values—have already been explicitly marked as missing.

When imputing data, it is important to keep a good record of the difference between values you have invented (imputed) and those that arrived with the original dataset. This record *might* take the form of an explicit annotation to each data item, depending on what your data formats enable. The most usual way to keep records is by maintaining versions of your data as you clean them in various ways, and maintaining (and versioning) explicit scripts that perform the modifications repeatably.

Generally, data comes grouped as many records or observations. The tabular form that we ultimately require for machine learning and many statistical purposes is clear this way. One row is an "observation," at least loosely, and each column represents a feature we wish, ideally, to have for every observation. Even data that is initially stored in a hierarchical or otherwise non-tabular structure needs to be translated to a record-oriented representation before we do most analyses on it. The initial form will still be partitioned in some record-like manner: maybe separate files, or separate top-level keys for nested data, or separate partitions based on some task-specific purpose.

The decision to impute values versus discard records need not be all or nothing. It might be the case that we have decided that some records are possible or desirable to save and others are not. Several considerations are generally present in our decision, whether done by record or for the problem generally. The predominant emphasis in these considerations assumes a machine learning use of a dataset; visualizations or analytics that are not "machine learning" per se worry about imputation much less often, but definitely sometimes. Some issues to consider include:

- Do you have *a lot* of data? If your data is limited, conserving every record possible can be especially important. Machine learning models, *mutatis mutandis*, are that much happier the more data they have to work with. If you have millions — or even tens of thousands — of records left after you discard those with missing data, you may be able to worry less about imputation.*effectiveness* If you only have hundreds of records, every one feels precious; of course, with fewer records, flawed imputation can also have a disproportionate effect.

- Do you have knowledge or suspicion that missing data occurs in a biased way? If the missing records are likely to concern observations that have a different characteristic or pattern than the overall dataset, it can be especially important to salvage them. Perhaps one sensor location or one time frame is closely associated with missing data. That location or time is likely to be needed to well capture some aspect of the domain modeled.

- Following on the bias issue, you may decide that it is OK to discard those records with missing data that belong to the "random flaw" subset, but that those records with systematic missing data are crucial since they address a different region of the parameter space of the problem.

- Do your records have many or few features? A record with five features and two of them missing is unlikely to retain much useful weight for good models. A record with one feature missing out of fifty or a thousand is much more likely to be worth remediating.

- What is the role of the missing value? If the target feature is missing from a supervised learning training set—i.e. for a classification or regression problem—imputation is very unlikely to do you much good. It is much more likely to be useful to impute an input feature. However, even there, the role of that input feature in the problem or domain can vary; a particular feature can be pivotal from a "business purpose" perspective, whether or not it is actually the most predictive feature. Imputing a feature of central task importance is generally unwise.

effectiveness

A well-known and compelling essay about how very large datasets turn out to solve many of our problems for us is The Unreasonable Effectiveness of Data (`https://static.googleusercontent.com/media/research.google.com/en//pubs/archive/35179.pdf`), by Alon Halevy, Peter Norvig, and Fernando Periera.

The first two sections of this chapter look at single-value imputation. This fits straightforwardly with what we always think of as imputation. The last section looks at oversampling and undersampling, which are whole-dataset modifications. Both organizationally and conceptually, it is worth addressing those under the topic of imputation. The goal with sampling is to produce a dataset that we believe better resembles the reality we are trying to model—exactly what imputation is about.

Typical-Value Imputation

And there's another marketing ploy
Typical girl gets the typical boy

–Ari Up, Paloma McLardy, Tessa Pollitt, and Viv Albertine

Concepts:

- Identifying values to impute
- Central tendency within a dataset
- Mean, median, geometric mean, and multi-modal data
- Population-based central tendency
- Neighboring data expressing a tendency

Pretty much the simplest thing we can do is assume a missing value is similar to the general trend for that same feature. In some cases, domain knowledge may inform us as to what a reasonable default is, in the absence of specific information about a particular record. Absent that background, however, the data that exists can provide guidance for imputation.

Typical Tabular Data

Let us look at the Dermatology Data Set (`https://archive.ics.uci.edu/ml/datasets/Dermatology`) available from the UCI Machine Learning Repository. This data contains 34 measurements of 366 patients, with each one diagnosed as having one of six skin conditions. Most of the features are ordinal coded measures of the severity of one feature observed.

We get this data in somewhat raw form. The `dermatology.data` file is a CSV with no headers. The `dermatology.names` file contains a bit more than its name might suggest. Beyond providing the feature names, it gives an additional exposition of the dataset, such as value coding, where unknown values occur, and a few other things, in prose. The `dermatology.py` file in this book's repository contains some moderate massaging of the data into a data frame.

```
from src.setup import *
from src.dermatology import *
df.iloc[:, [0, 1, 2, 3, -2, -1]].sample(6)
```

	erythema	scaling	definite borders	itching	Age
247	2	2	2	0	62
127	2	2	2	2	44
230	3	2	0	1	30
162	3	2	2	2	22
159	3	2	2	1	47
296	2	1	1	3	19

	TARGET
247	psoriasis
127	lichen planus
230	seboreic dermatitis
162	lichen planus
159	seboreic dermatitis
296	cronic dermatitis

A quick view of the sample rows does not reveal obviously missing data. We can investigate further to identify likely missing data. From the description provided, we know that observed severities are intended to be encoded as 0, 1, 2, or 3 (the feature "family history" as 0 or 1). Is anything outside this coding?

```
clean, suspicious = [], {}
for col in df.columns:
    values = df[col].unique()
    if set(values) <= {0, 1, 2, 3}:
        clean.append(col)
    else:
        suspicious[col] = values
```

Most fields are limited to the expected coding values.

```
print("No problem detected:")
pprint(clean[:8])
print(f"... {len(clean)-8} other fields")
```

```
No problem detected:
['erythema',
 'scaling',
 'definite borders',
 'itching',
 'koebner phenomenon',
 'polygonal papules',
 'follicular papules',
 'oral mucosal involvement']
... 25 other fields
```

A few other fields fall outside the coding set. However, one of them is TARGET, which contains only reasonable names and spellings of the several conditions diagnosed. Age, for the most part, also contains reasonable human ages, except one value of '?' is also present there. This is the manner in which this dataset encodes missing data.*missing*

missing

The Pandas library, in particular, by default recognizes a variety of string values as meaning "missing." You can manually configure, per column, what values count as missing within pandas.read_csv() and other functions that infer data types. As of this writing, and Pandas 1.0, these defaults are exactly these strings: '', '#N/A', '#N/A N/A', '#NA', '-1.#IND', '-1.#QNAN', '-NaN', '-nan', '1.#IND', '1.#QNAN', '<NA>', 'N/A', 'NA', 'NULL', 'NaN', 'n/a', 'nan', and 'null'.

Other libraries may or may not perform similar inference/guessing, and those that do will probably use a different collection of default strings. For data formats that directly encode floating-point values, often a NaN ("not a number") value, which is part of the IEEE-754 specification for floating-point numbers, is used to identify missing data. Philosophical attitudes vary about the correctness of this encoding, but you will definitely see it often. At other times, "special" values occur, such as -1 (hopefully for a measure that must be positive) or 99999 (hopefully for a measure expected to be orders of magnitude lower).

```
# Notice age has some expected ages and also a '?'
print("Suspicious:")
pprint(suspicious)

Suspicious:
{'Age': array(['55', '8', '26', '40', '45', '41', '18', '57', '22', '30', '20',
               '21', '10', '65', '38', '23', '17', '51', '42', '44', '33', '43',
               '50', '34', '?', '15', '46', '62', '35', '48', '12', '52', '60',
               '32', '19', '29', '25', '36', '13', '27', '31', '28', '64', '39',
               '47', '16', '0', '7', '70', '37', '61', '67', '56', '53', '24',
               '58', '49', '63', '68', '9', '75'], dtype=object),
 'TARGET': array(['seboreic dermatitis', 'psoriasis', 'lichen planus',
                  'cronic dermatitis', 'pityriasis rosea',
                  'pityriasis rubra pilaris'], dtype=object)}
```

Having identified the somewhat unusual value used by this dataset for missing data, we should often re-encode it using a more standard approach. In particular, converting the string value ages to floating-point numbers with NaN used for the missing data is a very common style, and one that Pandas treats in some convenient and useful ways. To accomplish this in Pandas, we first substitute a known "missing" value for the '?', then cast the column to floating-point. We can see that several rows have adjusted values.

```
# Assign missing ages marked with '?' as None
df.loc[df.Age == '?', 'Age'] = None  # or NaN
# Convert string/None ages to floating-point
df['Age'] = df.Age.astype(float)
# Display those rows with missing ages
df.loc[df.Age.isnull()].iloc[:, -4:]
```

	inflammatory monoluclear inflitrate	band-like infiltrate	Age	TARGET
33	0	0	NaN	psoriasis
34	0	0	NaN	pityriasis rosea
35	0	0	NaN	seboreic dermatitis
36	0	3	NaN	lichen planus
262	3	0	NaN	cronic dermatitis
263	2	0	NaN	cronic dermatitis
264	3	0	NaN	cronic dermatitis
265	3	0	NaN	cronic dermatitis

The question arises as to what value we might impute as "typical" for this dataset. 358 rows have specific ages, all in the reasonable range of human lifespans. Eight rows have missing values. There are a number of familiar ways of identifying the "central tendency" of a data collection. Ones that stand out are mode, median, mean, geometric mean, and less often, harmonic mean. In Pandas specifically, only the first three of these are built-in methods. For geometric mean or harmonic mean you will generally use scipy.stats.gmean or scipy.stats.hmean (neither is difficult to construct as a custom function). In a different programming language or tool, these details will vary, but the concept will be the same.

Geometric mean is useful when data covers several orders of magnitude. Often these are the same kinds of data you would plot using a log scale axis. Measurements concerning exponential growth are often appropriately "averaged" with geometric mean. Harmonic mean is useful when you are comparing *rates* of action. For example, if you have a feature that measures the velocity of some objects, the typical value is best measured as harmonic mean.

Keep in mind that these several averages are often numerically close to each other, and since an imputation is a guess to begin with, the choice among them *may* be striving for a *false precision.*

precision

False precision (also called overprecision, fake precision, misplaced precision, and spurious precision) occurs when numerical data are presented in a manner that implies better precision than is justified; since precision is a limit to accuracy, this often leads to overconfidence in the accuracy, named *precision bias.*

For data collections that have a more or less linear distribution, including a normal distribution, one of the more commonplace averages is probably appropriate. We might try the modal age of the patients as a good representation. We encounter in this dataset a multi-modal distribution, which is common in small data. Moreover, with ages between 0 and 80 years, and only 358 data points, the data is generally "lumpy." Mode is probably not a good approach (but could be if one value clearly predominated).

```
df.Age.mode()
```

```
0    40.0
1    50.0
dtype: float64
```

We can use a quick plot to get a better sense of the distribution of ages, and perhaps an idea about what value might be typical. Axis labels and ticks are omitted because we want only an overall sense of the distribution in our exploration.

```
(df.Age
    .value_counts()
    .sort_index()
    .plot(kind="bar", yticks=[], xticks=[],
        title="Age distribution of patients "
            f"({df.Age.min():.0f} to {df.Age.max():.0f})")
);
```

Age distribution of patients (0 to 75)

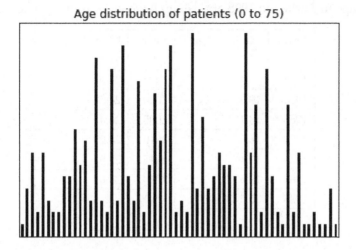

Figure 6.1: Age distribution of patients (0 to 75)

In this case, nothing particularly jumps out as a likely candidate. There are a few peaks only slightly less than the two modes, and no prevalent pattern to the noisy data.

Most likely mean or median are more representative. These values come out as reasonably close to each other here, although both are notably different from both modes.

```
df.Age.mean(), df.Age.median()
```

```
(36.29608938547486, 35.0)
```

However, we might also attempt to use domain knowledge to make more informed choices about a value to impute. For example, the metadata describing this dataset indicates that it was developed by several Turkish researchers and published in 1998. Patient confidentiality prohibits disclosure of more precise details, but we might consult historical demographic data, such as this table obtained from Statista (https://www.statista.com/), based on World Trade Organization datasets.

The median age in Turkey in 1998 appears to have been approximately 24 years old.

Year	Median Age	Year	Median Age
1950	19.7	1990	21.7
1955	19.4	1995	23.0
1960	19.6	2000	24.5
1965	18.4	2005	26.4
1970	18.5	2010	28.2
1975	19.1	2015	29.8
1980	19.5	2020	31.6
1985	20.5		

(Source: WTO, 2018; 2020 projected)

Of course, if our domain knowledge ran deeper than this population information, we might also have knowledge about general age correlations with skin conditions. As a non-expert, I tend to assume that such conditions generally increase with age, but good imputation should have a basis beyond only a vague hunch. For the purpose of this book, let us impute unknown values as the median age *within the data itself.*

```
df.loc[df.Age.isnull(), 'Age'] = df.Age.median()
df.Age.value_counts().head()
```

```
35.0    22
50.0    17
40.0    17
36.0    16
27.0    16
Name: Age, dtype: int64
```

Imputed 35-year-olds become a bit over-represented, but not dramatically so. And age-related tendencies should be middling for these imputed observations.

Locality Imputation

Trends and locality are clearly related, in some sense. For example, in a time series, the measurement taken at one particular minute is "local" to the measurement taken at the next minute by the same instrument. That is, assuming a roughly minute-scale measurement frequency; in a domain I worked in for a number of years—molecular dynamics—time steps are roughly femtoseconds (10^{-15}), and a minute is vastly outside the range of any achievable simulation. Conversely, in geology or cosmology, minutes are immeasurably small when sequencing epochs. In any case, linear or sequential locality is addressed in the next section on trend imputation.

Locality in general, however, is not specifically about sequence. For example, in a dimensional space—whether directly representing a physical space, or concerning a parameter or phase space—locality might simply be "closeness" in the space. Imputing values based on the other values that are nearby is often a reasonable way of filling in data we do not actually have. In some cases, locality-based imputation is more likely to represent the underlying data than is assuming a global default value.

For example, another dataset available from the UCI Machine Learning Repository is a collection of handwritten digits (`https://archive.ics.uci.edu/ml/datasets/Optical+Recognition+of+Handwritten+Digits`) that might be recognized by an optical character recognition application. These particular scanned images include anti-aliasing, so that the actual strokes in black ink are typically surrounded by gray pixels of varying darkness. While adjacent boundaries between dark and light do occur, often intermediate grays exist between black and white pixels. In photographic images, intermediate colors between regions of an image are even more common.

I have modified a subset of the UCI digit images by randomly dropping out some pixels. In this representation, a missing grayscale value is represented by -1. The actual scanned pixel values are between 0 (white) and 16 (black). Let us take a look at the dataset briefly. We can see that it is 50 samples of 8 × 8 images. Each of the positions in the 8 × 8 array is a small integer.

```
print("Array shape:", digits.shape)
```

```
Array shape: (50, 8, 8)
```

Each digit array has a few -1 values in it. We can get a sense of the missing data by visualizing the pixels with shades along with values. Several samples are shown, with each missing pixel containing an 'x' inside it.

```
show_digits(digits)
```

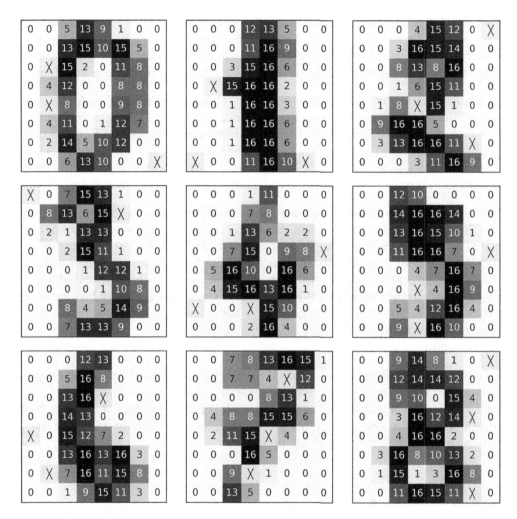

Figure 6.2: Visualizing some digits

If we wished to, we could apply sophisticated techniques for edge detection, convolutional filters, or the like, which might find better-imputed pixels. However, for this demonstration, we will simply assume each missing pixel is the mean value of its neighbors. Of course, whether to weight diagonals the same as horizontal and vertical neighbors is an additional decision. So is, potentially, a different weight for horizontal versus vertical, or up versus down, and so on.

```python
# Coded for clarity, not for best vectorized speed
# Function definition only; used in later cell
def fill_missing(digit):
    digit = digit.copy()
    missing = np.where(digit == -1)
    for y, x in zip(*missing):  # Pull off x/y position of pixel
        # Do not want negative indices in slice
        x_start = max(0, x-1)
        y_start = max(0, y-1)
        # No harm in index larger than size
        x_end = x+2
        y_end = y+2
        # What if another -1 is in region? Remove all the -1s
        region = digit[y_start:y_end, x_start:x_end].flatten()
        region = region[region >=0]
        total = np.sum(region)
        avg = total // region.size
        digit[y, x] = avg
    return digit
```

The function `fill_missing()` simply creates a single new digit based on adjacent digits. We can easily construct a new dataset by looping through the samples in the original one.

```python
new = np.empty_like(digits)
for n in range(new.shape[0]):
    new[n] = fill_missing(digits[n])

show_digits(new)
```

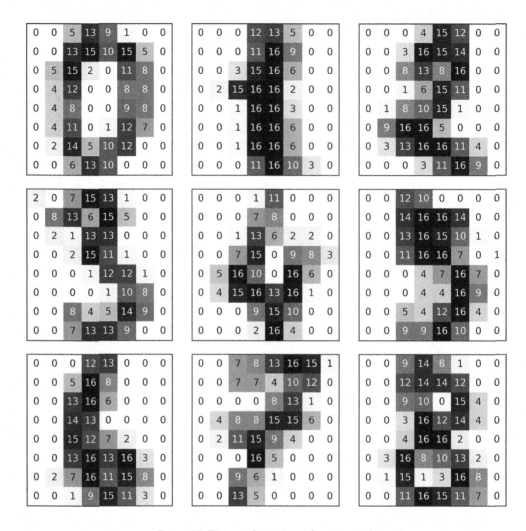

Figure 6.3: Digits with missing values imputed

As everywhere in this book, my intention is to promote thought about the best way to improve data quality, with the flawed resources available in actual data. The specific adjacency averaging that I perform in the sample code is *often* a reasonable approach—and apparently performs very well in the example—but you must always formulate a clear intention about what goal you have with your imputation; as well, think about how your particular approach might affect the modeling or analysis you perform later. Perhaps a different approach to imputation would work better with your selection of model.

Let us turn to trends in data, both time series and other kinds of linear trends.

Trend Imputation

The longer you stand in line, the greater the likelihood that you are standing in the wrong line.

–Anonymous

Concepts:

- Types of trends (regressions)
- Fill
- Linear
- Time-sensitive
- Non-local
- Correlated with another variable
- Working through a larger example: aggregation of timestamps by class
- Judging whether context is sufficient for imputation
- Static trend equivalent to central value imputation
- Trends other than time series
- Polynomial-fit trends imputation

The most obvious, and probably the most widely addressed, trend that data scientists use for imputation is time series data. If we make observations on a relatively regular schedule—every femtosecond, every second, every minute, every year, every century, or whatever—it is reasonable, to a first approximation, to guess that a missing observation is similar to the timestamped observations nearby to it. One very common use of trend imputation is in financial models; for example, market trades of securities may have irregular spacing of events (either missing data, or trades being less common than the tick frequency). However, the same concerns arise with many other domains as well.

There are several general approaches to trend imputation available. These include forward-fill, backward-fill, local regression, time-sensitive regression, non-local regression, and correlational imputation. One caveat in all the imputations I discuss in this section is that they cannot deal with high-frequency signals that have a shorter periodicity than the gaps in the missing data.

For example, if something can fluctuate on a stochastic 10-hertz frequency, one-second-spaced observations are going to be of little value for imputation. Obviously, to some degree it depends on the strength of overlapping signals, but this is a concern to keep in mind.

Types of Trends

Forward-/backward-fill: Assume that a missing value is the same as the value before/after it in the sequence. The Pandas `Series.fillna()` method can perform this imputation, as can the `tidyr` package's `fill()` function in the R tidyverse.

Local regression: Assume there is a continuous function connecting the observations adjacent to the missing one. Most of the time we simply assume a linear function; for example, we take the mean of those adjacent observations to fill the missing value. In concept, we can impute a value based on adjacent points being samples for a non-linear function, however.

Time-sensitive regression: Even if we look only at values adjacent to missing ones, if those adjacent values represent datetimes, we might take advantage of the actual chronological spacing of observations. If all observations are evenly spaced in time, this is moot. The general intuition here is that values are likely to change more in a longer time period than in a shorter one.

Non-local regression: Within a series, a regression can be global or windowed over a wider range than adjacent elements. Again, a linear regression is common, and is the simplest approach, but other functional forms for regression are possible as well. A global or windowed regression may be less sensitive to random local fluctuations in underlying trends. Of course, the missing datum might have been such a fluctuation itself, so this approach—and most others for trend imputation—amounts to a minor degree of smoothing of variability.

Correlation imputation: It may be that the data in one column (feature) with missing values is significantly correlated with the data in one or more other columns. If this is the case, it may be that models downstream should recognize the cross-correlation, for example by decomposition and dimensionality reduction. But as an initial imputation step, assuming values based on correlations is often useful.

In somewhat technical terms, we can note that imputation usually reduces heteroscedasticity since almost every kind of imputation follows a trend, not variability from that trend. For almost all data science purposes, that is desirable, or at least acceptable, but we should avoid stating many kinds of statistical generalizations on imputed data (usually using the raw data for those purposes instead).

***

Let us look at a very simple time series example first, to illustrate several of these approaches. We simply construct a small Pandas Series with date-level resolution, but uneven spacing of observation dates. The first observation has a dramatically different value than later ones, mostly to emphasize that the implied global slope is different from the local differential between elements.

```
date_series
```

```
2001-01-01   -10.0
2001-01-05     1.0
2001-01-10     2.0
2001-02-01     NaN
2001-02-05     4.0
dtype: float64
```

Forward- or backward-fill are straightforward.

```
date_series.ffill()   # or .bfill()
```

```
2001-01-01   -10.0
2001-01-05     1.0
2001-01-10     2.0
2001-02-01     2.0
2001-02-05     4.0
dtype: float64
```

Local regression, or called plainly "**averaging**," is also easy.

```
date_series.interpolate('linear')
```

```
2001-01-01   -10.0
2001-01-05     1.0
2001-01-10     2.0
2001-02-01     3.0
2001-02-05     4.0
dtype: float64
```

In Pandas (and in other tools), we can weight a trend based on time increments. This is still a local operation (in the sense of adjacent values), but it is a weighted average based on the greater nearness of 2001-02-01 to 2001-02-05 than to 2001-01-10. That is, the extreme value of -10 that is non-adjacent is not utilized.

```
date_series.interpolate('time')
```

```
2001-01-01    -10.000000
2001-01-05      1.000000
2001-01-10      2.000000
2001-02-01      3.692308
2001-02-05      4.000000
dtype: float64
```

Given that this series is monotonically ascending, we can perform a simplified regression merely by drawing a line from the initial point to the final point. This is not a least-squares linear regression, but it emphasizes the gap between uniform and time-based interpolation. The imputed value of 0.5 for February 1 might seem out of place, but if we visualize the global trend, it makes sense. The OLS (ordinary least-squares) value would also fall significantly below the time interpolated value, because one initial value is much lower than others later in the series.

```
plot_filled_trend(date_series)
```

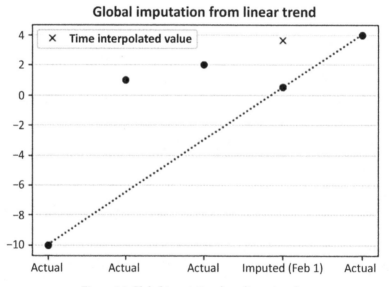

Figure 6.4: Global imputation from linear trend

We can also look for correlations among features to impute missing values. For example, in the dermatology data used earlier in this chapter, some observed features are clearly correlated with the Age feature that is occasionally missing. In this case, all of the medical observations are ordinal, but analogous approaches would apply to continuous features. In particular, the feature follicular horn plug is strongly (and monotonically) negatively correlated with patient age. We might simply assign each missing age based on the ordinal value of that other feature. Let us calculate the mean ages for each of the follicular horn plug degrees.

```
from src.dermatology import derm
feat = 'follicular horn plug'
age_groups = derm.groupby(feat).Age.mean()
age_groups
```

```
follicular horn plug
0    37.696429
1    20.400000
2    10.625000
3     9.750000
Name: Age, dtype: float64
```

A few lines of moderately dense Pandas code can assign to each missing Age based on the mean age of their grouping by the ordinal feature. It happens that in this particular dataset, all the missing ages are among patients with zero degree of "follicular horn plug," but other data would likely be different (or perhaps there is something in the collection or collation methodology that caused this correlation).

```
# The row labels for rows with missing Age
missing = derm.loc[derm.Age.isnull()].index

# Assign Age based on mapping the feature
derm.loc[missing, 'Age'] = derm[feat].map(age_groups)

# Look at filled data for a few features
derm.loc[missing, [feat, 'scaling', 'itching', 'Age']].head(3)
```

	follicular horn plug	scaling	itching	Age
33	0	2	0	37.696429
34	0	1	0	37.696429
35	0	2	2	37.696429

The precision at which Pandas calculated the mean age is not meaningful, but there is also no special benefit in explicitly reducing it.

A Larger Coarse Time Series

The City of Philadelphia, in the U.S. state of Pennsylvania, provides a wonderful resource called OpenDataPhilly (https://www.opendataphilly.org/), which is "a catalog of open data in the Philadelphia region. In addition to being the official open data repository for the City, it includes datasets from many organizations in the region." The dataset we work with in this section is valuable and of good quality, but it also contains enough nuance that a number of cleanup steps will be required to shape it for our purpose.

The particular real-world dataset we will discuss in this section concerns the tax-assessed market value of each property. I obtained this data by passing an SQL query over an HTTPS interface and getting back a JSON result. The particular query was:

```
SELECT parcel_number, year, market_value FROM assessments
```

A "parcel" is simply a tax/regulatory word for property under a common deed. I should be clear to note that OpenDataPhilly actually has complete information in this returned result (at the time of this writing), but I have artificially engineered a version with randomly missing values. The full data is in the file `philly_house.json` and the version with missing values is `philly_missing.json`, both in the repository for this book. Approximately 5% of the market values have been replaced with NaN for the missing data.

Understanding the Data

I believe the service limited results to fewer than the complete dataset; there are relatively few parcels included compared to the Philadelphia population. That question is not important for this section, but would likely be relevant to examine if we had other purposes in mind. Let us look at the dataset and do some basic forensics before imputation. It will take a number of steps to get "clean data" even when it was provided in rather good initial form.

```
parcl = pd.read_json('data/philly_missing.json')
parcl.sample(7, random_state=4) # Random state highlights details
```

	parcel_number	year	market_value
1862	123018500.0	2014	96100.0
3921	888301242.0	2015	15000.0
617	NaN	2018	0.0
1068	311033500.0	2018	16500.0
11505	888301508.0	2015	15000.0
3843	252327300.0	2014	NaN
10717	314204200.0	2016	41800.0

The general idea of the dataset is that each parcel has a market value in each of several years. We can see in the sample shown that some `parcel_number` values are missing and some `market_value` values are missing. The latter was in the data as I got it; each of those rows has some year, but a zero for market value. The missing market values were constructed by me artificially.

Let us get a sense of the distribution of these things.

```
nparcel = len(parcl[parcl.parcel_number.isnull()])
nmarket = len(parcl[parcl.market_value.isnull()])

print(f"All rows:  {len(parcl):>8,}")
print(f"No parcel: {nparcel:>8,}")
print(f"No market: {nmarket:>8,}")
```

```
All rows:    18,290
No parcel:    1,140
No market:      965
```

In the example, I have no idea why some results are returned with no parcel number, but under a stipulated goal of analyzing price trends over time, we cannot make any use of those. The missing parcel numbers are a characteristic of the data as I obtained it, not of my modifications. Let us discard them as unhelpful to our analysis. We also wonder, after this exclusion, what the typical price variation is for one property over the five years included. Perhaps we would like to know the standard deviation in terms of thousand-dollar groups. We calculate this in the next cell.

Notice that there are usually (but *not always*) five different years associated with each parcel. So the sum of the value counts shown partially below adds up to a little bit more than one-fifth of the total number of filtered rows.

```
parcl = parcl[parcl.parcel_number.notnull()]

print(f"Remaining rows: {len(parcl):,}")

stds = parcl.groupby('parcel_number')['market_value'].std()
(stds // 1000 * 1000).value_counts().head()
```

```
Remaining rows: 17,150
0.0         2360
7000.0       114
6000.0       109
2000.0       103
3000.0        83
Name: market_value, dtype: int64
```

It jumps out that the most common standard deviation, by far, seems to be the zero dollar range. Since we are rounding, that might be an actual zero, or it might simply be an amount less than 1,000 dollars. We should look more closely.

```
stds[stds == 0].count()
```

```
2309
```

The bulk of those parcels whose market value changed by a small amount in fact changed by exactly zero over the five years (at least as assessed). Moreover, the zero-change situation is around two-thirds of all the data. Of course, some of those zero-change parcels might have no change partially because they have missing data. Pandas usually ignores missing data for aggregations. It is not clear what the best remediation is for parcels that have, for example, four identical market values and one missing market value. Looking at a few of them can inform our intuition.

First, let us clean our data frame a bit more. Now that all the NaN values have been removed, we hope that all the parcel numbers are integers. We could also benefit from the years being actual years rather than merely integers.

```
parcl['parcel_number'] = parcl.parcel_number.astype(np.uint32)
parcl['year'] = pd.to_datetime(parcl.year, format="%Y")
parcl.head()
```

	parcel_number	year	market_value
0	213302600	2016-01-01	196800.0
1	213302600	2015-01-01	196800.0
2	213302600	2014-01-01	196800.0
3	213308200	2018-01-01	198000.0
4	213308200	2017-01-01	198000.0

Some slightly tangled Pandas code can tell us how often the zero-change parcels have missing data, and how much missing data parcels have. There are certainly other ways than the particular fluent code below to arrive at this answer, but the style is typical of data frame operations in many libraries, so it is worth understanding.

```
(parcl
    # Look at those parcels with zero STD among years
    # We calculated those standard deviations as 'stds'
    # The '.index' for non-deviation to find parcels
    .loc[parcl.parcel_number.isin(stds[stds == 0].index)]
    # Group by which parcel we are looking at
    .groupby('parcel_number')
```

```
        # We care about market values for parcel
        .market_value
        # Aggregation is count of different market values
        .agg('count')
        # Summarize rather than show individual parcels
        .value_counts()
)
```

```
5    1767
4     473
3      66
2       3
Name: market_value, dtype: int64
```

Removing Unusable Data

If fewer than four observations (years) exist, the parcel is not usable for the downstream analysis. This is a domain-specific judgment for this problem. Obviously, this is not any universal rule, but simply task-driven. We can remove those problem parcels with some more Pandas code. The following code is largely similar to the last example, but it uses descriptive temporary names rather than a fluent style. Neither style is per se better, but you will certainly encounter both in other data scientists' or developers' code.

One subtlety to notice in this code is that the Pandas .groupby() operation ignores missing data for aggregations, even just for counting. So if a group has three numeric values and two NaNs (that is, five rows matching the category generically), not only will .mean() give the average of the three non-missing values, but .count() will give the answer 3, not 5. The method .size() will include NaNs.

```
# Parcels that have no change between years (bool array)?
nochange = parcl.parcel_number.isin(stds[stds == 0].index)

# Parcel data grouped by parcel
by_parcel = parcl[nochange].groupby('parcel_number')

# Aggregate on number of market values and compare with 4
few_vals = by_parcel.market_value.count() < 4

# The parcel numbers that have fewer than 4 market values
few_index = few_vals[few_vals == True].index

# What are the actual row numbers we wish to drop?
```

```
drop_rows = parcl[parcl.parcel_number.isin(few_index)].index

# New name and DataFrame holds the non-dropped rows
parcl2 = parcl.drop(drop_rows)

# We trim from 17,150 rows to 16,817
parcl2
```

	parcel_number	year	market_value
0	213302600	2016-01-01	196800.0
1	213302600	2015-01-01	196800.0
2	213302600	2014-01-01	196800.0
3	213308200	2018-01-01	198000.0
...	...	...	...
18286	661010710	2016-01-01	215000.0
18287	661010710	2015-01-01	215000.0
18288	661010710	2014-01-01	215000.0
18289	661010720	2018-01-01	215000.0

16817 rows × 3 columns

Let us turn to actual trend imputation. By stipulation, when all but one year shows one common market value, the remaining year (with a missing value) should be imputed as the same value. In some sense this is the "null trend," but it is also the same action as the correlation imputation above. Treating the parcel number as a categorical variable (which it is "ontologically," albeit with many classes), what we impute is a *typical* value that is also exactly the mean, median, min, max, and mode for the class.

Imputing Consistency

The approach here is not the only possible one. For example, if we decided that housing values generally increased between 2014 and 2018 in Philadelphia, then even absent knowledge of a particular year for a particular parcel, we might impute that trend. However, this alternate approach is only easy to make sense of if the missing year is either the first or last one. If all of the 2014, 2015, 2017, and 2018 values are the same for a parcel, a linear global trend really will not inform us about that parcel in 2016.

```
# Aggregate group to find parcels w/ exactly four years
# The 'by_parcel' group already assumes no change
four_vals = by_parcel.market_value.count() == 4
```

```
# The parcel numbers that have 4 market values
four_index = four_vals[four_vals == True].index

# Row numbers of parcels to impute on
impute_rows = parcl2[parcl2.parcel_number.isin(four_index)].index

# Group parcels only for parcels with 4 market values
by_four = parcl2.loc[impute_rows].groupby('parcel_number')

# Impute the mean (or identically median, etc) to rows
new_vals = by_four.market_value.mean()

# A mapping of SOME parcel numbers to value
new_vals
```

```
parcel_number
42204300      30800.0
42205300      33900.0
42206800      30800.0
42207200      30800.0
                ...
888301511     15000.0
888301512     15000.0
888301814     15000.0
888301815     15000.0
Name: market_value, Length: 473, dtype: float64
```

There is a detail that the above code elided. We looked for places where one parcel has four non-missing values under the assumption that that probably means there is one NaN for some market value matching that parcel. However, technically that is not necessarily true. If a parcel has only four rows in total, that indicates an entire row is missing, not only the market value associated with that row. The next block of code fills in these common group values, but we add a couple of lines to show where it is simply reassigning the same value to the four existing rows.

In order to allow detection and display of the unusual condition we wish to note, the next code is an explicit loop. It is generally more idiomatic Pandas practice — or data frames generally — to vectorize the operation for speed. We could do that in Pandas using another `.groupby()` accompanied by a slightly magical `.transform(lambda x: x.fillna(x.mean()))`.

For fewer than 20,000 rows of data, the speed difference is not important, but for millions of rows it would be.

```python
# We keep a history of changes in different DFs
parcl3 = parcl2.copy()

# Loop through the new filled values by parcel
for n, (index, val) in enumerate(new_vals.items()):
    # Assignment will fill multiple rows, most redundantly
    parcl3.loc[parcl3.parcel_number == index, 'market_value'] = val
    # Did we start with only four rows in total?
    if len(parcl3.loc[parcl3.parcel_number == index]) == 4:
        print(f"Parcel #{index} has only 4 rows total (all
${val:,.0f})")
```

```
Parcel #352055600 has only 4 rows total (all $85,100)
Parcel #541286700 has only 4 rows total (all $116,600)
Parcel #621431100 has only 4 rows total (all $93,800)
```

The cleaning we have done in this section has been relatively detailed. We should check our work. We would like parcl3 to contain the same number of rows as parcl2 since the missing value imputation should not change that. We also know that there are 473 parcels that are acted on by the last bit of code. However, three of those were places where only four rows existed to start with. So if things went right, there should be 470 rows modified between the versions, in all cases substituting a value for a NaN.

```python
assert len(parcl2) == len(parcl3) == 16_817

(parcl3[parcl3.market_value.notnull() &
        (parcl2.market_value != parcl3.market_value)]
    .sort_values('parcel_number'))
```

	parcel_number	year	market_value
1733	42204300	2018-01-01	30800.0
3718	42205300	2017-01-01	33900.0
1306	42206800	2014-01-01	30800.0
1346	42207200	2014-01-01	30800.0
...	...	...	...
11517	888301511	2018-01-01	15000.0
11525	888301512	2015-01-01	15000.0
7802	888301814	2016-01-01	15000.0
14156	888301815	2015-01-01	15000.0

470 rows × 3 columns

Interpolation

The section has gone quite a long way before actually arriving at trend imputation. However, understanding datasets initially is always requisite, and other cleaning is very often required before we can perform trend imputation itself. Imputation requires a moderate degree of cleanliness before it becomes possible. Fortunately, the actual trend imputation is extremely compact in Pandas and other similar data frame tools.

Filling in values will require two steps in the approach we choose here. Linear (local) interpolation feels reasonable as an approach here. With only five timesteps, and most market values not actually changing at all in the dataset, any kind of global regression is not supportable for the example.

The default Pandas .interpolate() gives us *almost* what we want; however, it will not address a missing *first* element. Since it operates in a forward fashion, the method defaults to forward-fill for trailing elements. In order to ensure a first element is imputed as well, we need to follow up with a backward-fill.

There is a trick here to watch out for. If we simply interpolated on the entire data frame, that would likely fill in some values based on the prior parcel. Specifically, if the first year associated with a parcel is NaN, we would get a meaningless trend between the last value of the prior parcel and the first value of the next parcel. Hence we need to operate in a group-based way.

A simple preview of what we will do can be seen in a small Series, first with only interpolation, then adding back-fill.

```
s = pd.Series([None, 1, 2, None, 3, 4, None])
s.interpolate()
```

```
0    NaN
1    1.0
2    2.0
3    2.5
4    3.0
5    4.0
6    4.0
dtype: float64
```

```
s.interpolate().bfill()
```

```
0    1.0
1    1.0
2    2.0
```

```
3    2.5
4    3.0
5    4.0
6    4.0
dtype: float64
```

Let us put the pieces together. We first make sure we order correctly by parcel number and year, then interpolate, then back-fill.

```python
# Sort data to keep parcels together & years in order
parcl4 = parcl3.sort_values(['parcel_number', 'year'])

# Interpolate per group
parcl4['market_value'] = (
    parcl4
    .groupby('parcel_number')
    .market_value
    .transform(pd.DataFrame.interpolate))

# Back fill per group
parcl4['market_value'] = (
    parcl4
    .groupby('parcel_number')
    .market_value
    .transform(pd.DataFrame.bfill))
```

Now that we have (probably) completed our cleanup and trend imputation, we should do a sanity check on our data frame.

```python
print(f"Total rows after operations: {len(parcl4):,}")

# Overlooked missing data
parcl4.loc[parcl4.market_value.isnull()]
```

```
Total rows after operations: 16,817
```

	parcel_number	year	market_value
16461	571291500	2018-01-01	NaN

This final check reveals that there is one parcel for which only one year of data exists, and that hence has no trend to interpolate. Most likely we want to discard this row from our analysis as well. Before we leave this section, we can assure ourselves that this unusual row is not an artifact of our filtering and imputing, but is rather present in the original data itself.

```
# As read from disk (other than missing parcels)
parcl.loc[parcl.parcel_number == 571291500]
```

	parcel_number	year	market_value
16461	571291500	2018-01-01	NaN

Non-Temporal Trends

This book tries to use real-world data as much as possible. The odd accidents, patterns, and weird corners of real datasets are worth getting a feel for. Synthetic data—beyond the very short examples used to illustrate an API narrowly—risks missing some of the messiness. For this section, nonetheless, I invent a whimsical and fictional dataset that I believe has an interesting structure. Apologies go out in advance to the solid-state physicists or quantum chemists among my readers who might note that even a comic book metal cannot behave in the manner I purport.

Lex Luthor Laboratories has done a number of experiments that involve shining lasers at various forms of kryptonite, in their ever-nefarious efforts to defeat Superman and rule the world. In particular, they notice that many types of kryptonite gain a broad visual band of luminance when exposed to lasers of various wavelengths. Kryptonite being in scarce supply, they have not managed to test the behavior of all the element's types at all laser wavelengths. Moreover, the kilowatt lasers they used are each in some specific frequency, but they may hypothetically wish to develop weapons using different kinds of lasers than those used in the tests.

A data frame contains observations made by the lab. The units are measured in directional *candela* rather than overall *lumens* because lasers are focused in a single direction.

```
krypt = pd.read_fwf('data/excited-kryptonite.fwf')
krypt
```

	Laser_type_kw	Subtype	Wavelength_nm	Kryptonite_type
0	Helium-neon	NaN	632.8	Green
1	Helium-neon	NaN	543.5	Green
2	Helium-neon	NaN	593.9	Green
3	Helium-neon	NaN	611.8	Green
...	...	...	...	...
95	Excimer	ArF	193.0	Gold
96	Excimer	KrF	248.0	Gold
97	Excimer	XeCL	308.0	Gold
98	Excimer	XeF	353.0	Gold

	candela_per_m2
0	415.837
1	NaN
2	407.308
3	401.305
...	...
95	611.611
96	NaN
97	608.125
98	NaN

99 rows × 5 columns

A visualization will make it evident that, at least within the range of laser wavelengths tested, each type of kryptonite tested — green, red, and gold — seems to have a different, more or less log-linear response curve. It remains possible that xenologenetic metals, being what they are, will have surprising characteristics under untested wavelengths. At a first pass, though, we basically have a regression problem.

```
plot_kryptonite()
```

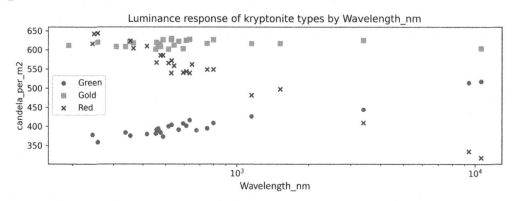

Figure 6.5: Luminance response of kryptonite types by wavelength

For this section, we are not necessarily interested in the full regression, but simply in imputing the *missing* observations. In the table and the plot, you can see that some lasers in the test suite do not have available data against some types of kryptonite. For example, the helium-neon laser at 1520 nm was only tested against gold and red kryptonite, and the CO_2 laser at 9400 nm was only tested against the green and red kryptonite.

```
(krypt[
    (krypt.Wavelength_nm > 1500) &
    (krypt.Wavelength_nm < 10000)]
.sort_values('Wavelength_nm'))
```

	Laser_type_kw	Subtype	Wavelength_nm	Kryptonite_type
5	Helium-neon	NaN	1520.0	Green
38	Helium-neon	NaN	1520.0	Red
71	Helium-neon	NaN	1520.0	Gold
6	Helium-neon	NaN	3391.3	Green
...	...	...	...	...
72	Helium-neon	NaN	3391.3	Gold
28	CO2	NaN	9400.0	Green
61	CO2	NaN	9400.0	Red
94	CO2	NaN	9400.0	Gold

	candela_per_m2
5	NaN
38	497.592
71	616.262
6	444.054
...	...
72	624.755
28	514.181
61	334.444
94	NaN

9 rows × 5 columns

While the two measures are directly computable from each other, electromagnetic frequencies in the visible range occupy a more linear numeric range, whereas wavelengths span several orders of magnitude. For our purposes, it might be friendlier to work with laser frequencies.

```
λ = krypt.Wavelength_nm / 10**9    # Wavelength in meters
c = 299_792_458                    # Speed of light in m/s
```

```
krypt['Frequency_hz'] = c/λ

# Plot frequency vs luminance
plot_kryptonite(df=krypt, logx=False,
                independent='Frequency_hz')
```

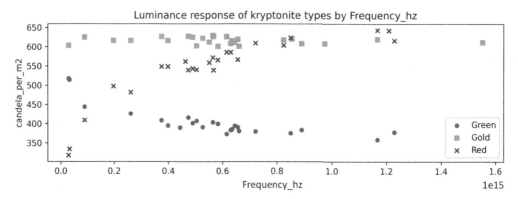

Figure 6.6: Luminance response of kryptonite types by frequency

Visually, on a linear-linear plot using frequency, there clearly seems to be bend in the response curve for red kryptonite, and perhaps for the green as well. Clearly the data is noisy, and does not closely match any smooth curve; whether this is because of the physical properties of the element or limitations in the experimental setup we do not know currently. With this motivation, we might perform a polynomial fit of order higher than one.

```
# Only perform the polyfit on the non-missing data
kr_vals = (krypt[krypt.candela_per_m2.notnull()]
           .sort_values('Frequency_hz'))

# Do a fit for each kryptonite color
for color in ('Red', 'Green', 'Gold'):
    # Limit to the color being fit
    kcolor = kr_vals.loc[kr_vals.Kryptonite_type == color]
    x = kcolor["Frequency_hz"]
    y = kcolor["candela_per_m2"]
    coef2, coef1, offset = np.polyfit(x, y, deg=2)
```

```
# Print out the discovered coefficients
print(f"{color:>5s} (hz → nit): "
      f"{coef2:.1e}*x^2 + {coef1:.1e}*x + {offset:.1e}")

# Use coefficients to fill missing values
kmissing = krypt.loc[krypt.candela_per_m2.isnull() &
                     (krypt.Kryptonite_type == color)]
x = kmissing.Frequency_hz
krypt.loc[x.index, 'candela_per_m2'] = (
                     coef2*x**2 + coef1*x + offset)
```

```
  Red (hz → nit): -2.6e-28*x^2 + 5.5e-13*x + 3.5e+02
Green (hz → nit): 1.4e-28*x^2 + -2.7e-13*x + 5.0e+02
 Gold (hz → nit): -4.1e-30*x^2 + 2.8e-15*x + 6.2e+02
```

Plotting again with the missing data imputed based on the polynomial fit, none of the new points appear obviously out of place. Whether they are *correct* is, of course, something that requires much more domain knowledge. At least our regression behaves as we expected it to.

```
plot_kryptonite(df=krypt, logx=False,
                independent='Frequency_hz')
```

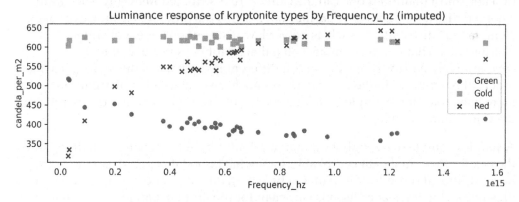

Figure 6.7: Luminance response with missing data imputed

By imputation, we have "filled in" all explicitly missing values, which makes many statistical tests and machine learning algorithms possible that are not without doing this. Let us turn now to a more global issue of sampling.

Sampling

Concepts:

- Categorical variables and discretized continuous variables
- Balancing target class values
- Sampling without replacement
- Sampling with replacement
- Oversampling by duplication
- Fuzzy statistical oversampling

Sampling is modification of a dataset in order to rebalance it in some manner. An imbalance can reflect *either* the data collection techniques used *or* the underlying pattern of the phenomenon you are measuring. This imbalance can be particularly clear when a variable is categorical and there is an obvious explicit count of the class distribution. A special kind of sampling is *time series resampling*, which is discussed in *Chapter 7, Feature Engineering*.

An imbalance can also be relevant where the distribution of a continuous variable is merely uneven. This is very common, since many quantities—in some sense, probably most quantities one can measure—are distributed unevenly, such as in a normal distribution or beta distribution. For this purpose, we exclude extremely "long-tailed" distributions such as power law distributions or exponential distributions. That is, a continuous value that simply has peaks within a comparatively narrow range presents a different issue than a value that spans many orders of magnitude. Often it is useful to transform a long-tailed distribution into a more linear one, for example by taking the log of the original values or discretizing the values into quantiles.

A simple example of a roughly normal distribution is human heights. Drilling into the details, the actual data is probably somewhat bimodal based on sex, and may have additional second-order patterns by nationality, age, and so on. For this simple illustration, the imbalance itself is sufficient for illustration. Obviously, humans vary in height, but even between the shortest newborn and the tallest adult, it is less than a 5x difference. Among adults only (excluding some very rare, very short people), it is almost always within 1.5x. In other words, height is essentially a linear quantity; but it is not one that is uniformly distributed.

The examples in this section will shift to using the R Tidyverse rather than Python. Python data frame libraries—both Pandas and others—make everything shown equally easy; the switch is made under the assumption that more readers are more familiar with Python, as an effort to encourage readers to think about the concepts rather than the libraries narrowly.

```
%load_ext rpy2.ipython
```

We can read in a dataset containing physical measurements of 25,000 (simulated) humans (http://wiki.stat.ucla.edu/socr/index.php/SOCR_Data_Dinov_020108_ HeightsWeights#References). For our purposes here, we just want to look at how height is distributed.

```
%%R -o humans
library('tidyverse')
humans <- read_csv('data/height-weight.csv')
humans
```

```
— Column specification —
cols(
  Height = col_double(),
  Weight = col_double()
)

# A tibble: 25,000 x 2
   Height Weight
    <dbl>  <dbl>
 1   167.   51.3
 2   182.   61.9
 3   176.   69.4
 4   173.   64.6
 5   172.   65.5
 6   174.   55.9
 7   177.   64.2
 8   178.   61.9
 9   172.   51.0
10   170.   54.7
# ... with 24,990 more rows
```

Dividing the heights into regular numeric increments, we definitely see a vaguely Gaussian distribution, at least inasmuch as middling heights occur much more often than the shorter or taller ranges.

Even so, all humans in this sample—and almost all adults generally—are in the narrow range from 153 cm to 191 cm.

```
humans.hist(figsize=(10,3), bins=12);
```

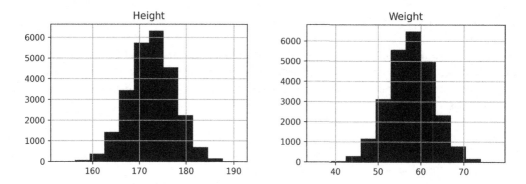

Figure 6.8: Histograms showing the distribution of height and weight

```
%%R
table(cut(humans$Height, breaks = 5))
```

```
(153,161] (161,168] (168,176] (176,183] (183,191]
      145      4251     14050      6229       325
```

If height were the target we were trying to predict from other features (for example, nutrition, nationality, gender, age, income, and so on), for many kinds of machine learning models, the rare classes ("very short", "very tall") would nearly or absolutely never be predicted from other features. There are simply too many people who are similar in those other measures to the small number of very short people (about 0.5% in the sample) that the default prediction would simply be "somewhat short" if not even just "average."

Note, however, that a similar problem exists if regions of the parameter space of the independent variables are imbalanced. For example, if Indonesia or the Netherlands each had only a few samples in the hypothetical training set (but other nations many), we would be able to make little use of the fact that residents of those countries (as of this writing) had the shortest and tallest average heights, respectively. Moreover, if the small number of samples included especially short Dutch people or especially tall Indonesian people, the presence of the class value might bias the prediction in exactly the opposite direction from what we would like.

Undersampling

The devil is in the details.

–Einstürzende Neubauten

Let us look at a dataset that uses actual categorical values rather than artificially discretized ranges. The UCI Machine Learning 1997 Car Evaluation Data Set (https://archive.ics.uci.edu/ml/datasets/Car+Evaluation) is useful here. The original dataset uses a variety of categorical words for ordinal values, such as the trunk being "small", "med", or "big", or the price of maintenance being "low", "med", "high", or "vhigh". These are converted to sequential integers for this book. However, the overall rating that we will focus on is left as descriptive words, even though it is also in an obvious implicit order.

```
%%R
cars <- read_csv('data/cars.csv',
                 col_types = cols("i", "i", "i", "i", "i", "i", "f"))
cars
```

```
# A tibble: 1,728 x 7
      price_buy  price_maintain  doors  passengers  trunk  safety  rating
          <int>           <int>  <int>       <int>  <int>   <int>  <fct>
 1            1               0      3           6      0       0  Unacceptable
 2            2               2      3           6      2       1  Acceptable
 3            2               2      5           2      1       1  Unacceptable
 4            0               1      3           2      2       1  Unacceptable
 5            2               1      5           2      0       1  Unacceptable
 6            3               1      2           6      2       1  Acceptable
 7            0               2      4           4      0       0  Unacceptable
 8            1               2      2           4      2       0  Unacceptable
 9            1               0      4           4      0       1  Acceptable
10            1               3      3           2      0       0  Unacceptable
# ... with 1,718 more rows
```

Imagine that we were trying to predict the "acceptability" of a car based on other recorded characteristics it has. It stands out that in the first ten rows, a large number are unacceptable. Let us look at the overall class distribution of the rating.

```
%%R
table(cars$rating)
```

```
Unacceptable    Acceptable    Very Good         Good
        1210           384           65           69
```

The evaluators of these cars are perhaps rather fussy in finding so very few of them good or very good. In any case, this shows a strong imbalance in the rating feature, which we will perhaps use as the target in our classification model. We would like to clean our training data in a manner likely to produce higher-quality models. Keep in mind that different specific modeling techniques are more, or less, likely to be improved by sampling techniques than others. For example, linear models are largely insensitive to class imbalance, while K-nearest neighbor models tend to be highly sensitive to these issues. But even within a generalization of that sort, different sampling, of different datasets and domains, will be effective to varying degrees. The choice of downstream model matters a lot.

If three things hold, undersampling is unproblematic:

- We have a great many rows in the dataset;
- Even the uncommon classes have a reasonable number of samples;
- The parameter space is well covered by the samples.

If we are lucky enough to have all these conditions hold, simply selecting a sample size of the smallest class is adequate. However, if we cannot reach these conditions — in particular, if the smallest classes are a bit too small — permitting a degree of imbalance is generally not terrible. 50:1 imbalance is likely to be a problem; 2:1 is likely to be unimportant. For our car evaluation, let us attempt to find 100 samples from each class, but settle for as many as we have. Having fewer than 100 samples of the uncommon classes in this dataset does not give us very much leeway.

```
%%R
unacc <- sample(which(cars$rating == "Unacceptable"), 100)
acc <- sample(which(cars$rating == "Acceptable"), 100)
good <- sample(which(cars$rating == "Good"), 69)
vgood <- sample(which(cars$rating == "Very Good"), 65)
samples <- slice(cars, c(vgood, good, acc, unacc))
samples
```

```
# A tibble: 334 x 7
```

	price_buy	price_maintain	doors	passengers	trunk	safety	rating
	<int>	<int>	<int>	<int>	<int>	<int>	<fct>
1	0	1	2	6	2	2	Very Good
2	0	0	4	4	2	2	Very Good
3	1	0	3	6	1	2	Very Good

4	0	0	5	6	1	2	Very Good
5	1	0	3	4	2	2	Very Good
6	1	1	3	6	1	2	Very Good
7	1	0	5	4	1	2	Very Good
8	1	0	4	4	1	2	Very Good
9	0	0	3	6	2	2	Very Good
10	1	1	4	6	2	2	Very Good

```
# ... with 324 more rows
```

Here we manually selected the number of rows available per class, and did not use higher-level libraries like DMwR (Data Mining with R), caret (Classification And REgression Training), or ROSE (Random Over-Sampling Examples), which would make the sampling somewhat more concise. These packages each include a variety of more sophisticated sampling techniques, some of which we will use shortly. In the Python world, the package imbalanced-learn is the go-to choice, and includes most of the techniques in the mentioned R packages.*packages*

packages

While there is much overlap between the tools available in R and Python, there are some differences in culture and focus between the languages and communities. On the one hand, R is most certainly more focused on statistics, and the breadth of libraries available in that area run deeper; the libraries for other areas are shallower in R, correspondingly.

Beyond the technical focus though, there is a notable philosophical difference in the programming language communities. Python tends to coalesce around common libraries with many contributors, or at least common APIs between libraries covering similar areas. R tends to grow many packages, each with relatively fewer contributors, with only partial overlap in functionality and less insistence on shared APIs among packages. NumPy, Pandas, scikit-learn, and much more narrowly imbalanced-learn, are "standard" APIs. In contrast, in R, data.table, data.frame, and tibble compete with varying APIs and advantages; more narrowly, DMwR, caret, and ROSE likewise compete.

Let us take a look at the distribution we obtained to make sure we did the intended thing.

```
%%R
samples %>%
  group_by(rating) %>%
  count()

# A tibble: 4 x 2
# Groups:   rating [4]
  rating           n
  <fct>        <int>
1 Unacceptable   100
2 Acceptable     100
3 Very Good       65
4 Good            69
```

Having only 60-some samples available at all from the uncommon classes is probably too sparse. To a large extent, a class having few samples simply cannot cover the parameter space of the features, no matter what technique we use. The 100 samples we have selected from the larger classes is not very much larger, but we can reasonably hope that since the underlying populations are much larger, and our sampling is unbiased, these samples are less likely to wholly miss parameter regions.

While sampling is imperfect, we can at least avoid a target imbalance that is likely to bias our model by combining undersampling with oversampling. Let us take 150 samples from each class by allowing replacement (and hence duplication from low-count classes).

```
%%R
# Find indices for each class (dups OK)
indices <- unlist(
  lapply(
    # For each level of the rating factor,
    levels(cars$rating),
    # sample with replacement 150 indices
    function(rating) {
      pred <- which(cars$rating == rating)
```

```
     sample(pred, 150, replace = TRUE) }))

# Check that we have drawn evenly
slice(cars, indices) %>%
  group_by(rating) %>%
  count()
```

```
# A tibble: 4 x 2
# Groups:   rating [4]
  rating          n
  <fct>       <int>
1 Unacceptable  150
2 Acceptable    150
3 Very Good     150
4 Good          150
```

Oversampling

> *God dwells in the details.*
>
> –Ludwig Mies van der Rohe (cf. Gustave Flaubert)

When data is plentiful, undersampling is a quick way of producing more balanced training data for machine learning models. Most often, datasets do not cover your parameter space so well that you can simply throw away training data with pure undersampling. Even if you have quite a few observations, even the common classes will cluster around a prototypic region of the high-dimensional space. If you need to evaluate the parameter space as sensitively as possible, discarding data is risky. Of course, it can also merely be the case that with the type of model and amount of computational resources you have, you simply cannot train a model on a full dataset; if so, undersampling has an independent appeal, and class sensitivity in doing it is entirely a good thing.

We have already seen how to perform the simplest kind of oversampling. In the car evaluation dataset, for example, we could simply sample with replacement up to the count of the most common class. Exactly that technique would create some noise in that most common class since some samples would be repeated and others omitted.*sampling*

> *sampling*
>
> The most straightforward approach to resampling per class does not differentiate the most common class from other classes. This means that if the most common class has 100 items, resampling with replacement will omit approximately 36 of them in the resampled version, and duplicate other items. In contrast, resampling to 100 items from a class that has only 10 initial items will with near certainty represent each item at least once.
>
> In concept, we could use extra code to do something somewhat more "fair." We would create a copy of the original data. Then we would sample only `max_class_size-current_class_size` items from each other class. Then we would combine the untouched original with the new samples. This at least would make sure that every original appears at least once in the resulting data. While this approach might be an improvement, it remains less nuanced than approaches like SMOTE, discussed below.

Another approach is simply duplicating uncommon classes as many times as are needed to make them reach approximate parity with the more common ones. For example:

```
# Read the raw data and count most common rating
cars = pd.read_csv('data/cars.csv')
cars2 = cars.copy()   # Modify a copy of DataFrame
most_common = max(cars2.rating.value_counts())

for rating in cars2.rating.unique():
    # A DataFrame of only one rating class
    rating_class = cars2[cars2.rating == rating]
    # Duplicate one less than overshooting most_common
    num_dups = (most_common // len(rating_class)) - 1
    for _ in range(num_dups):
        cars2 = pd.concat([cars2, rating_class])

cars2.rating.value_counts()
```

```
Unacceptable     1210
Good             1173
Very Good        1170
Acceptable       1152
Name: rating, dtype: int64
```

This approach brings each uncommon class as close to the frequency of the plurality class as is possible without being non-uniform in the duplication. That is, if we wanted *exactly* 1,210 `Acceptable` samples, we would duplicate some samples one more time than we had other samples. Allowing a very slight imbalance is a better approach.

More interesting than naive oversampling is a technique called **Synthetic Minority Over-sampling TEchnique (SMOTE)**, and a closely related one called **Adaptive Synthetic Sampling Method for Imbalanced Data (ADASYN)**. In R there are a number of choices for performing the SMOTE and similar techniques. Libraries include **smotefamily**, DMwR, and ROSE for a related but slightly different technique. For the next few code examples, however, we will use Python's imbalanced-learn instead, if only because there are fewer choices among the libraries needed.

While there are some technical differences among several techniques in the SMOTE family, they all are generally similar. What they do is generate *new data points* using K-nearest neighbor techniques. Among the minority samples, they look at the several nearest neighbors in the parameter space of features, and then create a new synthetic sample within that region of the parameter space that is not identical to *any* existing observation. In an informal sense, we might call this "fuzzy" oversampling. Of course, the class or target assigned to this synthetic point is the same as that of the cluster of minority class observations already existing. The bottom line is that this kind of oversampling with fuzziness in feature values usually creates much more useful synthetic samples than does a crude oversampling.

As discussed above, the cars rating classes are starkly imbalanced.

```
cars.rating.value_counts()
```

```
Unacceptable     1210
Acceptable        384
Good               69
Very Good          65
Name: rating, dtype: int64
```

Several similar oversampling techniques are available in imbalanced-learn. Read the documentation of the library for evolving details. All of them are built on top of the same scikit-learn API, and they may be included within scikit-learn pipelines and otherwise interoperate with that library. You do not need to use scikit-learn to use imbalanced-learn, except in the behind-the-scenes way that it utilizes K-nearest neighbors from that library.

Similar to the package name scikit-learn being imported under the module name `sklearn`, the installation package we use is named imbalanced-learn, but it is imported as `imblearn`.

```
# Only define the feature and target matrices, use in next cell
from imblearn.over_sampling import SMOTE

# Divide data frame into X features and y target
X = cars.drop('rating', axis=1)
y = cars['rating']

# Create the resampled features/target
X_res, y_res = SMOTE(k_neighbors=4).fit_resample(X, y)
```

Let us combine the features and target back into a DataFrame similar to the original.

```
synth_cars = X_res.copy()
synth_cars['rating'] = y_res
synth_cars.sample(8, random_state=2)
```

	price_buy	price_maintain	doors	passengers	trunk	safety
748	2	2	5	6	0	0
72	0	3	2	6	0	1
2213	3	0	2	4	0	2
1686	2	3	5	2	0	0
3578	0	0	4	6	1	1
3097	0	0	2	4	0	2
4818	0	1	4	4	1	2
434	2	3	5	6	2	0

	rating
748	Unacceptable
72	Unacceptable
2213	Acceptable
1686	Unacceptable
3578	Good
3097	Good
4818	Very Good
434	Unacceptable

As we wish, the classes of the target are exactly balanced. We could alter the sampling strategy not to require an exact balance, but in this case exactness is reasonable.

```
synth_cars.rating.value_counts()
```

```
Good            1210
Very Good       1210
Unacceptable    1210
Acceptable      1210
Name: rating, dtype: int64
```

A small point is worth noticing here. Unlike the several R libraries that perform SMOTE, imbalanced-learn retains the data type of the features. In particular, the ordinal integers of the features are kept as integers. This may or may not be what you want. Semantically, an evaluation of price_buy from "low" to "very high" could sensibly be encoded as a continuous value in the 0-3 range. However, the number of doors is semantically an integer. Still, if "more doors is better" for you as a consumer, there is likely no harm in a synthetic row with slightly nonsensible literal meaning.

More important than the direct interpretation of a given feature value is how useful the value is to your model. For many kinds of models, continuous variables provide more useful clustering, and most likely you will prefer to train on floating-point inputs. Let us cast our data types to floats and perform the resampling again, taking note of some of the new non-integral feature values.

```
cars.iloc[:, :6] = cars.iloc[:, :6].astype(float)
cars.head()
```

	price_buy	price_maintain	doors	passengers	trunk	safety
0	1.0	0.0	3.0	6.0	0.0	0.0
1	2.0	2.0	3.0	6.0	2.0	1.0
2	2.0	2.0	5.0	2.0	1.0	1.0
3	0.0	1.0	3.0	2.0	2.0	1.0
4	2.0	1.0	5.0	2.0	0.0	1.0

	rating
0	Unacceptable
1	Acceptable
2	Unacceptable
3	Unacceptable
4	Unacceptable

```
# Divide data frame into X features and y target
X = cars.drop('rating', axis=1)
y = cars['rating']

# Create the resampled features/target
X_, y_ = SMOTE().fit_resample(X, y)
pd.concat([X_, y_], axis=1).sample(6, random_state=4)
```

	price_buy	price_maintain	doors	passengers	trunk	safety
4304	1.0	0.158397	2.158397	6.0	2.0000	2.0
337	3.0	0.000000	3.000000	4.0	0.0000	1.0
2360	2.0	2.000000	3.247795	4.0	2.0000	2.0
3352	0.0	1.000000	2.123895	4.0	2.0000	1.0
2064	0.0	3.000000	4.000000	6.0	1.8577	2.0
4058	1.0	0.000000	3.075283	6.0	2.0000	2.0

	rating
4304	Very Good
337	Unacceptable
2360	Acceptable
3352	Good
2064	Acceptable
4058	Very Good

Exercises

For the exercises in this chapter, you will look first at evaluating the quality of imputed trends. In the second exercise, you will need to think about working with data that might be imbalanced in multiple features, not only in a single one.

Alternate Trend Imputation

In the kryptonite example in this chapter, we used a second-order polynomial fit on the input laser frequency to impute the missing values for candela per square meter. In some sense, it would definitely be simpler merely to use local interpolation, or even forward-fill or backward-fill. Most data frame libraries give us those local imputations "out of the box."

The dataset is available at:

```
https://www.gnosis.cx/cleaning/excited-kryptonite.fwf
```

You should quantify the differences between different imputation approaches. A good way to express the difference between samples is with root-mean-square deviation (RMSD), and for this exercise use that measure. Obviously, we do not know what the *correct* answer is for missing values, so we are only trying to evaluate how much different various approaches are from each other.

There are a number of differences you should measure and compare, for each color/ type of kryptonite and for the aggregate of all colors:

- The RMSD between *all* points (original and imputed) and the second-order polynomial fit function itself.

- The RMSD between the *original* points and:

  - A linear regression on them;

  - A second-order polynomial fit;

  - A third-order polynomial fit.

  - Some other regression that you find relevant (perhaps from a machine learning library).

- The RMSD for only *imputed* points between polynomial fits of degrees 1, 2, and 3, and a local interpolation based on neighbors only.

- The RMSD for *imputed* points only between polynomial fits of varying degrees and a simple forward-fill.

Describe what you feel is the best strategy to defeat that pesky Superman.

Balancing Multiple Features

The human height/weight data showed an imbalance in the numeric quantity `Height`. `Weight` shows a similar distribution. A version of this dataset with a fanciful target attached is available at:

    https://www.gnosis.cx/cleaning/height-weight-color.csv

This data adds a column called `Favorite` that is roughly equally balanced, and merely generated at random from the collection {red, green, blue}.

```
humcol = pd.read_csv('data/height-weight-color.csv')
humcol.sample(6, random_state=1)
```

	Height	Weight	Favorite
21492	176.958650	72.604585	red
9488	169.000221	79.559843	blue
16933	171.104306	71.125528	red
12604	174.481084	79.496237	blue
8222	171.275578	77.094118	green
9110	164.631065	70.557834	green

For this exercise, you wish to explore models to predict favorite color from height and weight. We saw earlier in this chapter the distribution of heights. Weight has a similar degree of imbalance between numeric ranges.

```
pd.cut(humcol.Weight, 5).value_counts().sort_index()
```

```
(44.692, 55.402]      125
(55.402, 66.06]      3708
(66.06, 76.717]     14074
(76.717, 87.375]     6700
(87.375, 98.033]      393
Name: Weight, dtype: int64
```

According to our stipulated hypothesis, height and weight might be predictive of favorite color. However, we also hypothesize that body mass index (BMI) might be predictive. This is deterministically derived from height and weight, but not according to the polynomial features derivation discussed in *Chapter 7, Feature Engineering*. Specifically, the BMI formula is:

$$BMI = \frac{kg}{m^2}$$

Your task is to create a new dataset with synthetic samples, in which height alone, weight alone, and BMI are each represented by a relatively equal number of observations. For this purpose, assume that height, weight, and BMI each divide into *five* classes that you might informally call, for example, "very short", "short", "average", "tall", "very tall", or similar names for the other features.

A simple way to approach this problem is simply to duplicate existing rows in a manner to increase the representation of their quantized classes. You might try that approach first. However, you should also try to use a technique such as SMOTE, ADASYN, or ROSE that generates novel synthetic samples that are *representative* of their height, weight, or BMI classes. As you generate these synthetic samples, you will need to assign an appropriate favorite color (this is straightforward when you merely duplicate rows; however, it will be more subtle as you create novel synthetic rows according to several different balancing requirements).

Given that the class imbalance is on the order of 100:1, but only among five classes per feature being balanced, each balancing operation, per feature, will increase the dataset size by approximately 4x. Think about whether those multiplications need to be chained, to produce a dataset approximately 4×4×4, or 64, times the original size. You should be able to arrive at a way of balancing independently by feature, thereby limiting the expansion to approximately 4+4+4, or 12, times the original size.

Oversampling up to, say, 300,000 rows is not unduly unwieldy. However, if you had started with more than 25,000 observations, the multiplication might be so. Assuming your initial oversampling indeed produces something on the order of 300,000 rows of data, undersample those 300k mostly synthetic samples down to only 100,000 in a manner that maintains rough class balance (precise balance is not required here; aim for less than 25% difference in row count per class).

As a final element of this exercise, if you are able to get to it, try to create an actual model of the relationship between height, weight, BMI, and the target favorite color. Specific modeling or machine learning techniques are outside the scope of this book, but they often are the purpose for which this book hopes to be helpful.

- How good of a prediction does your model make?
- *What* prediction does your model make? Which people prefer which color, and how strongly?
- Which feature is most strongly predictive?

As a hint, I will indicate that a relatively strong pattern is embedded in the favorite color assignment. There is a lot of noise and randomness in there as well, as you would expect if we had actual survey data about favorite color. But there are also patterns that most likely do not actually exist between physical measurements and this preference.

Denouement

Never answer the question that is asked of you. Answer the question that you wish had been asked of you.

–Robert McNamara

Topics covered in this chapter: Central Tendency; Correlated Tendencies; Trend Imputation; Locality; Undersampling; Oversampling.

In this chapter we looked at two related, but slightly different, main concepts. On the one hand, it is often useful to impute individual values where data is missing. When we do this, we can use a variety of patterns in the data and/or facts we know about the underlying domain that the data is drawn from. Sometimes we impute values based on what is typical for a given variable, sometimes conditioning typicality on a particular region of parameter space. Other times we find trends in data that can be sequenced in some manner, and impute based on those trends.

Under the second aspect, a kind of imputation occurs with sampling as well. In the case of oversampling, we straightforwardly impute entirely new synthetic samples, either simply by repeating existing ones or using aggregation techniques to extrapolate what is typical of an uncommon class. However, even in the case of undersampling, there is a kind of imputation going on. Undersampling a dataset does not change any individual values, but it absolutely changes the *distribution* of the remaining data. That is, after all, the whole point: we wish to create relative balance within a categorical or range variable that the original dataset does not follow.

For data science and data analysis, your burden is always to take the crude material that is presented to you in raw form, and give it a form suitable for modeling and analytic purposes.

In the next chapter, we move on to looking at *feature engineering* and creation of novel synthetic features.

7

Feature Engineering

People come to me as a data scientist with their data. Then my job becomes part data-hazmat officer, part grief counselor.

–Anonymous

Chapter 6, Value Imputation looked at filling in missing values. In *Chapter 5, Data Quality*, we touched on normalization and scaling, which adjust values to artificially fit certain numeric or categorical patterns. Both of those earlier topics come close to the subject of this chapter, but here we focus more directly on the creation of *synthetic features* based on raw datasets. Whereas imputation is a matter of making reasonable guesses about what missing values might be, feature engineering is about changing the *representational form* of data, but in ways that are deterministic and often information-preserving (e.g. reversible). A simple example of a synthetic feature is the construction of BMI (body mass index) in the prior chapter.

There are many ways we might transform data. In a simple case, we might transform a numeric or string representation of a datetime into a native representation that makes many operations easier. For strings, we might produce canonical representations and/or treat them as categories (also called **factors**). Moreover, a single string can often contain several meaningful but independent pieces of information that are more usefully treated as separate variables. For numeric values, at times transforming them into distinct ranges, and hence into ordinal values, can sometimes help reveal a pattern that is muddied by too much precision. Of course, quantization is not among the reversible transformations; but good practice continues to recommend versioning data and scripting transformations for repeatability.

While data type changes in the representation of individual features are important, we also sometimes wish to perform something more systematic with the parameter space and dimensionality of our dataset. One-hot encoding is a simple transformation that turns a single categorical feature into multiple numeric fields; this is often needed for specific statistical or modeling techniques. Polynomial features are synthetic features which combine multiple raw features in a manner that can often reveal meaningful interactions that cannot be seen in univariate features.

A completely systematic transformation is performed in a decomposition. **Principal component analysis (PCA)** and other techniques transform the entire parameter space in an information-preserving way. In itself, such a transformation does not gain or lose any information, but this is often coupled with *dimensionality reduction* where the bulk of the information can be gleaned from only a subset of these transformed dimensions. Depending on your purpose, such a transformation may make models more tractable and/or of better quality.

***

Before we get to the sections of this chapter, let us run our standard setup code.

```
from src.setup import *
%load_ext rpy2.ipython
```

```
%%R
library(tidyverse)
```

This chapter uses capabilities within scikit-learn more extensively than do other chapters. Everything that I demonstrate here using scikit-learn can certainly be accomplished in other ways as well. It just happens that scikit-learn builds in a great many of the tools one wants for feature engineering, in preparing data for a machine learning model. The APIs provided by scikit-learn are consistent and well-designed, so it certainly merits praise, in general, but the goal of this chapter is to explain underlying concepts.

Date/Time Fields

Time is a game played beautifully by children.

–Heraclitus

Concepts:

- Combining timestamp components
- Date/time operations in data frames

- Time deltas
- Duplicated timestamps (selection versus averaging)
- Resampling and grouping
- Interpolation at missing timestamps

As an example of date encoding that is not as immediately useful as we would like, let us return to the temperature readings that have been used elsewhere in the book. For the different purpose elsewhere, we simply provided a read_glarp() function that performed a minor amount of data cleanup within the function. For this section, we will do some similar operations from the raw data.

The temperature data consists of several files, each containing measurements for a different automated thermometer that (usually) takes a reading every three minutes. Looking at one of those, we see the contents are arranged like this:

```
%%bash
zcat data/glarp/outside.gz | head -5
```

```
2003 07 25 16 04 27.500000
2003 07 25 16 07 27.300000
2003 07 25 16 10 27.300000
2003 07 25 16 13 27.400000
2003 07 25 16 16 27.800000
```

These files have no headers, but the several columns correspond to what you would intuitively parse as dates in 2003 and 2004. We can read in the file as either space-delimited or as fixed-width, equivalently, for this particular format. Here we read it with Pandas as a space-delimited file.

```
temps = pd.read_csv('data/glarp/outside.gz',
                    sep=' ', header=None,
                    names=['year', 'month', 'day',
                           'hour', 'minute', 'degrees'])
temps.head(5)
```

	Year	month	day	hour	minute	degrees
0	2003	7	25	16	4	27.5
1	2003	7	25	16	7	27.3
2	2003	7	25	16	10	27.3
3	2003	7	25	16	13	27.4
4	2003	7	25	16	16	27.8

The particular problems or issues in this outside temperatures dataset are minor. However, there remain enough of them that it will allow us to use many of the most common techniques that you will need in working with time series data in general. The examples in this section all utilize Pandas, but other data frame libraries, in whatever language, will typically have similar capabilities.

Creating Datetimes

All the information we want is available in the data frame, but let us make it more useful. Many Pandas operations are especially convenient with DateTime indices, so we make that the index.

```
ts_fields = ['year', 'month', 'day', 'hour', 'minute']
temps.index = pd.to_datetime(temps[ts_fields])
temps.drop(columns=ts_fields, inplace=True)
temps
```

```
                          degrees
2003-07-25 16:04:00          27.5
2003-07-25 16:07:00          27.3
2003-07-25 16:10:00          27.3
2003-07-25 16:13:00          27.4
              ...             ...
2004-07-16 15:19:00          16.9
2004-07-16 15:22:00          16.8
2004-07-16 15:25:00          16.8
2004-07-16 15:28:00          16.4
169513 rows × 1 columns
```

Even though this data seems to be in time series order from a superficial look, there are many rows and it may not always be. Generally we would like to keep chronological data in order for many kinds of operations, including for producing graphs that might represent it. We could simply order the time series (the index in this case) as an idempotent operation, but before we do that, let us check whether that goal is already met.

```
temps.index.is_monotonic_increasing
```

```
False
```

We can probe into this by looking at the step differences—expressed in Pandas as a `Timedelta`—between successive rows.

```
increments = temps.index.to_series().diff()
increments[increments < pd.Timedelta(minutes=0)]
```

```
2003-10-26 01:01:00    -1 days +23:03:00
dtype: timedelta64[ns]
```

The index is not monotonic, and there is one backward jump (it occurs one hour earlier than the actual Daylight Savings Time adjustment that year, but is presumably still related). We should reflect on the fact that data that are ordered by some field values are not necessarily represented that way in their actual on-disk format. Many formats, such as SQL databases, perform all sorts of optimizations that can ignore ordering assumptions unless imposed. Before we look further, let us explicitly order the data by its DateTimeIndex.

```
temps.sort_index(inplace=True)
temps.index.is_monotonic_increasing
```

```
True
```

Imposing Regularity

As you may have determined in an exercise in *Chapter 5, Data Quality*, there are missing timestamps where we would expect in the general "every three minutes" pattern. Let us first verify that such gaps actually exist, then remediate them to produce a more regular time series. What we do here is clearly related to value imputation; it differs in "inventing" entire rows rather than only individual data points. Recall that three-minute increments over slightly less than a year adds up to about 170,000 expected observations.

```
increments = temps.index.to_series().diff()
gaps = increments[increments > pd.Timedelta(minutes=3)]
gaps
```

```
2003-07-26 19:28:00    0 days 00:06:00
2003-07-27 09:10:00    0 days 00:06:00
2003-07-29 08:28:00    0 days 00:06:00
2003-07-29 11:43:00    0 days 00:06:00
                          ...
2004-07-05 19:55:00    0 days 07:36:00
2004-07-06 09:28:00    0 days 00:06:00
2004-07-06 16:28:00    0 days 00:06:00
2004-07-14 04:04:00    0 days 00:06:00
Length: 160, dtype: timedelta64[ns]
```

So indeed we have some gaps in our measurements. They are not all that numerous; only about one in a thousand measurements are adjacent to time increments more than three minutes apart. We do, however, see that while most gaps are the loss of a single measurement—i.e. six minutes rather than the expected three—at some places larger gaps exist. A few large gaps exist; the longest one is over a day. Others are measured in hours or minutes.

```
with show_more_rows():
    print(gaps.sort_values(ascending=False).head(15))
```

```
2003-12-11 03:04:00    1 days 13:48:00
2004-04-28 00:31:00    0 days 13:06:00
2004-07-05 19:55:00    0 days 07:36:00
2003-12-18 09:25:00    0 days 06:33:00
2003-12-06 09:25:00    0 days 06:24:00
2003-12-29 08:46:00    0 days 06:03:00
2003-12-11 14:19:00    0 days 04:42:00
2004-04-04 03:01:00    0 days 01:03:00
2004-06-30 18:13:00    0 days 00:33:00
2003-11-24 08:04:00    0 days 00:30:00
2003-10-11 17:13:00    0 days 00:27:00
2003-12-13 17:10:00    0 days 00:15:00
2004-06-30 03:07:00    0 days 00:12:00
2004-06-22 10:16:00    0 days 00:12:00
2004-07-02 09:22:00    0 days 00:12:00
dtype: timedelta64[ns]
```

A typical small gap looks something like the example below. An observation was missed at `2003-07-26 19:25:00` that we would generally expect to be present. This is missing data, but by its implied absence relative to a predictable sequence rather than being explicitly marked with some sentinel.

```
temps.loc['2003-07-26 19:22:00':'2003-07-26 19:28:00']
```

	degrees
2003-07-26 19:22:00	27.5
2003-07-26 19:28:00	27.1

We can also look for cases where the gap between measurements is too short. There are few of them, but seeing those few will point to another problem.

```
small_steps = increments[increments < pd.Timedelta(minutes=3)]
small_steps.sort_values(ascending=False)
```

```
2003-10-03 12:04:00    0 days 00:02:00
2003-12-24 15:10:00    0 days 00:00:00
2003-10-26 01:01:00    0 days 00:00:00
2003-10-26 01:07:00    0 days 00:00:00
                              ...
2003-10-26 01:52:00    0 days 00:00:00
2003-10-26 01:55:00    0 days 00:00:00
2003-10-26 01:58:00    0 days 00:00:00
2003-10-26 01:31:00    0 days 00:00:00
Length: 22, dtype: timedelta64[ns]
```

The number of small gaps in the timestamps is only 22, but even more specifically, all of them except one are an actual zero time delta, which is to say duplicated datetime values. The one gap that is two minutes rather than the expected three will make the spacing of observations slightly irregular since later points will be at a one-minute offset from the expected position.

As a domain judgment, we will decide that a one-minute difference is not significant to any analysis or modeling we do on the data. However, this is a judgment that we need to make, and will not be universal to every dataset. In particular, when we regularize relative to missing observations below, we will also shift the imputed times of measurement for many observations. For events tied to specific times rather than patterns of change in the data, this shift would probably be unacceptable.

The next cell is also an opportunity to illustrate a nice feature of the Pandas API. We will look at a slice of data surrounding the two-minute gap, but the ends of the slice are times that do not actually occur in the data themselves. Pandas is clever enough to know about chronological order, and choose all index values that are *between* particular datetimes, even if the ends are not themselves present. We are also able to write datetimes as either actual datetime objects or as strings (in any of several guessed string formats; using ISO-8601 is always the best choice, where possible).

```
temps.loc['2003-10-03 11:57':'2003-10-03 12:08']
```

	degrees
2003-10-03 11:58:00	13.0
2003-10-03 12:02:00	12.8
2003-10-03 12:04:00	12.8
2003-10-03 12:07:00	12.8

Duplicated Timestamps

Here we encounter another problem that is not uncommon with time series data. A small minority of rows in our data are indexed by identical timestamps. We are fortunate in this dataset that there are only 41 problem rows out of 170,000, so almost any approach here is probably fine. Note that in many cases, additional columns may be part of the explicit or implicit key. For example, if the other location temperatures were aggregated with the outside temperatures, a tidy data frame could include the location as a categorical column; in that case, we would typically expect many duplicate timestamps, but only one per category/location.

```
# Show all rows that are part of duplicate set
# Other 'keep' options will drop some or all duplicates
temps[temps.index.duplicated(keep=False)]
```

	degrees
2003-10-26 01:01:00	1.9
2003-10-26 01:01:00	0.9
2003-10-26 01:07:00	1.9
2003-10-26 01:07:00	1.1
...	...
2003-10-26 01:58:00	0.1
2003-12-24 15:10:00	6.4
2003-12-24 15:10:00	20.9
2003-12-24 15:10:00	6.4

41 rows × 1 columns

Most duplicates have a small value difference, one degree Celsius or less. However, something peculiar happens at 2003-12-24 15:10:00. There are three different values recorded at that same moment, two of them 6.4°C, but the remaining one is 20.9°C. Both our domain knowledge of outdoor temperatures in Colorado in December and the pattern of the data itself would probably lead us to discard this clear outlier. Quite likely, since several instruments were recording, most of them inside a heated house, this 20.9 reading is a transposition with a measurement of a different thermometer.

One option for us is to use Pandas' method .drop_duplicates(). It gives us the option to keep the first row, keep the last row, or drop all rows with such ambiguity. We do not have a clear basis to decide among those options, but none would be harmful in this case, given the comparative infrequency of the duplicates. For example:

```
no_dups = (temps
            .reset_index()  # De-dup on named column
            .drop_duplicates(keep='first', subset='index')
            .set_index('index'))

print(f"Length of original DataFrame: {len(temps):,}")
print(f"Length of de-duped DataFrame: {len(no_dups):,}")

# Check if datetime index is now unique
no_dups.index.is_unique
```

```
Length of original DataFrame: 169,513
Length of de-duped DataFrame: 169,492
True
```

Another approach to de-duplication of duplicated timestamps is to group aggregate common values. For example, if we are not sure which measurement is to be preferred, we could take the mean of the several values. This is probably irrelevant for this specific data, and probably wrong for the case we noted with an obvious outlier among the duplicates. But let us look at the API anyway:

```
mean_dups = temps.groupby(temps.index).mean()

print(f"Length of mean-by-duplicate: {len(mean_dups):,}")
mean_dups.index.is_unique
```

```
Length of mean-by-duplicate: 169,492
True
```

Adding Timestamps

As we have noted, there are gaps in the time series data. Most are single missing measurements on the expected three-minute schedule, but one is over a day, and several are numerous hours. We also have the issue noted where one gap is two minutes long rather than three minutes, which we are aware of but will not treat as critical for the current dataset.

The typical way of adding more datetime rows is to resample the data to a desired frequency. For example, if we only wanted the temperature by month, but as a mean, we could do an operation like:

```
# See Pandas docs, it is easy to confuse M=month with m=minute
no_dups.resample('1M').mean()
```

index	degrees
2003-07-31	21.508462
2003-08-31	20.945075
2003-09-30	14.179293
2003-10-31	12.544181
...	...
2004-04-30	7.708277
2004-05-31	14.357831
2004-06-30	15.420425
2004-07-31	20.527493

13 rows × 1 columns

Intuitively, such a lower frequency resampling is very similar to grouping. We can get the same effect using .groupby(). Here we use slightly tricky code in that we want the months in chronological order rather than alphabetical; one way to get that is to include the number in the grouping, but then drop it.

```
# Groupby both month number and name
by_month = no_dups.groupby(
    [no_dups.index.month, no_dups.index.month_name()])
# The mean temperature over the month
by_month = by_month.mean()
# Discard the month number now that result is sorted
by_month = by_month.droplevel(0)
# Name the index
by_month.index.name = 'month_name'
by_month
```

month_name	degrees
January	0.433968
February	-0.209109
March	7.848025
April	7.708277
...	...

```
September   14.179293
  October   12.544181
 November    2.332037
 December    0.667080
12 rows × 1 columns
```

We have done something a bit different here in that the average is over a named
month rather than an actual chronological month. It makes little difference in this
example since our data ranges over almost exactly a year. However, even here, we
have averaged some numbers from July 2003 with some others from July 2004. If
that matters, we could include the year in the grouping as well to avoid that. Of
course, if we are looking for typical temperatures for a time of year, this may in
fact be closer to our goal for multi-year data.

Although the starting point is different, September and October show identical
means between the techniques (only July will be a little different). However,
downsampling to monthly data is really not our declared task. Rather we wish to
upsample slightly to fill in the missing three-minute increments. This is just as easy.
Recall that we have started out with 169,513 observations before this conversion to
a uniform three-minute frequency.

```
filled_temps = no_dups.asfreq('3T')
filled_temps
```

Index	degrees
2003-07-25 16:04:00	27.5
2003-07-25 16:07:00	27.3
2003-07-25 16:10:00	27.3
2003-07-25 16:13:00	27.4
...	...
2004-07-16 15:19:00	16.9
2004-07-16 15:22:00	16.8
2004-07-16 15:25:00	16.8
2004-07-16 15:28:00	16.4

171349 rows × 1 columns

The method .asfreq() has an optional argument to back-fill or forward-fill. We
have not used this, and therefore our data now contains a certain number of missing
values (marked as NaN). *Chapter 6, Value Imputation* discusses strategies for filling
and interpolation that we might use to guess values for the missing data.

We can see how many missing values there are:

```
sum(filled_temps.degrees.isnull())
```

```
1858
```

For the places where we added a single missing timestamp, any kind of filling or interpolation is probably sufficient. However, for the small number of larger gaps of multiple hours or even over a day, a linear interpolation almost surely does a poor job for the missing interval.

Remember the somewhat odd change in timestamp offset, where a single two-minute increment occurred? One or more of the other gaps righted the minutes-after-hour by the end of the time series, but some of the middle resampled measurements are shifted from their strict measurement time. One option here would be to *upsample* quite a bit to a one-minute frequency, and also combine that with a more sophisticated interpolation technique. Pandas provides—mostly by way of **SciPy**, if it is installed—a rich collection of interpolations: nearest, zero, slinear, quadratic, cubic, spline, barycentric, polynomial, krogh, piecewise_polynomial, pchip, akima, and from_derivatives.

One of these higher-order interpolations is likely to perform quite accurately on the few hour gaps, but obviously less well on the day-length gap. Let us upsample to one-minute frequency and then fill missing timestamps using spline interpolation.

```
one_minute_temps = no_dups.asfreq('1T')
one_minute_temps.index.name = 'Timestamp'
one_minute_temps
```

Timestamp	degrees
2003-07-25 16:04:00	27.5
2003-07-25 16:05:00	NaN
2003-07-25 16:06:00	NaN
2003-07-25 16:07:00	27.3
...	...
2004-07-16 15:25:00	16.8
2004-07-16 15:26:00	NaN
2004-07-16 15:27:00	NaN
2004-07-16 15:28:00	16.4

514045 rows × 1 columns

This high sampling frequency produces many rows and also many NaNs on the first pass.

```
one_minute_temps.interpolate(method='spline', order=3,
                              inplace=True)
one_minute_temps.head()
```

Timestamp	degrees
2003-07-25 16:04:00	27.500000
2003-07-25 16:05:00	27.082346
2003-07-25 16:06:00	27.079049
2003-07-25 16:07:00	27.300000
2003-07-25 16:08:00	27.072395

All values are filled with some imputed value here, but it is particularly interesting to look at the region around the missing day and a half at 2003-12-11.

```
(one_minute_temps
    .loc['2003-12-07':'2003-12-12', 'degrees']
    .plot(title="Spline interpolation of missing temps",
          figsize=(12,3)));
```

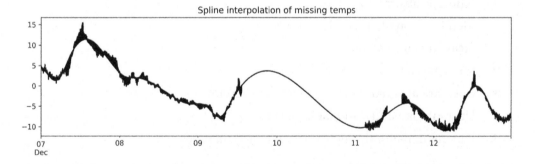

Figure 7.1: Spline interpolation of missing temps

It is easy to see where the smooth trend was interpolated/imputed versus the much messier raw data (even though two-thirds of the "raw" data is actually imputed, but very locally). While the long gap around 2003-12-11 may not be accurate, it is not implausible and should not unduly affect models of the whole dataset. There is even a smaller few-hour gap a few hours after the long gap that is clearly relatively close to what the missing data would have been.

Choosing the best interpolation technique is an art. A great deal depends on what cyclicities we expect in the time series data, if any. Indeed, it depends as well on whether the order of the data is a time series at all, or if it is some other type of sequence. The discussion in *Chapter 5, Data Quality* of detrending data is relevant. In the absence of domain knowledge that leads to an expectation of specific behavior, a simple linear interpolation of missing points limits the potential harm while not necessarily reaping much benefit. Where the data *is* time series data, using time-sensitive regression makes sense; see *Chapter 6, Value Imputation*. However, where you have an expectation of a more complex, but regular, pattern in the gaps, using an interpolation technique such as spline, polynomial, or piecewise polynomial is likely to provide better value imputation.

Let us turn to data that is encoded inside strings, even where numeric or datetimes hope to emerge.

String Fields

Language is conceived in sin and science is its redemption.
–Willard Van Orman Quine

Concepts:

- Numeric abstraction of text
- Identification of embedded numbers
- String distance measures
- Phonetic canonicalization
- Categorical versus small distinct value count
- Uncommon values and factor levels
- Parsing non-atomic fields into varying data types

Data contained in string fields can have numerous meanings. In the worst of cases, for us, words can express complex, nuanced, logically connected meanings. But data science has no interest in books, articles, nor even in short free-form annotations. We only like categorical, numeric, ordinal, and date/time data. *De minimis non curat lex.*

Of course **natural language processing** (**NLP**) is a genuine and important area of data science, data analysis, and machine learning. That cannot be an extensive topic of this particular book, but a general point can be. To become data, a prose text must be transformed.

Word counts are numbers. N-gram frequency—word or letter sequences considered as a unit—can be dimensions of a parameter space. Transformation probabilities of state transitions in a Hidden Markov Model of a text are simply vectors. Large vocabularies can be embedded in smaller vector spaces as synthetic dimensions. Perhaps existing sentiment analysis models can be used to generate numeric characterizations of sentences or other segments of prose text.

Before we get to a brief digression on just a few of the encodings we might use for NLP, let us look at simpler uses for text. A great many string fields are *very close* to being data. For example, integers or floating-point numbers might happen to be represented as strings. It is very common, for example, to come across string data that is clearly intended to represent numbers but merely has cosmetic issues.

Let us read in a very small tabular dataset similar to one shown in *Chapter 1, Tabular Formats.*

```
df = pd.read_fwf('data/parts2.fwf')
df
```

	Part_No	Description	Maker	Price
0	12345	Wankle rotary engine	Acme Corporation	$ 555.55
1	No.678	Sousaphone	Marching Inc.	$ 333.33
2	2468	Feather Duster	Sweeps Bros	$ 22.22
3	#9922	Area 51 metal fragment	No Such Agency	$9999.99

Underneath the features `Part_No` and `Price` we can clearly see the intention to represent an integer and a floating-point number, respectively. We simply have a bit of extra text in the strings of both columns that defeated automatic recognition of these types by the Pandas library. We can clean up the individual columns, then try again to convert to their desired types. While we are cleaning up, we might impose a slightly narrower restriction than Pandas (or other libraries) would infer by default. For our purpose, we assume that part numbers are always positive and no higher than 2^{16}, which is to say unsigned 16-bit integers.

```
# Regular expression to strip all non-digits
df['Part_No'] = (df.Part_No
                 .str.replace(r'[^0-9]', '')
                 .astype(np.uint16))

# Remove spaces or $ from start of strings
df['Price'] = (df.Price
               .str.lstrip("$ ")
               .astype(float))
```

```
df.dtypes
```

```
Part_No         uint16
Description     object
Maker           object
Price           float64
dtype: object
```

```
df
```

	Part_No	Description	Maker	Price
0	12345	Wankle rotary engine	Acme Corporation	555.55
1	678	Sousaphone	Marching Inc.	333.33
2	2468	Feather Duster	Sweeps Bros	22.22
3	9922	Area 51 metal fragment	No Such Agency	9999.99

Cleaning strings to allow them to convert to numbers can be fussy in its details, but in concept it does not amount to more than a little bit of eyeballing, and some trial and error, assuming each feature consists entirely of numbers "trying to get out." In the subsections below, we will look at ways to do more than this by imposing equivalences of strings, treating strings as categorical, and dividing string fields into implicit subfields (each perhaps of their own type).

If you do determine that conversion to numbers is appropriate, it is worth keeping in mind what *kinds* of numbers they are. The *Glossary* entry for NOIR provides discussion of nominal, ordinal, interval, and ratio variables. This consideration is, of course, worthwhile even when the native data format is already numeric. In the example above, (by stipulation) we might know that Part_No:100 was added to the catalog earlier than was Part_No:200, but not what time duration separates them. Part_No:99 might have been added at more of a (negative) gap from Part_No:100 than Part_No:100 is from Part_No:200. In this scenario, the variable is *ordinal*. In particular, we have no expectation that Part_No:100 + Part_No:200 has any specific relationship to Part_No:300 (nor any meaning at all). Of course, the numbers might also simply be random in relationship to catalog entry, and might best be left as strings.

In contrast to Part_No, we presume that Price entries will have ratio relationships among them. An item with Price:250 costs half as much as one with Price:500. If a buyer orders one Price:250 and one Price:500, they will generally be charged $750. Of course, that does not go so far as to indicate direct substitutability with the item that has Price:750, which the buyer does not want.

Fuzzy Matching

Sometimes we have a short string field that is meant to represent a nominal/ categorical value. However, with the vagaries of data acquisition, different strings might be entered for observations meant to contain the same nominal value. There are numerous ways that the characters of the string might go wrong. Extremely common problems are non-canonical capitalization and spurious spacing. For features that are intended to be nominal, simply lower- or upper-casing the raw strings, and removing all spaces (either from the padding or also interior, depending on the particular expected values), is often a good policy.

While simple canonicalization of spaces and case will reveal many intended equivalences, we might also look at the edit distance between possibly similar strings. An exercise in *Chapter 4, Anomaly Detection* had you play with this possibility. Simple typos and misspellings are often captured by a short Levenshtein distance between pairs of strings. There are two problems with this kind of comparison; the same issues apply to Damerau-Levenshtein, Hamming, Jaro-Winkler, or other edit distance measures as with Levenshtein. One problem is that distances are not transitive. If the edit distance between A and B is 5, and the edit distance between B and C is 5, then the distance between A and C can be anywhere from 0 to 10. If 6 is the threshold for "close enough equivalence," it may not be clear whether to consider B as "A-like" or "C-like," or both, or neither.

The greater problem with using edit distance is that it has quadratic complexity. That is — as the non-transitivity implies — the only way to find all similarities is to compare all the pairs of values to their respective pair edit distance. There may be a few shortcuts possible, for example if we identify collections of common prefixes, but generally we are required to accept this complexity. For the small example below, this would not be prohibitive, but for large datasets it would be.

Another approach that can often be useful is phonetic canonicalization. Often this approach is useful for names that may be transliterated in various ways, although the increasing prevalence of voice recognition systems with high fallibility probably presents additional opportunities. Most likely, voice recognition software will misidentify a word as something that sounds somewhat similar. While this approach may catch a class of typos as well, it is less consistent for that. The strings "GNU" and "GUN" are only one transposition apart, but their pronunciation is significantly different, for example.

A somewhat older (1918) phonetic canonicalization approach is called Soundex, and it works by substituting a common symbol for collections of similar sounds. For example, "b", "f", "p", and "v" are all encoded in the same way. Building on that system is the 1990 Metaphone.

Metaphone allows for more complex rules, such as looking at letter clusters that typically have a certain sound that is not simply the addition of the individual letter sounds, or dropping certain letters in the context of other adjacent ones. These techniques primarily rely on consonant sounds, and vowels are often dropped from the encodings.

Double Metaphone goes further than Metaphone, and tries to account for more irregularities in English where words are borrowed from Slavic, Germanic, Celtic, Greek, French, Italian, Spanish, Chinese, and other origins. This gives a relatively complex ruleset; for example, it tests for approximately 100 different contexts for the use of the letter C. However, the algorithm remains linear over any dataset size, and is generally sequential in coding individual words. The "double" in the name of this technique comes from the fact that it produces both a primary canonicalization and many times also a secondary one using alternate rules. This allows for a more flexible equivalence comparison. For example, the secondary encoding of *A* may match the primary encoding of *B*, which is at least a hint about similarity.

Let us illustrate with a specific example. We have a dataset that has a number of similar family names that come from various languages but may represent the same person, or the same family, modulo transcription differences. In this example, the names are labeled by "similarity group" for presentation purposes, but in real data you are unlikely to have anything analogous to this. Just to make it look a bit more like a typical dataset, an extra column with numbers is also included. Whether or not we manage to unify these different spellings of what might be the *same names*, names form nominal variables since there are finitely many.

```
names = pd.read_csv('data/names.csv', index_col='Group')
names.head(8)
```

Group	Last_Name	Other_Data
1	Levenshtein	103
1	Levenschtein	158
1	Levenstein	110
2	Hagelin	136
2	Haslam	105
2	Haugland	190
2	Heislen	181
2	Heslin	106

If we use the Python **Metaphone** package, we can use the function `doublemetaphone()`, which produces a pair of primary/secondary encodings for every input string (the secondary may be blank).

The `metaphone()` function in the same package, or most other canonicalization libraries, will produce a single string to represent an input string. The library Fuzzy is a faster implementation, but seems to be limited to ASCII inputs, which will not work with the accented characters in some of our test names. We add these canonicalizations to the data frame.

```
from metaphone import doublemetaphone

metas = zip(*names.Last_Name.map(doublemetaphone))
names['meta1'], names['meta2'] = metas
```

Let us look at the similarity group 6 here, which contains a number of spelling variations on the same name.

```
with show_more_rows():
    print(names.loc[6])
```

Group	Last_Name	Other_Data	meta1	meta2
6	Jeong	191	JNK	ANK
6	Jong	157	JNK	ANK
6	Chŏng	100	XNK	
6	Chung	123	XNK	
6	Jung	118	JNK	ANK
6	Joung	168	JNK	ANK
6	Chong	101	XNK	
6	Cheong	133	XNK	
6	Choung	104	XNK	

This very common Korean family name—in Hangul "정", IPA (international phonetic alphabet) "/dʒʌŋ/"—is transliterated to English in numerous different ways, according to different style guides, and during different times historically. You may encounter any of those listed, but they all refer to the same underlying name; or they do if they refer to Korean names. It gets complicated. In South Korea, "Jeong" is currently canonical; in North Korea, "Jong", is the current official transliteration.

As an example of the complication, the American feminist novelist Erica Jong is of Russian/Polish-Jewish ancestry, so you might expect her family name to have Yiddish origin. It turns out that it is actually that of her second husband, a Chinese-American psychiatrist. The Chinese name is distantly related to the Korean one, but certainly not a mere different transcription. Similarly, the German name of Swiss psychoanalyst Carl Gustav Jung is not related to the Korean one.

We see the canonicalization "ANK" for several of these, including the German name pronounced as "/jʊŋ/" (i.e. the "J" is pronounced similarly to an English "Y" in German, Yiddish, Swedish, Norwegian, Dutch, etc.).

There remain some name spellings where this technique does not unify them, even looking at secondary encodings. The initial "J" and the initial "Ch" are simply given a different representation. However, we have reduced many of the alternate spellings to a canonical representation. Let us look at another example. The former Libyan leader, (Muammar) Gaddafi, had a name that was transcribed in so many different ways by the English language press that the spelling variations became something of a humorous note. In Arabic it was "قَذَّافِي", in IPA it was "/gəˈdɑfi/" or "/gəˈdæfi/". Our double metaphone technique does quite well here, identifying nearly all variations as either the primary or secondary canonicalization. It may well be reasonable to your purpose to treat this as a common nominal value (the few encoded as "KTTF" will not be unified this way, nor will "KSF"/"KTSF", but all others can be). This is perhaps a better example than the many different individual people named "Jeong" (or some variant spelling) since almost any English news article, which is perhaps our hypothetical document corpus, that used any of these spellings referred to the same human person.

```
with show_more_rows():
    print(names.loc[5])
```

	Last_Name	Other_Data	meta1	meta2
Group				
5	Gadaffi	197	KTF	
5	Gadafi	189	KTF	
5	Gadafy	181	KTF	
5	Gaddafi	163	KTF	
5	Gaddafy	179	KTF	
5	Gadhafi	112	KTF	
5	Gathafi	187	KθF	KTF
5	Ghadaffi	141	KTF	
5	Ghadafi	152	KTF	
5	Ghaddafi	192	KTF	
5	Ghaddafy	122	KTF	
5	Gheddafi	142	KTF	
5	Kadaffi	139	KTF	
5	Kadafi	188	KTF	
5	Kaddafi	192	KTF	
5	Kadhafi	121	KTF	
5	Kazzafi	193	KSF	KTSF
5	Khadaffy	148	KTF	

5	Khadafy	157	KTF	
5	Khaddafi	134	KTF	
5	Qadafi	136	KTF	
5	Qaddafi	173	KTF	
5	Qadhafi	124	KTF	
5	Qadhdhafi	114	KTTF	
5	Qadhdhāfi	106	KTTF	
5	Qadthafi	186	KTF	
5	Qathafi	130	K0F	KTF
5	Quathafi	145	K0F	KTF
5	Qudhafi	158	KTF	

To round out our encoding, let us look at the few other names that have similar sounds, in several groups. Feel free to skim the next example; confessedly it enables jokes about Levenshtein distance and the author's last name.

```
with show_more_rows():
    print(names.loc[names.index < 5])
```

	Last_Name	Other_Data	meta1	meta2
Group				
1	Levenshtein	103	LFNXTN	
1	Levenschtein	158	LFNXTN	
1	Levenstein	110	LFNSTN	
2	Hagelin	136	HJLN	HKLN
2	Haslam	105	HSLM	
2	Haugland	190	HKLNT	
2	Heislen	181	HLN	
2	Heslin	106	HSLN	
2	Hicklin	151	HKLN	
2	Highland	172	HHLNT	
2	Hoagland	174	HKLNT	
3	Schmidt	107	XMT	SMT
3	Shmit	167	XMT	
3	Smith	160	SM0	XMT
3	Smitt	181	SMT	XMT
3	Smit	192	SMT	XMT
4	Mertz	173	MRTS	
4	Merz	116	MRS	
4	Mertes	178	MRTS	
4	Hertz	188	HRTS	

All of the Smith-like names can be unified as "XMT", although we have to look at both the primary and secondary encodings to do so. The H-initial names do not strike us as necessarily all the same to start with, but we see some overlaps. Disappointingly, "Mertz" and "Merz" are not unified this way, notwithstanding that in German or Yiddish this author's last name was probably a historical misspelling of "Mertz".

The above examples of unifying nominal values focused on person names—family names in particular—but the technique is general to other cases where phonetic confusion or substitution might have occurred in the representation of categorical values.

Explicit Categories

Conceptually, there is a difference between a variable that merely has a small number of measured values and one that is actually categorical. Factor (categorical) variables allow us to express an intention about their use more accurately, but also enable a few additional APIs and performance optimizations. Most frequently, factors are associated with data stored as strings, but that need not be the case; the data type alone does not determine the matter. For example, we might have data on the houses in a housing development that looks like this:

Lot #	Address	Acres	House Style
32849	111 Middle Rd	2	37
34210	23 High St	1	21
39712	550 Lowe Ave	3	22
40015	230 Cross St	1	21
32100	112 Middle Rd	1	14
30441	114 Middle Rd	2	22

We can use a small amount of domain knowledge to make a judgment on the nature of each feature. In particular, we can probably assume that Lot # is meant uniquely to describe a property. The Address is presumably similar. The fact that one field is an integer and the other a string is not as important as is the intent that the value represents something distinctive about each record. Even if one lot might occasionally be subdivided into multiple addresses, and other lots might be undeveloped with no address, generally we expect approximate distinctness of the values. The values may not be entirely unique across records, but they tend in that direction. These are not good candidates for factors.

Let us think about house style and lot size (in acres) next. The house style is presumably selected from among a relatively small number of stock floor plans the developer has available. It is encoded as an integer, but it might well have been a short name used for the same intent (e.g. "Tudor Revival 4 BR"). We may need to account for future data in which houses were built on custom plans—or in any case, plans not from the developer's portfolio—but that could be encoded with a name like "CUSTOM" or a sentinel number like -1. Most likely, the house style is best described as a categorical variable.

The variable Acres could mislead us if we only look at the data currently present. It is an integer with even fewer different values than House Style has. As domain knowledge, we know that new developments commonly are divided into fixed plot sizes (1-3 acres is unusually large for residential houses, but not absurd). However, over time, lots may become subdivided or aggregated in units that do not match the original allocations. The owners of 114 Middle Rd might sell 0.35 acres of their land to the adjacent owners of 112 Middle Rd, leaving both with non-integer and uncommon lot sizes. Most likely, we do not, in fact, wish to encode this variable as categorical, even though its initial values might suggest such. Probably floating-point numbers are most appropriate despite the variable holding only integers currently.

***

In an exercise in *Chapter 4, Anomaly Detection*, you were shown a dataset with a number of human names, many of which are probably misspellings of more common intended names. Using Pandas first, let us read in the data, then discard rows with uncommon names, then convert the string column Name to a categorical variable.

```
humans = pd.read_csv('data/humans-names.csv')
humans
```

	Name	Height	Weight
0	James	167.089607	64.806216
1	David	181.648633	78.281527
2	Barbara	176.272800	87.767722
3	John	173.270164	81.635672
...	...	...	...
24996	Michael	163.952580	68.936137
24997	Marie	164.334317	67.830516
24998	Robert	171.524117	75.861686
24999	James	174.949129	71.620899

25000 rows × 3 columns

For this purpose, we simply do not wish to look at rows with names occurring fewer than 10 times. We can see that this keeps the large majority of rows, but 417 are removed from the 25,000.

```
name_counts = humans.Name.value_counts()
uncommon = name_counts[name_counts < 10]
humans = (humans
            .set_index('Name')
            .drop(uncommon.index)
            .reset_index())
humans
```

	Name	Height	Weight
0	James	167.089607	64.806216
1	David	181.648633	78.281527
2	Barbara	176.272800	87.767722
3	John	173.270164	81.635672
...	...	...	...
24579	Michael	163.952580	68.936137
24580	Marie	164.334317	67.830516
24581	Robert	171.524117	75.861686
24582	James	174.949129	71.620899

24583 rows × 3 columns

At this point, there are 18 unique names remaining, as seen below. They are stored slightly inefficiently as separate strings for each one, but in general all Pandas operations will behave perfectly fine. We might, for example, group by name to do some other operation. Moreover, libraries like scikit-learn will generally be happy to treat a collection of distinct strings as categorical (for many models; others will need a numeric encoding). Converting to factors in Pandas does little more than optimize storage size and make some selection operations faster. These are worthwhile goals, but have little effect on the available APIs. We will see below that R's Tidyverse is somewhat more customized to factors.

```
humans['Name'] = humans.Name.astype('category')
humans.Name.dtype
```

```
CategoricalDtype(categories=['Barbara', 'David', 'Elizabeth', 'James',
                             'Jennifer', 'Jessica', 'John', 'Jon',
                             'Joseph', 'Linda', 'Marie', 'Mary',
                             'Michael', 'Patricia', 'Richard', 'Robert',
                             'Susan', 'William'],
                  ordered=False)
```

Nothing about using this DataFrame really changes. In particular, you can pretend that Name remains a string field, but filters will run faster. As we see above, the dtype now exposes the category values as well, but the same information is generally available with Series.unique() even for string columns (albeit needing a linear scan of the entire column for strings, but looking up a single existing data structure for categorical columns).

```
humans[humans.Name == 'Mary']
```

	Name	Height	Weight
19	Mary	170.513197	71.145258
35	Mary	175.783570	73.843096
54	Mary	166.074242	70.826540
61	Mary	175.258933	78.888337
...	...	...	...
24532	Mary	172.602398	72.602118
24536	Mary	172.159574	70.383305
24547	Mary	173.902497	71.545191
24549	Mary	169.510964	71.460077

1515 rows × 3 columns

Let us look at the same dataset using R, which treats what it calls "factors" as more special. Albeit, in R as well, it is easy to convert back and forth between factor variables and their underlying data type (often underlying strings, but we treat integers, or even floats, as factors at times).

```
%%R
humans <- read_csv('data/humans-names.csv')
humans

— Column specification —
cols(
  Name = col_character(),
  Height = col_double(),
  Weight = col_double()
)

# A tibble: 25,000 x 3
   Name     Height Weight
   <chr>     <dbl>  <dbl>
 1 James      167.   64.8
 2 David      182.   78.3
```

```
 3 Barbara      176.    87.8
 4 John         173.    81.6
 5 Michael      172.    82.8
 6 William      174.    70.7
 7 Elizabeth    177.    81.2
 8 Joseph       178.    78.3
 9 Jessica      172.    64.5
10 William      170.    69.2
# ... with 24,990 more rows
```

In this Tidyverse version of our dataset, we will do something modestly different than we did with Pandas. First we will use `mutate_at()` in very much the same way as we did with `.astype()` in Pandas. Next we use a custom facility of factor variables. Here, all uncommon names are not discarded but are lumped together as a common value `"UNCOMMON"`. This allows us to retain the other associated data columns (which obviously would have been possible in Pandas, but slightly less concise).

```
%%R
# Make the column Name into a factor variable
humans <- mutate_at(humans, vars(Name), factor)

# Any values occurring fewer than 100 times will be
# aggregated under the factor level "UNCOMMON"
humans['Name'] <- fct_lump_min(humans$Name, min = 100,
                          other_level = "UNCOMMON")

humans
```

```
# A tibble: 25,000 x 3
   Name        Height Weight
   <fct>        <dbl>  <dbl>
 1 James        167.    64.8
 2 David        182.    78.3
 3 Barbara      176.    87.8
 4 John         173.    81.6
 5 Michael      172.    82.8
 6 William      174.    70.7
 7 Elizabeth    177.    81.2
 8 Joseph       178.    78.3
 9 Jessica      172.    64.5
10 William      170.    69.2
# ... with 24,990 more rows
```

The only visible change is that the column type has changed, but this lets us ask about the levels of the factor variable, whereas the same call produces NULL for character columns.

```
%%R
levels(humans$Name)
```

```
 [1] "Barbara"   "David"     "Elizabeth" "James"    "Jennifer" "Jessica"
 [7] "John"      "Jon"       "Joseph"    "Linda"    "Marie"    "Mary"
[13] "Michael"   "Patricia"  "Richard"   "Robert"   "Susan"    "William"
[19] "UNCOMMON"
```

Here again, not all that much has changed in the tibble API. The ability to use fct_lump_min() and similar functions is specific to factor columns, but accessing them remains the same as before (just faster).

```
%%R
humans %>% filter(Name == "UNCOMMON")
```

```
# A tibble: 417 x 3
   Name     Height Weight
   <fct>     <dbl>  <dbl>
 1 UNCOMMON   172.   76.5
 2 UNCOMMON   167.   60.3
 3 UNCOMMON   182.   85.2
 4 UNCOMMON   176.   72.3
 5 UNCOMMON   174.   82.1
 6 UNCOMMON   170.   66.8
 7 UNCOMMON   171.   60.0
 8 UNCOMMON   171.   73.9
 9 UNCOMMON   171.   80.4
10 UNCOMMON   177.   73.3
# ... with 407 more rows
```

Let us take a look at the distribution of observations now that uncommon names have been included in the catch-all "UNCOMMON" factor level.

```
%%R
ggplot(humans, aes(y = Name)) + geom_bar(stat = "count")
```

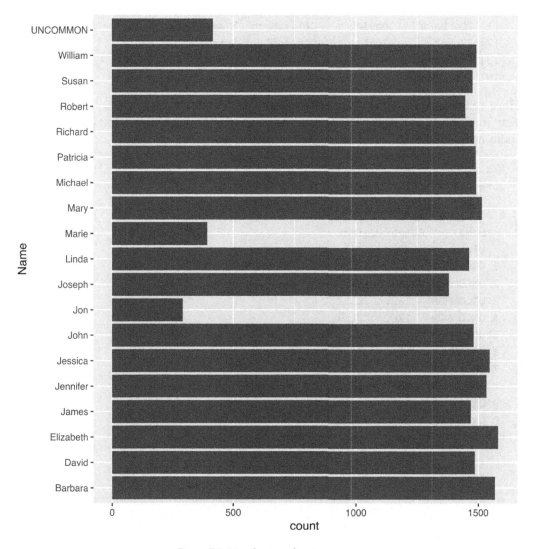

Figure 7.2: Distribution of name counts

In the next section, strings are considered again, but in the sense they are used in natural language processing, as texts of human languages which we might transform into numeric representations.

String Vectors

Get rid of meaning.

–Kathy Acker

Concepts:

- Bag-of-words
- Word2Vec
- Cosine similarity
- Stop words, tokenization, lemmatization

Natural Language Processing (NLP) is a large subfield of data science. The topic is deserving of numerous good books of its own, and fortunately many indeed exist. For this book, we want to look only at one niche area; how can you encode strings of natural language into numeric features that machine learning models can accept as inputs and that statistical techniques can operate on?

Ordered historically, and in sophistication, there are two main methods of transforming a natural language text into a vector. In the simplest case, we can use a technique called "**bag-of-words**." This is simple enough as a technique that we can easily create this representation ourselves with a few lines of code. The idea is first to construct a vocabulary for the entire corpus; that is, simply a collection of all the words it contains. Then we can represent each text within it by a vector of the length of the vocabulary, with each component dimension indicating the count of that word. It should be obvious that this can produce large vector sizes as corpora, and hence vocabularies, grow in size. Even though it loses order of words, this encoding can be quite effective in producing useful vectors capturing semantic distinctions.

For a highly simplified example, suppose you have several pet stores in your town. Each publishes a catalog, with varying numbers of mentions of the two words "dog" and "cat." Having a particular kind of pet (among these) yourself, you wish to determine which is likely to be more relevant for your pet care needs. The vectors we generally use in NLP are likely to have hundreds or thousands of dimensions rather than two.

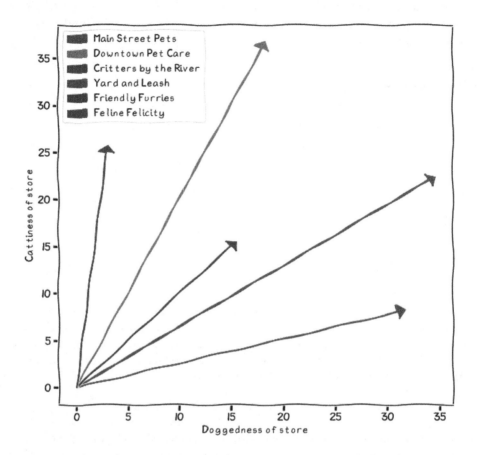

Figure 7.3: Pet store vector space

In order to keep vocabularies at least relatively manageable, we can reduce words to simpler form. We can discard punctuation and *canonicalize* case to arrive at fewer words. Moreover, using the NLTK (Natural Language Toolkit) package, we can remove "stop words" – those usually small connecting words, pronouns, and a few others, that add little to the general semantics of a sentence. Clearly, these are often necessary for clarity of human communication, but a vector representation of meaning usually does better without them. For a simple example, let us choose a famous and powerful poem by an unfortunately politically authoritarian poet.

```
# William Butler Yeats
second_coming = """
Turning and turning in the widening gyre
The falcon cannot hear the falconer;
Things fall apart; the centre cannot hold;
```

```
Mere anarchy is loosed upon the world,
The blood-dimmed tide is loosed, and everywhere
The ceremony of innocence is drowned;
The best lack all conviction, while the worst
Are full of passionate intensity.

Surely some revelation is at hand;
Surely the Second Coming is at hand.
The Second Coming! Hardly are those words out
When a vast image out of Spiritus Mundi
Troubles my sight: somewhere in sands of the desert
A shape with lion body and the head of a man,
A gaze blank and pitiless as the sun,
Is moving its slow thighs, while all about it
Reel shadows of the indignant desert birds.
The darkness drops again; but now I know
That twenty centuries of stony sleep
Were vexed to nightmare by a rocking cradle,
And what rough beast, its hour come round at last,
Slouches towards Bethlehem to be born?
"""
```

The first step is to determine the simplified words, and thereby the vocabulary, for our vector encoding. First the poem itself is reduced to a sequence of more canonical words. This is a form of *tokenization*, but a very simplified form.

```
def simplify_text(text):
    stops = nltk.corpus.stopwords.words('english')
    words = re.findall(r'[a-z]+', text.lower())
    return [w for w in words if w not in stops]

poem = simplify_text(second_coming)
poem[:6]
```

```
['turning', 'turning', 'widening', 'gyre', 'falcon', 'cannot']
```

From here we would like a mapping from the vocabulary to index positions within the vector. The position of any particular word representation in the vector is irrelevant for this purpose, since each makes up an orthogonal axis of the vector. For example, it doesn't matter if "gyre" was chosen to be the second or sixth or twentieth element of the vector.

Our goal will be to encode each fragment using such a vector. Trivially, a fragment might be a single word, but it might be a line, a paragraph, a stanza, or whatever other division we like. The below code first creates a mapping of words to index positions, then generates the bag-of-words vectors.

```python
word2ndx = {w:n for (n, w) in enumerate(set(poem))}
print(f"Vector dimensions={len(word2ndx)}")

def make_vector(words, word2ndx=word2ndx):
    # Generate the vector of zero count per dimension
    vec = np.zeros(len(word2ndx), dtype=np.uint16)
    for word in words:
        # we might ignore unknown word or attempt
        # to canonicalize it, here we raise exception
        assert word in word2ndx
        n = word2ndx[word]
        vec[n] += 1
    return vec

list(word2ndx.items())[:5]
```

```
Vector dimensions=84
[('centre', 0), ('loosed', 1), ('blank', 2), ('falconer', 3),
('moving', 4)]
```

To illustrate this bag-of-words vectorization technique, we can encode each stanza as a vector.

```python
for i, stanza in enumerate(second_coming.split('\n\n')):
    print(f"Stanza {i+1}:")
    print(make_vector(simplify_text(stanza)))
```

```
Stanza 1:
[1 2 0 1 0 0 0 2 0 0 0 0 0 0 1 0 0 0 1 0 0 0 0 0 1 0 1 1 1 1 0 1 0 0 1 0
 1 1 0 1 1 0 2 0 0 0 0 0 0 0 1 0 0 0 1 1 1 1 0 1 0 0 1 1 0 1 0 0 0 0 1
 0 0 0 0 1 0 1 0 1]
Stanza 2:
[0 0 1 0 1 1 1 0 1 1 1 1 1 1 0 1 1 2 0 1 1 1 1 1 0 1 0 0 0 0 2 0 1 1 0 1
 0 0 1 0 0 1 0 1 1 1 1 2 1 1 1 1 0 1 2 1 0 0 0 0 1 0 1 1 0 0 1 0 1 1 2 1 0
 1 1 1 1 0 1 0 1 0]
```

These vectors represent a distinction between the "meaning" of the two stanzas. Surprisingly to me—I did not realize until writing this paragraph—there are no word repetitions other than the stop words. Within each stanza, various words are repeated, albeit only ever twice, not more than that. As human readers, we certainly get a different "feel" from each stanza and would characterize its overall meaning differently.

Generally a more powerful vectorization technique than bag-of-words is **Word2Vec**. This model allows you to create vectors of arbitrary dimensionality; but more importantly than that alone, Word2Vec uses a two-layer neural network that actually looks at the context of each word as defined by the words surrounding it. This winds up producing vectors that are curiously meaningful. Some commonly cited examples are the subtraction and addition of vectors with different components of their meaning. For example, trained on a large, typical English-language corpus, we will likely see:

$$(cat - dog) \approx (kitten - puppy)$$

Or:

$$(china - beijing) \approx (turkey - ankara)$$

Depending on the corpus used in training, the second might be thrown off by the additional meaning of "turkey" as a flightless bird eaten especially in North America. But then, "china" is also a word for porcelain dishes, which could have a similar homonym effect.

Building on Word2vec is an improved version, called a "paragraph vector" by its original inventors, Quoc Le and Tomas Mikolov, but called **Doc2Vec** in the gensim package we utilize here. Gensim is a very useful NLP package for Python that contains a number of useful NLP modeling tools; it is well-optimized for speed in its underlying libraries. Also worth investigating is spaCy, which has a similar purpose, but with more pre-built models. For many purposes, either vectorization is mostly similar; Doc2Vec primarily adds the ability to tag each document (e.g. a sentence, or a paragraph, or a stanza, or an entire book) by some attribute such as its author. This tagging allows additional methods that characterize a tag (i.e. author) overall and compare it to other tags or novel texts.

For this discussion, we will look at a collection of 14,485 tweets about airlines. A corpus larger than the single poem we used above is useful, but there is no reason we could not use that in a similar way. This dataset has a number of things in addition to the tweets themselves.

Two such fields are name (of the account) and airline. The latter is somewhat redundant since it is determined based on the Twitter @ tag that the user themselves attached. Let us look at a few to get a sense.

```
db = sqlite3.connect('data/Airline-Tweets.sqlite')
cur = db.cursor()

sql = """
SELECT name, airline, text
FROM Tweets
"""
cur.execute(sql)
tweets = cur.fetchall()
pprint(tweets[5000:5003], width=60)
```

```
[('Paul_Faust',
  'United',
  '@united Love to report how horrible this flight is to '
  "your team. Let's make it worse...as they get to my "
  'seat...out of all snacks'),
 ('Jennsaint8',
  'Southwest',
  '@SouthwestAir any chance they will change this to '
  'include Northeast airports?  JetBlue has.'),
 ('_stephanieejayy',
  'Delta',
  '@JetBlue do you have any afternoon flights going from '
  'BQN to JFK? I only seem to find early morning flights.')]
```

It would definitely make sense to tag this corpus using the author; however, since each author will have written relatively few tweets, the more frequently occurring airline names are perhaps more interesting to use. This choice is not too important for this book, but just something to illustrate. We will use both tags to show the API.

```
from gensim.models.doc2vec import Doc2Vec, TaggedDocument

docs = []
for (author, airline, msg) in tweets:
    td = TaggedDocument(simplify_text(msg), [author, airline])
    docs.append(td)

# Require words occur at least 4x, Look 2 words to each side
# The produced vector is 10 dimensional
model = Doc2Vec(docs, vector_size=10, window=2, min_count=4)
```

Let us see how large our vocabulary is under the minimum count requirement and also look at a few of the example words.*stems* The ordering of words in the vocabulary is again of no significance, as it was not with bag-of-words. There are several thousands of words in the vocabulary, but we reduce the representation to an arbitrary dimensionality. Here we choose 10 dimensions, which is probably sufficient for these fairly stereotyped messages. A wider corpus with more semantic variation would probably benefit from higher dimensionality (the default if not specified is 100).

```
print("Number of words:", len(model.wv.vocab))
list(model.wv.vocab)[:7]
```

```
Number of words: 3359
['jetblue', 'new', 'ceo', 'seeks', 'right', 'balance', 'please']
```

stems

Identification of *words* is itself an important area of NLP. Inflectional forms of the "same" word are often best treated as the same base form. This is done either by stemming or by lemmatization. Stemming tries to identify a few letters making up a morphological root of a word by removing common affixes. Lemmatization goes further by using both grammatical context and phonemic relations. For example, a lemmatizer might canonicalize "dove" as a verb as "dive" (i.e. jump) but "dove" as a noun as "dove" (i.e. a bird). Either technique would tread the word "seek" in the example as being identical to "seeks", "seeking", et cetera.

The purpose of this code we have run is to now be able to represent any string we might create as 10 numeric features. Novel strings may only utilize terms in our vocabulary, but Gensim provides a mechanism to construct a larger vocabulary along with the model, including words that do not occur in the initial training set. Let us first look at the vector for an existing tweet, then for a novel message.

```
msg = tweets[11_001][2]
print(msg)
model.infer_vector(simplify_text(msg))
```

```
@AmericanAir thank you for responding rather quickly btw
array([ 0.01165844,  0.00964975, -0.08577796, -0.03201848,  0.00883767,
        0.13692749,  0.06367198,  0.02911634, -0.00109272, -0.16733222],
      dtype=float32)
```

Below we create a short novel message and obtain its vector. These dimensions have no particular meaning, but we are able to measure the relationships between them. We can also store this synthetic data in intermediate datasets that might be used for downstream modeling techniques; this latter is the most common use for this transformation.

```
badservice = model.infer_vector(['bad', 'service'])
badservice
```

```
array([-0.03352741,  0.0146618 , -0.03105226,  0.036326  ,  0.05287395,
        0.05780041, -0.05203189,  0.07293667, -0.01861257, -0.13574287],
      dtype=float32)
```

The Gensim library provides a rich set of functions to compare these representations, using cosine similarity (the cosine of the angle between two vectors) and other techniques. Just as one example, let us see which single words are closest to my short message, "bad service". A small note is that I have frozen this next output; the neural network underlying Doc2Vec has state randomization, so each time it is trained, different vectors, and different connection weights in the underlying neural network, are produced. Here I display the result from one particular run, but other runs will vary in details.

```
model.wv.most_similar(['bad', 'service'])
```

```
[('terrible', 0.9658449292182922),
 ('clients', 0.9587224125862122),
 ('management', 0.9491853713989258),
 ('greeting', 0.9436992406845093),
 ('msy', 0.9382249116897583),
 ('pathetic', 0.9378621578216553),
 ('dropped', 0.9307988286018372),
 ('keeping', 0.9277007579803467),
 ('lack', 0.924517035484314),
 ('telling', 0.9227219223976135)]
```

Most of those words are directly negative; the ones that seem neutral or positive probably occur mostly in contexts that negate their ordinary meanings in some sense. For example, perhaps "management" is usually surrounded by negative adjectives in the tweets. We can also utilize the tags to get vectors that simply represent the collection of texts associated with the tag, as we do in the next cell.

We could make measurements from these vectors in the parameter space to those for additional airlines, or to particular texts expressing a sentiment, and this would illustrate the similarity of those various vectors.

```
airlines = ('Delta', 'United', 'JetBlue')
delta, united, jetblue = (model.docvecs[x] for x in airlines)
print(f"Delta:\n{delta}\n")
print(f"United:\n{united}\n")
print(f"JetBlue:\n{jetblue}\n")
```

```
Delta:
[ 5.578579    2.0885715 -5.8722963 -5.2461944  4.862418    6.6500683
  3.054988    2.5725224  3.1206055 -9.660177 ]

United:
[ 0.62689006  2.9862213  -10.10382    -7.578535   -0.44318137
  3.9621575   2.9998243  -0.11659689 -2.9283297  -7.8558965 ]

JetBlue:
[ 0.04514389  0.03341183 -0.02691341  0.01708637  0.02028313 -0.03833938
 -0.0415993  -0.04835104 -0.05358113 -0.03369116]
```

How similar are what people tweet about these airlines, as a per-airline comparison?

```
from scipy.spatial.distance import cosine
print(f"Delta  | United  | {cosine(delta, united):.3f}")
print(f"Delta  | JetBlue | {cosine(delta, jetblue):.3f}")
print(f"United | JetBlue | {cosine(united, jetblue):.3f}")
```

```
Delta  | United  | 0.239
Delta  | JetBlue | 0.930
United | JetBlue | 0.787
```

We can see that Delta and United are quite similar in this analysis, but Delta and JetBlue are nearly as distant in vector space as is possible. That is, a value of zero would mean identical "sentiment" vectors, while a value of one would be maximally different. This is a good time to continue thinking about vector spaces in an abstract sense.

Decompositions

After the entropy is accounted for, all that is left is noise.

–David Mertz

Concepts:

- Principal Component Analysis and other decompositions
- Whitening
- Dimensionality reduction
- Visualization with t-SNE and UMAP

A highly dimensional dataset—whether of high dimension because of the initial data collection or because of creation of extra synthetic features—may lend itself less well to modeling techniques. In these cases, it can be more computationally tractable, as well as more predictive, to work with fewer features. Feature *selection* is mostly outside the scope of this book, but is discussed briefly in the below section on *Polynomial Features*, which is the technique that increases the number of synthetic features most dramatically.

However, one special kind of "feature selection" is a **decomposition** of the parameter space of a feature set. These techniques presuppose that all features have been numerically encoded in some manner, perhaps via the technique discussed below in the *One-Hot Encoding* section. A decomposition creates synthetic features in a sense, but what it really does is create a new orthonormal basis (new axes) of the parameter space. The transformation in a decomposition is information-preserving and reversible *if* you keep the same number of dimensions as in the prior dataset. However, the purpose of a decomposition is most often to perform *dimensionality reduction*. When a decomposition is performed on multi-dimensional data, it concentrates the entropy of the data into the initial dimensions, leaving much less information content in the remaining dimensions; often, discarding the higher-numbered dimensions does little harm to modeling metrics, or indeed improves them.

The most common, and oldest, decomposition technique is principal component analysis (PCA), which was first developed by Karl Pearson in 1901. We will primarily focus on PCA in this section, but just keep in mind that other techniques might prove more powerful for specific datasets and domain characteristic distributions of values. Some of these other techniques include non-negative matrix factorization (NMF), latent Dirichlet allocation (LDA), independent component analysis (ICA), and t-distributed stochastic neighbor embedding (t-SNE). The last listed technique, t-SNE, is not reversible, however, so is not quite accurately characterized as a decomposition, but it *is* a dimensionality reduction that is very often useful for visualization, and we will look at an example of that. Conveniently, all of these decompositions (as well as others) are provided by scikit-learn; each is certainly available in other libraries as well, of course.

Rotation and Whitening

As an initial example, let us look at a dataset with just two features, and perform a decomposition on it. When we perform a decomposition we emphasize the "most important synthetic axes." The result of this for PCA specifically is that, by definition, the variance decreases with each successive PCA feature. Whitening and sphering are synonyms meaning re-scaling these synthetic features.

With a decomposition, there can be a secondary de-emphasis of some features that is too strong. It depends on the specific kind of model used, but for many models a numeric feature ranging from 0 to 100 will simply have more effect than a feature varying from 0 to 1 just because it contributes *bigger* numbers to the calculation. Usually it is better to let a model select the importances of features than to judge them in advance with feature engineering. That is, a decomposition — or other feature engineering technique — might give a synthetic feature a numeric scale greater or less than some other feature, and hence a corresponding default weighting. It is best to avoid that, as we do below.

```
from src.whiten import data, show

# Only two initial features for illustration,
# but in general we would have a high dimensionality
show(data, "Parameter space for two features",
    "Raw Feature 1", "Raw Feature 2")
```

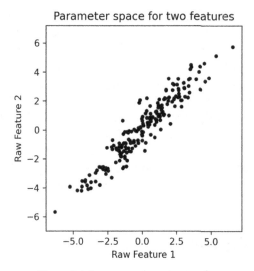

Figure 7.4: Parameter space for two features

Here we have two features that are obviously pretty strongly correlated. In particular though, we notice that the variance is greater along a diagonal of roughly 45° than along the observed axes. PCA will reorient the data to make this axis of variance (i.e. the most entropy) the primary component.

```
from sklearn.decomposition import PCA
show(PCA().fit_transform(data),
     "PCA Components", "Synthetic Axis 1", "Synthetic Axis 2")
```

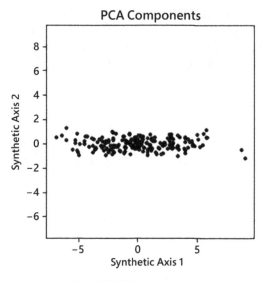

Figure 7.5: PCA components

We looked at scaling in more detail in *Chapter 5, Data Quality*. We could use those standard techniques to scale this "flattened" data, but this concern is common enough in PCA transforms that scikit-learn builds in an argument to do it automatically. This often saves us the need to rescale data a second time after the transform, and is generally a cleaner approach.

```
show(PCA(whiten=True).fit_transform(data),
    "Whitened Components", "Synthetic Axis 1", "Synthetic Axis 2")
```

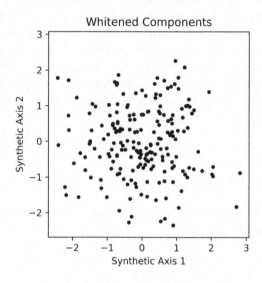

Figure 7.6: Whitened components

The use of "whitening" is closely analogous to the distinction between "white noise" and "pink noise" in acoustics and spectral analysis. Both kinds of noise represent a wide range of frequency values, but "pink" overemphasizes the red end of the visual spectrum. Similarly, a non-whitened PCA would overemphasize one particular axis.

Dimensionality Reduction

While a change to the orthonormal basis might in itself aid machine learning models, the more common use of decomposition is to reduce the number of dimensions while still retaining most of the information. As an example, let us use the widely available Wisconsin Breast Cancer dataset. This can be obtained from the UCI Machine Learning Repository, from Kaggle, or included with scikit-learn and other data science libraries. In summary, this dataset contains 30 numeric measurements of tumors, with a target characterization as benign or malignant.

It has 569 observations that are relatively well balanced between the target classes (212 malignant, 357 benign).

```
cancer = load_breast_cancer()
X_raw = StandardScaler().fit_transform(cancer.data)
y = cancer.target
```

If we try to make a prediction using a typical machine learning model, we can do *pretty well* with a naïve approach. In order to illustrate this, we perform a train/test split to avoid overfitting the specific data used to train the model. This is outside the direct scope of this discussion, but a line of code below performs that. We can also reduce the dimensionality using PCA, and the effect on the model quality is interesting. For this discussion, we will try selecting just one principal component, only two components, and four components, derived from the original 30 features. We whiten in each case to preserve scales of dimensions (this is generally moot for the PCA1 case).

```
X_pca1 = PCA(n_components=1, whiten=True).fit_transform(X_raw)
X_pca2 = PCA(n_components=2, whiten=True).fit_transform(X_raw)
X_pca4 = PCA(n_components=4, whiten=True).fit_transform(X_raw)
```

Using our three candidate feature matrices, let us see how well the corresponding K-neighbors models perform.

```
for X in (X_raw, X_pca1, X_pca2, X_pca4):
    X_train, X_test, y_train, y_test = (
        train_test_split(X, y, random_state=1))
    model = KNeighborsClassifier().fit(X_train, y_train)
    accuracy = model.score(X_test, y_test)
    error_rate = 100*(1-accuracy)
    print(f"Features | {X.shape=}\t| {error_rate=:.2f}%")
```

```
Features | X.shape=(569, 30) | error_rate=4.90%
Features | X.shape=(569, 1)  | error_rate=9.79%
Features | X.shape=(569, 2)  | error_rate=6.99%
Features | X.shape=(569, 4)  | error_rate=4.20%
```

An error rate of 4.90% on the raw data is not too unreasonable. In any case, let us consider that a baseline. With only one principal component, the error rate jumps to 9.79%; this is surprisingly good given how much information we discarded, and is better than we could have done utilizing any single raw feature. If we keep two principal components, the error rate falls to 6.99%, which is a sensible intermediate value.

However, what is intriguing is that with four principal components, we actually get a slightly better error rate, of 4.20%, than we achieved with the complete raw data. In essence, after the bulk of the entropy in the data is accounted for, all that is left is random noise.

This contrast between "entropy" and "noise," while accurate, is also meant as a playful phrasing. Entropy and noise are treated as synonyms in many contexts, although "information content" is actually closer to the meaning of entropy. But the underlying point is that some of the variability in observations is due to the underlying natural (or artificial) phenomenon, and some of it is due exclusively to the random variation of sampling a finite population. Dimensionality reduction via decomposition has a tendency to pick out the signal from the noise. I will note that there remains trial and error here; for example, choosing five or six components rather than four becomes worse than the raw data again (on this exact model algorithm, with this exact train/test split, with these exact hyperparameters, et cetera).

Let us return to exactly what PCA does as a transformation. It simply determines multipliers for each of the raw dimensions to linearly derive the principal components. For example, in the breast cancer dataset, each observation is a vector of 30 numbers. Each of those numbers is multiplied by some constant, and those 30 products are added together to make up component 1. Likewise for component 2, with different multipliers. Let us create a table of these multipliers for n_components=3 to illustrate.

```
pca3 = PCA(n_components=3).fit(X_raw)
pd.DataFrame(pca3.components_.T,
          index=cancer.feature_names,
          columns=['pca_1', 'pca_2', 'pca_3'])
```

	pca_1	pca_2	pca_3
mean radius	0.218902	-0.233857	-0.008531
mean texture	0.103725	-0.059706	0.064550
mean perimeter	0.227537	-0.215181	-0.009314
mean area	0.220995	-0.231077	0.028700
...	...	...	...
worst concavity	0.228768	0.097964	-0.173057
worst concave points	0.250886	-0.008257	-0.170344
worst symmetry	0.122905	0.141883	-0.271313
worst fractal dimension	0.131784	0.275339	-0.232791

30 rows × 3 columns

In other words, we can use the `.transform()` method of the fitted PCA object, but we can equivalently just perform the same calculation in plain NumPy.

```
row0_sk = pca3.transform(X_raw)[0]
row0_np = (pca3.components_ * X_raw[0]).sum(axis=1)
print(f"Row 0 as transform: {row0_sk}")
print(f"Row 0 as mul/sum:   {row0_np}")
```

```
Row 0 as transform: [ 9.19283683  1.94858307 -1.12316599]
Row 0 as mul/sum:   [ 9.19283683  1.94858307 -1.12316599]
```

Visualization

For different purposes, utilizing a different decomposition can be useful. Principal component analysis, however, remains the first technique you should try in most cases. One special use is when we want to generate useful visualizations of high-dimensional parameter spaces into the two or three dimensions we can actually represent spatially. **T-distributed Stochastic Neighbor Embedding (t-SNE)** is a nonlinear dimensionality reduction technique for projecting high-dimensional data into two or three dimensions. Similar objects are modeled by nearby points and dissimilar objects are modeled by distant points, with high probability.

As an example of this visualization technique, let us look at a collection of 1,797 handwritten digits scanned as 8×8 grayscale pixels. This collection is one of those published in the UCI Machine Learning Repository and distributed with scikit-learn. What this amounts to is a 64-dimensional parameter space for the various pixel values. Relatively simple models like logistic regression can get good results in predictive accuracy on this dataset; convolutional neural networks do even better. Let us look at a few sample scans and import the underlying data.

```
digits = get_digits()
```

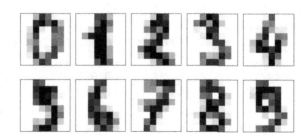

Figure 7.7: Sample digits

We might try to simplify this 64-dimensional parameter space using PCA. That will indeed get us a two-dimensional visualization that shows reasonable differentiation of digits in this projected parameter space. There is certainly, for example, a region toward the top center of the plot below that is dominated by the digit 0. At the same time, there is strong overlap between the regions where digits occur, and somewhat loose differentiation.

```
pca_digits = PCA(n_components=2).fit_transform(digits.data)
plot_digits(pca_digits, digits, "PCA")
```

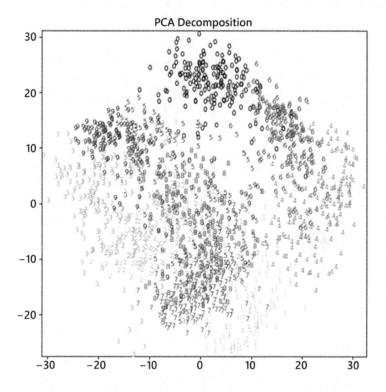

Figure 7.8: PCA decomposition of digit space

The scale units of the PCA dimensionality reduction, and those below of other techniques, have no specific numeric meaning. They are simply artifacts of the algorithms, but produce differentiated numbers that can be plotted, or used in statistics or modeling.

In contrast, using t-SNE we achieve a much stronger result for this visualization. Correspondingly, modeling based on this projection will provide much more to work with. In this example, t-SNE plus logistic regression does not perform better than the logistic regression on the full feature space, but it is not that much worse with far less underlying data used to represent each observation. The cluster of 0 digits at the center left, for example, is extremely strong, with a large gap between those and any other digits. A few others are less well separated, but in the ways we would tend to expect; a 9 drawn a certain way strongly resembles a 3, for example.

```python
tsne_digits = TSNE(random_state=1).fit_transform(digits.data)
plot_digits(tsne_digits, digits, "t-SNE")
```

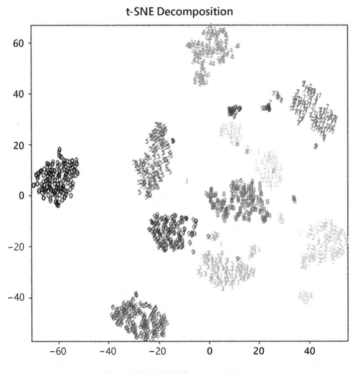

Figure 7.9: t-SNE decomposition

Uniform Manifold Approximation and Projection for Dimension Reduction (UMAP) is another technique with a similar motivation (but very different math) as t-SNE. UMAP often has additional advantages. Specifically, the distance *between* clusters — not only the closeness of observations *within* a cluster — is roughly preserved by UMAP, whereas t-SNE simply does not attempt to do that. In this particular scanned digits example, UMAP produces even tighter clusters than does t-SNE as well.

In fact, the clusters are tight enough that it is difficult or impossible to distinguish the many overlain digits within each cluster.

```
from umap import UMAP
umap_digits = UMAP(random_state=1).fit_transform(digits.data)
plot_digits(umap_digits, digits, "UMAP")
```

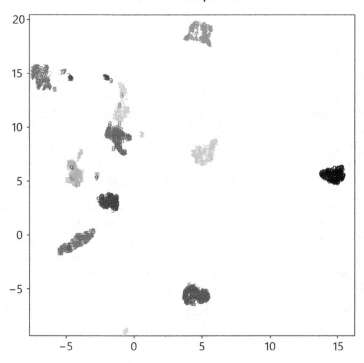

Figure 7.10: UMAP decomposition

In using a decomposition technique to generate synthetic features, you are not, of course, limited to using only those features. Depending on your specific needs, it can make sense to utilize a top few decomposed dimensions, but also add those into the same intermediate dataset with some original raw features, with one-hot-encoded features, with polynomial features, or with other types of synthetic data. This task-specific construction of a dataset is likely to be most effective for the particular purpose you have in front of you. Obviously, a lot of gut feeling, some reasoning, and a lot of trial and error are needed to arrive at the best data to work with.

Let us look at turning continuous measurements into ordinal data, which can often increase the power of models.

Quantization and Binarization

I only like two kinds of men, domestic and imported.

–Mae West

Concepts:

- Decreasing granularity
- Balancing bin size
- Setting thresholds

There are times when continuous—or even simply ordinal—data is more usefully represented by a small number of levels. At the limit of that, we may reduce a numeric range to just two values: True/False or 1/0 generally, but other values can work. At this limit, *quantization* is known as *binarization*. Using a quantization transformation is often useful when data as represented has more precision than is genuinely meaningful—either from the perspective of the accuracy of measurements, or from the perspective of utility to our data science task.

As a simple example for this section and the next one, I will use the results of a survey I conducted on students in a half-day tutorial on scikit-learn I gave at a conference. I sometimes use this same data in other training as a quick dataset for performing machine learning. What is presented here removes some of the features, but retains those useful for these sections. Like all data, this dataset is messy; some cleanup was done, but a few elements were deliberately eschewed to provide you a real-world mess (but not *too dirty* to be useful).

```
survey = pd.read_csv('data/ML-survey.csv')
survey.sample(6, random_state=1)
```

	Language	Experience	Age	Post_Secondary	Success
95	C++	1.0	57	12	7
44	Python	7.0	24	11	5
56	R	2.0	46	9	10
97	Python	2.0	23	3	5
69	Python	5.0	53	4	8
114	Python	25.0	76	23	1

This data is simple enough. Some biographic data was collected about tutorial attendees, and they were asked to evaluate how successful the tutorial was on a 1-10 scale. A tiny bit of domain knowledge will tell you that on ratings like this the distribution of responses is highly skewed. In essence, a 9 or 10 is a strong positive, and anything 7 or less is negative. A response of 8 is moderately positive. Perhaps one might hope for more uniformity across the range, but human psychology and a history of social pressures around how to respond to such evaluations make this so. These data follow this familiar pattern.

```
(survey
    .Success
    .value_counts()
    .sort_index()
    .plot(kind='bar', title="Distribution of Ratings"));
```

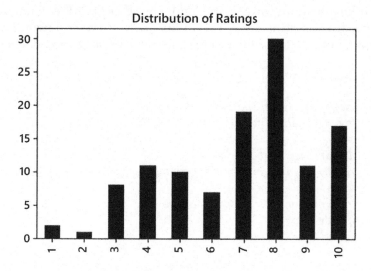

Figure 7.11: Distribution of ratings

Given the distribution of data, the known psychology of ratings, and a stipulated analytic purpose, we wish to treat the rated success simply as a binary value. This can be done very easily in Pandas—or almost identically in every other data frame library—by a simple comparison that creates a Boolean array.

These Boolean arrays are often used as filters or masks, but they can equally provide perfectly good values directly.

```
survey.Success >= 8
```

```
0        True
1        True
2        True
3        False
        ...
112      False
113      True
114      False
115      True
Name: Success, Length: 116, dtype: bool
```

If you are working with raw arrays, in NumPy or other libraries, you may wish to use the scikit-learn class `Binarizer`. This utility always expects a two-dimensional matrix as input, but a matrix with a single column is perfectly acceptable.

```
from sklearn.preprocessing import Binarizer

# Set threshold anywhere *between* 7 and 8
binary_rating = Binarizer(threshold=7.5)

# Pass 2-D DataFrame, not Series
success = binary_rating.fit_transform(survey[['Success']])

# Maintaining versions is good practice
survey2 = survey.copy()
survey2['Success'] = success
survey2
```

	Language	Experience	Age	Post_Secondary	Success
0	Python	20.0	53	13	1
1	Python	4.0	33	7	1
2	Python	1.0	31	10	1
3	Python	12.0	60	12	0
...	...	...	...	...	...
112	Python	4.0	35	4	0
113	Python	3.0	44	6	1
114	Python	25.0	76	23	0
115	Python	25.0	75	12	1

116 rows × 5 columns

Binary values are well-suited for the Success measure. For other columns, we would like to treat them somewhat differently. Let us look at how the amount of post-secondary education of attendees was distributed; we will treat it somewhat differently.

```
(survey2
    .Post_Secondary
    .plot(kind="hist", bins=20,
        title="Distribution of Education"));
```

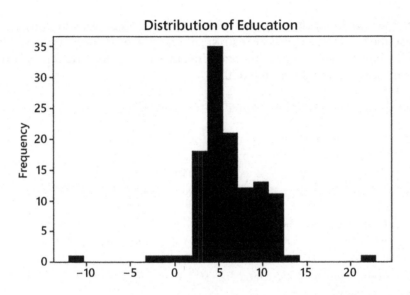

Figure 7.12: Distribution of education

There are two apparent outliers in the data. One respondent claimed 23 years of post-secondary education. That same respondent happens to be visible above as row 114, and the respondent reported being 76 years old. Given that the survey intention and description were along the lines of noting a doctorate or equivalent profession degree as 10 years, the 23 is somewhat suspicious; possibly this same person has a Ph.D., M.D., and J.D. to add to that number, but more likely there was some failure in communicating the intention, or an entry error. Nonetheless, for our binning, we will just stipulate that that person will go in the most-education category.

The second outlier is -12, which is simply a nonsensical value. The intention, in any case, was that no college education would be noted as zero, not by some subtraction for years-until-college. Perhaps a third-grader attended and felt that was the best description. Or again, more likely there was a data entry error. We will simply code this as the least-education category, in this case. For another purpose, you might reflect on techniques discussed in *Chapter 6, Value Imputation* to treat the illegal value. Rather than preserve the exact years of education, we will only store values corresponding to "least-education", "mid-education", and "most-education" — numerically coded just as 0, 1, and 2. Our project documentation should describe this mapping.

To divide the data into roughly equally sized bins based on the amount of education, we can use the scikit-learn class KBinsDiscretizer. As elsewhere in the scikit-learn API, we first create a parameterized instance of the class, then perform a .fit_transform() to transform the data.

```python
from sklearn.preprocessing import KBinsDiscretizer

# Create a binner with 3 balanced bins
edu_bin = KBinsDiscretizer(n_bins=3,
                           encode='ordinal',
                           strategy='quantile')

# Bin the Post_Secondary column
level = edu_bin.fit_transform(survey2[['Post_Secondary']])

# In this version, rename the binned field "Education"
survey3 = survey2.copy()
survey3['Education'] = level.astype(np.uint8)
survey3.drop('Post_Secondary', axis=1, inplace=True)
survey3.sample(8, random_state=2)
```

	Language	Experience	Age	Success	Education
24	Python	3.0	28	1	0
89	Python	12.0	46	0	2
28	Python	3.0	31	1	1
56	R	2.0	46	1	2
2	Python	1.0	31	1	2
53	Python	10.0	3	1	2
45	Python	1.0	31	0	2
79	JavaScript	1.0	32	1	1

We can see generally that Education values are 0, 1, or 2 as anticipated. We can look in more detail to see what cut-offs were selected and how many respondents fall into each category.

Note that although I am describing these as categories (and expect a mapping documenting the keys), these are clearly ordinally arranged, not categorical.

```
print("Education cut-offs:")
print(edu_bin.bin_edges_[0], '\n')
print("Count per bin:")
print(survey3.Education.value_counts())

Education cut-offs:
[-12.          4.33333333    7.          23.          ]

Count per bin:
2    44
0    39
1    33
Name: Education, dtype: int64
```

For education, we allowed the utility to decide the cut-points for balanced bins. However, perhaps we would rather divide into fixed numeric ranges for a particular feature. Let us try that approach for the Experience value (intended to reflect years of programming experience). KBinsDiscretizer can simply be instantiated with different parameters to achieve this. Again we need to document that numbers 0, 1, 2, 3, and 4 are used to denote experience ranges rather than raw years; however, here we retain the same column name in the new dataset version.

```
# Create a binner with 5 bins of same numeric range
exp = KBinsDiscretizer(n_bins=5,
                       encode='ordinal',
                       strategy='uniform')

# Bin the Experience column
exp_level = exp.fit_transform(survey3[['Experience']])

# Retain the Experience name, but new meaning
survey4 = survey3.copy()
survey4['Experience'] = exp_level.astype(np.uint8)
survey4.sample(8, random_state=3)
```

	Language	Experience	Age	Success	Education
83	MATLAB	1	37	0	2
5	Python	0	32	1	0
6	Python	0	34	0	2
42	MATLAB	0	31	0	2
100	Python	0	47	0	2
97	Python	0	23	0	0
40	Python	1	33	1	2
25	R	0	36	1	0

The result of using the "uniform" strategy for binning produces strongly imbalanced bins. However, that is perfectly reasonable in many cases, including most likely this one. In our broader purpose, rounding the amount of experience to rough multiples of 5 years might be a good simplification. If we varied this technique modestly, we could make those cuts at exactly 5 years, but approximately that range was obtained by regularly cutting the data itself.

```
print("Experience cut-offs:")
print(exp.bin_edges_[0], '\n')
print("Count per bin:")
print(survey4
        .Experience.value_counts()
        .sort_index())
```

```
Experience cut-offs:
[ 0.    5.4 10.8 16.2 21.6 27. ]

Count per bin:
0    93
1    14
2     4
3     1
4     4
Name: Experience, dtype: int64
```

In each of the prior quantizations, we encoded values as ordinals. However, another approach is sometimes better. We might consider the different numeric ranges of a value as genuinely categorically different, rather than as ordinals or even as purely quantitative. Education was treated in an ordinal way, since the increments were uneven. But experience is simply continuous but quantized. To an approximation, recovering the original measurement is simply multiplying each value by 5.4, in that case.

For certain measurements, different values may reflect different domains or regimes. For those, we can use one-hot encoding, which is discussed in the next section but is available as a parameter of `KBinsDiscretizer` as well.

Although I believe it is fanciful for this example, let us stipulate that "Young", "Mid_Age", and "Old" tutorial attendees are wholly different kinds that we wish to distinguish (your author will be lumped into the last of those domains). Before we do that, however, we have to handle a data quality issue. Some age values look suspicious.

```
survey4.Age.describe()[['mean', 'min', 'max']]
```

```
mean      36.965517
min        3.000000
max       99.000000
Name: Age, dtype: float64
```

```
survey[survey.Age < 10]
```

	Language	Experience	Age	Post_Secondary	Success
53	Python	10.0	3	9	9
85	Python	3.0	3	10	6

There was conceivably a 99-year-old in the tutorial, but there were certainly no 3-year-old attendees. Although the 99-year-old was *probably* an inaccurate entry, the 3-year-olds are provably wrong from the data itself, since their programming experience and post-secondary education each exceed their age. I will assume that these are 30-something attendees who made data entry errors, and impute an age of 35 to both of them (not far from the median or mean age of all attendees, which I might also reasonably use).

```
# Create next version and impute for bad data
survey5 = survey4.copy()
survey5.loc[survey5.Age == 3, 'Age'] = 35

# Create a binner with 3 bins to 3 columns
# Note: a sparse array with "onehot"
age_bin = KBinsDiscretizer(n_bins=3,
                           encode='onehot-dense',
                           strategy='quantile')

# Bin and split the Age column
age = age_bin.fit_transform(survey5[['Age']])
```

```
age = age.astype(np.uint8).T
survey5 = survey5.assign(Young=age[0],
                         Mid_Age=age[1],
                         Old=age[2])
survey5.drop('Age', axis=1, inplace=True)
survey5.sample(8, random_state=4)
```

	Language	Experience	Success	Education	Young	Mid_Age	Old
13	Python	0	0	2	0	1	0
2	Python	0	1	2	0	1	0
25	R	0	1	0	0	1	0
16	Python	0	1	0	0	0	1
19	Python	0	0	1	0	0	1
79	JavaScript	0	1	1	0	1	0
5	Python	0	1	0	0	1	0
24	Python	0	1	0	1	0	0

Having created synthetic columns for age ranges using one-hot encoding, this is a good point to turn to the next section that discusses one-hot encoding in general. We will continue to work with this survey dataset that we have massaged and transformed in stages.

One-Hot Encoding

If once a man indulges himself in murder, very soon he comes to think little of robbing; and from robbing he next comes to drinking and Sabbath-breaking, and from that to incivility and procrastination. Once [begun] upon this downward path, you never know where you are to stop. Many a man has dated his ruin from some murder or other that perhaps he thought little of at the time.

–Thomas de Quincey

Concepts:

- Avoiding artificial ordering
- Synthetic boolean features

Very commonly, we work with features that have a number of class values encoded in them. For many models or other statistical techniques, we require features to be encoded as numbers. An easy way to do that is by encoding values as numeric ordinals. For example, in the survey data, we *could* encode the language feature by mapping Python=1, R=2, JavaScript=3, and so on. While those values are numeric, we often get better quality if we do not impose an artificial ordering to the categories. Different programming languages have no inherent or obvious ordering among them.

The encoding of class values may not be as meaningful strings, but may already use a range of small integers. This can falsely suggest ordinality to a variable. We should consult documentation and domain knowledge to determine if that is a reasonable interpretation for a particular feature. Symmetrically, of course, strings sometimes actually do encode clearly ordinal values; e.g. "Poor", "Good", "Best" in an evaluation of something (the meaningful order is unlikely to be the "natural" order of those strings, such as alphabetical).

To encode one feature with multiple values, we can transform it into multiple features, one for each class value. The "one-hot" in the name of this encoding indicates that exactly one of these new features will have a one, and the others will be zeros (or alternately True/False, depending on your programming language and library). The favorite programming language column of the survey dataset is a good candidate for one-hot encoding.

In Pandas, the `get_dummies()` function transforms a data frame into one-hot encoding. In scikit-learn, the class `OneHotEncoder` performs the same task, but is not limited to working with Pandas (anything matrix-like works). In both APIs, you have a variety of options to provide the naming of the new features, whether to use dense or sparse arrays for storage, whether to omit one category (to reduce multicollinearity), and in Pandas which columns to encode. By default, Pandas will look for all string or categorical columns, but you can tweak that; for example, you may want to force one-hot encoding of an integer column.

For presentation, we display a transposed data frame with a sample of a few rows and the encoded language features as rows. We can see that most samples (here shown as columns) have a 1 in the `Lang_Python` feature, and 0 for other features.

A few of the samples have their "one-hot" in a different feature.

```
survey6 = pd.get_dummies(survey5, prefix="Lang")
survey6.sample(10, random_state=3).T.tail(8)
```

	83	5	6	42	100	97	40	25	115	103
Lang_C++	0	0	0	0	0	0	0	0	0	0
Lang_JavaScript	0	0	0	0	0	0	0	0	0	0
Lang_MATLAB	1	0	0	1	0	0	0	0	0	0
Lang_Python	0	1	1	0	1	1	1	0	1	0
Lang_R	0	0	0	0	0	0	0	1	0	1
Lang_Scala	0	0	0	0	0	0	0	0	0	0
Lang_VB	0	0	0	0	0	0	0	0	0	0
Lang_Whitespace	0	0	0	0	0	0	0	0	0	0

The scikit-learn API is similar to other transformers we have looked at. We simply create a parameterized instance, then fit and/or transform data using it. Under this API, the metadata such as suggested feature names lives in the encoded object and the raw encoded data is a plain NumPy array.

```
from sklearn.preprocessing import OneHotEncoder
lang = survey5[['Language']]
enc = OneHotEncoder(sparse=False).fit(lang)
one_hot = enc.transform(lang)
print(enc.get_feature_names())
print("\nA few encoded rows:")
print(one_hot[80:90])
```

```
['x0_C++' 'x0_JavaScript' 'x0_MATLAB' 'x0_Python' 'x0_R' 'x0_Scala'
 'x0_VB' 'x0_Whitespace']

A few encoded rows:
[[0. 0. 0. 1. 0. 0. 0. 0.]
 [0. 0. 0. 0. 0. 0. 0. 1.]
 [0. 0. 0. 1. 0. 0. 0. 0.]
 [0. 0. 1. 0. 0. 0. 0. 0.]
 [0. 0. 0. 1. 0. 0. 0. 0.]
 [0. 0. 0. 1. 0. 0. 0. 0.]
 [0. 0. 0. 1. 0. 0. 0. 0.]
 [0. 0. 0. 1. 0. 0. 0. 0.]
 [0. 0. 0. 0. 1. 0. 0. 0.]
 [0. 0. 0. 1. 0. 0. 0. 0.]]
```

With our transformation, we have arrived at a dataset with more features, but ones better suited to our downstream purposes. Let us look at just one row since the DataFrame has become too wide to display easily in this space. The particular encodings we have performed all give us small, non-negative integers, in this example, but this could easily be combined with other continuous numeric variables, perhaps with those scaled to a similar numeric range as these small numbers.

```
with show_more_rows():
    print(survey6.loc[0])
```

```
Experience          3
Success             1
Education           2
Young               0
Mid_Age             0
Old                 1
Lang_C++            0
Lang_JavaScript     0
Lang_MATLAB         0
Lang_Python         1
Lang_R              0
Lang_Scala          0
Lang_VB             0
Lang_Whitespace     0
Name: 0, dtype: int64
```

One-hot encoding is one small step toward increasing dimensionality with synthetic features. Next we turn to a truly giant leap with polynomial features.

Polynomial Features

In the final analysis, a drawing simply is no longer a drawing, no matter how self-sufficient its execution may be. It is a symbol, and the more profoundly the imaginary lines of projection meet higher dimensions, the better.

–Paul Klee

Concepts:

- Generating synthetic features
- The curse of dimensionality
- Feature selection

Generating polynomial features can create a large number of new synthetic features. The basic idea behind this transformation is simple: we add new features that are the multiplicative product of up to N of the existing features. In the scikit-learn version we will use in this section, `PolynomialFeatures` does a multiplication of all combinations of parameters (up to specified degree). It is, of course, easy enough to create multiplicative, or other, combinations of features manually. The `PolynomialFeatures` wraps up identifying all combinations and providing a general transformer object with useful metadata, in one API that is familiar to users of other scikit-learn classes.

Constructing polynomial features is often the main reason we need subsequently to winnow features using feature selection. Reducing 30 raw features to 15, for example, is unlikely to be hugely important to most models. But reducing the 496 synthetic features in the below example becomes important to both the power of a model and computational resources used. If we construct a much larger number of synthetic polynomial features, the imperative for feature selection becomes that much stronger. It is quite common that a combination of polynomial expansion combined with feature selection produces greatly stronger models than raw features can.

Scikit-learn provides a detail about whether to create the squares (or cubes, etc.) of single features, which is not terribly important in an overall data pipeline most of the time. I generally feel there is no harm in including those terms, and occasionally there is benefit. If the `interactions_only` option is not used, the number of produced features is:

$$\#features = N + N + \frac{N \times (N - 1)}{2} + 1$$

For example, for 30 raw dimensions, we obtain 496 polynomial features, at degree 2; for 100 raw features, we get 5,151. In this section, we return to the Wisconsin Breast Cancer dataset also used earlier in this chapter. Recall that it has 30 numeric features (and one binary target).

```
cancer = load_breast_cancer()
X_raw = MinMaxScaler().fit_transform(cancer.data)
y = cancer.target
```

Generating Synthetic Features

Creating the polynomial features is simply another transform, much like all the other transformers in scikit-learn that we have looked at in this book. We only pay much attention in this section to the degree 2 polynomial, but for an illustration of the growth of synthetic features, several degrees are created in the loop below. We create both a dictionary of transformers and another of the resulting X arrays. While generating them, let us display how highly dimensional these synthetic features are.

```
poly = dict()
X_poly = dict()

print(f"Raw data set shape:  {cancer.data.shape}")

for n in [2, 3, 4, 5]:
    poly[n] = PolynomialFeatures(n)
    X_poly[n] = poly[n].fit_transform(X_raw)
    print(f"Degree {n} polynomial: {X_poly[n].shape}")
```

```
Raw data set shape:  (569, 30)
Degree 2 polynomial: (569, 496)
Degree 3 polynomial: (569, 5456)
Degree 4 polynomial: (569, 46376)
Degree 5 polynomial: (569, 324632)
```

Tens or hundreds of thousands of features are simply too much to be amenable to good modeling or analysis. Even the 496 features in the second-order polynomial are a bit shaky in practical terms. The degree 2 may not overwhelm memory (obviously it depends on the number of rows; this example is small), but it almost certainly will lead to the curse of dimensionality and models will be ineffective.

Let us take a look at what these synthetic features contain and how they are named. Since we have already scaled the original features into the interval [0, 1], the multiplicative combinations will remain in that range. We *could* scale the polynomial data again to re-normalize, but it will not be crucial in this case.

We can name these synthetic features however we like, of course; but `PolynomialFeatures` provides a convenient set of suggestions based on the raw feature names.

```
names = poly[2].get_feature_names(cancer.feature_names)

row0 = pd.Series(X_poly[2][0], index=names)
row0.sample(8, random_state=6)
```

```
mean compactness^2                       0.627323
radius error worst perimeter             0.238017
smoothness error worst concavity         0.090577
mean compactness worst concavity         0.450361
perimeter error                          0.369034
area error fractal dimension error       0.050119
radius error concavity error             0.048323
mean fractal dimension symmetry error    0.188707
dtype: float64
```

I chose a particular random state that gets a representative collection of feature names. In particular, some features are named as being a power of raw features, such as `mean compactness^2`. Others are simply the raw features themselves, such as `perimeter error`. Most of the synthetic features are multiplications of two raw ones, such as `smoothness error worst concavity` or `mean compactness worst concavity`. In concept, synthetic features representing ratios of features might be valuable as well, but they are not produced automatically. For multi-word feature names, it might be aesthetically preferable to use a delimiter like an asterisk or a comma rather than a space, but in any case, a multiplication is what is signified by those latter names.

With higher-order polynomials, the names of features grow more complex as well, of course. Varying combinations of up to four raw features are combined, including powers of individual raw dimensions as possible terms.

```
names = poly[4].get_feature_names(cancer.feature_names)
row0 = pd.Series(X_poly[4][0], index=names)
row0.sample(6, random_state=2)
```

```
mean texture mean symmetry concavity error worst fractal dimension
0.000884
mean texture mean perimeter mean smoothness
0.007345
mean concave points compactness error worst perimeter^2
0.114747
```

```
fractal dimension error worst radius worst perimeter worst symmetry
0.045447
mean compactness mean fractal dimension worst area worst compactness
0.133861
mean area worst compactness worst concave points^2
0.187367
dtype: float64
```

***

R mostly makes it similarly easy to generate polynomial features. A *formula* is a nice bit of R syntax that makes it concise to generate all the interaction terms. However, including the powers of the raw terms becomes somewhat cumbersome to express in a formula. It is possible, but a support function helps get it right. With a much simpler dataset, the below code generates degree 3 polynomial features from a tibble. The actual logic is no different with a higher-dimension X, merely the display is cleaner with this small example.

```
%%R
X <- tibble(A = c(0.2, 0.3, 0.4),
            B = c(0.1, -0.3, 0.5),
            C = c(-0.2, 0.3, 0.1))
formula = ~ .^3
poly2 <- as.tibble(model.matrix(formula, data=X))
poly2
```

```
# A tibble: 3 x 8
  '(Intercept)'     A     B     C 'A:B' 'A:C' 'B:C' 'A:B:C'
          <dbl> <dbl> <dbl> <dbl> <dbl> <dbl> <dbl>   <dbl>
1             1   0.2   0.1  -0.2  0.02 -0.04 -0.02  -0.004
2             1   0.3  -0.3   0.3 -0.09  0.09 -0.09  -0.027
3             1   0.4   0.5   0.1   0.2  0.04  0.05    0.02
```

This example represents three rows of data, each one containing each of the three raw features, the pairwise product of each of the three raw features, and the product of all three raw features.

Feature Selection

Simply *having* a huge number of synthetic features is not yet of great utility, since to utilize them we probably have first to discard most of them. The "curse of dimensionality" can refer to several related problems with highly dimensional data.

In essence, model effectiveness and statistical meaning can become much worse as the number of parameter dimensions becomes too large.

 A very rough rule of thumb is that the number of columns should be no more than one-tenth the number of rows. This ratio depends upon the kind of model used, but different choices impose a stricter requirement than the rule of thumb, which is best treated as a lower bound. Moreover, even for datasets where you may have millions of observations, an approximate maximum of several hundred dimensions should be a goal.

In deep neural networks, which are a special kind of machine learning design, you will sometimes encounter an input layer with higher dimensionality than this rule of thumb suggests. However, even there, the initial layers of such a network almost always serve to reduce dimensionality. Effectively, networks *learn* how to perform feature selection in their training. Hidden layers of neural networks often have hundreds of neurons, but rarely thousands. Often even deep networks, with many layers, have fewer than hundreds of neurons in each layer.

This is where *feature selection* comes in. We need to decide which of our numerous (mostly synthetic) features genuinely help our model, and which simply add noise. For a comparison, let us try to model the breast cancer data under various transformations. We also introduce selection of only the "best" features in this approach.

There are a number of approaches we can use to select the best features. The very simplest of these is univariate modeling of the predictive strength of each feature on its own. This is what is performed, for example, within scikit-learn by `SelectKBest`. In the presence of a huge number of features, this is sometimes a reasonable approach. However, a much more powerful technique is to eliminate features recursively based on a specific model object (i.e. a class and a collection of hyperparameters).

Within scikit-learn, `RFE` and `RFECV` perform recursive feature elimination. The latter class is more precise and much slower. The class name abbreviates "recursive feature elimination and cross-validation". Plain RFE already repeatedly trains a model with decreasing numbers of features (e.g. 496 models trained for the degree 2 polynomial breast cancer data). RFECV takes that a step further by using feature importance under several different train/test splits and choosing the plurality order. By default that is five folds, and hence five models for each number of features considered (e.g. 2,480 models trained for the degree 2 polynomial). Robustness under subsampling gives a reasonably strong confidence in the evaluation.

Within R, the caret package contains the pair of functions `rfe()` and `rfeControl()` to perform recursive feature elimination, optionally with cross-validation.

A limitation to keep in mind is that not all types of models provide a ranking of feature importances. For example, that concept is not relevant in the K-neighbors models that we used in illustrating decomposition for dimensionality reduction. Linear models provide coefficients, which are sufficiently equivalent to feature importances that they are also utilized in recursive feature elimination. In those models where we do not have explicit feature importances, it is still possible to do univariate feature selection and try various numbers of features that are strongest in a univariate correlation. It is certainly possible — even likely — that a reduced feature set will achieve a better metric this way. We simply have less scaffolding to support the search, in that case.

Let us look at a model type that exposes feature importances, and recursively eliminate features from the 496 in our degree 2 polynomial synthetic dataset. We set a number of hyperparameters to the model, and the specific feature selection and metric evaluation will vary if different ones are used. A few parameters at the end simply control execution context, and are not material to the model algorithm itself (i.e. using multiple CPU cores or initializing in a particular random state).

```
model = RandomForestClassifier(n_estimators=100, max_depth=5,
                               n_jobs=4, random_state=2)
```

The next few lines of code have a lot to understand in them. We create an instance of the RFECV class that is parameterized with the particular estimator we wish to train repeatedly. In this case it is a random forest classifier (with specific hyperparameters), but any kind of model that exposes feature importances is equally suitable. We then fit the incorporated model numerous times, both as we decrease the number of features and also as we exclude folds for the cross-validation. Data about every one of these fitting and implicit scoring operations is stored in attributes of an RFECV instance, and are available for later inspection.

The most crucial attribute retained is the *support*, an array indicating which features are included in the optimal subset and which are not. We can use that attribute to filter the larger initial matrix to only include the columns that prove more useful to include than to exclude. That is saved as `X_support` in this code; we look at its shape to see that we have reduced features.

```
rfecv = RFECV(estimator=model, n_jobs=-1)
best_feat = rfecv.fit(X_poly[2], y)
X_support = X_poly[2][:, best_feat.support_]
X_support.shape
```

```
(569, 337)
```

Here we can compare the quality of several different candidate feature sets. We fit against the raw data, then against the full polynomial data, then finally against that subset of columns of the polynomial data that passed feature elimination. Each time, a new model is fitted, then scored against split out test data. Note that we used the entire dataset in the RFECV to determine the best N (337 in our case), but the trained model we use for scoring only has access to the training rows to assure this is not simply overfitting.

```
for X in (X_raw, X_poly[2], X_support):
    X_train, X_test, y_train, y_test = (
        train_test_split(X, y, random_state=42))
    model.fit(X_train, y_train)
    accuracy = model.score(X_test, y_test)
    error_rate = 100*(1-accuracy)
    print(f"Features | {X.shape=}\t| {error_rate=:.2f}%")

Features | X.shape=(569, 30)  | error_rate=2.80%
Features | X.shape=(569, 496) | error_rate=1.40%
Features | X.shape=(569, 337) | error_rate=0.70%
```

The error rate achieved by these different approaches is illuminating. Even with the raw features, the random forest model we use here is superior to the K-neighbors used earlier in this chapter. More relevant here is that we see a greatly improved error rate by using the polynomial features; we see a dramatically still better error rate when we winnow down those features only to those that are more predictive. In some cases we will select an order of magnitude fewer features than we started with to get a better metric result. Here it is only a moderate reduction in the number of features; the important element is that accuracy is thereby improved.

Another useful attribute created by the RFECV selection is the grid scores. These are the metric score obtained after each feature is successively eliminated. Or more accurately, it is the mean of the score under each fold excluding a portion of the data from the training. In any case, we see here a typical pattern. For very few features, the accuracy is low. For a moderate number it achieves nearly the best metric. Over the bulk of different feature counts, the metric is roughly a plateau. Choosing any N of those initial features along the plateau will provide a similar metric. Some particular number is optimal under the particular selection search, but often the exact number depends on small details such as random initializations. At times there is also a pattern wherein some range of number of features is clearly preferable, with a clear decline for additional features.

```
(pd.Series(best_feat.grid_scores_)
    .plot(figsize=(10, 2.5), linewidth=0.75,
        title="#Features vs. Accuracy on 2-Polynomial Data"));
```

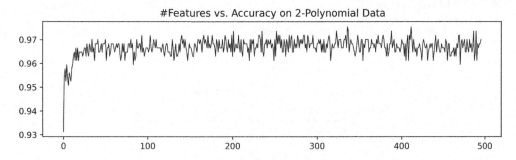
Figure 7.13: Features versus accuracy on 2-polynomial data

Choosing a number of features near the start of the plateau reduces the size of synthetic data needed, but you must judge whether the plateau has an obvious start.

Exercises

The exercises below ask you to look for "continuous-like" results in discrete events, and then symmetrically to treat continuous or frequent events as measures of coarser time units. Both of these modifications to create synthetic features are commonly useful and appropriate in real-world datasets.

Intermittent Occurrences

This chapter discussed imposing regularity upon timestamp fields, but this exercise asks you to reverse that goal, in a way. There are times when events are inherently erratic in occurrence. For example, a Geiger counter measuring radiation produces a "click" (or other discrete signal) each time a threshold is reached for ionizing radiation being present. Similarly, we could measure the timestamp when each new bud appears within a grove of trees; the frequency of occurrences would correspond in some overall way to the growth rate, but the individual events are stochastically distributed. Other phenomena — for example, the Covid-19 pandemic (currently underway, at the time of this writing), with new diagnoses on particular days within each geopolitical region — have similar discrete events that indirectly define an overall pattern.

An artificial dataset is provided that contains events measured by any of five instruments over the one-year interval covering 2020. The recording of events occurs only at exact minutes, but that does not preclude multiple events occurring during the same minute. In general, the typical event frequency for each instrument is less frequent than once per minute. The five instruments are simply named as "A" through "E". You are free to imagine this data describing one of the phenomena mentioned above, or whatever other domain you wish.

The dataset is available at:

```
https://www.gnosis.cx/cleaning/events.sqlite
```

Records within the dataset will resemble the following few.

Timestamp	Instrument
2020-07-04 11:28:00	A
2020-07-04 11:29:00	B
2020-07-04 11:31:00	C
2020-07-04 11:34:00	D
2020-07-04 11:28:00	A
2020-07-04 11:34:00	A

Notice that the data do not necessarily occur in chronological order. Moreover, the same timestamp may contain multiple events, either from the same or a different instrument. For example, in the table, `2020-07-04 11:28:00` measured two events from instrument A, and `2020-07-04 11:34:00` measured one event from instrument A and another event from instrument D. There are approximately one million events recorded in total.

Each instrument exhibits a different pattern in relation to time sequence. Create however many synthetic features you feel are necessary to reasonably characterize the behaviors in numeric form. However, *do* think of features as numbering in tens or hundreds, not in hundreds of thousands. Put these features into a tidy data frame that might be used for further statistical analysis or machine learning techniques. This data frame will have columns corresponding to the synthetic features you have decided to utilize.

Attempt to characterize the behavior of each instrument in general terms, using prose descriptions, or perhaps using mathematical functions. Be as specific as you feel the data warrants, but also describe the limitations or uncertainties of your characterization as well as possible.

Characterizing Levels

In this exercise, use the same dataset as in the prior exercise, which is available at:

```
https://www.gnosis.cx/cleaning/events.sqlite
```

As described above, each of five instruments measures discrete events occurring at specific timestamps. Events are discerned at one-minute accuracy, and the time series covers calendar year 2020. Some minutes have multiple events (from either the same or different instruments), and some have no events.

Your goal in this exercise is to characterize each day of the year according to whether it is "low", "medium", or "high" in event frequency. You should characterize this quantized level both per individual instrument and for the day as a whole. You should decide what quantization strategy is most appropriate both for the cumulative frequencies and the per-instrument frequencies. Your choice of strategy is likely to depend upon the different distributions of events per each instrument.

You may assume that all five instruments measure something roughly commensurate in aggregating them. For example, if these events are the detection of a new bud on a tree — per one example in the previous exercise — the different instruments might be measuring different groves (but not buds versus leaves versus fruits, for example).

If you feel that the quantization of low/medium/high is not well suited to one or more of the instrument event distributions, characterize what problem or limitation you feel applies, and try to think of an alternate approach to characterizing the instrument behavior.

Denouement

> And this old world is a new world
> And a bold world
> For me
>
> –Nina Simone

Topics covered in this chapter: Date/Time Fields; String Fields; String Vectors; Decompositions; Quantization; One-Hot Encoding; Polynomial Features.

This chapter looked at many approaches to *inventing new features*. This stands in contrast to *Chapter 6, Value Imputation*, which was about *inventing data points*. Both techniques are important in their own ways, but they do something conceptually different. It often happens that the way we collect data, or are provided it, does not represent the most meaningful content of that data, yet better representations lurk within what we have.

Three general themes were presented in the creation of synthetic features. In one case, we sometimes have a single feature that, as represented, combines two or more basic features that can be easily pulled apart and represented separately. Similarly, but moving in the other direction, sometimes a small number of components that are directly present may be better combined into a single feature. A clear example for both of these moves is a datetime value that might be either several components, such as year, month, hour, or minute, or might be a single value.

As a second theme, we looked at the parameter space in which observations live as vectors. As an abstract mathematical entity, the initial observations need not form the orthonormal basis (the dimensions) of an observation vector. Often transforming the basis of the parameter space produces dimensions that are more useful for statistics and machine learning. However, it is worth remembering that after such transformations, the synthetic features rarely have any human-meaningful sense to them, but are exclusively numeric measures.

As a third theme, we looked at synthetic features that emerge from the interaction of an initial feature with either its domain of values or with other initial features. Intuitively, there are quantities that are never directly measured: "heat index" is an interaction of summer temperature and humidity; "body mass index" is an interaction of human weight and height. At times, the interactions are more informative than are those things we directly measure. Using polynomial feature engineering, we can explore the space of all such interactions, but with the pitfall of sometimes arriving at unworkably many features. In that last circumstance, feature selection comes to our rescue.

PART IV

Ancillary Matters

Closure

What You Know

This book hopes to have shown you a good range of the techniques you will need in preparing data for analysis and modeling. We addressed most of the most common data formats that you will encounter in your daily work. Hopefully, even if you use file or data formats this book could not specifically address, or even did not have the opportunity to mention, the general concepts and principles laid out will still apply. Only some libraries and interface details will vary. Particular formats can have particular pitfalls in the ways they facilitate data errors, but, obviously, data can go bad in numerous ways independent of representations and storage technologies.

Chapters 1, 2, and *3,* respectively, looked at tabular, hierarchical, and "special" data sources. We saw specific tools and specific techniques for moving data from each of those sources into the *tidy* formats that are most useful for data science. Most of the examples shown used Python libraries, or simply its standard library; a smaller number used corresponding tools in R; and from time to time, we looked at other programming languages that one might use to perform similar tasks. Relatively often, I found it relevant to show command-line oriented techniques and tools that I, myself, often use. These are very commonly the simplest ways to perform some initial analysis, summarization, or pre-processing. They are available on nearly any Unix-like system, such as Linux, BSD, OS X, or the Windows Subsystem for Linux. However, I hope to have inspired ideas and conceptual frameworks for readers to utilize in approaching their data, much more than simply to have introduced those specific libraries, APIs, and tools I chose for my examples.

Past the ingestion stages, with sensitivity to some issues characteristic of their formats, we get into the many stages — ideally pipelined once they reach actual production — of identifying and remediating problems in data. In terms of identification, there are two general types of problems to look for, with many nuances among each. On the one hand, we might look for this or that individual datum — one isolated reading from one particular instrument, for example — that went wrong in some manner (recording, transcription, tabulation, and so on).

At times, as *Chapter 4* focused on, we can identify — at least with reasonable likelihood — the existence of such problems. On the other hand, we may have more systematic problems with our data which describe the collection of all (or many) observations rather than individual data points. Most of the time, this comes down to *bias* of one sort or another; at times, however, there are also patterns or trends in data that are real, genuine, and reflect the underlying phenomena, but that are not the "data within the data" that most interest us. In *Chapter 5*, we looked at both bias and at techniques for *normalization* and *detrending*.

Having identified bias and discardable trends, the next stage of your pipeline will be — broadly speaking — *making up data*. I have emphasized throughout the book that versioning data and writing repeatable scripts or automated workflows is essential to good data science. When you impute values (*Chapter 6*) or engineer features (*Chapter 7*), you should always be conscious of the fact that the data is no longer *raw* but rather processed; you should be able to recover each significant stage in the pipeline and repeat all transformations. The assumptions you make about what values are *reasonable* to invent are always subject to later revision as you learn more. But there are absolutely times when data is missing — either absent in the raw data or determined to be sufficiently unreliable by analysis — that imputing good guesses about the missing data is good practice. Moreover, sometimes fields should be normalized, combined, and/or transformed in deterministic ways before final modeling or analysis.

The chapters of this book are arranged in something resembling the order of the stages of the pipelines you will develop in your data science practice. Obviously you need to determine which specific formats, techniques, and tools are relevant for your specific problems. Still, in rough order, these stages will be similar to the order of this book. I have drawn examples from numerous different domains, and used data of different "shapes." Nonetheless, of course, your domain and your problem is, in many or most ways, entirely unlike those in the examples I have presented. I hope and believe you will find conceptual connections and food for thought from these other domains. The tasks facing you are far too broad and diverse to reduce to a small set of recipes, but they nevertheless fit inside a fairly small number of conceptual realms and overall purposes.

What You Don't Know (Yet)

Almost nothing you have read in this book addresses which statistical tests or which machine learning models you should use. Whether a support vector machine, or a gradient boosted tree, or a deep neural network (DNN) is more applicable to your problem is something I am agnostic about throughout.

I have no idea and no opinion about whether a Kolmogorov–Smirnov, Anderson–Darling, or Shapiro–Wilk test better tests for normality of your dataset (although from my sample, one might conclude that your test should have two mathematicians in its name). You should read other books to help you with those judgements.

Juxtaposed with this deliberate limitation is the fact those choices are mostly irrelevant to data cleaning. Regardless of what models you utilize, or what statistics you apply, you want the data that goes into them to be as clean as is possible. The entire pipeline this book recommends, and describes the stages of, will be both necessary for every analytic or modeling task, and be also nearly entirely the same, regardless of that final choice for the next stage of your pipelines. However, this paragraph comes with a tentative caveat.

A spectre is haunting the data science zeitgeist—the spectre of automation. Perhaps a large portion of data cleaning would be better performed by very clever machines—especially deep neural networks that are starting to dominate every domain—than by human data scientists. In fact, my original plan for this book was to include a chapter discussing using machine learning for data cleaning. Perhaps a complex trained model could make a better judgement of "anomaly" versus "reliable data" than can the relatively simple techniques I discuss. Perhaps additional layers in a deep network can implicitly separate signal from noise, or detrend the *uninteresting* parts of the signal. Perhaps normalization and engineered features are nothing more than much cruder versions of what a few fully connected, convolutional, or recurrent layers near the input layer of a DNN will do automatically.

These ideas of automation of data cleaning represent intriguing possibilities. As of right now, the contours of that automation are uncertain and in flux. A number of commercial cloud services—as of the middle of 2021—offer frontends and "systems" whose superficial descriptions make them sound similar to this spectre of automation, at least at the level of an elevator pitch. However, in my opinion, as of today, these services do far less in reality than their marketers insinuate: they are simply an aggregation of enough clustered machines to try out the same models, hyperparameters, data cleaning pipelines, etc. that you might perform sequentially yourself. You can—and quite likely should—rent massive parallelism for large data and sophisticated modeling pipelines, but this is still somehow ontologically shy of machines genuinely guiding analytic decisions.

Anything I might have written today on data cleaning automation would be out of date in a year. Still, look for my name, and the names of other data scientists who think about these issues, when you look for future writing, training materials, lectures, and so on. I hope to have much more to say about these ideas elsewhere. And look at the details of what those cloud providers genuinely offer by the time you read this; my caveats may become less relevant over time. I hope my recommendations throughout this text, however, will remain germane.

Glossary

Ontology recapitulates philology.

–Willard Van Orman Quine (c.f. Ernst Haeckel)

Accuracy

In a classification model, there are numerous *metrics* that might express the "goodness" of a model. Accuracy is often the default metric used, and is simply the number of right answers divided by the number of data points. For example, consider this hypothetical *confusion matrix*:

Predicted/Actual	Human	Octopus	Penguin
Human	5	0	2
Octopus	3	3	3
Penguin	0	1	11

There are 28 observations of organisms, and 19 were classified accurately, hence the accuracy is approximately 68%. Other commonly used metrics are precision, recall, and F1 score.

Related concepts: F1 score, precision, recall

ActiveMQ

Apache ActiveMQ is an open source message broker. As with other message brokers, the aggregations of messages sent among systems is often a fruitful domain for data science analysis.

BeautifulSoup

Beautiful Soup is a Python library for parsing and processing HTML and XML documents, and also for handling not-quite-grammatical HTML that often occurs on the World Wide Web. Beautiful Soup is often useful for acquiring data via web scraping.

Berkeley DB

Berkeley DB is an open source library for providing key/value storage systems.

Big data

The concept of "big data" is one that shifts with time, as computing and storage capabilities increase. Generally, big data is simply data that is too large to handle using "traditional" and simple tools. What tools are traditional or simple, in turn, varies with organization, project, and over time. As a rough guideline, data that can fit inside the memory on a single available server or workstation is "small data," or at most "medium-sized data."

As of 2021, a reasonably powerful single system might have 256 GiB, so big data is at least tens or hundreds of gigabytes (10^9) in size. Within a few years of this writing, the threshold for big data will be at least terabytes (10^{12}), and already today some datasets reach into exabytes (10^{18}).

Big-endian (see Endianness)

Data arranged into "words" (typically 32-bits), or other units, where the largest magnitude component (typically a byte) is stored in the last position.

BSON (Binary JSON)

BSON is a binary-encoded serialization of JSON-like documents.

caret (Classification And REgression Training)

The R package caret is a rich collection of functions for data splitting, pre-processing, feature selection, resampling, and variable importance estimation.

Cassandra

Apache Cassandra is an open source distributed database system that uses the **Cassandra Query Language** (CQL), rather than standard SQL, for queries. CQL and SQL are largely similar, but vary in specific details.

Categorical variable (see NOIR)

Related concepts: <u>continuous variable</u>, <u>interval variable</u>, <u>nominal variable</u>, <u>ordinal variable</u>, <u>ratio variable</u>

chardet

The `chardet` module in Python, and analogous versions in other programming languages, applies a collection of heuristics to a sequence of bytes thought likely to encode text. If the protocol or format you encounter explicitly declares an encoding, try that first. As a fallback, `chardet` can often make reasonable guesses based on letter and n-gram frequencies that occur in a different language, and which byte values are permitted by a given encoding.

Chimera

In Greek mythology, a chimera is an animal combining elements of several dramatically disparate animals; most commonly, these include the head of a lion, the body of a goat, and the tail of a snake. In adapted uses as a generic but evocative adjective, anything that combines surprisingly juxtaposed elements together can be called *chimerical*; or metaphorically, the thing might be called a *chimera*.

Column

A single kind of data item that may have, and usually has, many exemplars, one per *row* (a.k.a. sample, observation, record, etc.). A column consists of ordered data items of the same data type but varying values. A number of synonyms are used for "columns" with slightly varying focus. *Features* emphasize the way that columns are used by machine learning algorithms. *Field* focuses on the data format used to store the data items. *Measurement* is used most often when a column collects empirical observations, often using some particular instrument. *Variable* is used when thinking of equational relationships among different columns (for example, independent versus dependent).

Overall, columns and rows form *columnar* or *tabular* data.

Synonyms: <u>feature</u>, <u>field</u>, <u>measurement</u>, <u>variable</u>

Comma-separated values (CSV)

A representation of columnar data in which each line of text is separated by a newline character (or **carriage return**, or **CR**/LF). Within each line, data values are separated by commas. Values separated by other delimiters, such as a tab or |, are also often informally called **CSV** (the acronym, not the full words).

Variations on the format use several quoting and escaping conventions. String data items containing commas internally need to be either quoted (usually with quote characters) or escaped (usually with backslash); but if so, those characters, in turn, require special behaviors.

Continuous variable (see NOIR)

Related concepts: categorical variable, interval variable, nominal variable, ordinal variable, ratio variable

Coreutils (GNU Core Utilities)

A collection of shell-oriented utilities for processing text and data. The subset of these tools that was formerly contained in the separate textutils package, in particular, is relevant to processing textual data sources. These tools include cat, cut, fmt, fold, head, sort, tail, tee, tr, uniq, and wc. Other command-line tools such as grep, sed, shuf, and awk are also widely used in interaction with these tools.

Corpus (pl. corpora)

Corpus is a term from linguistics, but is used also in related natural language processing (NLP). It simply refers to a large "body" (the Latin root) of text covering a similar domain, such as a common publisher, genre, or dialect. In general, some sort of modeling or statistical analysis may apply to a particular body of text and, by extension, to texts of a similar domain.

CouchDB

Apache CouchDB is an open source document-oriented database. Internally, data in CouchDB is represented in JSON format.

CrateDB

CrateDB is an open source document-oriented database. CrateDB occupies an overlapping space with MongoDB or CouchDB, but emphasizes real-time performance.

Curse of dimensionality

The phrase "curse of dimensionality" was coined by Richard E. Bellman in 1957. It applies to a number of different numeric or scientific fields. In relation to machine learning, in particular, the problem is that as the number of dimensions increases, the size of the parameter space they occupy increases even faster. Even very large datasets will occupy only a tiny portion of that parameter space defined by the dimensions. Models are fairly uniformly poor at predicting or characterizing regions of parameter space where they have few or no observations to train on.

A very rough rule of thumb is that you wish to have fewer than one-tenth as many dimensions/features as you do observations. However, even very large datasets perform best if feature engineering, dimensionality reduction, and/or feature selection can be used to reduce their parameter space to hundreds of dimensions (i.e. not thousands; often tens are better than hundreds).

However, as a flip side of the curse of dimensionality, we also sometimes see a "blessing of dimensionality." Linear models especially can perform very poorly with only a few dimensions to work with. The very same types of models can become very good if it is possible to obtain or construct additional (synthetic) features. Generally, this blessing occurs when models move from, for example, 5 to 10 features, not when they move from 100 to 200 features.

As John von Neumann famously quipped: "With four parameters I can fit an elephant, and with five I can make him wiggle his trunk."

Data artifact

An unintended alteration of data, generally as a consequence of hardware or software bugs. Some artifacts can be caused by flaws in data collection instruments; others result from errors in transcription, collation, or data transfer. Data artifacts are often only detectable as anomalies in a dataset.

Data frame

A data frame (sometimes "dataframe") is an abstraction of tabular data provided by a variety of programming languages and software libraries. At heart, a data frame bundles together multiple data type homogeneous series or arrays (columns), enforcing a few regularities:

- All *columns* in a data frame have the same number of data items within them (some might be explicitly a "missing" sentinel).

- Each column has data items of the same data type.

- Data may be selected by indicating collections of rows and collections of columns.

- Predicates may be used to select row sets based on properties of data on a given row.

- Operations on columns are expressed in a *vectorized* way, operating conceptually on all elements of a column simultaneously.

- Both columns and rows may have names. In some libraries, rows are only named by index position, but all name columns descriptively.

Popular data frames libraries include Python Pandas and Vaex, R data.table and tibble, Scala DataFrame, and Julia DataFrames.jl.

data.frame

The data frame library that is included with a standard R distribution. The R standard data.frame is the oldest data frame object for R and remains widely used. However, either the Tidyverse tibble or the data.table library are generally preferable for new development, having been refined based on experience with data.frame.

See also: data frame, data.table, tibble

data.table

A popular data frame library for R. Philosophically, data.table tries to perform filtering, aggregation, and grouping all with standard arguments to its indexing operation. The data.table library has a somewhat different attitude than the Tidyverse, but is generally interoperable with it.

See also: tibble, data.frame

Dataset

A dataset is simply a collection of related data. Often, if the data is tabular, it will consist of a table, but it may be a number of related tables. In related data that is arranged in hierarchical or other formats, one or more files (in varying formats) may constitute the dataset. Often, but not always, a dataset is distributed as a single archive file containing all relevant components of it.

Denormalization

Denormalization is the duplication of data within a database system to allow for more "locality" of data to queries performed. This will result in a larger storage size, but in many cases, also in faster performance of read queries. Denormalization potentially introduces data integrity problems where data in different locations falls out of sync.

DMwR (Data Mining with R)

The R package DMwR includes functions and data accompanying the book *Data Mining with R, Learning with Case Studies*, by Luis Torgo, CRC Press 2010. A wide variety of utilities are included, but from the perspective of this book, it is mentioned because of its inclusion of a SMOTE implementation.

DOM (Document Object Model)

The Document Object Model (DOM) is a language-neutral application programming interface (API) for working with XML or HTML documents. While the specification gives a collection of method names that might be implemented in any language, the inspiration and style is especially inspired by JavaScript.

Domain-specific knowledge

Much of data science, including even that part of it concerning this book's topic, cleaning data, can be driven by *"the shape of the data itself."* Certain data items may follow patterns or stand out as anomalous on a purely numeric or analytic basis. However, in many cases, accurate judgements about which data is important, or which is of greater importance, lies not in the data themselves but in knowledge we have about the domains the data describe.

Domain-specific knowledge—or just "domain knowledge"—is what informs us of those distinctions that the data alone cannot reveal. Not all domain knowledge is extremely technical; the term might refer to topics that are more "common sense" as well. For example, it is general knowledge that outdoor temperatures in the northern hemisphere are usually higher in July than in January. A dataset that conflicted with this background knowledge would be suspicious even if the individual data values were all, in themselves, in a reasonable numeric range. Bringing that very common domain knowledge to a problem is important, where applicable.

Equally, some domain knowledge requires deep subject area expertise. Data in a psychological survey might show particular population distributions of subscales from the Minnesota Multiphasic Personality Inventory (MMPI). Some distributions might be implausible and indicate likely data integrity or sample bias problems, but a specialized knowledge is needed to judge that. Or radio astronomy data might show particular emission frequency bands from distant objects. A specialized knowledge is needed to determine whether that is consistent with expectations of Hubble redshift distances or might be data errors. Likewise in many domains.

Eagerness

In computer programming and computer science, sometimes the words "*lazy*" and "*eager*" are used to distinguish approaches to solving a larger problem. Commonly, for example, an algorithm might transform a large dataset. An eager program will process all the data at once. In contrast, a lazy program will only perform an individual transformation when that specific result is needed.

See also: laziness

Elasticsearch

Elasticsearch is a search engine based on the Lucene library. As part of implementing a search engine, Elasticsearch contains a document-oriented database or data store.

Endianness

Endianness in computer representations of numbers is typically either **big-endian** or **little-endian**. This refers to the scaled magnitude of composite values stored in a particular order. Most typically, the composite values are bytes, and they are arranged into "words" of 16-bits, 32-bits, 64-bits, or 128-bits (i.e. 2, 4, 8, or 16 bytes per word).

For example, suppose we wish to store an (unsigned) integer value in a contiguous 32-bit word. Computer systems and filesystems typically have an addressing resolution of 1 byte, not of individual bits directly, so this is 4 such slots in which scaled values may be stored. For example, we wish to store the number 1,908,477,236.

First, we can notice that since each byte stores values 0-255, this is a reasonable way to describe that number:

$$1{,}908{,}477{,}236 = (52 \times 2^0) + (13 \times 2^8) + (193 \times 2^{16}) + (113 \times 2^{24})$$

Storing values in each of the 4 bytes in the word could use either of these approaches:

Byte-order	Byte 1	Byte 2	Byte 3	Byte 4
Little-endian	52	13	193	113
Big-endian	113	193	13	52

Historically, most CPUs used only one of big-endian and little-endian word representation, but most modern CPUs offer switchable *bi-endianess*. Likewise, many libraries such as NumPy allow flexibility in reading and writing data of different endianness in storage format.

Formats other than computer words used to store numeric values may also be endian. Notably, different date formats can be big-endian, little-endian, or indeed *middle-endian*. For example, ISO-8601 date format prescribes big-endianness, for example, 2020-10-31. The year represents the largest magnitude, the month the next largest, and the day number the smallest resolution of a date. The extension to time components is similar.

In contrast, a common United States date format can read, for example, October 31, 2020. A spelled-out month name indirectly represents a number here (numbers are also used with the same endianness and different delimiters; for example, 10/31/2020). From an endianness perspective, this is middle-endian. The largest magnitude (year) is placed at the end, the next largest magnitude (month) at the start, and the smallest magnitude (day) in the middle. Clearly, a *different* middle-endian format is also possible, but is not widely used (for example, 2020 31 Oct).

Much of the world outside of the United States uses a little-endian date representation, such as 31/10/2020. While the specific values in the representation of October 31 would disambiguate the endianness used, for dates such as October 11 or November 10, this is not the case.

F1 Score

In a classification model, there are numerous *metrics* that might express the "goodness" of a model. F1 score blends *recall* and *precision*, avoiding the extremes that occur in certain models, and is often a balanced metric. F1 score is derived as:

$$F1 = 2 \times \frac{precision \times recall}{precision + recall}$$

Related concepts: accuracy, precision, recall

Feature (see Column)

Synonyms: column, field, measurement, variable

Field (see Column)

Synonyms: column, feature, measurement, variable

Fuzzy

Fuzzy is a Python library for analyzing phonetic similarity in English texts.

GDBM (GNU dbm)

GDBM is an open source library for providing key/value storage systems.

General Decimal Arithmetic Specification

The General Decimal Arithmetic Specification is a standard for implementation of arbitrary precision base-10 arithmetic and numeric representation. It incorporates configurable "contexts", such as rounding rules in effect. The Python standard library `decimal` module, in particular, is an implementation of this standard.

Gensim

Gensim is an open source Python library for NLP, specifically around unsupervised topic modeling. Gensim contains an implementation of the word2vec algorithm and a few closely related variants of it.

Gibibyte (GiB)

Metric prefixes are standardized in the International System of Units (SI), by the International Bureau of Weights and Measures (BIPM). Orders of magnitude— powers of 10—are indicated by prefixes ranging from *yotta-* (10^{24}) down to *yocto-* (10^{-24}). In particular, the multipliers of 10^3 (*kilo-*), 10^6 (*mega-*), and 10^9 (*giga-*) are *almost* right for dealing with typical quantities seen in computer storage.

However, for both historical and practical reasons, bytes of memory or storage are typically expressed as multiples of 2^{10} (1024) rather than of 10^3 (1000). These numbers are relatively close, but while it is common to misname 2^{10}, 2^{20}, and 2^{30} as *kilobyte*, *megabyte*, and *gigabyte*, these are wrong. Since 1998, the International Electrotechnical Commission (IEC) has standardized the use of *kibibyte* (KiB), *mebibyte* (MiB), and *gibibyte* (GiB) for accurate description of these powers of 2. For larger sizes, we also have *tebibyte* (TiB), *pebibyte* (PiB), *exbibyte* (EiB), *zebibyte* (ZiB), and *yobibyte* (YiB).

ggplot2

A popular book, *The Grammar of Graphics (Statistics and Computing)*, by Leland Wilkinson (ISBN: 978-0387245447), first published in 2000, introduced a way of thinking about graphs and data visualizations that breaks down a graph into components that can be expressed independently. Changing one such orthogonal component may change the entire appearance of a graph, but will still reflect the same underlying data in a different manner.

The R library `ggplot2` attempts to translate the concepts of that book into concrete APIs, and has been widely adopted by the R community. The Python libraries **ggplot**, to a strong degree, and **Bokeh** and **Altair**, to a somewhat lesser extent, also try to emulate Wilkinson's "grammar." Altair is, in turn, built on top of **Vega-Lite** and **Vega**, which have a similar goal to JavaScript libraries.

Glob

A common and simple pattern matching language that is most frequently used to identify collections of filenames. Both the Bash shell and libraries in many programming languages support this syntax.

GQL (Graph Query Language)

Graph Query Language is a (pending) standard for querying graph databases, based on the Cypher language developed by Neo4j for their product.

Gremlin

Gremlin is a graph query language, distinct from GQL. Queries in Gremlin emphasize a "fluent programming" and functional style of description of nodes and classes of interest.

Halting problem

The halting problem is probably the most famous result in the theory of computation. Alan Turing proved in 1936 that there cannot exist any general-purpose algorithm that answers the question "Will this program ever terminate?" For some programs, it is provable, of course, but in the general case it is not. Even running a program for any finite amount of time, N steps, does not answer the question, since it might yet terminate at step $N+1$.

In slightly more informal parlance, saying that a given task is "equivalent to the halting problem" is an idiomatic way of saying that it cannot be solved. At times, the phrase is used as a speculation about the difficulty of a problem, but at other times a mathematical proof is known that shows that solving the novel problem would imply a solution to the halting problem. Within this book, the phrase is used only in the strict sense, but with an affection for the jargon of computer science.

h5py

H5py is a Python library for working with hierarchical datasets stored in the HDF5 format.

HDF Compass

HDF Compass is an open source GUI tool for examining the content of HDF5 data files.

Hierarchical data format (HDF5)

The Hierarchical Data Format (HDF5) is an open source file format that supports large, complex, heterogeneous data. HDF5 uses a hierarchical structure that allows you to organize data within a file in nested groups. The "leaf" of a hierarchy is a dataset. An HDF5 file may contain arbitrary and domain-specific metadata about each dataset or *group*. Since many HDF5 files contain (vastly) more data than will fit in computer memory, tools that work with HDF5 generally provide a means of lazily reading content so that most data remains solely on disk unless or until it is needed.

Hyperparameter

In machine learning models, a general model type is often pre-configured before it is trained on actual data. Hyperparameters may comprise multipliers, numeric limits, recursion depths, algorithm variations, or other differences that still make up the same kind of model. Models can perform dramatically differently with different hyperparameters.

Idempotent

Idempotence is a useful concept in mathematics, computer science, and generally in programming. It means that calling the same function again on its own output will continue to produce the same answer. This is related to the even fancier concept in mathematics of an attractor.

Imager

Imager reads and writes many image formats and can perform a variety of analysis processing actions on such images programmatically within R. Images within the library are treated as 4-dimensional vectors with two spatial dimensions, one time dimension, and one color dimension. By including time as a dimension, imager can work with video as well.

imbalanced-learn

imbalanced-learn is an open source Python software library for sensitive oversampling data. It implements the SMOTE (Synthetic Minority Oversampling TEchnique) and ADASYN (Adaptive Synthetic) variations of those algorithms, as well as undersampling techniques. In the main, imbalanced-learn emulates the APIs of scikit-learn.

Imputation

The process of replacing missing data points with values that are likely, or at least plausible, to allow machine learning or statistical tools to process all observations.

Interval variable (see NOIR)

Related concepts: categorical variable, continuous variable, nominal variable, ordinal variable, ratio variable

ISO-8601

ISO-8601 (Data elements and interchange formats – Information interchange – Representation of dates and times) is an international standard for the representation of dates and times. For example, generating one while writing this entry, using Python:

```
from datetime import datetime
datetime.now().isoformat()
```

```
'2020-11-23T14:43:09.083771'
```

jq

jq is a flexible and powerful tool for command-line filtering, searching, and formatting JSON, including JSON Lines.

JSON (Javascript Object Notation)

JSON is a language-independent and human-readable format for representation of the data structures and scalar values typically encountered in programming languages. It is widely used both as a data storage format and as a message format to communicate among services.

Jupyter

Project Jupyter is an open source library, written primarily in Python, but supporting numerous programming languages, to create, view, run, and edit "notebooks" for *literate programming*. This book was written using Jupyter Lab, and its notebooks can be obtained at the book's repository. In literate programming, code and documentation are freely interspersed while both rendering as formatted documents and running as executable code. Whereas R Markdown achieves similar goals using lightly annotated plain text, Jupyter uses JSON as the storage format for its notebooks.

Jupyter supports both the somewhat older "notebook" interface and the more recent "JupyterLab" interface. Both work with the same underlying notebook documents.

Kafka

Apache Kafka is an open source stream processor. As with other stream processors, and related message brokers, the aggregation of messages sent among systems is often a fruitful domain for data science analysis.

Kdb+

Kdb+ is a column-store database that was designed for rapid transactions. It is widely used within high-frequency trading.

Laziness

In computer programming and computer science, sometimes the words "lazy" and "eager" are used to distinguish approaches to solving a larger problem. Commonly, for example, an algorithm might transform a large dataset. An eager program will process all the data at once. In contrast, a lazy program will only perform an individual transformation when that specific result is needed.

See also: eagerness

LMDB (Lightning Memory-Mapped Database)

LMDB is an open source library for providing key/value storage systems.

Lemmatization

Canonicalization of words to their grammatical roots for natural language processing purposes. In contrast to stemming, lemmatization will look at the context a word occurs in to try to derive both the simplified form and the part of speech.

For example, the English word "dog" is used both as a noun for the animal, and occasionally as a verb meaning "annoy." A lemmatization might produce:

```
we[PRON] dog[VERB] the[DET] dog[NOUN]
```

Related concept: stemming

Little-endian (see Endianness)

Data arranged into "words" (typically 32-bits), or other units, where the largest magnitude component (typically a byte) is stored in the earliest position.

MariaDB

MariaDB is a popular open source relational database management system (RDBMS). It uses standard SQL for queries and interaction, and implements a few custom features on top of those required by SQL standards. At a point when the GPL-licensed MySQL was purchased by Oracle, its creator Michael (Monty) Widenius forked the project to create MariaDB. Widenius' elder daughter is named "My" and his younger daughter "Maria."

MariaDB is API- and ABI-compatible with MySQL, but it adds a few features such as additional storage engines.

See also: MySQL

Matplotlib

Matplotlib is a powerful and versatile open source plotting library for Python. For historical reasons, its API originally resembled MATLAB's, but a more object-oriented approach is now encouraged. Numerous higher-level libraries and abstractions are built on top of Matplotlib, including Basemap, Cartopy, Geoplot, ggplot, holoviews, Seaborn, Pandas, and others.

Measurement (see Column)

Synonyms: column, feature, field, variable

Memcached

Software that keeps key/value associative arrays in memory for the purposes of caching or proxying slower server responses. Although contents of a memcached server are transient, snapshotted contents may be useful to analyze for data science purposes.

Metaphone

Metaphone is an algorithm for the phonetic canonicalization of English words, published by Lawrence Philips in 1990. The same author later published Double Metaphone, and then Metaphone 3, each of which successively better takes advantage of known patterns in words derived from non-English languages. Metaphone, and its followups, are more precise than the early Soundex developed for the same purpose.

Mojibake

Mojibake is the nonsensical text that generally results from trying to decode text using a character encoding different from that used to encode it. Often this will produce individual characters that belong to a given language or alphabet, but in combinations that make no sense (sometimes to humorous effect). The word comes from Japanese, meaning roughly "character transformation."

MonetDB

MonetDB is an open source column-oriented database management system that supports SQL and several other query languages or extensions.

MongoDB

MongoDB is a popular document-oriented database management system. It uses JSON-like storage of its underlying data, and both queries and responses use JSON documents. MongoDB uses a distinct query language that reflects its mostly hierarchical arrangement of data into linked documents.

MySQL

MySQL is a widely popular open source relational database management system (RDBMS). It uses standard SQL for queries and interaction, and implements a few custom features on top of those required by SQL standards. At a point when the GPL-licensed MySQL was purchased by Oracle, its creator Michael (Monty) Widenius forked the project to create MariaDB. Widenius' elder daughter is named "My" and his younger daughter "Maria."

See also: MariaDB

Neo4j

Neo4j is an open source graph database and database management system.

netcdf4-python

netcdf4-python is a Python interface to the netCDF C library.

Network Common Data Form (NetCDF)

NetCDF (Network Common Data Form) is a set of software libraries and machine-independent data formats that support the creation, access, and sharing of array-oriented scientific data. It is built on top of HDF5.

NLTK (Natural Language Toolkit)

NLTK is a suite of tools for natural language processing in Python. It includes numerous corpora, tools for lexical analysis, for named entity recognition, a part of speech tagger, stemmers and lemmatizers, and a variety of other tools for NLP.

See also: gensim, spaCy

Node.js

Node.js is an open source, standalone JavaScript interpreter that runs outside of embedded JavaScript in web browsers. It can be used at the command line in the manner of scripting languages, with an interactive shell, or as a means to run server processes. The Node.js environment comes with an excellent package manager called npm (Node Package Manager) that allows you to install additional libraries easily (much like pip or conda for Python, RubyGems for Ruby, Cabal for Haskell, Pkg.jl: for Julia, Maven for Java, and so on).

Nominal variable (see NOIR)

Related concepts: categorical variable, continuous variable, interval variable, ratio variable

NOIR (Nominal, Ordinal, Interval, Ratio)

The acronym NOIR is sometimes used as a mnemonic for different feature types. This is the French word for "black" but is especially associated, in English, with a style of "dark" literature or film. The acronym stands for Nominal/Ordinal/Interval/Ratio.

Nominal or *ordinal* variables simply record which of a finite number of possible labels a data item records. This is sometimes called the *classes* of the variable.

Ordinal variables express a scale from low to high in the data values, but the spacing in the data may have little to no relationship to the underlying phenomenon. For example, perhaps a foot race records the first place, second place, third place, etc. winners, but not the times taken by each. First place crossed the line before second place, but we have no information on whether it was milliseconds sooner or hours sooner. Likewise between second and third position, which might differ significantly from the first gap.

The last variable types are *continuous* variables, but *interval* and *ratio* variables are importantly different. The difference is in whether there is a "natural zero" in the data. The domain zero need not always be numeric zero, but commonly it is. Acidity or alkalinity measured on the pH scale has a natural zero of 7, and generally values between 0 and 14 (although those are not sharp physical limits). If we used the pH measure as a feature, we might re-center to numeric zero to express actual ratios (albeit log ratios for this measure). It is reasonable to treat pH as a ratio variable.

As an example of an interval that is not a ratio, a newspaper article claimed that the temperature on a certain winter day, in some city, was *twice* as hot as in average years based on an artifact of the Fahrenheit scale in which a difference was between 25 °F and 50 °F. This is nonsense as a ratio. It is perfectly useful to talk about the *mean temperature* or the *standard deviation* in temperature, but the numeric ratio is meaningless (in Celsius or Fahrenheit; in Kelvin or Rankine, it's minimally meaningful, but rarely used to describe temperatures in the range that occur on the surface of the earth). In contrast, the *ratio variable* of rainfall has a natural zero, which is also numeric zero. Zero inches (or centimeters) of rain means there was none. 2 inches of rain is twice as much water falling as 1 inch of rain is.

NumPy

NumPy is an open source Python library for fast and vectorized computations on multi-dimensional arrays. Nearly all Python libraries that perform numeric or scientific computation rely on NumPy as an underlying support library. This includes tools in machine learning, modeling, statistics, visualization, and so on.

Observation (see Row)

Synonyms: record, row, sample, tuple

Ontology

Ontology in philosophy is the study of "what there is." In data science, an ontology describes not only what class/subclass and class/instance relationships exist among entities, but also the kinds of features an entity has. Perhaps most importantly, an ontology can describe the kinds of relationships that can exist among various entities.

When different kinds of observations can be made, describing the particular collection of features that pertain to that observation, and the particular data types and ranges of permissible values each can take on, is an element of the ontology of the data. Different tables, or data subsets, may have different feature sets and hence a different ontological role.

Ontology can be important for categorical data especially. Some labels may be instances of other labels, for example, with varying degrees of specificity. If one categorical variable indicates that the entity is "mammal," another that it is "feline," and another that it is "house cat," those are all possibly descriptions of the identical entity under different taxonomic levels, and hence part of the ontology of the domain.

The relationships among entities can sometimes be derived from the data themselves, but often requires domain knowledge. These relationships can often inform the kinds of models or statistical analysis that make sense. For example, if the *entity* underlying a collection of data is a medical patient, parts of the ontology of the domain might concern whether several different features observed were collected with the same instrument, or from the same blood sample, or whether the observations were made on the same day. Even though the features might measure very different quantities, the "same-day" or "same-instrument" relationships can inform analysis.

See also: taxonomy

Ordinal variable (see NOIR)

Related concepts: categorical variable, continuous variable, interval variable, ratio variable

OrientDB

OrientDB is an open source, multi-model database management system. It supports graph, document, key/value, and object models. Querying may use either Gremlin or SQL.

Orthonormal basis

Within a highly dimensional space, specifically a parameter space, the location of an observation point is simply a parameterized sum of each of the dimensions. For example, if we measure three features in an observation as having the values a, b, and c, we can express those measurements in 3-D parameter space, with orthogonal unit vectors $\vec{x}$, $\vec{y}$, and $\vec{z}$, as:

$$observation = a\vec{x} + b\vec{y} + c\vec{z}$$

However, the choice to represent the observation using those particular unit vectors, $\vec{x}$, $\vec{y}$, and $\vec{z}$ is somewhat arbitrary. As long as we choose any orthonormal basis—that is, N mutually perpendicular unit vectors—we can equally well represent all the relationships among observations. For example:

$$a\vec{x} + b\vec{y} + c\vec{z} = a'\vec{x}' + b'\vec{y}' + c'\vec{z}'$$

Decompositions are a means of selecting an alternate orthonormal basis that distributes the data within the parameter space in a more useful way. Usually, this means in a way concentrating variance within the initial *components* (lowest numbered axes).

Pandas

Pandas is a widely popular, open source Python library for working with data frames. The name derives from the econometrics term "panel data." Pandas is built on top of NumPy, but adds numerous additional capabilities. One of the great strengths of Pandas is working with time series data. But as with the underlying NumPy array library and other data frame libraries, most operations on columns are fast and vectorized.

Parameter space

The parameter space of a set of observations with N features is simply an N-dimensional space in which each observation occupies a single point. By default, the vector bases that define the location of a point correspond directly with the features themselves. For example, in analyzing weather data, we might define "temperature" as the x-axis, "humidity" as the y-axis, and "barometric pressure" as the z-axis. Some portion of that 3-D space has points within it, and they form some pattern or shape that models might analyze and make predictions about.

Under decompositions of the features, we might choose a new orthonormal basis in which to represent the same data points in a rotated or mirrored N-dimensional space.

Parquet

Apache Parquet is an open source, column-oriented data storage format that originated in the Hadoop ecosystem, but is widely supported in other programming languages as well.

PDF (Portable Document Format)

Portable Document Format is a widely used format used to accurately represent the appearance of documents in a cross-platform, cross-device manner. For example, the same document will look nearly identical on a computer monitor, a personal printer, or from a professional press. Fonts, text, images, colors, and lines are some of the elements PDF renders to a page, whether displayed or printed. PDF was developed by Adobe, but is currently governed by the open and freely usable standard ISO 32000-2.

Pillow (forked from PIL)

The Python Imaging Library reads and writes many image formats and can perform a variety of processing actions on such images programmatically within Python.

Poppler

An open source viewing and processing library for Portable Document Format (PDF). In particular, Poppler contains numerous command-line tools for converting PDF files to other formats, including text. Poppler is a fork of Xpdf that aims to incorporate additional capabilities.

See also: Xpdf

PostgreSQL

PostgreSQL is a widely popular, open source relational database management system (RDBMS). It uses standard SQL for queries and interaction, and implements custom features and numerous custom data types on top of those required by SQL standards.

Precision

In a classification model, there are numerous *metrics* that might express the "goodness" of a model. Precision is also called "positive predictive value" and is the fraction of relevant observations among the predicted observations. More informally, precision answers the question "given it was predicted, how likely is the prediction to be accurate?".

For example, consider this hypothetical *confusion matrix*:

Predicted/Actual	Human	Octopus	Penguin
Human	5	0	2
Octopus	3	3	3
Penguin	0	1	11

In a binary problem, this can be expressed as:

$$\text{Precision} = \frac{true\ positive}{true\ positive + false\ positive}$$

For a multiclass problem, as in the confusion matrix, each label has its own precision. Given the 8 true humans in the dataset, 5 of them were correctly identified. However, 2 non-humans were also so identified; in other words:

$$\text{Precision}_{human} = \frac{5}{5 + 2} \approx 71\%$$

An overall precision for a model is often given by averaging (weighted or unweighted) the precision for each label.

Related concepts: accuracy, F1 score, recall

PyTables

PyTables is a Python library for working with hierarchical datasets stored in the HDF5 format.

Query planner

When a query is formulated against a database, whether using SQL or another querying language, the database management system (DBMS) will internally create a set of planned steps involved in executing that query. Many DBMSs can expose these plans prior to executing them; users can use this information to judge the efficiency of database access (and possibly modify queries or refactor the databases themselves).

A query planner will make decisions about which indices to use, in what order, the style of search and comparisons across data that may live in many tables or documents, and other aspects of how a query may be executed efficiently. When accessing big datasets, the quality of a query planner can often differentiate different DBMSs.

R Markdown

R Markdown is a format and technology for *literate programming*. In literate programming, code and documentation are freely interspersed while both rendering as formatted documents and running as executable code. Whereas Jupyter notebooks, which have many of the same qualities, are stored as JSON documents, R Markdown is purely an extension of the easily human-readable and editable Markdown format, which lightly annotates plain text with regular punctuation characters to describe specific visual and conceptual elements. With R Markdown, code segments are also included as plain text by indicating their sections with a textual annotation.

RabbitMQ

RabbitMQ is an open source message broker. As with other message brokers, the aggregations of messages sent among systems is often a fruitful domain for data science analysis.

Ratio variable (see NOIR)

Related concepts: categorical variable, continuous variable, interval variable, nominal variable, ordinal variable

Recall

In a classification model, there are numerous *metrics* that might express the "goodness" of a model. Recall is also called "sensitivity." It is the fraction of true occurrences that are identified by a model.

For example, consider this hypothetical *confusion matrix*:

Predicted/Actual	Human	Octopus	Penguin
Human	5	0	2
Octopus	3	3	3
Penguin	0	1	11

In a binary problem, this can be expressed as:

$$\text{Recall} = \frac{true\ positive}{true\ positive + false\ negative}$$

For a multiclass problem, as in the confusion matrix, each label has its own recall. There are 8 true humans in the dataset, and 5 of them were identified correctly. However, 3 humans failed to be identified (in the whimsical example, all were predicted to be octopi); in other words:

$$\text{Recall}_{human} = \frac{5}{5 + 3} \approx 62\%$$

An overall recall for a model is often given by averaging (weighted or unweighted) the recall for each label.

Related concepts: accuracy, F1 score, precision

Record (see Row)

Synonyms: observation, row, sample, tuple

Redis (Remote Dictionary Server)

Redis is an open source, in-memory key/value database. Redis supports numerous data types and data structures, including strings, lists, maps, sets, sorted sets, HyperLogLogs, bitmaps, streams, and spatial indices.

Relational database management system (RDBMS)

An RDBMS is a system for storing data and implementing the relational model developed by E. F. Codd in 1970. Under this relational model, data is stored in tables, with each row constituting a *tuple* of values, the keys to those values named by the columns of the table. The term "relational" in the name pertains to the fact that data in one table may be *related* to data in other tables by declaring *foreign key* relations and/or by performing *joins* in the query syntax.

For several decades, all RDBMSs have supported the SQL querying language, sometimes with optional extension syntax related to their additional features or data types. Often, but not quite always, RDBMSs are used on multi-user distributed servers, with *transactions* used to orchestrate write actions among those multiple users.

Popular RDBMSs include PostgreSQL, MySQL, SQLite, Oracle, Microsoft SQL Server, IBM DB2, and others.

Requests

Requests is a full-featured, open source HTTP access library for Python. It is not included in the Python standard library, but is ubiquitous and generally preferred to tools included with minimal Python distributions.

REST (REpresentational State Transfer)

REST is a software educational style that normatively describes patterns of interactions between HTTP servers and clients. The adjective *RESTful* is also frequently used. Under this style, the HTTP methods GET, POST, PUT, and DELETE are clearly separated by their intended functions. A main emphasis of the style is *statelessness*: each request must contain all information needed to elicit a response, and that response should not be dependent on the sequence of prior actions that client made.

rhdf5

rhdf5 is an R library for working with hierarchical datasets stored in the HDF5 format.

rjson

rjson is an R library for working with JavaScript Object Notation (JSON).

ROSE (Random Over-Sampling Examples)

ROSE is an R package that creates synthetic samplings in the presence of class imbalance. It serves a similar purpose to SMOTE oversampling.

Row

A collection of data consisting of multiple named data items pertaining to the same *entity*. Depending on the context, the entity can be defined in various ways. For an object in the physical world, for example, it is common in scientific, and other, procedures to take a number of different measurements of that same object, and a row will describe that object. In simulations or other mathematical modeling, a row may contain the results of synthetic *sampling* of possible values. Considered from the point of view of the actual storage of the data, a focus on the *tuple* or *record* structure of the row are more emphasized.

The named data items collected about a single row are generally indicated in the *columns* of the data. Each column may have a different data type within it, but each different row within that column will share the data type but not generally the data value.

Synonyms: observation, record, sample, tuple

rvest

The rvest package for R is used to scrape and extract data from HTML web pages.

Sample (see Row)

Synonyms: observation, record, row, tuple

Scikit-learn

Scikit-learn is a wide-ranging open source Python library for many machine learning (ML) and data science tasks. It implements a large number of ML models (both supervised and unsupervised), metrics, sampling techniques, decompositions, clustering algorithms, and other tools useful for data science. Throughout its capabilities, scikit-learn maintains a common API; many additional libraries have chosen to implement identical or compatible APIs as well.

Scipy.stats

Scipy.stats is a Python module in the NumPy ecosystem that implements many probability distributions and statistical functions.

Scrapy

Scrapy is a Python library for spidering and analyzing collections of web pages, including a high-performance engine to coordinate retrievals of many pages.

Seaborn

Seaborn is a Python data visualization library based on matplotlib. It provides a high-level interface for drawing attractive and informative statistical graphics.

SeqKit

SeqKit is a toolkit for manipulating files in the FASTA and FASTQ formats, which are used for storing nucleotide and protein sequences.

Signed integer

An integer represented in computer bits of some specific length. In signed integers, one bit is reserved to hold the sign (negative or positive) of an integer. The largest integer that can be represented, for N bits storing a number, is $2^{N-1} - 1$. The smallest integer that can be represented is -2^{N-1}.

The sizes of integers in many programming languages match the sizes of memory units in modern CPUs, and can be 8-bit, 16-bit, 32-bit, 64-bit, or 128-bit. Other bit lengths are rarely defined.

In data formats and databases, sizes might be defined by a number of decimal digits rather than binary bits. Some programming languages, such as Python, TCL, and Mathematica in their default integers, and numerous other programming languages using specific libraries, allow for arbitrary-precision integers that have no size bound. They do this by dynamically allocating more bits to store larger numbers as needed.

See also: unsigned integer

Solr

Apache Solr is a search engine based on the Lucene library. As a part of implementing a search engine, Solr contains a document-oriented database or data store.

spaCy

spaCy is an open source software library for advanced natural language processing. It is focused on production use and integrates with deep-learning frameworks.

SPARQL Protocol and RDF Query Language

Had J. B. S. Haldane lived later, he might have commented that free software developers have "an inordinate fondness for recursive acronyms" (YAML, GNU, and so on). SPARQL is a query language for RDF (Resource Description Framework), or the "semantic web." It has been implemented for a variety of programming languages. SPARQL expresses queries in the form of "subject-predicate-object" triples. This has some similarity to key/value stores, but more to graph databases.

Sphering (see whitening)

Normalization of data under a decomposition.

Synonym: whitening

SQLAlchemy

SQLAlchemy is a Python library that provides an "object-relational mapping" between the tabular and relational structure of RDBMS tables and an object-oriented interface.

SQLAlchemy can use drivers for all popular SQL databases, and exposes a variety of methods for manipulating their data within Python.

SQLite

SQLite is a small, fast, self-contained, high-reliability, full-featured, SQL database engine that stores multiple data tables in single files. Bindings to access SQLite (version 3) are available for all popular programming languages. The library also comes with a command-line tool and shell for manipulation of data using only SQL.

State machine

A "finite-state machine," "finite automaton," or simply "state machine" is a model of computation in which the focus moves among a finite number of states or nodes based on a specific sequence of input.

STDOUT / STDERR / STDIN

In Unix-like command shells, there are three special files/streams called "standard output," "standard error," and "standard input." They are ubiquitously abbreviated as "STDOUT," "STDERR," and "STDIN" respectively. Composed command-line tools treat these streams in special ways, and they are utilized widely. In particular, STDOUT is usually "data" output, while STDERR is usually "status" output, even though they may appear interspersed in terminal sessions.

Stemming

Canonicalization of words to their grammatical roots for natural language processing purposes. In contrast to lemmatization, stemming only treats words individually without their context, and hence can be less accurate.

Related concept: lemmatization

Structured data

While the term "unstructured data" is often used, it is somewhat of a misnomer. "Loosely structured," or "semi-structured," would be more accurate. For example, the paradigmatic example of textual data is at very least structured by the particular sequence in which words occur.

Quite likely, it is further organized by sequences belonging to chapters, separate messages, or other such units (themselves likely structured by sequence), and moreover usually a variety of metadata, such as author identity, subject line, forum, and thread, also pertain to the text itself.

Tab-separated values (TSV; see Comma-separated values)

Delimited files where tabs are used as the line delimiter.

Tabula

Tabula-java is the underlying engine for the GUI tool Tabula. Other bindings include *tabula-extractor* for Ruby, *tabula-py* for Python, *tabulizer* for R, and *tabula-js* for Node.js. The engine and the tools that utilize it provide interfaces to extract tabular data represented in PDF documents.

Taxonomy

Taxonomy is, in some sense, a special aspect of ontology; it describes the hierarchical relationships among categories of entities. Some labels may be instances of other labels, for example, with varying degrees of specificity. If one categorical variable indicates the entity is a "mammal," another that it is "feline," and another that it is "house cat," those are all possibly descriptions of the identical entity under different taxonomic levels, and hence part of the ontology of the domain.

While taxonomy is largely narrower than ontology, taxonomy also tends to indicate a focus on the more global level of the domain, not a narrow region of that domain. When one speaks of a taxonomy, it generally indicates an interest in all the relationships among all the classes of entities, and an expectation that those relationships will be tree-like and hierarchical. One might describe *ontological* features of a single entity, or a small collection of entities, but a taxonomy will normally describe the entire domain of all possible entities.

See also: ontology

tibble

The R library tibble is an implementation of the data frame abstraction, but one that tries to do *less* than other libraries. Quoting from the official documentation:

> *Tibbles are data.frames that are lazy and surly: they do less (i.e. they don't change variable names or types, and don't do partial matching) and complain more (e.g. when a variable does not exist). This forces you to confront problems earlier, typically leading to cleaner, more expressive code.*

See also: data.frame, data.table

Tidyverse

The Tidyverse is a collection of R packages that share a common philosophy of API design and that are designed to work well together. Core libraries of the Tidyverse are ggplot2, dplyr, tidyr, readr, purrr, tibble, stringr, and forcats. A variety of other optional packages are also designed to work well with the base collection.

At core, the Tidyverse has an attitude of making data into "tidy" forms, in the sense discussed at more length in *Chapter 1, Tabular Formats*. As well, the tools within the Tidyverse lend themselves to composition by piping data between methods in a "fluent programming" style.

Tuple (see Row)

Synonyms: observation, record, row, sample

Unsigned integer

An integer represented in computer bits of some specific length. In unsigned integers, no bits are reserved to hold the sign (negative or positive) of an integer, and hence only number zero through a maximum size can be represented. For N bits storing a number, the largest number representable is $2^N - 1$.

Sizes of integers in many programming languages match sizes of memory units in modern CPUs, and can be 8-bit, 16-bit, 32-bit, 64-bit, or 128-bit. Other bit lengths are rarely defined. In data formats and databases, sizes might be defined by a number of decimal digits rather than binary bits.

Some programming languages, such as Python, TCL, and Mathematica in their default integers, and numerous other programming languages using specific libraries, allow for arbitrary-precision integers that have no size bound. They do this by dynamically allocating more bits to store larger numbers as needed.

See also: signed integer

Variable (see Column)

Synonyms: column, feature, field, measurement

Web 0.5

The term "Web 0.5" is a neologism and back-construction from the term "Web 2.0." The latter became popular as a term in the late 2000s. Whereas Web 2.0 was meant as an evolution of the World Wide Web into highly interactive, highly dynamic, visually rich content, Web 0.5 is meant to hearken back to the static, compact, and text-oriented web pages that were developed in the early 1990s. The writer Danny Yee publicized this term, to the minor extent it is used.

Web 0.5 web pages are intended primarily for human readership, in contrast to RESTful web services, which are primarily intended to communicate data among computer servers and applications. Their simplicity, however, also makes them easily accessible to web scraping techniques, where relevant.

Whitening

Normalization of data under a decomposition. Transformations such as Principle Component Analysis (PCA) reduce the variance of each subsequent component successively. Whitening is simply rescaling the data within each component to a common scale and center.

Synonym: sphering

XML (eXtensible Markup Language)

XML is a markup language that defines a grammar for representing documents and ancillary schema languages for defining dialects within that broad grammar. The content of XML is always text, and is, in principle, human-readable while also enforcing a strict structure for automated processing. In essence, XML defines a hierarchical format in which arbitrary elements may be arranged.

XML is used widely in domains such as internal formats for office applications, for representing geospatial data, for message-passing among cooperating services, for scientific data, and for many other application uses.

Xpdf

An open source viewing and processing library for Portable Document Format. In particular, Xpdf contains several command-line tools for converting PDF files to other formats, including text. The Poppler fork aims to incorporate additional capabilities that the Xpdf authors consider out of scope for that project.

See also: Poppler

YAML

YAML is, light-heartedly, an acronym for either "YAML Ain't Markup Language" or "Yet Another Markup Language." It is intended as a highly human-readable and human-writable format that can represent most of the data structures and data types widely used in programming languages. Libraries supporting the reading and writing of YAML from or to native data structures are available for numerous programming languages.

Share your experience

Thank you for taking the time to read this book. If you enjoyed this book, help others to find it. Leave a review at `https://www.amazon.com/dp/1801071292`

packt.com

Subscribe to our online digital library for full access to over 7,000 books and videos, as well as industry leading tools to help you plan your personal development and advance your career. For more information, please visit our website.

Why subscribe?

- Spend less time learning and more time coding with practical eBooks and Videos from over 4,000 industry professionals

- Improve your learning with Skill Plans built especially for you

- Get a free eBook or video every month

- Fully searchable for easy access to vital information

- Copy and paste, print, and bookmark content

Did you know that Packt offers eBook versions of every book published, with PDF and ePub files available? You can upgrade to the eBook version at packt.com and as a print book customer, you are entitled to a discount on the eBook copy. Get in touch with us at customercare@packtpub.com for more details.

At www.packt.com, you can also read a collection of free technical articles, sign up for a range of free newsletters, and receive exclusive discounts and offers on Packt books and eBooks.

Other Books You May Enjoy

If you enjoyed this book, you may be interested in these other books by Packt:

Clean Code in Python. - Second Edition

Mariano Anaya

ISBN: 978-1-80056-021-5

- Set up a productive development environment by leveraging automatic tools
- Leverage the magic methods in Python to write better code, abstracting complexity away and encapsulating details
- Create advanced object-oriented designs using unique features of Python, such as descriptors
- Eliminate duplicated code by creating powerful abstractions using software engineering principles of object-oriented design
- Create Python-specific solutions using decorators and descriptors
- Refactor code effectively with the help of unit tests
- Build the foundations for solid architecture with a clean code base as its cornerstone

Machine Learning Using TensorFlow Cookbook

Alexia Audevart

Konrad Banachewicz

Luca Massaron

ISBN: 978-1-80020-886-5

- Grasp linear regression techniques with TensorFlow
- Use Estimators to train linear models and boosted trees for classification or regression
- Execute neural networks and improve predictions on tabular data
- Master convolutional neural networks and recurrent neural networks through practical recipes
- Apply reinforcement learning algorithms using the TF-Agents framework
- Implement and fine-tune Transformer models for various NLP tasks
- Take TensorFlow into production

Pandas 1.x Cookbook - Second Edition

Matthew Harrison

Theodore Petrou

ISBN: 978-1-83921-310-6

- Master data exploration in pandas through dozens of practice problems
- Group, aggregate, transform, reshape, and filter data
- Merge data from different sources through pandas SQL-like operations
- Create visualizations via pandas hooks to matplotlib and seaborn
- Use pandas, time series functionality to perform powerful analyses
- Import, clean, and prepare real-world datasets for machine learning
- Create workflows for processing big data that doesn't fit in memory

Packt is searching for authors like you

If you're interested in becoming an author for Packt, please visit authors.packtpub. com and apply today. We have worked with thousands of developers and tech professionals, just like you, to help them share their insight with the global tech community. You can make a general application, apply for a specific hot topic that we are recruiting an author for, or submit your own idea.

Index

A

accuracy 266, 427
Adaptive Synthetic (ADASYN) 341, 439
alternate trend imputation 345, 346
Apache ActiveMQ 427
Apache Arrow 43
Apache Avro 43
Apache Cassandra 43, 428
Apache Hive 53
Apache Parquet 42, 52-54, 448
Apache Pig 53
Apache Solr 455
Apache Spark 53
application programming interface
    (API) 433
arrow package 53
autocorrelation 267-271, 280
averaging 315
awk 64

B

bag-of-words 379
bcolz 44
Beautiful Soup 137, 427
Benford's law 244, 245
Berkeley DB 128, 428
Bespoke validation 282
  collation validation 283-287
  transcription validation 287-291
bias 233-236
  detecting 236-240
biasing trends 233
  comparison, to baselines 240-244
big data 428

big-endian 428, 434
binarization 398
Binary JSON (BSON) 121, 428
binary serialized data
    structures 165-169
Body Mass Index (BMI) 220

C

canonicalization 456
carriage return (CR) 430
Cartopy 87
Cassandra Query Language (CQL) 428
categorical variables 429
channel manipulation 159, 160
character encodings 175-181
chardet module 180, 429
chimera 429
classes 445
Classification And REgression
    Training (caret) 337, 428
class imbalance 246-253
Cloudera Impala 53
collation validation 283-287
column 429
command-line scraping 146, 147
comma-separated values
    (CSV) 9, 10, 430
  advantages 18-21
  disadvantages 13-18
  sanity check 10-12
  textual data 13
concatenated JSON 83
configuration files 108
  concepts 108
Configure Unify Execute (CUE) 93

content delivery network (CDN) 252
continuous variables 430
Coreutils 430
Corpus 430
correlation imputation 314
CouchDB 121, 430
CrateDB 121, 431
cuDF 58
curse of dimensionality 413, 431
custom text formats 170
  character encodings 175-181
  structured log 171-174
cyclicity 267-271

D

Dask 14, 19, 58
data artifact 431
database management system
    (DBMS) 450
Database Manager (DBM) 128
data characterization
  exercises 291-293
data formats 42, 43
  HDF5 44
  NetCDF-4 44
data frames 55, 56, 432
  in Derived Wrappers 58, 59
  in Pandas 58, 59
  in Scala 56, 57
  in Spark 56, 57
  in Vaex 59, 60
data frames, in R
  data.table 63
  Tidyverse 61, 62
Data Mining with R (DMwR) 337, 433
dataset 433
data.table 63, 432
Data Types 78-82
Date/Time fields 353, 354
  datetimes, creating 354, 355
  duplicated timestamps 358, 359
  regularity, imposing 355-357
  timestamps, adding 359-363
datetimes, creating 354, 355

decomposition 388
deep neural network (DNN) 424
denormalization 433
Derived Wrappers
  data frames 58, 59
detrending 269
dimensionality reduction 391-394
directed acyclic graph (DAG) 58, 71
discovered cycles 278-281
distributed Stochastic Neighbor
    Embedding (t-SNE) 394
DNA Data Bank of Japan (DDBJ) 283
Doc2Vec 383
Document Object Model (DOM) 433
document-oriented databases 121-123
  CouchDB 121
  CrateDB 121
  denormalization 125, 126
  discontents 125, 126
  Elasticsearch 121
  missing fields 123-125
  MongoDB 121
  Solr 121
Document Type Definition (DTD) 100
domain knowledge trends 271-278
domain-specific knowledge 433
double Metaphone 368
dplyr 61
duplicated timestamps 358, 359

E

eagerness 434
Elasticsearch 121, 434
endianness 434, 435
  little-endian 434, 442
  big-endian 428, 434
entropy 393
Excel
  tidy data 65, 66
Exchangeable Image File Format (Exif)
    161
explicit categories 372-379
eXtensible Markup Language
    (XML) 99, 100, 459
  user records 100-102

F

F1 Score 436
factor 351, 375
  weighting 262-266
factor levels 246
false precision 306
fastparquet 53
feather 43
feature 436
feature selection 413-417
  decomposition 388
feature selection models
  limitations 415
Federal Information Processing
    Standards (FIPS) 89
field 436
filled area
  exploring 130
fixed bounds 205-210
Flat Custom Formats 109, 110
fonetika 223
formula 413
forward-/backward-fill 314, 315
Fuzzy 369, 436
Fuzzy matching 367-372

G

General Decimal Arithmetic
    Specification 436
Gensim 436
Geographic Information Systems
    (GISes) 85
GeoJSON 85-88
geometric mean 305
ggplot2 437
Gibibyte (GiB) 437
Glob 437
global imputation
  from linear trend 316
GNU dbm (GDBM) 128, 436
Graph Query Language (GQL) 119, 437
Gremlin 119, 438

H

h5py 46, 438
Hadoop File System (HDFS) 53
halting problem 438
harmonic mean 305
HDF Compass 438
Hierarchical Data Format
    (HDF5) 42-44, 438
  tools and libraries 45-50
hierarchical formats
  missing data 196
HTML tables 137-140
hyperparameters 439

I

idempotence 439
image formats 153
  channel manipulation 159, 160
  metadata 161-164
  pixel statistics 156-159
image metadata 153, 155
imager library 154, 439
imbalanced-learn package 337, 439
imputation 439
  alternate trend imputation 345, 346
  correlation imputation 314
  global imputation, from linear trend 316
  locality imputation 309-312
  trend imputation 313, 314
  typical-value imputation 301
independent component analysis
    (ICA) 389
INI files 109, 110
International Bureau of Weights and
    Measures (BIPM) 437
International System of Units (SI) 437
Internet Engineering Task Force (IETF)
    73
interquartile range (IQR) 211-218, 260
interval variables 439
ISO-8601 440

J

Japan Electronic Industries Development Association (JEIDA) 165
JavaScript Object Notation (JSON) 73-75, 440, 453
  Binary JSON (BSON) 121, 428
  concatenated JSON 83
  Data Types 78-82
JSON Lines 82-85
JSON Schema 92-98
  length-prefixed JSON 83
  missing data 196
  Newline Delimited JSON (ndjson) 82
  Not-a-Number (NaN), handling 78-82
  rjson 453
jq 75, 440
JSON Lines 82-85
JSON Schema 92-98
Jupyter notebooks 440, 450

K

Kafka 441
kdb+ 43, 441
Keyhole Markup Language (KML) 85, 102-107
key/value store 127-130

L

larger coarse time series 317, 318
  consistency, imputing 322-324
  data 318, 320
  interpolation 325, 327
  unstable data, removing 321, 322
latent Dirichlet allocation (LDA) 389
laziness 441
lemmatization 385, 441
length-prefixed JSON 83
levels
  characterizing 418
libxml2 101
libxslt 101
Lightning Memory-Mapped Database (LMDB) 128, 441
little-endian 434, 442

locality imputation 309-312
local regression 314

M

machine learning (ML) 454
machine learning (ML) model
  applying 256, 257
MariaDB 43, 442
Matplotlib 442
measurement 442
Memcached 127, 442
metadata 161-164
Metaphone 368, 443
metaphone() function 369
Michelson-Morley experiment 221, 222
Minnesota Multiphasic Personality Inventory (MMPI) 434
miscoded data 201-204
missing data 191, 192, 228-232
  in hierarchical formats 196
  in JSON 196
  in sentinels 197-200
  in SQL 192-196
misspelled words
  exercise 223, 224
Mojibake 176, 443
MonetDB 43, 443
MongoDB 121, 443
multiple features
  balancing 346-348
multivariate outliers 219-221
MySQL 30, 443

N

National Center for Supercomputing Applications (NCSA) 44
National Oceanic and Atmospheric Administration (NOAA) 198
natural language processing (NLP) 364, 379, 430
Natural Language Toolkit (NLTK) 380, 444
Neo4j 119, 444
NetCDF-4 44
  tools and libraries 45-50**

netcdf4-python 46, 444
Network Common Data Form
    (NetCDF) 42, 44, 444
Newline Delimited JSON (ndjson) 82
Node.js 444
Node Package Manager (npm) 444
noise 393
Nominal, Ordinal, Interval, Ratio
    (NOIR) 445
nominal variable 444
non-local regression 314
non-negative matrix factorization
    (NMF) 389
non-tabular data 140-146
non-temporal trends 327-331
normalization 254, 255
NoSQL databases 119
   concepts 120
   key/value store 127-130
Not-a-Number (NaN) 78, 191
   handling 78-82
NPY parser
   enhancing, exercise 182, 183
NumPy 87, 445
   NPY format 166

O

observation 445
one-hot encoding 407, 408, 409
ontology 446
optical character recognition (OCR) 154
ordinal variables 445, 446
ordinary least-squares (OLS) 316
OrientDB 119, 447
orthonormal basis 447
outliers 211
   interquartile range (IQR) 216-218
   Z-Score 211-215
oversampling 339-344
   oversampled polls, exercises 294, 295

P

Pandas 447
   .melt() 7
   .to_datetime() 26

.astype() 27
.sample() 39
.read_parquet() 54
sentinel values 198
.describe() 230
.autocorr() 280
.fillna() 314
.interpolate() 315, 325
.groupby() 321
.drop_duplicates() 358
.get_dummies() 407
data frames 58
paragraph vector 383
parameter space 448
parcel 318
pdftotext tool 148
PIL 154
Pillow 154, 448
pink noise
   versus white noise 391
pixel statistics 156-159
polynomial features
   constructing 410
   generating 410
   synthetic features 411, 413
Poppler 148, 448, 460
portable document format
   (PDF) 148-153, 448
positive predictive value 449
PostgreSQL 30, 449
precision 449
principal component analysis
   (PCA) 389, 459
PROJ 87
Protocol Buffers 43
pyarrow 53
PyTables 46, 450
python-Levenshtein 223

Q

quantization 398-406
query planner 450
quiet NaN
   versus signaling NaN 195

R

R
  SQL data, reading 34, 35
RabbitMQ 450
Random Over-Sampling Examples
     (ROSE) 337, 453
Raster 153
ratio variable 451
Ray 58
RDF Query Language 455
recall 451
record 451
record separator-delimited 82
regularity, imposing 355-357
relational database management
     system (RDBMS) 29, 442-452
relational model
  creating 131, 132
Remote Dictionary Server (Redis) 127,
     452
Representational State Transfer
     (REST) 74, 452
Requests library 137, 452
rhdf5 46, 453
ribosomal RNA (rRNA) 283
rjson 453
R Markdown 450
rotation 389
row 453
R package stringdist 223
R tibbles 15
rvest package 137, 453

S

sample 453
sample weighting 263-266
sampling 332-334
Scala
  data frames 56, 57
scaling 254, 255
  scaling layer 262
  techniques 257-262
Scikit-learn 454
Scipy.stats 454
Scrapy 137, 454

Seaborn 230, 454
sensitivity 451
sentinels
  missing data 197-200
  sentinel value 191
SeqKit 454
  using 284
Shapely 87
signaling NaN
  versus quiet NaN 195
signed integer 454
Solr 121
Soundex 367
spaCy 383, 455
Spark 19
  data frames 56, 57
sparklyr 53
SPARQL Protocol and RDF Query
     Language (SPARQL) 119, 455
spectre of automation 425
sphering 389, 455
spreadsheets
  disadvantages 21-28
SQLAlchemy 30, 455
SQLite 42, 50-52, 456
SQLite3 30
SQL RDBMS 29, 30
  massaging data types 30-34
StandardScaler 258
statelessness 452
state machine 456
STDERR 456
STDIN 456
STDOUT 456
stemming 385, 456
string fields 364-366
  explicit categories 372-379
  Fuzzy matching 367-372
string vectors 379-387
structured data 456
structured log 171-174
Structured Query Language (SQL) 29
  disadvantages 36-41
  missing data 192-196
  tidy data 67

support attribute 415
synthetic features
  generating 411, 413
Synthetic Minority Over-sampling
    TEchnique (SMOTE) 341, 439

T

tab-separated values (TSV) 457
Tabula 148
  tabula-extractor 148
  tabula-java 148, 457
  tabula-js 148
  tabula-py 148
  tabulizer 148
Taxonomy 457
t-distributed stochastic neighbor
    embedding (t-SNE) 389
Thrift 43
tibble 458
tidy data 4-9
  from Excel 65, 66
  from SQL 67
Tidy Geography 88-92
tidyr package 8
Tidyverse 61, 458
time-sensitive regression 314, 315
timestamps, adding 359-363
tokenization 381
Tom's Obvious, Minimal Language
    (TOML) 108-113
transcription validation 287-291
trend imputation 313, 314
trends
  types 314
tuple 458
type affinity 51
typical tabular data 302-308
typical-value imputation 301

U

undersampling 335-338
Uniform Manifold Approximation and
    Projection (UMAP) 396
unit in the last place (ULP) 258

unsigned integer 458, 459
user interface (UI) 28

V

Vaex 14
  data frames 59, 60
variables 459
vectorization techniques
  bag-of-words 379
  Word2Vec 383
visualization 394-397

W

Wayback Machine 137
Web 0.5 459
web scraping 136, 137
  command-line scraping 146, 147
  HTML tables 137-140
  non-tabular data 140-146
Web traffic
  scraping, exercise 183, 185
whitening 389, 391, 459
white noise
  versus pink noise 391
Word2Vec 383

X

Xpdf 148, 448, 460

Y

YAML Ain't Markup Language
    (YAML) 108, 114-118, 460

Z

Zarr 44
Z-Score 211-215

Made in United States
North Haven, CT
27 November 2022